ROLE CALL: A GENERATIONAL ANTHOLOGY
OF SOCIAL AND POLITICAL BLACK ART & LITERATURE

ROLE CALL: A GENERATIONAL ANTHOLOGY OF SOCIAL AND POLITICAL BLACK ART & LITERATURE

edited by
Tony Medina
Samiya A. Bashir
Quraysh Ali Lansana

with a foreword by Haki R. Madhubuti

Third World Press
Chicago, Illinois

Third World Press, Chicago, Illinois 60619
© 2002 by Tony Medina, Samiya A. Bashir, Quraysh Ali Lansana

Library of Congress Cataloging-in-Publication Data

Role Call: A Generational Anthology of Social and Political Black Art & Literature /
edited by Tony Medina, Samiya A. Bashir and Quraysh Ali Lansana
     p. cm.
       ISBN 0-88378-238-3 (alk. paper)—ISBN 0-883-78239-1 (pbk.: alk. paper)
        1. American literature—African American authors. 2. African Americans—
Literary collections. 3. Social problems—Literary collections. 4. American literature—20th century. 5. Politics—Literary collections. 6. Blacks—Literary collections. I.
Medina, Tony.

PS508.N3 R64 2002
810.8'0358—dc21

              2001045718

Printed in the United States of America

10 090 08 07 06 05 04 03 02   10 9 8 7 6 5 4 3 2 1

Design: Washington Design, Brooklyn, NY
Michele Y. Washington & Emily Punjavilasluck
COVER IMAGE:
"Handful" by Kenneth L. Addison, mixed media batik
LEFT, FRONT INSIDE JACKET:
Pilot Want Her Wings, by Torkwase Dyson, oil on canvas
EDITOR PHOTO:
by Cheryl L. Minor
RIGHT, BACK INSIDE JACKET:
Miss Eve, by Kenneth L. Addison, monoprint collage
BACK COVER IMAGE:
Jigga Who, by Navin June Norling, mixed media on wood

LIBATION

creator, god/s, goddess/es, deities, prophets, saints,
earth, sun & moon, stars & planets, fire, water, ether, air, metals.
universal knowledge and truth.
the most positive and divine aspects of the ancestors of each of the contributors to this work.
all of our mothers and fathers whose deeds and misdeeds have shaped us.

we call the deities, spirits and saints of love, war, fertility, science, dance, art, song,
harvest, sex, creativity, mathematics, commerce, politics, destiny, life, death.

we pray that we have and will continue to live and create, giving proper respect
in the perpetuity of artistic, intellectual, physical and political action.
we pray that all of our creative endeavors assist in the elevation of our immediate
and universal lineages-those who we follow and those yet to come.
we give thanks to the goddesses and gods who have been there since the beginning
and helped our ancestors move and persevere throughout the diaspora,
through the most severe oppression and detachment.

we continue to call those deities, spirits and saints,
those indigenous to our homelands and traditions
and those we've met during our journeys, who assist in our survival and upliftment.

we recall the rhythms, tones and movements of our earliest rituals.
we give thanks for all things great and small.

we dedicate this book to our ancestors, those related by blood and by struggle,
who passed on during the making of this book:

Gwendolyn Brooks
Jacob Lawrence
Raymond R. Patterson
Safiya Henderson-Holmes
Dudley Randall
Wilson L. Driver
David Earl Jackson
Barbara Christian
John Biggers
Tito Puente
Aaliyah Haughton
Russell Hutchison
Belle Lawrence
Jasmine Houston
Tony Medina, Sr.
Jenese Aileen Russell Woodson

for them, for us, for you, for everyone that we can not name,
this is our offering.

Contents

WHAT IS THE ROLE OF TODAY'S **EMERGING YOUNG ARTISTS IN** THE CURRENT STRUGGLE FOR EQUALITY AND JUSTICE?

HOW DO THE VOICES OF THE **NEXT GENERATION** DEFINE THE ISSUES AND POLITICS OF TODAY?

contents

3 THE ROLE CALL

contents

4 **ROLE CALL** IS AN EXPLORATION OF OUR **CURRENT CULTURAL LANDSCAPE IN POETRY, FICTION, ESSAYS, VISUAL ARTS AND THEATER-ON-THE-PAGE.**

contents

5 ROLE CALL IS A LITMUS TEST OF—AND A CALL TO ARMS TO— A GENERATION GROWN FAT ON THE LIMITED FREEDOMS WON BY THE CIVIL RIGHTS STRUGGLE.

contents

6 ROLE CALL
TAKES ON RACE, SEXUALITY, EDUCATION, NATIONALISM, SPIRITUALITY, AIDS, GLOBALIZATION, HIP HOP AND THE PRISON INDUSTRIAL COMPLEX.

contents

contents

7 ROLE CALL IS A JOURNEY THROUGH THE TROPICS OF BLACK RAGE, BLACK LOVE AND BLACK FIRE.

contents

BLACK FIRE

Shouts outs
Acknowledgments

The Generation Now

Welcome to today's thoughts and words. Welcome to young minds free and liberated enough to write, illustrate, think, act, publish and publicly state what is on their young fired up minds. Flashback to the 1960s: I remember, oh so well, being literally beat up in print by the cultural watchers and police who felt that my works and the works of others were too angry, too ghetto, too rude, too Black and we were too young to have anything meaningful to add to the cultural dialogue of the time. However, the killer criticisms were mean spirited remarks like, "this is not poetry, it is the scribbling of an angry, out of control man," or something just as crude and fearful.

Well, this angry young man has grown into a rather balanced elder who is still an angry poet, activist and witness who understands the unique power of words. I also remember when we used to be "Negroes," a European-American invention three steps from some white plantation whose minds had been programmed to think of themselves as creatures less than lovers and lower than the newest ideas of whatever white person, generally connected to some university or think tank who sought to build a reputation, career or get rich stepping on Black bodies by attempting to define Black folks less ready for western "civilization." In reality, in the United States, others have always defined us. The poets, writers, artists and musicians of the sixties, i.e., the Black Arts Movement, changed all of that forever!

Back to real time. Back to the year of September the eleventh, the year of name calling and asking the wrong question. We received the completed galley of this powerful book in August, a month before the attack on America that reshaped both the physical and mental landscape of our country for the foreseeable future. Therefore the writers herein do not address themselves to that unfortunate tragedy. However, *Role Call* does, with clarity and passion, take on serious subjects of racism, sexism, the economy and class issues, homophobia, love or lack thereof, the problems of being young, bright and ambitious in a fastly aging country, questions of family and much more.

Role Call is to this generation what *Black Fire* was to mine. It is encyclopedic in its scope and includes close to all of the major and emerging young writers making their mark today. Reading this significant work, one immediately notices the impact of Gwendolyn Brooks, James Baldwin, Margaret Walker, Amiri Baraka, Sonia Sanchez, John Oliver Killens, Lucille Clifton, Melvin B. Tolson, Nikki Giovanni, Mari Evans, June Jordan, Kalamu ya Salaam, Alice Walker, Ishmael Reed, Audre Lorde and hundreds of black and non-white writers and poets out of the struggles of the 1960s and before. *Role Call* is a fair and nearly exhausted representation of the ideas, activism and vision of the mosaic of young voices speaking their names.

To know one's name, i.e., one's true consciousness, is not easy or an automatic end—game in a culture that bases its ultimate value on the accumulation of money and cultural and political acculturation. However, these young writers, poets, musicians, and visual artists have truly benefited from the strong literary and artistic legacy which they inherited. It is with great pleasure, and in keeping with the mission of Third World Press, that we publish *Role Call*. The editors—Tony Medina, Samiya A. Bashir and Quraysh Ali Lansana—must be congratulated for their diligent work, careful eyes, rigorous editing, unique design and their unquestionable love of literature, life and their people that is on display in this powerful book.

It is indeed with young poets and writers like them that we see possibilities and unlimited sun rises. After the tragedy of September 11, 2001, it is somewhat comforting to know that we have young women and men who view life in all its rudeful and beautiful complexities and are on the offense to not only solve problems but be themselves the actors in the solutions. These young writers, for the most part, do not buy into American victimization of non-whites and see writing as a way to confront the many questions that require progressive minds and acts.

in this universe
the magic   the beauty   the willful act of explaining
the world and you;
the timeless   the unread   the unstoppable fixation
with language and ideas
the visionary   the satiable equalizer screaming for
the vitality of dreams   interrupting false calm
demanding fairness and a new, new world are the
poets and their poems
writers and their fiction and prose,
visual artist and their colors and smiles,
our well spring,
our memory,
our tradition.

Haki R. Madhubuti
Poet, educator, essayist, and
Founder and publisher of Third World Press

CALL & RESPONSE

If we have learned anything from the '50s and '60s,
it is that we need an organized, collective response
to our oppression.
-Toni Cade Bambara

We begin with a call.

Try to make our way through the changing same of American life, comfortable with shopping malls and cable, McRibs and organic free-range chicken, capitalism consolidating its economic strength on a global scale. Planes drop out the sky. Poets drop like flies. We weep over Diana and Jon-Jon, nose deep in the Post, *stepping over bloodstains on the front stoop. We be walking up to the stage, self-conscious, egocentric, pulling a pawn shop microphone out a black leather case, straightening out the shirt, clearing the throat.*

With a calling,
Djembe and bata drums say come!
> The ancestors call.
> We respond.
> The circle widens.

Remember:
Give and forgive. Gather hands.
Cull the collective fruit and harvest,
carving memory.

Come together—a wide-hipped squat before the fire—there are stories to tell.

We create and destroy, love and fight, work to transcribe the thinkspeak of the tribe. We work the knots out of shoulders, caress cheeks with love, braid hair, stop, point up to the sky when the stars come out.

We begin with a callin. Yarnspinnin.
Talkin ain't no more than opening your mouth.
Walkin ain't nothing but putting one foot
in front of the other—
again and again and again.

We come with a calling, an offering.

We trade and barter.
We build ladders, as well as fly.
Find abundance amongst scraps,
Create from plenty plentymo'.

Each one of us comes with the word sculpted
into many things trying to become one.

The slave interrogates the slave:
What is social? What is political?
What role do artists play in society?
What role does society figure in our art?
Should it remain detached, separate from the community?
                    What are we communicating?

The ancestors call.
We respond with a rap, a sermon, a painting or song, a poem, a photograph, a
sheet of music. We respond onstage at an open mic, at the monkey bars in the
schoolyard.

The ancestors call.
We hear the hush, the whisper,
feel the vibration, the stillness,
the calm, soothing silence that asks us to come.

We began with that clarion to call us all to task.
The response is what we remember, what we refuse to forget.

We come together from different aesthetic camps, varying schools of thought
and form. We play together, alone, with each other, off each other. We want to
come back, come home, recreate community.

It begins with a call to unity, a regrouping after decades
of political and aesthetic division individualistic isolation.

We know that it is increasingly difficult
to survive within the reordering of imperialism.
            We know that it isn't finished.
                    We aren't finished yet either.

We hear our call. We know our role.
This is our response / ability.

What are we writing?
What are we doing?
(besides bum rushin the couch)
Are we awake?
Are we listening?
        Are you?

Who is present?
        Raise ya hands in the air!
Who's here?
        Say it loud! I'm Black and I'm...
        Uh huh.
                Thought so.

Tony Medina, Samiya A. Bashir, Quraysh Ali Lansana
Brooklyn, New York, 2002

Having been given, I must give.

Paul Robeson

ROLE CALL: A GENERATIONAL ANTHOLOGY OF SOCIAL AND POLITICAL BLACK ART & LITERATURE

WHAT IS THE ROLE OF TODAY'S EMERGING YOUNG ARTISTS IN THE CURRENT STRUGGLE FOR EQUALITY AND JUSTICE?

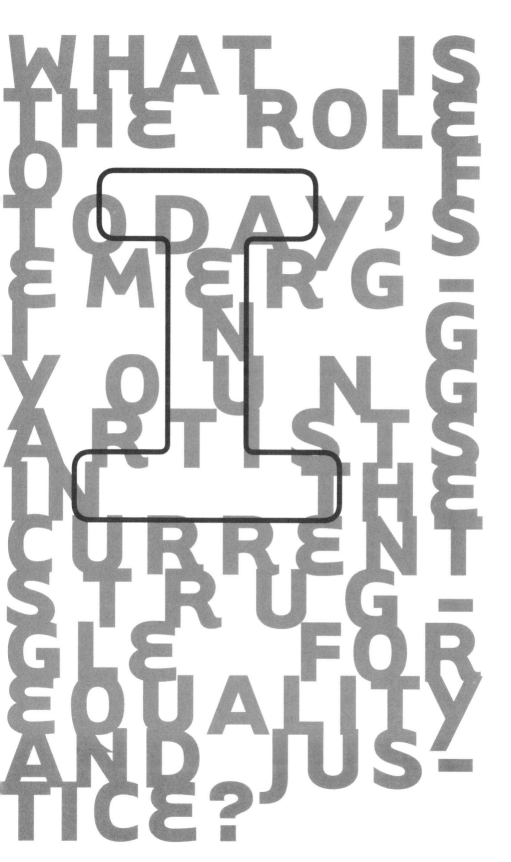

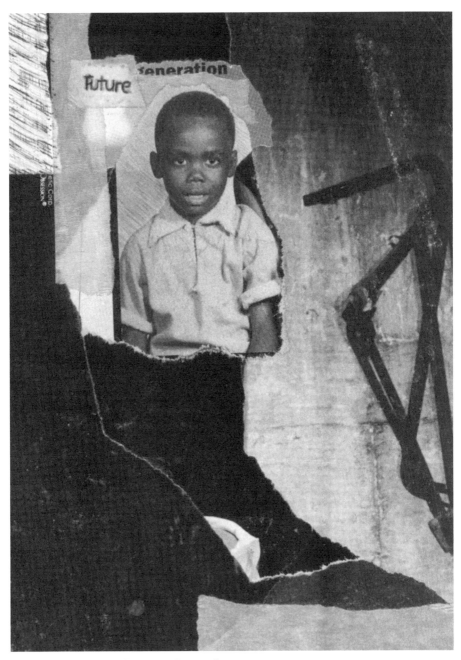

John Abner—**Future Generation** collage

I Write

Because somewhere in Soweto there is a small, brown girl who looks like me.

Her hair sings with the sun.

She is wearing clothes with no name.

She is beautiful.

She is hungry, like her sister in South Carolina.

They are cold, and possibly my cousins. They are hungry.

I cannot finish my family tree. It stops somewhere in South Carolina.

> Because somewhere in Atlanta, there is a soldier named Mutulu.
>
> He lives in a cage. His dreadlocks do not see the sun.
>
> He is wearing clothes with numbers.
>
> He has not touched a breast in fourteen years.
>
> He is lonely.

Because many brown people do not own guns.

Because they may not use them if they did.

Because between candy bars, Sundiata chain smokes his way through the day.

Because Assata and Nehanda cannot come home.

Because some of us collect stamps instead of weapons.

We are foolish.

> Somewhere in St. Croix, there is a fine Black man.
>
> His eyes dance. He wears nothing.
>
> He is at least as beautiful as god.
>
> I am afraid the fine man and god will hurt me.
>
> I cannot submit. When I get on my knees, I am wordless.
>
> When I lay under him on hot nights, trying to receive all that is good in him,

I scream too loud. Then, he thinks I belong to him. He is strong.
He cannot love me. When he leaves, he takes god with him.
We are hurt.

Somewhere in San Francisco, there is a father
confusing his daughter with his wife. His breath stinks.

Because his little girl learns about lust between her father's legs.
Because he waited for her inside her house and did not stop when she cried.
Because an old woman cannot walk down the street alone at night.
Wearing whatever she pleases. We are cold.

Somewhere in Chicago, there is a small black boy who did not make it through the night.
His hands are soft. He is wearing a toe tag. His mother has been crying for years.
Because he does not belong in a refrigerator.
Because no sterile white sheet can cover his pain.
Because life and death hurt.

Askhari

sankofa

tell of a whole song coming
forgotten libations
remembered opening
horizons of new breath
promised from our children's mouths

we gather at the river places
embroider our selves tighter
in the empty seasons
sew the middle fabric
with reinforced seams
elders at the edge
as the sky rains
sequins of color
straw and feathers
journey us home

Pamela Plummer

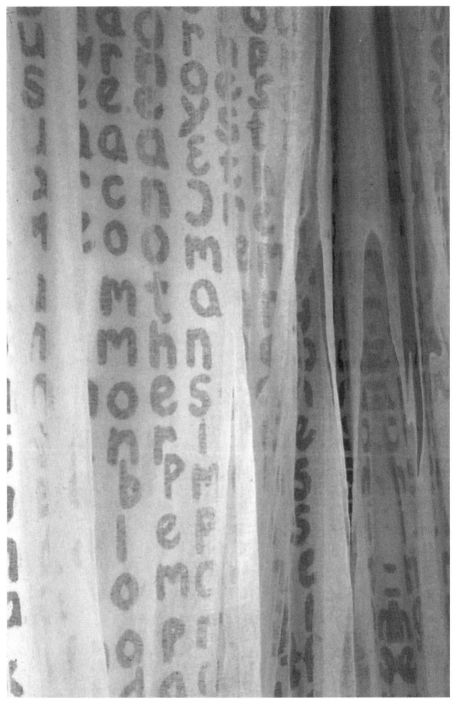

Kim Mayhorn—**Aya** installation detail

Incantation for the Word

Shi-shi   shah-shah   shi   she-eeh
is the music of divination powder
Tákátákátákátáká
      is the music of palm nuts conversing/(ikin)
      Ikin can
      speak of a certain matter burrowed in sand
      Ódu is the music of
      Omolú is the music of
                that speech

And we arrived with these pronouncements
circling a wooden tray
circling those signatures (who summon the true name of things)
like coded messages from birds soaked
with the dew of universe
archetypes & all
           past present & therefore
                  future
           many languages with rhythm & all
           even tonal
           circling a wooden tray
           tray whose circular implies
              WORLD
And it is word who causes this dance
And there are rhythmic leaps into
the sweetness of abundance into
the iron crest of creativity
And there are herbs which cause the invisible to manifest

And it is word who causes this dance
Tákátákátákátáká
is the music of palm nuts conversing/(ikin)
Yes we can initiate a dialogue between known &
unknown
between those who flow round jagged stones of ignorance
river-like
like wise fish
we can bring messages regarding history
the ineffable speech of music
the music of verse
vibration from spirits through ripples
rhythm residing deep among the lushness
An old beaded crown invokes the power of poem
— in an incantation we can

      Ódu is the music of
      Omolú is the music of
              that speech
     Shi-shi   shah-shah   shi   she-eeh
           shshsh!

Adrian Castro

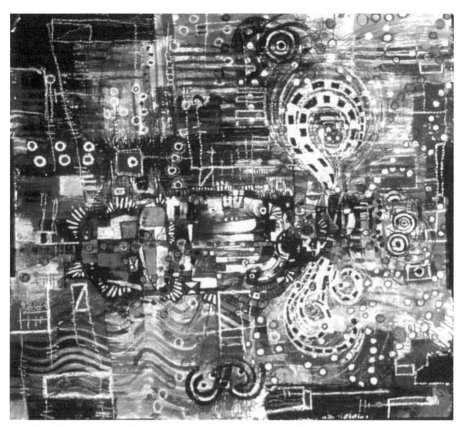

Eric Mack—**Percussion Permeates** mixed media on canvas

How MUSIC Relates to the Brain

In the study of how music relates to the brain, it has been determined that the human being is, in fact, a musical being. This is to say music is not merely an activity; it is rather an expression of faculties intrinsic to the human brain. The apparatus of the brain which transmits music is largely the same apparatus through which language is transmitted, an apparatus located in both the left and right hemispheres of the brain. Yet the right hemisphere is endowed with an auditory cortex containing important links responsible specifically for perceiving, remembering and enjoying music. Links to be distinguished from those located in both the left and right hemisphere responsible for speech and general auditory function.

Naturally, these regions of the brain, like all other aspects of our organism, will atrophy if not given suitable work. Thus, it can be said the brain must be given sufficient harmonic, melodic and temporal content to be considered adequately nourished.

The same way one can observe a direct correspondence between the modern scourge of cancer and other health abnormalities with the imposed societal dependency on packaged food, one can see that as music has been reduced to a consumable commodity there has been an observable degeneration in every aspect of society's musical intelligence, an intelligence inseparable from the general intelligence of the brain. As corporations continue to dominate the collective musical experience of society they are, in effect, interfering with many aspects of the brain's evolution. Furthermore, these conditions have created a sort of cultural amnesia in which music in its former, more significant meaning has been forgotten. In *The Music of Africa*, Professor J.H. Kwabena Nketia provides a variety of descriptions of social/musical modes of perception which will provoke a sense of depravation and, hopefully, profound interest in any cognizant victim of American pop culture.

In any society where authentic community has not been entirely eradicated, music remains a vital means by which a culture transmits wisdom, vitality, and values to itself. In some cultures, parents traditionally sing songs of love and endearment to their infants and young children. Whereas, in a society under the mass-hypnotic control of a gigantic spectacle of hyper-consumption, children are subject to the random causality of the mass media and a music industry which has fallen almost entirely under the yoke of mega-conglomerates who have subsumed the production of alums with a wide range of other entirely unrelated industries—i.e. snack food, water utilities, etc. It is entirely fair to say that in the business of music, social considerations are entirely irrelevant, there are only charts and graphs indicating profit lost or generated.

This vapid, disconnected concept of music and culture is, here in the new millennium, utterly estranged from an ancient understanding which viewed music as a reflection of the vibrational nature of reality. What is by now perceived as an ordinary major scale—do re mi fa so la ti do—was at one time known by performers of sacred music as the reflection of the law of octaves, a metaphysical principle relevant not exclusively to the discipline of music but more extensively on the cosmic and micro-cosmic scales of reality.

While there are still those musicians who use music as a vehicle of transformation they are relegated to the underground of those vast areas under the total control of the Spectacle. Those messengers of truth who share the highest utterances in their music can be found in those increasingly obscure regions where cultures remain which have not been fallen under the psycho-spiritual manacles of modern consumption. I leave you with an excerpt from Mali's Afel Bocoum Alkibar's "Buribal" (Friendship):

> You Destroyer of the forest
> I will not recall you
> You who have never planted a tree
> You are excluded
> You who know that the trees
> Have all been generous,
> I will recall you and thank you

Jeremiah Hoseah Landes

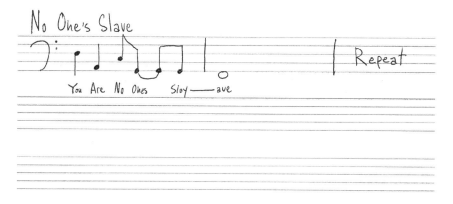

Jeremiah Hoseah Landes—**No One's Slave** musical composition

From Girl in the Mirror:
Three Generations of Black Women in Motion

Some say our story begins in the middle of an ocean, in the belly of a monster, at the mercy of demons. Others say that we began with a hammer and a nail; that we laid our bodies down and raised cities along our spines. But I say it goes deeper than that, deeper than cotton fields and human cargoes, the thick and heavy links of a history we're constantly trying to break, to desire. The urge that stirs you in the middle of the night, grabs you by the spine and jerks you upright. The story begins here, when we realize that we are no longer asleep and the beat of our hearts sounds just like the beat of a far away drum. And it is at this moment of unrest, when our hearts refuse to allow us to be still, that we realize what we must do, which is gather ourselves up and move.

Natasha Tarpley

Dear **Mama**

I am kneeling
under the umbrella tree
with a piece of paper and stub of pencil.
Since I have learned to write,
angels crowd my shoulders
like Missy's wedding shawl.

Mama, when I am writing
seems like flight enters my bones.
I'm planning what the note will say
for our crossing over to Jordan.
I suspect we will look into the river
see our faces, see our hands,

even see our wide-long feet
wavering on the water
and claim ourselves,
this body belongs to me,
these are my wide arms,
my knobby knees, my knotted hair.

Mama, I come here on Sundays at sunrise
practicing the plan. First I write
my name, Willa May, then I write Free.
I plant seeds. Then I speak it.
I say Willa May, Free to the leaves, to acorns,
to butterflies staring on the grass blades.

The soil under my heels starts whispering,
nudging me to stand, get moving, walk.
Seems like I can't stay on the ground long,
those angels that swoop around my pencil,
are the same ones fluttering about my knees,
scattering dreams everywhere.

Angela Shannon

I Am My Mother

if she had gone the other way
if I had met her someplace else
we might have recognized each other

the slight sway of our hips
make men want more
than just words from our mouths
in the cross-reference of rumba and reggae

seen raining from the tips of our foreign fingers
pasting a collage of cultures cut from storybooks
that speak nothing of girls with no fathers
and no laughter to lead them
into a language of their own

My mother painted these words on my hands
from faraway places like Montreal and Brazil
she cut me in pieces
I am learning to forgive her
in the way that daughters will always forgive their mothers
for stepfathers with errant fingers
and for the list of other silences I am chewing the bitter memories

I am my mother

Staceyann Chin

sticks and stones

this pen
feels good
in my hand.

it's exalting to watch
letters form words—

who says
the page is silent?

my words scream
and sob, cackle and crash,
chatter and hiss. they slide
into each other. bumping
sounds on the paper. they scratch
deep itches. paper cuts come
from words.

Kim Louise

Kim Mayhorn—**"A Woman was Lynched the Other Day..."**
installation detail

Case of Blues

Daddy carried his leather satchel from Watts to St. Louis to Memphis.
He said it was a case of blues, played its contents on his Mama's antique upright,
in two-part harmony, kept it at his feet as he sucked rib juice from long bones,
crooned on sun-splashed porches, and sprawled in beds on the questionable side
of county lines.

His case lured him down shaded dirt roads, along gravel covered lanes
where farm girls in see-thru shifts leaned against breezes, gathered apples,
hung moons and hoisted suns. Their young hands scrubbed his shirts,
pulled feathers from scalded hens to make his meals.

Whatever he wanted was in that case of blues.

Respect:
he stroked it from ivory, strummed it from old guitars, hummed
tear-stained melodiesuntil his blues sat upright, slipped down from
dusty rafters, and arched their willowy bodies along honky-tonk walls.

He sang of their meetings in freight yards and cotton fields, in meadows
where white sheets spoke, and ropes danced in trees eager to snap his neck.
He sang of fleshy women with talcum-laced breasts and arms wrapped in lilac water,
until his notes softened the images of torn black skin, rebellious black men
cradled in dirt in lonely churchyards, beneath tangled weeds.

While he sang
his blues would touch his face, kiss his hands, then tuck themselves away in his case
as he slid his long, heavy shoes across the dance floor one more time, maybe twice,
whiskey and the sultry rhythm of a screaming sax on his breath,
his breath on the damp neck of a juke joint harlot.

As the music died, he gripped his case, dragged his shadow across the smoky room
past garish red smiles and contorted limbs, out to draped moonlight and hissing
darkness, leaving behind a piece of himself swaying in the memory of his blues.

Gina M. Streaty

Homage to **Leonardo Drew's Number Eight**
Installation, St. Louis
Art Museum

So this is your art, a black man's art,
this mass hanging from ceiling to floor,
this rage of tattered ropes, bird carcasses,
burnt feathers molting into steely cargo.
I can't ignore this ugliness you've turned
inside out, anger made palpable
coiled cords of sooty rope twining around
raccoon and porcupine skulls, animal hides
and antlers torn, fractured shards in this
assemblage, wood ruptured in it too,
the whole heft of it black, painted black
the ripped rags, deer bones. What
made you build this? What drove you
to salvage the accidents others spurn
turn them into this dense wall no one
can pass by, turn from? Uncomprehending,
I stop and breathe a hard breath
before your amalgam of rope, wood, paint,
your loom of blistered discards.

Allison Joseph

Dumas

the eagle shall die
pierced &

plummeting
    twisting
        turning
    blindly
        burning
the dome shall fall
its high whiteness turned to dust
the final cleansing
        we shall be avenged
and in that time our beating wings
shall be a Black shadow
upon the fading earth. The flight
of our soaring souls shall echo
the path of the sun across the
face of God.
        we shall be beautiful

Jabari Asim

So dark
I can't see my hands.
A feeling now
on the river.
A barely perceptible wind
down over it
a certain smell
as of growing old.
You must
believe me
I have no way
to prove this.
Dark.
You,
      with your tiny instruments
fluttering
ungodly
mastering a movement
catching the whispers
with your net
like a diction,
you must
believe me.
You
with your
busy work — the stitching
                    of air on air with your thread of listening —
how is that made to measure?

I wanted to know
where the song was from.
What if the book said
to look
in the mud?
You must
believe me. There was once
a story here. I have
no way to prove this.
Is there a spotted nest?
Is there a mud fortress carved by slow water?

Shane Book

Sheila L. Prevost—**The Poet** oil on canvas

The Good Doctor Writes

Dear Mr. President,

Due to your capacity as the Supreme Elected Judge of Poeticity, I am writing you as regards my non-selectioning as the new Poet Laureate of these continuously United States. Although the various variables variances have me somewhat bewildered, I am none the less firm in celebrationing the inevitable prescribing of this eventuality under God of man. Due to the excelling genius of my poetitude, and my diverse mental-cultural backgrounds(s), I anticipate my effective institutioning into this Due-Processionary capacity. Once so constituted I will (of course) designate the foundation of INTERIOR-MANUALS(S) for the revivalizing of Accentuated-Syllabic Poetics, and establish IAMBIC ENERGY CLUBS for the prevention of Lower Moodiness. Through the appropriate certifications, the Spiritual Void of Free Verse, and Overeating can be avoided. I will also refrain from the haphazard metering arising out of the Differential Equational, Problems associated with Out-of-Bounds Languaging and the lack of a Frameworkable American Prosody(s)'s. The immediate fitting of such structures(s) of office should ensure the total preventioning of Diseased Sonneting and Explicit Lyrics. The non-allowance of ill advised Poeting will also facilitate the reaching of a Philosophical State of Community Affairs. Please be advised(ed) that all attempts at Personal Hypnosis(s) will fail, due to my immunization against the harmingness of Projectable, Blue, and Green Brainwaves. I eagerly await your
Response(s)'s.

Sincerely, your Humble Servant,

THE HONORABLE REV. DR. EZRA EMILY POE III, LT.

P.S. Thanks for the chocolates.

DJ Renegade

After the Verdict

There is the tumult
Of quiet fear in the air
The dark goddesses
Have reached down
Snatched up
The scales of justice
Rent them—
Flung them to the earth
In a shower of mettle
That turns to fire
In the eyes, hearts
Of the dispossessed.
They have flung wide
Their patient veils
Raged at the sun—
Accused her of sheltering
The criminals in her light,
While the night
Begs to come on—
To enter here
Dark and hot like a shiver
Of reproach,
Fiery and cold like stones
Of retribution
From which we downtrodden
Will build again
Magnificent cities
To settle slowly
On the scorched bones
Of our enemies

G. Winston James

larry (for the brother who was featured on 60 Minutes on December 13, 1992)

I come to do dis...
to be here
to not go away
to be right in yo face and let you
know what you have created.
you will not sweep me under no carpet.

> i will smoke reefah in yo face
> drink liquor in yo face
> ask all of you for money
> each and every time i see you and
> don't care that it bothers you.
> i am here;
> alive,

accounted for, surviving and uninterested in
yo disinterest; you will not be able to ignore me.
i will pee on yo lawn
shit down yo backstairs
i will vomit in the street next to yo lexus.
you can call me crazy,
call me insane,
call me a disgrace to my race and I will
laugh and drink gin;
i am what you are—garbage. the whole world is garbage.
ny, dc, calcutta, somalia, bangladesh, yugoslavia, the whole world
is under the guidance of the garbage company.
they drive trash trucks called
aircraft carriers and dump their garbage everywhere.
they come dressed in camouflage uniforms and are deeply into
recycling this garbage. we are up to our ears in fuckin
garbage and nobody give a damn.
so let me walk crooked and drink liquor,
yell and smoke reefah,
do what i want to do,
when i want to do it,
where i want to do it until the disinterested get
interested; this is my manifesto;
this ain't no garbage.

Brian Gilmore

Johnalynn Holland—**Kofi** black and white silver gelatin print

Harbors and Spirits

(for Alice Allen, Mom)

Black man's days are chains.
Slaves are his days,
and ships.

Cold dawn.
War ravaged land.
Black mothers
gather children.
Their clear gaze and
strong hands.
This is our
journey of dreams.

Black man's days are chains.
Ships and slaves
packed in sweat.

Shadows of waves/followed
us here. Whip music,
nine-tailed cat songs.

Ten acres in the crack
be/hind a mule's ear.
My Daddy's dead.
My Momma's cross the sea.
Ain't got nobody
to speak one damn word for me.

We work.
A rat rotates in
side our belly.
Put our blood

on the counter.

Trumpeter
trumpeting blood in a
floodsong floodsong of feelings.
This is our
journey of dreams.

Train.
Sippi shack on tracks.
We passengers,
dead moons in our eyes.

We party.
Whisky kills you.
Wine makes you crazy.
Smack makes you lazy.
Crack kills you baby.

Sour city.
These winds
blast you white to the bone.

1930.
You are born in
sippi dreams.
We colored folks
carry Jim Crow in
our pockets.
Cracker mouth/a
guillotine of censorship.
We guard our heads.

26

Whip cracks
leave blues echoing
generations of song but
raisins are
leather sacks/breathe tough life.
This is our
journey of dreams.

Black man's days are chains.
Slaves are his days,
and exile.

1949.
we cover waterfronts.
Sweet Home Chicago.
Chitown alleys.
You carry a blues
rag to cover your face/
to clean white homes.
O what kind of place can this be?

Tall buildings.
A wall/blocking dreams.
Pain forms boots and gloves
for your hands/legs/feet.
Your mask of subservience
wears threadbare.

1962.
weary days.
Long nights.
I am born.
Blues warmth.
Your womb
severed with
a surgeon's knife.
My soul in
side your cry.

I am two.
Daddy gone.
You tend memory.
Wasted breath.

In your path I walk.
Cold winds rock
my asthmatic lungs.
His shadow: my veil.

A love supreme.
Trane is blowing.
Trane is blowing.
Trane is blow/ing.
Trane is blow/ing:
leaves/a natural mystic.
Bloodlines recovered
from white shores.
Trane is blowing.
Sand from a
lost shore. Salt
from seas crossed.
Sheets of sound
we rap a
round.
Trane is blow/ing.
Frag/ments of
dreams. Pin/drops
of pain worry
our need.
A love supreme.
A love supreme.
Col/trane is
blow/ing.
Rose petals
lift to blood
mist.
Fiery rhythms.
Fragile beats.
Eat beets and taps yo feets.
Col/trane is
blow/ing.
Cinders lift
from hearts.

1987.
Tonia.
She touches.

I am 27.
She touches.
The hard shell.
The kernel of tenderness.
Love and sticky blues.
Iron hurt.

I wait
on this shore.
My body harbors
spirits but
my soul, exile.
I search for
the song home.
This is our
journey of dreams.

when will we witness
the boomerang's return?
Is my heart a curve?
When will drum
skin melt under pounding hands?
Are beats memory?

Who shall we send?
Who will go for us?

Our hearts fat.
Our ears heavy.
The nation mourns.

Da
created the earth/
a fish he pilled
   from his vagina.

Fish swimming
black night river.
A phallus.
The long Nile.

Leonel Rugama knew.
Heroes never said

they would die for their
country; they just died.
So he died.
So we die.
He saw a
black man throw
himself into the
Siquia River,
throw himself,
down there in Bluefields/in
to a river.
He knew:
dreams are rivers,
nightmares in dreams,
but other dreams and other rivers.

In this journey,
we have rhythm/
even in death.
Pennies dance
on our eyelids.
Toes move.

Water doesn't harm us.
Black woman:
keeper of rhythm.
Her songs
are water.
Black woman:
a quilt that soaks
up rain and sun.

Her common womb
   multiplies children.
Her words glue
   will and blood.
With steepled hands,
she cuts down
our enemies.
She testifies,
sings this
journey of dreams.

Mother, mamma,
ma'm, the land
restore my sight.
Torch of warriors,
slaves, sharecroppers.
Heat of hands.

Dawn/a few hours away.
Light/on missionary roads.
Day carries a burden of roots.

1990.
Rivers pass where
I am just arriving.
In my path I walk.
I breathe.
Che.
I shall make a
reliquary of his asthmatic lungs.
They are drums to
breathe me a new life.

Mother, mama,
ma'm: you are thin and weary.
But you endure.
Your gray hair
steels my heart.
Reflects our ancestry.
I forget but I always return.

I reach a shore.
Antoney, Isabell and Pedro are
three tortoises in the mud.

I put them in shells/set
them out to sea.
I sing, dance and drink them to
Guinea.

I remove my veil/toss
into the ocean.
I fish for our unborn heart.

I leave Whitman's
captain dead on the shore.
I steer my dreams
and move outward/in
to deeper water.
I am a dolphin arcing
from sea to sea.

Jeffery Renard Allen

Coltrane Spoke to Me One Night

What came out of his horn
was murderous, the world
come undone in the belly
of his song. Sound
cursing the night
for centuries of insomnia,
the mirror persecuting
the image, crucified
and lied to, tied
to railroad tracks
of bones, at the bottom
of the sea, wrapped
around the earth
like moss on stone,
this is the breaking off
of locks and chains,
this is the skin toughening
up to break the needle,
this is what it means
to be alive, awake, sober,
feeling the welts and whip
marks evaporate from the flesh.
We are numb and feeling,
We know what death tastes like
We will stay a while
and be your worse nightmare
if that's what it takes
to sing our song.

Tony Medina

The Role Call

Any half-decent rapper
Can conjure the dead,

Can reach into graves
And accuse God

Of Indian giving.
The trick is ancestral,

No more magic than memory's
Hidden strings & chains.

Trust me,
We haven't forgotten a name.

Say them. Raise your hands.
Holler at me!

Thomas Sayers Ellis

II

HOW DO THE VOICES OF THE NEXT GENERATION DEFINE THE ISSUES AND POLITICS OF TODAY?

John Abner—**America in Control** collage

on the use of
charliebrown/teachatalk
(why little token franklin had sat at the back of the class?)

an un/acculturated demagogue of a southeastern region bluesese
molasseslike dispenser drip drawl
(huh?)

spook rednecks headchecked for severe lacerations of mis/learnings
peculiar institutions higher matriculations
(whut is hiiiiigh...whut is hiiiiyer?)

wah wah waaah   wah wah wah waaaah
(yes ma'am!)

and eloquently thinking that i surpass societal norms
leaning on the everlasting arm of the queen's best missionary english

my religion, indeed a pidgin/patois
all the hipburds speak it, my niggerish* chicness pervades my punctuates

waah waah waah   wah wah wah wah waah wah wah waah (knaimtaukinbout'?)
wah wah waah wah waaah waaah wah wah wah waah waaah   (knameen'?)

do you understand eloquent robeson /othello to your ol' man ribbuh auditory recep-
tacle?
crisp and concise in my enunciation. i hears in my inner ears and some
choose to mishears

(like when you thinking you speaking your cleverest elizabethan prose & they
nose/eyes squint like
E   X   C   U   S   E   M   E?
que usted dijo?
ce vous a dit?
was sie sagte?)
your klingon tricoder deciphers...no hablaste?
(don'tchunnerstand?!)
waah   waah   wah   wah   wah...?
spoken on my best colonpoul behaviour, w/ my carltonbanks profile
fit for an otis graham entrance into your nathan harem
trying to impress, my hillary huxtable lisp   &   s h   i   iii ii i i ii i   t

wah   wah wah   wah waah waah wah wah   wah wah   wah
wah waah wah   waah   waah   wah w   ah
wah   wah   wah
waah wah waah waah ...
(yes ma'am)
wah wah wah wah wah wah waah wah wah waah waah wah wah waah

(knaimtaukinbout'?)

r.c. glenn

*note: a mixture of s.eastern regional bluesese, pickaninny and yiddish.

Music, man,
what is it gonna be?

How do you start to talk about anything invisible? Cuz when was the last time you saw some music? Those markings on a page like this. That doesn't seem to be music. So sound / that which is gotten aurally / from here to here to the ear / sonics. And to the point any finger would not do it justice either. No finger stretches that far, that deeply. So approach with caution, with respect and also cunning. Go into it as you would a forest / head cocked, intuiting hints or changes in wind direction. Sound, a heavy thing now/ notice we don't have earlids, no real, natural protection from aural attack. This is important, perhaps even paramount. We are at the mercy of sound / of music. It comes and goes as we step, sleep or repose / forget about escape / think only of survival. Sound. There are frequencies that can induce vomiting / tones so low they bypass the ear canal and move directly to the internal organs / black peoples love of the bass. There are tones so high that exposure to them for longer than a minute would drive you stark raving mad / I say loony. We have no earlids, no escape from sound or from volume. We need not all these weapons of war like tanks and fighter planes and missles and such. All of those take up too much room / cost way too much to maintain, and are sloppy at best. Sound is of the cleanest element. There is nary a trace left over / nary an image. Entire cities could be controlled by sonics. Sound waves from every mountain top and ravine. Clean, punishing, exacting. So you wanna be a rock and roll star? That's cute. Music. Somehow denoting organization / the interlocking of rhythm, melody and harmony / that which is pleasing to the ear. But is that all of music? Rhythm, melody and harmony? Twelve notes to our western octave? Is that all of what music is? Is music that which is played on fancy, expensive instruments designed specifically for the purpose of accessing those twelve notes, those variations on the harmony? Is that music? This is not exactly rhetorical, I am truly interested myself. Sound. / again it squeezes in whether you want it to or not. Its nature is inquisitive, stealthlike. So how do you pit music side by side with sound? Can they mingle? Have a drink together? Does one take over where the other has left off, or is it more subtle, more sexual? Of course I tend to bond with the latter idea. The idea that you can't or shouldn't attempt to make the clear distinction. Ever been sitting at your window, dreaming about whatever, and hear what sounds like an achingly long note held on a trumpet, then ten seconds later gives up the ghost to what it is / a slow-in-coming-to-stop delivery truck down on the block. Or the way your portable fan magically locks with the hot new drum-and-bass track playing on your stereo. These elements can and do congeal. Neither one saying they are better than the other. And that is where things get interesting/ unpredictable / imposing. At that point where control and surrender entwine. Music / communication / the telling of a story, the manifestation of an internal impulse. Music / communication/the telling of a story, the manifestation of an internal impulse. Music to weep to, music to kill to, music to think to. Sound / the fragments last seen floating off the coast of Australia / the infinite webs of street activities collaged / another form of harmony. A symphony for an instant. So you want to be a rap star? That's cute. But all of this actually does something to us. This organizing of sound elements and calling it music, and performing it in some way, shape, or form for others to use. Cuz we do use it/ it is functional. It does act on our consciousness in some way. There are ghosts attached / vapors which are set into motion when this music hits the air. It does things. Ghosts. Spirits. Things unseen. Things for good and bad if those terms still fancy you. Layers upon layers of complexities all acting with or without our full comprehension. Music of the spheres / celestial sounds. A bass player in New York attempting to heal the world with bow and string. A deep listening / a contemplation and obsession with the interior and its manifestation in real time using sound. As the terrain just expands and expands. To envelop. If you are a musician, is it your duty to ask the questions? Is it your duty to be aware that you are setting forces into motion? Depends on the game I guess. Depends on what camp you're trying to impress. For some it is a business and nothing more, for others it is life or death. Each has its own set of standards and rules of conduct. And do we as listeners have the right to expect the truth from our musicians or assume it's all entertainment anyways? Where would you be without music? How many moments in your life have been soundtracked by that certain song? Will you ever forget it? Those unspoken thoughts before a feeling sets in. Is there a storehouse from which to draw? Whose job is it to attempt a translation? Who will pick up the baton? Not under some banner called jazz, or funk, or classical, but of life. The mystery of the black notes. The mystery of the air and great symphonies. The moment of creation and timing / improvisation. The breath / the heart and the mind, working in consort for another form of speaking. It is a lifetime challenge to actually trust the unknown / sound / reverberations. Some say the music is already there and it's up to us to pick it out, give it a life of its own. To improvise, to improve, to provide. Above and beyond style / above and beyond looking dapper and talking about deals. Above and beyond the worry of being misheard for noise or confusion. There is something solid inside. Go in and have a peep / go on. Tell me what you feel, cuz that is the language we answer to here. And all of this as old as the hills and will no doubt endure for as long as there are creatures that traverse the earth. And who are you to delve for the emotionality, for the pure note. Ah, to utter knowledge of purity, very touchy indeed. Maybe one note at any given time is all that matters. Just clues now, set up along the road / markers to gauge ones travels. Music as pathway to emotions, a strong arm to steady you. A way in. It's so rare to hear it alluded to, hinted at. It's even more rare to see it attempted, the knife edge of the moment, where jewels await. Forgive me for being so mystical, i'm only trying to be plain. Honest. Close your eyes, close your mouth / tell me what you feel / no don't. Don't say a word, just open the ears further. Take the energy usually reserved for the voice and apply it to the ears. Let them be your guides now / trust em now / maybe it really is life and death...

Morgan Michael Craft

Sheila L. Prevost—**The Rapper** oil on canvas

Guernica

Survivors will be human.
—Michael S. Harper

It's all there in black
and white: someone
has done it again.

We have lynched a man

in a land far-off
like Texas, hog-tied
and -wild

to the back of a car.

There's a word I have been
searching for
in the sand but cannot find.
*
At five o'clock in the afternoon

we play ball, hard,
in Spanish
until we bruise

No trash
talk, no beautiful
rejections-just these

shots, the smooth
skull of the ball
and that

slant Andalusian light
*
Nearby they are burying
the boy beaten
by the gang-nobody

knows him, everyone
calls the killers by name.

role call

Names. With handcuffs some
manage to hide

their faces like furnaces

failing-first flame, then smoke
and now only cold.
*
It shifts, this light,
its bruised eye shines

above our heads.
Before us the horse,
javelin-tongued, about

to whinny a word-
that wildness in the eyes.
Again, the bull

horning in-how many
has he drug
silent into swamp

or south, whether of States
or Spain?
If it moans

like a man it must
be a man.
*
One day the writer
The painter rose

excused himself from the table
at which he no longer

could sit still.
Still sit.

Bought him a one-way
billet, boarded the train

or the boat bound

for Paris

land of red and blue
*
Dragged awake by mid-day
light, hunger
sweating my sheets.

We go out into heat. Sit
shaded and peeled the shrimp
we will eat, and laugh.

Seafood fresh as a wound.
*
Precious South,
must I save you

or myself?
On the day of the saint

we watch from the terrace
trying not to toss

ourselves over like flowers.
In the arena

the bulls bow, and begin.
Above the roar the victor

Will save
the ear, the living leather.

Kevin Young

We play in the Do-It-Yourself family rooms, attics and
garages that never get done. That pink stuff is just like cotton candy. EXCEPT IT ITCHES. *On muggy days when the wind*
IS RIGHT, OUR EYES BURN AND WATER. OUR BARE ARMS AND LEGS
itch. Everywhere you look is pink and hazy from the factory just outside town. THAT STUFF IS JUST LIKE COTTON CANDY.
EXCEPT IT ITCHES.

Kate Rushin

reтireꝺ, **ronald reagan sits in his dayroom and wonders**

where she comes from, this little salvadoran girl, the one with the missing hands and the hole in her head that perches her frame on the bedspread. why is she always there pointing a bloody stump at his face? he was horrified, "it's that kid again. who told her she could come on my set? who gave her a day pass? this is my production, dammit!"

but she was the first of many visitors, laughing open a mouthful of blood, of birds that turned into stealth fighters whipping around the ranch, committed to bombing runs just above his head.

the kid always bought back new things. one day, a coca field stretched under her sandaled feet and invaded his living room, another time she wore the word contra carved into her tiny bird winged chest, and then there was that time she called for mama, and a huge dollar bill appeared with ronald's face where washington's should be. on wednesdays, that north guy would float through the bedroom ceiling on a parachute made of crackpipes. north would spread his arms wide, his chest filled with eyes staring through bars where his medals used to be, and sink down through the floor.

LBJ appeared on tuesday afternoons after lunch, would share a stogie with him and reminisce. In an effort to cheer him up, he would say things like, "hell. you got it easy, man. how'd you like to see platoon after platoon of em' file by, bungee stick torn and bullet holed, all of them with their bloody hands, screaming 'why? why? why?' with each salute?"

one day, ron is being wheeled onto the porch for some after-dinner fresh air when he caught sight of nixon sitting on the railing.

"i don't know what's wrong with you reagan. lookit me for chrissakes. we

both got blood on our hands, but one bungled up robbery, and i get labeled
the biggest crook in the country. you get away with murder (no pun intended)
and everybody still loves you when you field a few softball questions on
court tv. cheer the hell up. you got out with your balls intact."

serenity was ava gardner in a silver gown, slowly stroking his temples.

"what's the matter baby?"

"it's those damn ghost actors, ava. they act like it's grand central station
or something. when do i get my own goddam dressing room?"

but that kid. that kid was gonna have to go. last time she tried to speak, a
million children's voices rained on him like god's spit, whispering
"desaparecidos, desaparecidos" and with that she sprouted wings of giant
crinkled greenbacks and hovered over him with death in her eyes.

every night, ronald dreamed that he would wake from a dream of missile silos
circling the globe, the globe morphing into his disembodied skull, his skull
a swarming pit of nations that curse his soul, trigger his defense systems
that bring all the warheads crashing toward his disintegrating brain, that
wakes him up in the middle of the night screaming his lines with more
conviction than ever before, "mommy, mommy, where's the rest of me?"

and there, right above his head would hover a kite attached to his shallow
breath, a cloud of salvadoran/guatemalan/watts/cabrini/johannesburg
children, a flock of swollen bellies and bullet-smothered skins, an ocean of
small hands reaching down, waiting for ronnie to come out, to play.

Tyehimba Jess

blood *and* wine

my cries sampled on FM radio
the wai-wai-wicki-wailing at
the walls built up around my heart
an unnatural protection

my nails scratch
at packed tight masonry bricks
i didn't know i could build

it becomes harder to distinguish
between the free and plenty samples
and the costly real deal

i don't know if i'm crying
or if i've cut to commercial

concentrate

there is a fresh water pond
where i wash my hands and feet
cover my head and shoulders
before i kneel

there are grooves
worn places where my fists
assume their position
regularly-i know this place well

wai-wai-wicki-wailing at my wall
the echo of the auction block
driving me mad
the proctors & the gamblers sell
my sorrow back to me

the drumbeat
of my own highly pressurized heart in the
background, my own brother giving the pitch

at such an incredibly low price
i can hardly wai-wai-wicki-wait
to go in and buy it

quick fix distraction from my cry
waiting on the rainbow takes patience
a certain faith that tears can be filtered
through mortar and bricks
a certain trust that will keep me from running
to the store cash in hand
knowing if someone is selling my pain
in one aisle
they will surely sell some relief
in the next

Samiya A. Bashir

Corporate America
Comes to **El Barrio**

for Sandra Maria Esteves

It was a sad day
In the ghetto
When
Doña Cuca's Spanish
Restaurant
closed its doors
for the very
last time
Only memories
Of the greasy
Caribbean Cuisine
Would remind
Its old customers
Of what was
El Flavor del Barrio
Cause Corporations
Monetary Transformers
Or better yet
Devils in disguise
Had moved into
The poor neighborhood
Little/Overweight/Balding
Gringos had discovered gold
in them there ghettoes
Black folk were destitute
but damn
Tons of cash
Were being spent
On hole-in-the-wall
Establishments
Mr. big bucks "Rob-a-fella"
brought corporate America
to the needy citizens
of El Barrio

It was legendary
Clean
Immaculate and spacious
It could seat
One hundred and fifty
In the worst part of the hood
It was Economics
At its best!
It was the one and only
Magnifico
"Mac-cuchifritos"
Spanish Fast Food with style
Where all the workers
Had Latino Names
Like Juana, Maria, Jose, Pedro, Juan
And let's not forget our
faithful Affirmative Action
government appointed quotas
immigrant worker:
Chuy Jose De La Cruz Montessori Edward Olmos
Lopez Anthony Martin Puente
Even poor white trash
Were given full employment
Just as long as they spoke
In a terrible stereotypical accent
        "Olay! My naymo is Bob Smith
        Komo están ustedes! Si no ganamos
        No cobramos! Tienes un perro
  En tus pantalones! Would you like to try the special?"
Behold the ninth wonder
Suburban rich big wigs
Drove distances
To experience the gutter
Taste the magic
The feel of Mac arroz con gandules
Mac pernil
Mac alcapurria
Mac relleno de papa
Mac empanadilla
And everyone's favorite
Mac platanos/Mac plantains
Viejos, campesinos, jibaros

All complained
Of the new Yanqui
Business invasion
But their cries
Were short lived
For they eventually died
Like Doña Cuca
Leaving the youth
And future generations to believe
That being Latino lies
In a Styrofoam container.

Shaggy Flores

Calida Garcia—**Jobless** oil on canvas

The **Bird Cage** Bunch

for all those who don't believe in the freeze

and if you still
think that life is nothing
but absolute fun
one endless party of people
spacing out in the twilight zone
bones pop-locking to the bitter sweet
beat of disco-punk-funk
man it's rocking
slowly shocking lethal shit
inside your brain baby
maybe you don't believe that
when they drop the bomb on
the white boy
you too will be burned

Charlie R. Braxton

SURVIVORS

standing in the checkout line

the sister in front of me
pulls out a brand new book of food stamps

and eyes from all directions
cashier
bagboy
people in line behind me

> but not the white woman in the next line
> who softly whispers
> this will be with stamps

but eyes from all other directions

piercing
cutting
slashing
stabbing this sister
maiming her self pride
murdering her self esteem
mutilating her self respect

then i hear whispers behind me
the whispers you hear
when you know people are talking about you
but are too scared to say that shit out loud
whispers

reform
work like the rest of us

role call

laying up making babies
and this one...

        who me?

...probably has those damn food stamps too!

and i/we turned around

me and my feet
tired from working two jobs
to pay my half of the ghetto rent
me and my momma's back
strong from picking a bale of cotton a day
that provide us with still separate and unequal opportunity
load our mind guns with intellectual blanks
and march us to the front lines of the workforce
to be gunned down by part-time no-time hard-times
sister-soldiers, stronger bolder
surviviors
of the constant flurry of lies and misrepresentations
fired from the automatic image weapons of television networks
and media conglomerates
aimed at assassinating the realities of African American families in America
survivors
of the systematic destruction of our famlihoods
survivors
of the covert and overt racism of today

we are survivors
and descendants of survivors
of the war against our civil rights
descendants of survivors
of the post-reconstruction holocaust
descendants of survivors
of slavery in America
descendants of survivors
of the colonization of our mothers
the colonization of the motherland

and the colonization of the planet
that we are alive is a victory!

the cashier
not recognizing the sister
as the survivor she was
asked
WILL THAT BE WITH FOOD STAMPS?
the sister closed her eyes
looked into the mirror of her soul
saw herself
her mother
grandmother
great grandmother
other mothers
kissing white asses generation after generation
and she can't even use the stamps to buy toilet paper
with which to wipe her own
sister/soldier
felt the eyes
piercing
cutting
slashing
stabbing

WILL THAT BE WITH FOOD STAMPS?

she took a deep breath, smiled and said
for herself, for all of us
NO, I'LL BE PAYING WITH REPARATIONS

Kysha N. Brown

Renaldo Davidson—**Faces** oil pastel on paper

Callin Out Ya Uncle

Ya Uncle aint nuthin but a
A RED WHITE AND BLUE
  CESSPOOL
RACIST SWINE

CORRUPT CAPITLIST TROLL
A WAR MONGREL
HATIN ON LOVE WITH HIS
CHITTLIN BREATH
CRABNATION NOTIONS
  WANNABE MASSACHARLIE TO THE WORLD
PERPETRATIN A FREE & EQUAL SOCIETY

YA UNCLE GAVE BIRTH TO A
CORNUCOPIA OF ELECTED MUDSLINGERS
  DERELICTS & RANCID BRAIN BEAURACRATIC OAFS

SNOWSNAKES WITH ENOUGH VENOM TO ANNIHILATE
  ALL OTHER CULTURES
YA UNCLE IS A
DOOKY MOUF DERILICT SPEWIN & FOAMIN GREEN BILE
  FROM ANAL LIPS

A JEDI MIND TRICKSTER—

"We interrupt this program to bring you frontline news...
  Our Military Campaign has brought Friendly Casualities
  up to 10,000 but we will continue our Peace Initiatives
  now back to Survivors who Wanted to be Millionares"

UNCLE GREEDY RODENT
UNCLE DESTRUCTION

UNCLE SHARK TEETH PIRRANAH
UNCLE TOXIC WASTE KEEPER
UNCLE EMBRYONIC MUTATIONS

UNCLE INVENTOR OF TIE A YELLOW RED
  OR ANY OTHER COLOR RIBBION AROUND A PROBLEM
  WITHOUT SOLVING THA MUTHAFUCKA

UNCLE ENGRAVER OF YAKTY YAK YANG YANG DOUBLETALK

"We interrupt once again to bring you more frontline news...
Friendly Fire has brought the causualty number up to 1 million
  but we will continue our Peace Iniatives...Stay tuned as we bring you lost
episodes of I Dream of Jeanie"

Tish Benson

returned to sender

for Diallo and Dorismond

More than blood binds you. There is
The apple, bitten and browning.
There is flight. There are frank phone
Chords, wrapped long. There is Holy,
State of our union, leaking. There is lead.

We mourn you as if twice dead:
One, first slain with Toussaint:
The other, ancestor, long before ghost.
But what do we enshrine?
More than your blood blackens sidewalks.

There is the bird's tendency to soar,
The offense of your tongues
And movement. There is the
Threat of kin at floodgates.
There is keeping on.

The scent of menace is more than my own
Dark surface, swirling to target. There is
Gunsmoke settling. Warning floating red
Across waves. There is a sickening silence
Before the reckoning morn.

Mendi Lewis Obadike

Dear Daddy

e. st. louis, jan. 1960

i hope you are doing well.
the coat you sent me fit girt well
and the suit you sent girt
was a perfect fit on me.
i need a new coat (bad)
and girt needs a long-sleeved sweater
for a twelve year old.
we all need shoes;
donnell's soles have just come off.
did you get the Christmas card
we sent you?
maybe we can come and visit
for the summer.
P.S. i will be seventeen on friday.
your daughter, eva.

Andrea M. Wren

REBA is a STATE CHILD and what you call *fast.* She wears SHORT, TIGHT, straight skirts and smokes cigarettes on the corner under the firehouse tree. She styles her hair in a French Roll. She comes to my house to teach me how to do the *Boogaloo, the African Twist and the Philly Dog* (banned in three states). My grandfather says: *Reba is too grown for you. I don't think she should come here anymore.* The next thing I hear, **Reba is pregnant and tries to kill herself.** I never ask anyone to my house again. Reba is too grown.

Kate Rushin

BERNEATHA'S STORY
for Ntozake

mama may have a Cadillac / but i got me a Rolls / Rolls Royce his real name be 'Toine / but we all know Rolls go better wit Royce than Antoine do / n 'sides / i just like sayin it.

i know mama didn't want her 'Neatha to turn out turnin tricks / just like her / a 10 dollar ho wit a 20 dollar rent bill ain't no real mama's dream but / sometimes / 'specially these times / i ain't all sure my mama wuz real / but / i just gotta check my scars

mama wuz always half there n half not there / kinda like me but soon / jesus soon / i don't gotta be there no more neither / i don't gotta be here no more.

mama always be wantin me to talk to her bout sumptin but i ain't never had nuthin to say / come on 'Neatha / talk to mama tell / mama all about it [1] / she say after she sell me off to Cadillac for a five dollar vile o' crack / or any other mens what come in wit a 2 finger bottle of gin / tell / mama all about it she say / n then she'd pass away into her snow covered dreams

Papa may have a kingdom but he never come to save me.
i didn't never know my daddy / sheeit / i don't think my mama knew my daddy she wuz basin at the time / but i used to dream my daddy was a king in afrika / like that greasy ol' sign in Big Bobby Jr.'s Fish House / The Great Kings of Africa / yeah my daddy wuz a king n if i knew one thing from kinneygarten storytime it's dat ain't no princesses live like i do.

once my daddy come to see 'bout me / cuz a' course he would it's just africa's a long way away / he'd throw his spear / or whatevah / so hard it'd go through that pimp Cadillac's heart n come out the other side n me n mommy wd go back to his kingdom / away from all the white horses n glass pipes from broken noses black eyes n blood between my thighs n i'd go to school somewhere wouldn't none a them girls never laugh at me no more / but

god bless the child that's got her own my mama used to say when i wuz older 'fore she sent me to the back room / Are you my daddy? / huh, i used to ask that to every john she made me take, it wuz all of 'em by time i wuz nine i didn't want to miss my ex-cape / but mostly they just say yeah, sugar, i'll be yo daddy / come on ova heah n give ol poppa a kiss / n then they'd want me to kiss 'em in places my real daddy wouldn't never 'llow / course now that i'm 15 n grown i don't know bout that no more.

I got my own man now mama, I never wanted yours. I gotta Rolls n he don't put me in check near as much as yr Cadillac. But I'm tired mama. I wish I cd tell you how tired, how tired I be when the mornin comes. It's time I got my own now mama, n what I want is sleep. But mama's gone now. They said it wuz that gay disease that ain't so gay no more, n i ain't got nuthin left to live for.

mama i didn't never have the chance to be the child that's got her own / 'til now / i'm comin to you mama wanna tell you all about it / this baby girl here got sumpn too / finally / that's all her own / i got 26 pills i been savin since the day you left me mama / they tole me i got that shit too / just like you mama / i'm comin / wanna tell you all about it

hope it's quick / not like you mama / it's the only thing i ever had that's mine / 26 pills / im'a take 'em 1 by 1 wit this vial a 'caine / i cain't wait to see you mama wanna finally put a rest to both our pain

one. i'm comin to you mama / are you there? are you there?
two. i still love you mama / mama i need you / wanna tell you all about it
three. i got 26 sumpns i can finally call my own mama / mama

are you there?

Samiya A. Bashir

1 *Mama's quotes are used from "Crack Annie," by Ntozake Shange*

Excerpt from
Monster

Beula: Oh, there goes Mommy's baby! C'mere, Theresa. Look, Scotty, dere's Mommy's baby comin' in. Wait, wait, don't go to your room so quick. Come give Mummy a kiss. No? You don' wan' give Mummy kiss? Well that's alright. Mummy loves you. You may not love Mummy, but Mummy loves you.

Look, Scotty, you see how pretty my baby is? Oh, what you mean don't call you baby? As long as I live, you always be Mummy's baby, right, Scotty? Look at her. You see her? See she's grown tall, right? She'll probably be tall like my mama Sophie, but too bad she don't like to dress. *(Beat)*

Theresa, how come you don't like to dress up? Me and your grandmother always dressed. Always. Eva told me, said if Marsha didn't wear a dress at least once a week, she'd kill her. And Marsha ain't pretty. Oh shit-where's Eva? Oh, she and Ray went to her place? Good. All that psoriasis and stuff. I mean you pretty. And you don't take care. I mean she actually looks nasty. But even she tries to take care with her appearance. Scotty, you tell Theresa, tell her that men like feminine girls, right? Don't they? They like girls to dress up ... You would think that I don't buy her clothes or nothin', her dressin' the way she does, right? And in all black like that?

(To Theresa) Theresa, you fifteen years old dressin' in all that stuff. No, no wait a minute. Don't go to your room when I'm talking to you. I'm just telling you for your own good. Now, I'm glad you're smart and all *(to Scotty)* oh God, she's smart, but she's runnin' down there to that ole Village listenin' to the ole weird music.

Here, show Mummy how you dance. Go get music and show me and Scotty how you dance. *(Theresa says no)* No. You see, Scotty, you see? And she stays locked in that room in there listening to that stuff-ole weird music with the lights off or she reads all the time. What Scotty? You think she looks good? Yeah, she looks good to you? Scotty thinks you look good Theresa. He thinks you pretty. He thinks you dressed up in ole that black look'n like walkin' death looks good. He thinks you pretty. Well pretty is as pretty does. You walk around here sullen and lookin' at me like you looking at me now-like i shouldn't enjoy myself. Well I enjoy myself Theresa. Goddamn right! Yes, goddamn, take a drink and yes Scotty is my man. Oh you gettin' mad? I don't care nothin' about you gettin' mad. Look at you, dressed up like some old bull dyke. You disgust me. You really do. Nobody's good enough for you, right? You so above it all, right? Winfred asked you out. Just to go to the movies. You'd think he asked you to marry him, the way you acted. That's all, but no. He doesn't "share your interests." You mean he ain't like them freaks you hang with in that ole friggen Village. *(Beat)* Well let me tell you somethin' baby. I may not be a young woman, but men still like me. A lot of 'em are young men. A lot of them much younger than you, Scotty. Young. And when I was young I was way better lookin' than you. Ran rings around you. I was pretty as hell. You ain't in my league. You ain't in my league now. As a matter of fact, lemme hear you say it. That's right. You are not in my league. *(Beat)*

You come in here all nasty after you had your good time in your "East Village." *(Beat)* Scotty, you think she's pretty, huh? Dat's what you think? Well you don't know her. You don't know. So you get the fuck outta my house and tell Eva and Ray don't come back in here tonight either. I'm sick of all a y'all. Just get out. Theresa you go on to your room, I'm sick of you. Tryin' to take my man from me, my own daughter. Haven't you taken enough, goddamn you? Haven't you taken enough?

Dael Orlandersmith

Who's Afraid of a BLACK GRRRL REVOLUTION?

A Problackgrrrl-Feminist Founder's Statement on the Black Grrrl Revolution Struggle

Who's Afraid of a Black Grrrl Revolution? Those who maintain white male, white female, and black male dictated social systems, structures, and order. Those who hate a Black Grrrl for being "stuck up" and "self absorbed" enough to resist, outsmart, and overcome her multiple oppressions. Those who hate a Black Grrrl confident. Those who hate a Black Grrrl proud. Those who hate a Black Grrrl too successful. Too educated. Too cute. Too free. Shit, those who hate a Black Grrrl for fucking eating every day. For having shoes. For having decent shelter. Those afraid of a Black Grrrl Revolution just love the romanticized notion of Black Grrrl suffering. Love to hear of us raising twenty kids on four dollars a week and never miss a day of church. Love us to NEED them.

And why are they afraid of a Black Grrrl Revolution? Cause a Black Grrrl Revolution requires a full on eradication of all forms of oppression and folks just want to eradicate the oppressions that affect them—the white, the male, the privileged. Cause folks just can't bear the thought of living a life void of the right to oppress in some capacity. Well, perhaps those afraid of a Black Grrrl Revolution are merely addicted to some form of privilege and are just not ready to let it go. Perhaps those afraid of a Black Grrrl Revolution are more self-serving than apathetic. Perhaps. Well, then it's the folks who could not care less about a Black Grrrl Revolution who are in straight up collusion with oppression.

Who could not care less about a Black Grrrl Revolution? Smug motherfuckers so filled up with their own privilege and popular causes could not care less that Black Grrrls suffer every form of a global human oppression. Could not give a fuck that Black Grrrls live lifelong slow deaths buried under the weight of deferred dreams in serving blackmalewhitemalewhitefemalekind. Those same hypocrites who march for Mumia yet go on with their days and sleep tight at night when little Black Grrrls are gang raped in school. Those same hypocrites who iconize urban superstar rapists and talk shit about taking down the world bank-yet when and how do they support-not pimp, not profit from-but SUPPORT the independent and unadulterated visions of Black Grrrls? No, they just keep on building new and improved establishments for Black Grrrls to file for-scrub up for-type for-manage for-sing for-dance for.

And they could not care less that Black Grrrl brilliance goes unrecognized, could not care less as long as they all remain white or male or privileged on the backs of Black Grrrls.

How do they try to prevent a Black Grrrl Revolution? By perpetuating Black Grrrl exhaustion and broken heartedness. By convincing Black Grrrls that they cannot do anything on their own. By devising of new establishments for Black Grrrls to accessorize. By denying Black Grrrls access to the ol' white boy, ol' white girl, and ol' black boy networks. By denying Black Grrrls access to information, to resources, to love, to truth, to honesty, to energy, to spray paint, to the turntables, to the mic, to the academy, to feminism, to liberation, to the tools of revolution. By calculatively ignoring how drained Black Grrrls are and still making demands on our cultural capital.

Now what happens when a Black Grrrl takes her crumbs and makes a cake, self educates, savvily allocates the 30 cents she makes on every dollar, overcomes their every attempt on her spirit, and utilizes all that space so graciously provided her by systematic isolation to create, name, fund, foster, conceptualize, and contextualize a Black Grrrl Revolution? They try to kill her. Kill her because somebody's got to be David if they are all to be Goliath. Kill her because somebody's got to be willing to play the part of the least valued if they are all to play the more valued. Kill her because somebody's got to be the volunteer if they are to be the owner. Kill her because somebody's got to do the legwork if they are all to be the visionaries. And in a white supremacist-light supremacist-patriarchal-capitalist-biphobic-homophobic-ageist (i.e. anti-blackgrrrl) world, it just must seem logical to the users and benefactors of privilege to just offer up Black Grrrls as the sacrificial lamb for their freedom, their privilege, their success, their survival.

How do they try to kill a Black Grrrl Revolution? Ten times out of ten they fire the bullet at the Darkest and/or Loudest Black Grrrl. La Negra Bruja, La Negra Revolucionaria, La Prietta Bata. Focus the red light of hate right at her forehead and then hate her even more for alluding, for surviving. All day, every fucking day, alluding their hate that aims to kill. Hate a Black Grrrl for fighting for her name. Hate a Black Grrrl for fighting for her right to exist fully on her own terms. Hate a Black Grrrl for getting out of line. Hate a Black Grrrl for being difficult. Hate that a Black Grrrl is the one who put the three words Black Grrrl Revolution together. All their Hate Hate Hate Hate Hate Hate Hate Hate Hate Hate Hate Hate Hate Hate Hate Hate Hate Hate Hate Hate Hate that drives them to try to kill a Black Grrrl Revolution.

Their weapons of choice when trying to kill a Black Grrrl Revolution? Slander, scrutiny, withdrawing and withholding of energy, envy, imbalanced competitiveness (cause privileged folks competing with multiply-marginalized folks is a little imbalanced, no?) discrediting, ignoring, assaults, insults, slighting, condescension, sexual-social-cultural rape, manipulation, dismissiveness, hypocrisy, erasure. But their all time favorite weapon of choice is reverse psychology. Convince a Black Grrrl that she's already liberated, that she's being greedy, that she's asking for too much, that she's conceited, that she's selfish, that she has an attitude, that one Angela, that one Alice, that one Oprah is one too many. Convince a Black Grrrl that being high up in their structures is the same thing as spearheading her own vision. Convince a Black Grrrl that it's all just one big coincidence, just one big fluke, that there hasn't been a genre, a global philosophy, a global movement rooted in, based on, and coming from the context of all grrrls of color and many languages. Convince a Black Grrrl that she's crazy for desiring a movement of her own. Convince a Black Grrrl to kill herself and ease their oppressor load. Then they all just sit back and jack and jill off in bliss as a Black Grrrl invisibilizes herself, plays herself down, takes back seat, beats herself up, negates herself, martyrs herself all in the name of trying to convince them that she is none of the things she's being accused of, all in the name of trying to convince them that she is not them-the oppressors and the privileged. Folks hate when Black Grrrl will and Black Grrrl brilliance outdoes their oppression and privilege. So they press the heel harder, pull the rank tighter, hoping to kill even the very possibilty of a Black Grrrl Revolution.

Now why would they want to kill even the very idea of a Black Grrrl Revolution? Because the anti-blackgrrrls can't HEAR a Black Grrrl. Because the anti-blackgrrrls can't SEE a Black Grrrl. Because the anti-blackgrrrls want Black Grrrls to remain wrapped up in struggles that liberate everyone else except for Black Grrrls. And even as anti-blackgrrrls march thousands deep demanding an end to all kinds of brutality that affects and/or kills whitemalewhitefemaleblackmalekind, even as the anti-blackgrrrls fight among and teargas each other, they all unite on the frontline to kill even the very idea of a Black Grrrl Revolution. And sometimes the anti-blackgrrrls are Black Grrrls.

Who's afraid of a Black Grrrl Revolution? In the end it doesn't matter who's afraid of a Black Grrrl Revolution because there will never be a free world without one. Because a free world is the one reality that cannot be created by walking around, walking over, and ignoring the most marginalized of Black Grrrls. Because a full on eradication of all oppression can not and will not be achieved without addressing every form of oppression to which the most marginalized of Black Grrrls are subject. So of all the freedom fighters, the militants, the liberals, the progressives, the radicals, the nationalists, the marxists, the thisxists and the thatxists I dare ask Who's down for a Black Grrrl Revolution?

Brigette M. Moore

What It's Like to Be a Mixed Girl
(For Those of You Who Aren't)

for Patricia & Mikaela Smith

well, i've got to say, it's people claiming
you're torn between tragic paths
when you know exactly where you walk
it's hair pulled out by girls who see
stuck up high yellow bitch
stamped on your breath
it's brothers blurting
damn i thought you was white
then asking for your phone number
it's being painted with zebra stripes
with brushes that assume you're confused
it's classical & hip hop cymbals clashing
it's you & your brothers
calling each other "nighonk"
because neither epithet fits
it's comparing yourself to
chocolate/vanilla swirl pudding pops so
you don't carry the weight of
in-between & enslaved fractions for names
it's your coworker's bottom lip dropping low
when you hang Audre Lorde's picture above your desk
it's recognizing a bass-filled moan
rolling into a phone's receiver from your mouth
it's questions, transitions, connections
it's tackling which hair moisturizer won't make
greasy clumps or itchy scalp with no help from momma
it's dreaming your hair curls in proportion to
your miraculously darkened skin, then
waking up when your voice reminds you
You're Black.

Tara Betts

GROWING *Wild*

Every which way and all over the place is how my hair wills to be/It strains against braids and barrettes, rebels against the comb and brush because it must be free/To twirl, spiral, wave and curl itself into formlessness like water, like wind, like fire, like me.

Masters of hair manipulation, my mother, grandmother, aunties, cousins and even the older girls who pass the day at the black-topped playground down the hill and a multitude of other self-proclaimed experts vow to know just how to fix my wild, frizzy, curly hair-more water on the brush, Vaseline, setting lotion, coconut oil, or maybe tighter braids. I am the middle child, the one in the first grade. I listen patiently and stare at the ground as strangers finger and stroke my hair making remarks trying to describe and define it: fuzzy, fluffy, puffy, wooly. My mom always tells them that I was born with a head full of hair. That getting my hair done each morning is our biggest battle.

When she washes it on Saturday mornings pouring entire pitchers full of water over my scalp, every drop disappears into the sopping, spongy mass that coils into the drain and rests against the cool, silvery steel of the kitchen sink. And there are so many people waiting, wishing they could get their hands on my head to really and finally do something with it.

"What a waste. To have all that hair and not know what to do with it." These are the words I hear from the girls on the playground, the ones who don't want it to rain and mess up their shiny pressed and curled hairstyles. The ones who pretend to cut my hair with make believe scissors. There are girls with longer hair, especially the Puerto Rican girls. There are girls with thicker braids and fatter double twists than mine, but no one else's hair breaks free from braids and twists or frizzes and curls right back up after spending two hours on humungous rollers under a hot dryer and being blown straight with an even hotter blow dryer that makes me jump every time the air hits my scalp.

Every morning, after long battles to keep newly braided strands from unraveling and popping off the barrettes and plastic bobbles on black elastic, I am finally released from the vice grip of my mother's knees to head out for school or the playground. But by the time I get home, my hair is loosed—has freed itself or been emancipated by curious hands that just want to see or touch all that hair.

My hair, like me, is wild—longing to be whatever it is. To explore and stretch out. To take up as much room as it needs wherever and whenever. When I can't take it anymore, the pulling and tugging, the jerking and tearing away of tangles, the fixing of my hair and therefore me, I rebel. At the foot of the steps one Saturday morning, I tell my mother I am not getting my hair done anymore.

"Not getting your hair done? Sit your behind down here," she says while pointing to the space on the floor between her knees, "and pass me the No More Tangles and the big comb out of that bag."

After a few attempts at raking through the jungle that is my morning hair with the massive, black, plastic comb, I am squirming, eyes pooling with water from straining to remain in their sockets. I whine and wince, unable to sit still. My mother has had it, too. She is "sick of fooling with this mess."

"We're going to the hair salon," she tells me.

I am full of relief and feeling special when I climb into the car next to her to go to the salon because it is just the two of us, and I feel that I have finally been heard and understood.

Central Avenue has big stores and little shops lined up on both sides of the busy street, one after another for miles. I am full of maybes on the way. Maybe the people in Scarsdale know how to fix my hair. Maybe they will give us the right spray or a magic cream or a special comb. Maybe they will make my hair do what Lisa Fontanella's does when she bends forward and brushes her hair upside down without catching a snag and flips it over her back where it just lies there all smooth and shiny on her navy blue vest.

In front of where we are parked is a giant picture window that says Garden of Eve with a big red apple painted on the glass that makes me think of the poison apple in Snow White and the Seven Dwarfs. I cup my hands around my face and press against the glass to see inside. There are women sitting under dryers reading magazines and smoking cigarettes and others are having their nails done. They are not little girls like me.

"Come on," my mother says holding the door. A warm rush of smoky air tinged with the cocoa smell of Mommy's hands catches the breeze.

We are heading for a lady with hair like mine, but she is not black like Mommy and me. Mommy is moving as if everyone in the place is not staring at us, so I decide to do the same thing. Her hand is gripping mine with the all too familiar, "Don't' say a word. Just ignore them. We belong here just as much as anyone else," signal that I know so well.

"May I help you?" the curly headed woman says.

"I called about my daughter's hair."

They have plastic covered chairs that go up and down and round and round. Once I am in one of the chairs, my mother leaves me there with all the ladies. They don't speak to me.

While she washes my hair, I study the tiny star dangling from the chain around her neck. After she finishes, she leads me back to the swivel chair and raises an eyebrow and exhales a deeply drawn breath as if to say something, but nothing comes out. It takes what feels like days to get the tangles out in tiny sections, but it doesn't hurt at all. It is like magic. Overjoyed, I think this is the best thing that has ever happened to me and to my hair. I fight back a wide smile and make a mental note to tell my mother how to do it just the lady does it.

She parts my hair right down the middle and makes two big ponytails, one left, one right with giant rubber bands. She braids them and rubber bands the ends. Then she cuts them off. I sit, bewildered.

My braids are on the counter, just like that. I think she will put them back. No words have passed between us. Not even one. When she is finished cutting and combing, I am nearly hairless except for the curly cap left covering my scalp like forest floor moss.

When my mother comes back for me, I am sitting under a tall lamp with a long neck that bends and has a red bulb that beams down on my head. It feels like sunshine. I sit motionless and speechless under the fake sun hoping my mother will tell the lady that she has to put my braids back on, but she just fingers my tiny curls.

"You mean to tell me her hair is still wet? She's been in here for over an hour already," my mother says just before she moves her hand away to fish around in her brown leather handbag. I trace the big gold initials on the clasp with my eyes as she walks toward the register, JEM. I know what the first and last letters stand for, but not the middle one.

"How much?" she asks the lady.

"Eighteen dollars."

"The sign says ten."

"Yes Ma'am. Ten and up. It took me nearly an hour just to comb the tangles out, Ma'am."

"You don't have to tell me. Who do you think has been combing the tangles out of her hair for the last six years?"

She pays the lady. I want her to buy a magic spray or cream or something, anything to put my braids back on my head. Instead, she marches back to where I am seated and pulls me by one arm toward the door. My braids are still on the counter, but we are moving fast and Mommy is mumbling about how white folks must think she has all the time and money in the world.

All I can think about is that we are leaving my hair. In the car, I strain my neck trying to keep the salon from fading from view, but I don't dare say anything when my mother is on fire. At the traffic light, I decide it's worth the risk, so I spit it out, "We left my hair there?"

"Your hair? What are you talking about?"

I begin to cry when she tries to explain that my hair looks nice like this. That it is really cute. Really. That now we won't have to spend all of that time messing with my hair every morning, but all I want is my hair. There's nothing she can do about it now she tells me. She says that I should have spoken up when I had the chance. When was my chance?

The short walk to school on Monday stretches for miles; only, this time no one is staring or making remarks about my hair. My hands are as preoccupied as my mind as they search nervously for what had once been a part of me. I take up less space and exist quietly where once I had sprawled my entire self loosely through the air, spilling over the sides of time and exploring space in free flowing spirals. Like my hair, I am cut off.

I am silent, enraged, exposed, and defeated by the solution to the problem of having hair that was too big, hair that belonged neither here nor there, hair that would not conform or cooperate with the expectations and demands of others, hair that would not stay in place, hair that would not be controlled, hair that stood up and out and commanded attention.

Carol Smith Passariello

Kenneth L. Addison—**Braiding Rituals** mixed media collage

Poem Where My Mother and Father are Absent

My sisters and I
on the winding path:
the side of the mountain
leading to the river.

One of us getting sick
in the back of Aunty's car;
all of us swaying together
unable to stop.

Our nakedness,
white as sunlight;
a fisherman and his son
watching: our small bottoms

emerging from clear water,
smooth stones underneath;
our submerged bodies
exposed to no one.

Aunty scrubbing
against harder rocks,
trying to get stains out;
her girlfriend fixing lunch.

My sisters and I
running with outstretched arms;
the river calling us
to come back in,

to stay among reeds,
stay floating
in its steady stream,
not return to the house

of broken windows,
thorn-covered walls,
the empty porch swing
creaking in the wind.

Shara McCallum

The Zoo

I was always embarrassed
going to the zoo
my mother was fat
her boyfriend had blurry tattoos
on his arms.
He never liked us
and dragged along
some of his own kids
to hate us even more.
He would get drunk
and curse loudly at us.
I walked ahead,
my brother lagged behind,
my mother never said anything.
I saw him punch her
in the mouth
the one time she did.

We never had money
to buy anything in the gift shop
we were always just looking.
My brother stole
a tiny plastic polar bear once.
He ran to me and unclasped his fist
to show me as we walked to the car.
He even let me hold it
while he sat on my lap.
We snuck it back and forth
and never told anyone.
I don't know why
We would go.
Trying so hard to do
what seemed so easy
for everyone else.

She is still missing that tooth.

Melanie Hope

Celebration

Summer days disrupted by trickster's
hand at play. Someone's child, brother,
son dressed all in red fell across
cement of a brownstone stoop.
Bullet casings sprayed over the ground.
One can hardly see the blood on his
clothes except for the outlines of an
unknown country gathering width across
his back. The old men who witness
his fall, stand back, afraid.
Grapevine hurricane of children
talking among themselves rushing
past fear or reason to see the fallen
one. It's almost like going to a party,
the excitement lights their faces.
A block away robust sounds of gospel
music burst through the air like trumpets.
A weird epiphany it's churchtime in the streets
and worshippers stand, arms raised with their
mind on the lord, unaware a child
dies in full view, while they celebrate.

Jacqueline Johnson

Black or American

I love Alana. I just wish she didn't live in Harlem. My Brooklyn ass is tired of making the hour trip uptown just to get some.

If it wasn't for her, I would have been in Flatbush when the news broke instead of standing here on this train platform feeling for the first time like an outsider amongst my own kind.

"Reparations brother!" Someone shouted, patting me on the back. They were all shouting, frantically congratulating each other, celebrating the passing of S9821-the reparations bill that promises to compensate American citizens of African descent for years of unpaid slave labor.

I have been deemed ineligible.

"Hello?" I said walking closer to the train exit to get better cell phone reception.

"Nigel? It's Alana."

I didn't answer. I was still fuming from our argument this morning.

"Nigel, can you hear me?" I heard her sigh but I still didn't answer. "I'm sorry. I didn't mean to be so..."

"Insensitive," I said coming to her rescue. "That's what I'd call it. When your girlfriend tells you she thinks it's extremely fair that you can't be compensated because your parents were born in Jamaica, that's called being insensitive."

Now she was quiet. I leaned against a poster of an enlarged subway map and waited for her to speak. Two trains had come and gone. I was already late to work.

"You can have some of whatever money I get. At least I have slave ancestors on one side of my family, so I can get half of the $500,000. I don't know, the newscasters on CNN said the rules were very specific and complicated."

"No thanks," I said to both Alana and the man passing out free t-shirts with a mule on the front and the words "40 Acres" on the back.

"Come on Nigel, you can borrow some for your..." Borrow? I immediately cut her off.

"Which half of you is going to submit the claim? The white half or the black half? Or are you still hanging on to 'other'?"

She hung up. I knew that would end the conversation.

I don't even feel like going to work now. The whole white office will be talking or trying not to talk about the bill. Ever since it was introduced, my co-workers and I tip-toe together, making small talk about current events but always careful not to mention what it's opponents call the "Boat Bill."

I choose going home over work. My block is 95 percent West Indian, so I know there will be someone to empathize with me. I brace myself for the massive crowd awaiting me on the next train. I don't care how hard I have to push to get on, I can't stand being surrounded by all these liberated cotton slave blacks any longer. Sugar cane enslaved too.

The conductor doesn't have to announce the stops for me to know that I'm getting closer to home. As the train makes its way downtown and into Brooklyn, the emotional energy in my car drops from elation to surprise to guilt to overwhelming disappointment and anger.

"Flatbush Avenue!" announced the conductor.

"Welcome home," I say aloud.

It's as if the Harlem celebration happened in a foreign country. This train platform is devoid of happy shouts and dancing people. No one's passing out free t-shirts or embracing strangers with congratulatory hugs.

I make my way up the stairs and out on to the street. I'm hit with the warm smell of just-baked plantain tarts and the sound of dance hall music from the man on the corner peddling mixed tapes. The street is saturated with makeshift grocery stores and delis, patty shops and a host of crowded, overstocked stores no one has ever heard of.

"What does reparations mean?" Asks Malcolm, whose 15 year old ass should be in school.

"It means we gettin paid son!" says Akiel jumping up and down. He's the eyes and ears of the block. "We gettin paaaiiidd!"

I interrupt their conversation and run down what I know to be the truth.

"Yo, how you jus gonna walk up on niggas and casually drop some shit like that?" I'm shocked that Akiel is so unaware. The announcement has been all over the news. I expect that from Malcolm, but not from Akiel.

"It's true," I tell them. It feels good to have someone to share my misery with. "We can't have not one single penny of that money. We can't even get the free college education or down payment on a house or any of that other free shit that would make our lives easier."

Akiel slams his bottle of carrot juice on the brick-faced apartment building behind us. Malcolm just stares at the bleeding cut on Akiel's hand and says nothing. I don't say anything either because I don't have anything to say.

*   *   *

I never expected to be barred from compensation. If I had known my American citizenship would be cast aside, I wouldn't have voted for the Reformist party or helped the great-grandson of the late Al Sharpton in his efforts to get every single black citizen to support the Boat Bill. It was largely due to my neighborhood's grass-roots campaign that Sharpton landed appearances on numerous t.v. and radio shows, begging black people to rally behind our new female president and Reformist congressmen.

"It will help strengthen and revitalize the black community!" he urged. "Renew our sense of pride! Finally legitimize our plight," he proclaimed. Liar. The bill has done nothing but deteriorate what was left of our community.

It's been six months and four days since the reparations bill was enacted into law. Since that time, I've come to hate any black American as defined by the language in the Boat Bill. Up in Harlem, they hate us West Indians and down here in Brooklyn, we hate them cotton-pickin niggas.

I refuse to go anywhere near Harlem, not even to see Alana. Somehow and for some reason, we're still together. Although I don't see how because she's become more intolerable ever since she discovered that she too is ineligible to receive compensation. That $250,000 that she was so willing to share with me, lend to me...It was whisked away from her because she's not a full 3/4 black. When I found out all I could say was, "Princess, you can't complain. That is an extremely fair clause."

The only thing we seem to agree on these days is that the entire bill is one big catch 22. I've been familiarizing myself with the provisions of the appropriations process. I need to be thoroughly informed for the upcoming Senate hearings (they just want to see us dance and sing for our supper), which are being held in response to what the white supremacy groups coined the BLACKout. Africans, West Indians, mulattos, octoroons, Native Americans (what? you think they're not part of us?), Spanish speaking people of color, and all others conveniently excluded from America's so called apology, are refusing to work.

I was glad my mother happily accepted the challenge. I hate the family she works for and the fact that my mother is their mother for hire. But she's so attached to those kids, she feels like she's abandoned them.

"Let it go Ma," I said trying to absolve her of the unnecessary guilt. "It's about time we started using that 'one nation under God, indivisible' shit to our advantage." She frowned at my language and waved me out of her kitchen with one hand.

I ran into the living room, grabbed today's newspaper and rushed back into the kitchen to show my mother that the BLACKout has the entire country thrown off.

"See, it's working," I said pointing to the front page story and picture. I began reading the article, "The whole New York City transit system has come to a halt." She didn't say anything but her eyes said read on, so I did.

"People of color were the train conductors, bus drivers, subway booth attendants and everything in between. Other large cities are also experiencing the results of this massive Boat Bill backlash. Atlanta, Los Angles and Philadelphia have no cab service and have been stripped of their migrant workers, housekeepers, secretaries, airport crews, trashmen, janitors, nannies and free jailhouse labor." My mother just nodded her head and waved me out of her kitchen again. I smiled at her and understood that she had heard all she needed to hear to legitimize her refusal to work.

I've been trying to explain the significance of this to Alana for over 20 minutes, but her non-white, non-black ass can't seem to understand.

"You and your blanket generalizations. My mom's a financial analyst." That would be her black half. "And my dad is..." she stopped.

"Do you ever actually listen or do you just wait for the pause in conversation? It's a modern day slave revolt! We been serving them for years. Serve, serve, serve. Then they say we'll do you a favor and free you. But most of us are still stuck serving them in some way. And now they realize that not only did we build this country, but we've kept it going." I stood up and started pacing because I was getting excited. I couldn't just sit still and look at her barely there black face anymore. Damn, her mom must have had some white features to pass on too.

"Are you into that people of Israel religion again?"

"Israelites, baby."

She started to speak but I shh'd her and turned up the volume on the television so we could hear President Charlene Duffy try to kiss and makeup. The more she talked, the more she rationalized the provisions for eligibility, the more I realized that America never meant to truly repay us for its sins.

I began comparing what President Duffy said to my Senate hearing notes. Ineligible: any persons with ancestors who were free at any time before the enactment of the Emancipation Proclamation; any persons whose parents or grandparents were not born in the United States of America; any person who has or persons whose parents have been engaged in anti-government activities or activities that threaten the national security of the U.S. (e.g., members of the Nation of Islam, Black Panthers, draft dodging); any persons who have lived outside of the U.S. for a period of time exceeding two years for reasons other than military duty or employment assignments.

We continued watching, but I don't think Alana is listening anymore. Her nervous twitch is kicking in, causing her to braid and unbraid her wavy dirty-blond ponytail. I ignored her and continued comparing the president's words to my notes. Eligibility Requirements for Payment: anyone wishing to claim the full $500,000 and reparations benefit package must be able to prove slave lineage both paternally and maternally; $250,000 is granted per parent provided the person submitting the claim did not violate any provisions outlined in sub-section 29A. Households with an annual income of over $70,000 are only eligible for non-monetary compensation, e.g., free college tuition (public institutions only) and up to $20,000 in grant money for a down payment on a home.

"That's it! I'm out!!!" I yelled.

"Stop screaming! Everyone doesn't want to hear your business." Alana said annoyed.

"Nuttin will change!!!" I yelled some more. It's my house, why I should I be quiet? "I don't belong here anymore. I'm moving to Jamaica. Come, we'll stay at my grandmother's."

She started crying and sputtering words I couldn't understand. Finally she calmed down enough to speak clearly. "You're leaving?"

I kneeled down in front of her. "You know how I am star. Me never beg no one for a ting. I not startin now." I tried to get her to look at me, at least glance at me so I could read her eyes. All I got was a scrunched up brow, which usually meant that my in and out patois was getting on her nerves.

"I'm staying Nigel," she finally said.

At first I didn't understand her decision. I just couldn't understand why someone would want to stay in a country where people were ignorant enough to believe that a nationality is a race. Where black Americans can't be compensated for the unjust society that they've lived in all their lives simply because they have a fusion of cultures.

But for Alana, there was no fusion. American culture was the only one she had ever known, felt, believed in, fought against and formed her identity in. For the first time, my contempt for her switched to pity.

I passed the airline pack of peanuts to the man sitting on my right. I wonder if he's going home or if he's like me-leaving home to go home. He asked if Jamaica was my final destination. I told him yes.

"Know what I love best about Jamaica?" he asked me.

"What's that?"

"In Jamaica you're accepted as a man because you're a man. You don't have to prove it like you do in the states."

"True," I said. "But the worst part is having to prove you're black."

Jill Robinson

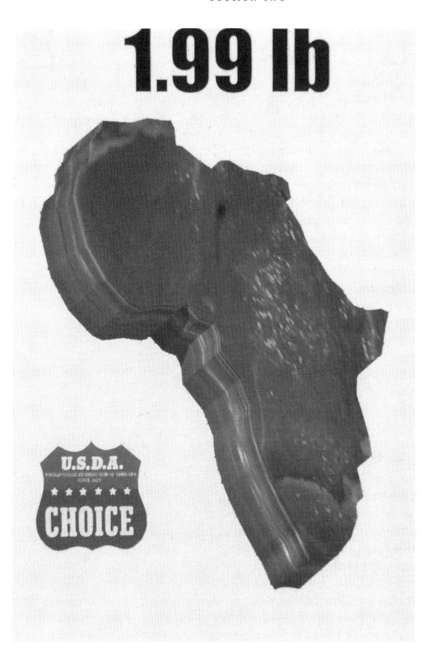

Derrick Adams—**Untitled** (from *The Consumer* series) manipulated digital print

WHAT I *Am*

Fred Sanford's on at 12
& I'm standing in the express lane (cash only)
about to buy Head & Shoulders
the white people shampoo, no one knows
what I am. My name could be Lamont.
George Clinton wears colors like Toucan Sam,
the Froot Loop pelican. Follow your nose,
he says. But I have no nose, no mouth,
so you tell me what's good, what's god,
what's funky. When I stop
by McDonalds for a cheeseburger, no one
suspects what I am. I smile at Ronald's poster,
perpetual grin behind the pissed-off, fly-girl
cashier I love. Where are my goddamn fries?
Ain't I American? I never say, Niggaz
in my poems. My ancestors didn't
emigrate. Why would anyone leave
their native land? I'm thinking about shooting
some hoop later on. I'll dunk on everyone
of those niggaz. They have no idea
what I am. I might be the next Jordan-
god. They don't know if Toni Morrison
is a woman or a man. Michael Jackson
is the biggest name in showbiz. Mamma se
Mamma sa mamma ku sa, sang the Bushmen
in Africa. I'll buy a dimebag after the game,
me & Jody. He says, Fuck them white people
at work, Man. He was an All-American
in high school. He's cool, but he don't know
what I am, & so what. Fred Sanford's on
in a few & I got the dandruff-free head
& shoulders of white people & a cheeseburger
belly & a Thriller CD & Nike high tops
& slaver's dead & the TV's my daddy-
          You big Dummy!
Fred tells Lamont.

Terrence Hayes

80

Kraig A. Blue—**My Environment** oil on canvas

Justice in the Techno Age

It was a carefully constructed plan
All loop holes called into action
All justifiable lies put to the test
All rules implemented to
Barricade rubber-stamped killers

It was a show of farce
A test of wills, cunningness, connivery
A pushing of the proverbial envelope

> Standing at the front of the conference room,
> pointer in hand,
> pointing at the image projected
> through the overhead projector

> *This is how we shoot an innocent*
> *Black pedestrian in front of his home*
> *And, get away with it*

> *This is how we gang up on*
> *The unknowing bystander*
> *Holding a sandwich,*
> *In the middle of the night,*
> *And use him for live target practice*

> *Notice how we didn't even have to do one day of community service.*

Nancy Mercado

Theodore A. Harris—**Arriving with Orders from Shaka Sankofa (Gary Graham)** collage

war PIGS

in a post war half awakened sleep
dreams consist of mushroom clouds
crying babies and dead bodies
machine gun salutes and maniacs
carrying hearts for souvenirs

amputated children yell for help
while lucky men come out
with their arms and legs
hunted by agent orange
on foreign lands flags wave for other countries
controlled by coups, world bank loans funding
armies with international conspiracies, hordes
of masked men fight seven year wars with no sunlight
clouds of death cover the villages for weeks, weeping
mothers holding their children in the palm of their hands
tears hold keys to life and secrets to death,

napalm nightmares h-bomb
hiroshima afternoon massacres
the sky turned the color of
dark purple, the moon
gave highlights through the clouds

it looks like death smiling upon us
the absence of hope lingering in the air
the stench of dead cows fouling the lungs
of breath taking survivors on the blackest day
when the sun rose
it rose a bloody red

s.r. bonafide

Cheney and Mandela:
Reconciling the Truth about Cheney's Vote

Newark, NJ, August 2000: We did not know then what we know now. We did not know that his statesmanship would be legendary, outstripped only by his forgiveness. We did not know he would be president, or that he could survive 27 years of imprisonment to walk free again. And in our nation, where athletes are superstars, we did not know that Americans would one day shower Nelson Mandela with ticker tape like the Yankees fresh from winning the pennant.

When congressman Dick Cheney voted against a 1986 resolution calling for the release of Nelson Mandela and the recognition of the African National Congress, Americans did know that this man had been waiting decades for his freedom. In a larger sense, so had all black South Africans. The tenets of American democracy—one man, one vote—were denied to the majority of citizens, along with the most basic economic and educational needs. Yet Republican vice-presidential candidate Cheney still defends his vote, saying recently on ABC's "This Week," that "The ANC was then viewed as a terrorist organization. I don't have any problems at all with the vote I cast 20 years ago." What, then, does this tell us about what information Mr. Cheney considers before he takes a decision? And what the long term consequences are likely to be, and on whom?

By no means were Mandela or the ANC universally viewed as "terrorists, evidenced by the fact that the vote on the resolution was 245 to 177 in favor, still shy of the two-thirds needed to override

President Reagan's veto. Mandela and his longtime friend and colleague ANC Secretary General Oliver Tambo pondered deeply before advocating violence as even a limited tactic of the ANC. In a 1958 conversation with economist Winifred Armstrong, they reflected on their belief that "If you sow violence, you reap violence." Armstrong, who has lived, traveled and written extensively about Africa, noted that "Mandela and colleagues thought ahead, and considered the impacts on all of the players, not just the home team."

As South Africa's Truth and Reconciliation Commission has revealed, much to the consternation of all involved, the ANC's armed wing committed acts of violence including bombings, as did the government. In fact, while the United States maintained diplomatic ties with South Africa, former president P. W. Botha ordered the 1988 bombing of the South African Council of Churches in Johannesburg. Twenty-three people were injured. Other government operatives did far worse for decades, killing and maiming everyone from political activists to infants.

Mandela made choices no man should ever have to make about whether to lead a people into bloodshed for a just cause. In an interview with Time magazine shortly before he received the Nobel Peace Prize in 1994, Mandela said that former ANC president and Nobel winner "Chief Albert Luthuli believed in nonviolence as a way of life. But we who were in touch with the grassroots persuaded the chief that if we did not begin the armed struggle, then people would proceed without guidance."

Dick Cheney has had to make life-and-death choices as well. His handlers are burnishing his star in large part based on his role in the Gulf War, a conflict which took on an elephant-and-flea aspect as American tanks literally rolled over fleeing Iraqui soldiers. Now, in the most American of parlays, Cheney has come back, briefcase in hand, to help Iraqui oil interests rebuild. Both partisan allies and veteran journalists call him a civil man, an intelligent man. But while people deride knee-jerk liberalism, there is such a thing as knee-jerk conservatism as well, as evidenced by the laundry list of Cheney votes on issues from armor-piercing bullets to defunding the preschool program Head Start.

America prides itself on its just wars. World War II produced what many now call "The Greatest Generation," and the Revolutionary War birthed us. But every battle leaves scars, some deeper than others. Even America could not accomplish its revolution without a full-fledged war. Nelson Mandela, through a mix of violence even he loathed and hard-won prison diplomacy, accomplished that. Rather than a terrorist, I wager most Americans—even some compassionate conservatives—would consider him a hero of democracy. As the Republicans gather in Philadelphia, we should think clearly about how we define democracy, how inclusive it is, and how far in the future our leaders must look to make the right choices for our nation, and the world.

Farai Chideya

Cleaning the
White House Latrine:
THE LAST YEARS OF CLARENCE THOMAS

Supreme Court Justice Clarence Thomas retired today, loosening the noose around Black people's necks. Upon stepping down from the bench, the graying Thomas said to Colin Powell, anchor of the new *Essence* half-hour celebrity talk show co-produced by Oprah Winfrey and Bill Cosby, "I took a wallop from black people all my life. Whites were the only one's that truly embraced me... I mean when I reached out to Anita—"

"You mean with the Coke bottle," Powell interjected.

In another clip from the interview a somber Powell pressed, "You regret being called a Tom."

"My mother should've named me something else. She should've seen it coming!"

What was most penetrating about Powell's interview was that he got Thomas to reveal never-before-mentioned secrets about his past, an experience he had with J. Edgar Hoover which appears in his newly released memoir *Cleaning the White House Latrine* which says it all, proving to be most compelling and revealing. "We saw each other on occasion. But I was an idealistic youth, fresh out of law school and I just couldn't wear garter belts, they made my legs itch and I could barely get my feet into them pumps. They killed my corns. You should've seen the blisters on my toes, all swolled up and pulsating! Looked like corn-on-the-cobs!"

Toward the end of the segment Powell and a camera crew escorted Thomas to a cemetery where he broke down in front of two unmarked graves believed to be where his mother & sister ended up after their long bout with welfare. A broken-down Thomas said through a rain forest of crocodile tears, "To my mother and sister who I left on welfare...ignore what happened, I was on my period."

Tony Medina

THE FURTHER ADVENTURES OF TUTOR THE TURTLE

Treasent-treasent Treezle-troam
Time for this one to come home...

After all I have told you, Tutah,
Are you sure you want to be black in America?

    Well, gee, Mr. Wizard, times have changed.
    It might be a little tough, but I'll be down
    with the brothers—they'll show me the ropes.

But, Tutah, look—the Republicans are on the rampage,
white people, in general, seem like dangerous playmates,
and the black community is riddled with...with
self-inflicted wounds!

    Yet and still, Mr. Wizard, I would be African-American.
    I've read about Fanny-Lou Hamer and Malcolm.
    Black people are bold and resilient and I wanna be one.

    I wanna raise up like Michael Jordan and blow jazz
    with Wynton Marsalis and...and...

What, Tutah, what!!?

    And I wants ta get funked up, Mr. Wizard-P-funk: The BOMB!

Alright, Tutah, remember if you hear any noise
it's just me and the boyz:

        {the incantation}

Two parts laugh and three parts pain
Cutting lash and hard-won gain

Thumpin' bass and rumble drums
Dr. King and drive-by guns

Skin of dark and spark of eye
Ella's grace and Pippen's glide

Purple Heart and might of back
Time for Tutor   to   be   BLACK!

{Tutor, transformed, disappears into America.   Ten minutes pass.}

HELP MR. WIZARD!

Tim Seibles

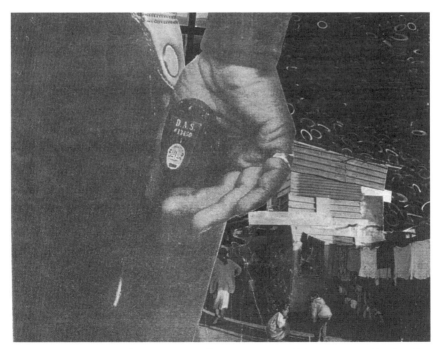

Theodore A. Harris—**The Cross, The Gun, Necklacing and Black People** collage

The Bush Boys

A Cowboy son
With no Indians to chase
Wears snake skin boots to bed
Sleep in soft leather chaps
And masturbates
To the whispers of death row

Next to twirling spurs
Sleeps a wife
Night gowned and powdered pretty
Grace Kelly to his Gary Cooper
One cowboy's palm strokes
Foreskin
Panting while another black man's heart
Tapers slow
In Texas

In Florida
A Sheriff packs his daddy's pistol
He is pattyroller searching
Everglades for runaways
Lusting for the rope
His humid breath
Leaks tobacco
Kisses his wife on her Mexican brown lips
As he tightens a noose
He grows hard for the smell
Of more wetbacks and white trash
Necks
Stretching like the black ones
His daddy used to
Brake.

Kelly Norman Ellis

Turtle **Eggs**

I'm laying on a beach in Mexico, just staring at the horizon when this white, gung-ho surfer dude comes up to me and says, "Blissed out, huh?" "Yes," I say, to which he responds by sitting down and telling me how he's traveled the world, but it's his first time to Mexico. "It's beautiful.—but would be even better," he adds, "if they had some environmentalists." "What?" I asked, eyeing him strangely, but believing he's found a fellow confidante, he continues. "The other day I went surfing on this practically deserted beach and I met two Mexican boys who tried to impress me by showing me some rare turtle eggs. They also told me turtle eggs are considered a delicacy to eat. But I got mad and told those boys that if they continued eating the eggs, turtles are going to become extinct."

It's obvious to me that the gung-ho surfer man is proud of his statements and thinks I share his perspective. Instead, I say, "Mexico is poor and the people's priorities are shelter and eating and until the quality of life for poor people is improved, they won't look after and care for the environment." Startled as if by a wave of politics—surfer dude rapidly removes himself—which brings me back to another point in my own Brooklyn neighborhood where, on a Sunday morning, I'm awakened at 9am by sounds of an electric saw and my neighbor's two agitated Rottweilers who are barking from yards over into my bedroom window—After working all night and feeling jolted out of a bartending stupor I rise, open the window wider, and yell, "Shut those fucking dogs up—and turn the goddamn saw off! It's 9am Sunday morning and people are trying to sleep!?" My neighbor barely responds and continues to saw, which brings me back to another point which I hate to say, hate when it's said about Asians, Blacks, Puerto Ricans, Irish, Italians and Jews but it's true—WHITES REALLY RUIN NEIGHBORHOODS.

Five years ago, when I moved in, my neighborhood was eclectically mixed with Blacks, Latinos, and White working class and it was quiet. No we didn't all get along, but it was quiet. Then three years ago-we were discovered as Manhattan's cheaper alternative, and suddenly there are Whites everywhere buying and renovating half-million dollar homes a block away from the projects—Whites who have replaced the indigenous Latino Cuchi Frito shops and cafe con leche with strict cappuccino —

Whites with dogs of every shape and size without leashes, allowed to run free, not understanding everyone in the free fucking world doesn't enjoy or love puffy wuffy.

There was a time in recent past when I lived and left my house in relative ease, but now, since the neighborhood changed, I'm accosted at the front door by two leashless, glaring rottweilers and an owner who's half a block away. When I complain he explains to me, like one of those new-agey permissive parents, how his obnoxious, tantrum-riddled rottweilers are just babies. Not only is my street littered and peppered with dog shit—property values are up! So that once moderately priced apartments are twice the price and artists are moving to Queens.

The Whites have also brought with them these strange little shops and restaurants, where you can't get a meal or sandwich for under $10, so that a meal around the block, offering a minute green salad, can cost upwards of $20 and there is still strangely nothing to eat. They're also into beautifying and improving the environment. Suddenly, there are private gardens cropping up everywhere, construction at every hour—morning, day, noon, and night—and every once-abandoned, dilapidated, warehouse is now considered a billion trillion dollar site—with ultra thin, Vanna White looking show room models and agencies like Ma Bell, Con Edison, and cable—once scarce—are now eager to please, and on once quiet, relatively clear streets there's traffic—tourists arriving by bus loads, carrying maps, eating at outdoor cafes and staring as I pass by in my casual Sunday sweats.

My new neighbors, like parents are also angry, righteous, and entitled—forming block parties, coop boards and offering millennial visions to determine the future of our neighborhood. One of my friends, who is White and lives next door, is out one day picking up the trash, trying to beautify the neighborhood. He looks at me strolling by and says, "Why don't Blacks do more? Why don't they care about the neighborhood?" I try to respond, as if for the entire race, not withstanding my experience is as far from the projects as it is from that of the Whites populating our neighborhood. Impatiently I explain, as I did to the gung-ho surfer, "Because we don't own half million dollar homes, and landlords exploit us. Until our everyday concerns for survival are met we can't care about the neighborhood." My neighbor looks at me unconvinced, half perplexed, as if we were discussing something as removed and distant as turtle eggs found by children on a Mexican beach.

Pamela Sneed

Mother Tongue:
unman chant

the *tin-tin-tin* follows
ca-*tuun-tuun*-cata-*TAN*
and I see myself
in the space between the hits
      it's not
      how fast I play - it's not
      my speed
      no eastern notation
      no western idealism
how I hear
is where I place myself
before the - *CaTUUN* - comes down -
piri - piri - piri - pown - skirts around the beat
before the beat
comes down surrounding every sound I found
myself inna place
where I laughed at familiar *off*
      I know *off* so well
      I breathe its edge so good
      when I smell its presence it zooms
      through pores, through blood - traveling...
                gouging out river-*POW! pam-pam*
              para-po / para-po! CHAM!
              CHEEEEEEEI or NO!
              Ga Tho --------
              Ga Tho --------
              GARA PA or no!

timbale to my bone
stirring slow familiar home
salsero to the beat
the one I come from - street but
street I be
tho not in me - I pray these knees
my bended pleas - to hear me I - tho lost...
              would stray inside you any day... / *bata-shun!*
              oron - oh no!
              sal sorro - no...soy yo / de tu...this

thing I know - so well...I don't

mother tongue who fails me so...I
mother tongue inside me - *YO!*
mami ton son - suro no AYYY!
mama cuun-CON torro soy...san -
gre de...san - gre tuyo - pero no! ...I know

no hay són puro de YO...
no pure song...of me...
no tongue...of you...
I am *no* where I know - where?
where I can be solo BORI-coro
de mi...   AIY - AIY - Yoooooo / CO-RO
     YAI - YAI - Yoooooo / ROYO
     NO - NO - Yorro Mas
     No Man No / Know Me? No,
     No Soy Yo...

a man once unmanned
  will man what is man
but once he is manned
  a man will unman

me llamo Llame-e-e-e-e-e
  un hombre sin nombre
me llama Llame-e-e-e-e-e
  y ahora soy hombre

i live as a ma-a-a-a-n
  a man of no name
my name is Unma-a-a-a-n
  unman i remain

Edwin Torres

The POWER
of the Press

I recently read an e-mail report from the Zora Neale Hurston Festival down in Florida. The writer was reporting on Kalamu ya Salaam's talk on technology, and of ya Salaam's oft-repeated words about how we, as black literati, should know and own the mechanisms of producing our work. As a black lesbian publisher putting out books by and for black lesbians, I fully grasp and wholeheartedly agree with his views. She who owns the press has the power of the press.

It matters who publishes. The literary world is full of stories like this one: author, rejected by hundreds of presses, decides to self-publish because same author believes there's an audience for the work. Author sells thousands of copies, mainstream press notices and picks up author for major book deal, author and publisher live happily ever after. Except most of those authors are men, and most of those presses are out to cash in.

Publishing used to be about getting the new and unique into the marketplace of ideas; now a lot of publishing is done according to the marketability of a book. Recent articles on the future of book publishing in *The New Yorker* and *The New York Times* stated that manuscripts submitted to mainstream presses currently undergo a profit-and-loss analysis before the press decides on manuscript acceptance. Remarkably, the chain bookstores are part of that process. Some mainstream presses ask the chains for advice on book titles, cover design and whether they think a manuscript will sell.

Book publishing began as an elite business for two main reasons: Books cost money, something men, especially elite men, always made more of, and because those who read were elite—typically white, male, wealthy, and above all, educated. For a long time, white women were not allowed education, under the arguments that it would reduce their femininity, that it might be harmful to their brains, that they were not biologically capable of learning things beyond cooking and sewing, and that since they better served society in the home, education about the world outside was unnecessary.

Education for blacks was denied even longer for many of the same reasons; too much learning might cause blacks to break out of their place in society. It was illegal for black children to go to public schools well into the 1900s. But with the availability of cheap paper, and the advent of public education, books became accessible to the white masses, and later, everybody else.

Alternative presses arose as a counter to commercial publishing. In order for their differing world views to be heard, "avant-garde" authors began self-publishing, and eventually those authors began publishing others' work as well. Their concern was more for culture than commerce, a concern which has continued to this day. As Robert McLaughlin states in his history of the alternative press, there are two publishing philosophies: "The one thinks literature is important to make a buck; the other thinks literature is important to change the world." Those out to change the world were mainly male and white; women and blacks were poorly represented in the early 1900s.

The Women in Print Movement was a result of the second wave of the women's movement and was exemplified by a flurry of pamphlets and newsletters geared to keeping women in the know. Eventually these pamphlets and periodicals were compiled into anthologies, and women's presses branched out into poetry, fiction, specialized anthologies and more.

The first press in the United States that published books by women of color for women of color, Kitchen Table: Women of Color Press, began for the same reasons the alternative presses began way back when for, as Barbara Smith said, "our need for autonomy, our need to determine independently both the content and conditions of our work, and to control the words and images that are produced about us." By 1980, feminist presses, i.e., white feminist presses, had begun to address the issue of racism within the women's movement by publishing "special issues," much like black gay and lesbian writers are being anthologized today within white gay publishing. Recognition came in the occasional short story or poem and that was, for many years, white feminists' way of acknowledging that black women were indeed women too, possibly with their own set of issues to deal with. I remember when I first came out in 1980. I looked for images of black lesbians in feminist literature and rarely found them. In the *Original Coming Out Stories*, for example, there were two women I could identify as nonwhite in a collection of 41 stories—one black and one Latina.

With the recent demise of Kitchen Table, black feminist nonfiction is mainly getting published by university presses, and black lesbian authors have discovered that trying to get published is as hard as ever. Many black presses won't publish work by women, much less lesbians, and many white feminist and lesbian presses won't take a chance on a new black author, reasoning that the press won't know how to market the book and will consequently lose money. Obviously some alternative presses are headed the same way the commercial ones are: the bottom line is financial and not cultural. There were a few feminist publishers committed to publishing the varied voices of women of color, but they are few and far between. In an anthology workshop conducted by a white woman in 1997, I learned that editors need to be sure to include one or two voices of color within the pages for the sake of politics. Black women's realities remain in the margin of many feminist books published today.

Many more black gay men's books are published than black lesbian books. It's an economic fact: men have more money—and access—for publishing than women. This goes for straight people, too. Black gay men find it hard to get published by white gay presses, just as black lesbians search for a home with a white, lesbian-owned press. Issues of class, race, gender and sexualities all play historic and current roles in that drama.

Most mainstream presses are now owned by entertainment conglomerates. such as Time/Warner, General Cinema, Viacom (Paramount), MCA (Universal Studios). Those corporations don't look to culture; they look to the bottom line. The bigger companies want profit margins of 12 percent and up, just like their profits on the other entertainment media they own. They see books as disposable entertainment to be treated like a movie, newspaper, or video. This does not bode well for serious, literary publishing.

After winning the two Lammy awards in 1998, I picked up a distributor, an alternative one. The first few months were great, since I'd had standing orders with the chains, and the

chains had refused to sell to me unless I had a distributor. After a year, though, my sales reports confirmed the standard practice of returns; 50 in one month means I lose $1,000. In December 2000, my distributor dropped me from its rolls; I don't think I was a profitable enough risk. So now I'm doing more handselling and book events, the way I started in 1997.

I sold books this way: I held signings in cities where the book's contributors lived, thus generating its own audience. I began to keep track of addresses and phone numbers. Black lesbian social groups helped tremendously with publicity by generating word-of-mouth sales, and sponsoring book signings in their cities.

I've also made alliances with many white gay women, women who own bookstores that came about during the Women in Print movement, women who've had a couple of decades of the theory of coalition building pushed into their brains. Interestingly, a few of these women knew the theory, but eschewed (by their actions) the practice, but most white women's bookstore owners that I've encountered were eager to add Red-Bone Press titles to their stock. When I would contact a black lesbian social group to ask about hosting an event, I'd hold the reading in local feminist bookstores, thus helping build some sort of coalition between black and white women in their communities.

When I called black bookstores to place the book in their stores, I was frequently met with hostility: "That kind of book won't sell here." This says a lot for the topic of race solidarity; sexuality seems to be one of the great dividers, at least in the publishing world. Qevin Oji of black gay-owned grapevinepress agrees: "In my humble opinion, black bookstores are the greatest and most unexpected censors of black gay and lesbian publishing, simply by refusing to stock the book for their lesbian and gay customers. In a sense, we can't 'come home' because there's nothing on the shelf that speaks specifically to who we are."

It's a wonder why I'm in this business, but I get affirmation every time I sell a book. It comes in the faces and voices of the women: when they tell me how long it took them to walk in the store just to buy it, what a treasure it was just to hold it, they couldn't imagine that there was a book out there just for them. So I believe my work is necessary, and well-appreciated. For now I continue to rely on the network of customers and independent women's and gay bookstores I've built and work on adding black bookstores to the mix.

Lisa C. Moore

Sheila L. Prevost—**Lethal** oil on canvas

Invasion of the Body Snatchers

A lot of yelling and violence. The wars.
You bled all over each other.

You thought you understood what money meant,
what money wanted, but you never imagined.

The things done for the sake of country.
For the sake of race.
Labor.
The carefully broken wheel of class.

You all had been so energetic and determined—
so plump with what we named "Freedom."

It must have been torture to keep it up.

When the televisions first came on
you were ready to sit down and watch.
You must have been almost praying

for someone to save you, to make it
so nobody needed to worry. We had
cleared the way with religion. There
wasn't any big hurry, but

by the time there were 3 stations and color
it seemed like you really wanted it

our way   to see and believe, to
laugh, laugh, laugh, to become

a Christian shopper
another day   another dollar:

That's easy enough to remember.
And shopping is a kind of prayer   a wish
for better things.

And gosh, look how bright it stays out there!
All the friends want cable now.

Shouldn't everyday be as Saturday as this–

The sun so blonde it's making everybody blind.

Do you ever catch yourself wondering
what they're thinking—other people,
how they keep coming to work so calm?

Some   you used to know. Some
were just like you. Remember:

those soaring conversations? Your hands
the speed of words,

as though you could actually
hold them? Your ideals—
the will to do Good, to claw
evil's clean-cut company face, the
we shall overcome and all that.

Well, you needed to be born again—well   you were.

Sometime between civil rights and *Oprah*,
somewhere between Vietnam and Desert Storm.

Remember how Baghdad lit up that first night, all the "sorties"
and here, the yellow ribbons—

weren't you   almost feeling   glad?

You think all this has something to do with Republicans?

Look at your watch,
how those thin hands move you around—
it's like you're floating, like you're
not really here now.

You think there's something strange in the water?
You think there's some new germ in the air?

Think fewer trees   just mean   fewer birds?

You have   no idea.

Tim Seibles

ROLE CALL III

ROLE CALL IS A ROLL CALL OF A NEW GENERATION OF BLACK ARTISTS AND WRITERS

THE ROLE CALL

JOHN ABNER has exhibited his work at The Brecht Forum Gallery in New York City, and his murals appear through out the city of Philadelphia. **STARR ACHÉ** is a writer, performer and activist of Haitian descent whose has been published in *Shadowbox*, a magazine of hip hop culture and politics. **DERRICK ADAMS'** art is a meditation on the active relationship between pop-cultural images and personality development: it interrogates the assumption that images are "uninterrupted" or pure and works toward exposing their perversion. He has exhibited at Rush Arts Gallery, Marymount College Gallery, Lowe Gallery and Gallery Annex. **JENOYNE ADAMS** is a writer, poet, and dancer as well as a 1998 PEN Center USA West Emerging Voices Fellow. A member of the World Stage Anansi Writer's Workshop in Leimart Park, in Los Angeles, C.A., she is the author of the novel, *Resurrecting Mingus*. **KENNETH L. ADDISON** has had his work exhibited at Pro Arts Gallery 2000, Triton Museum of Art, The Gallery Theater at Skyline College and Odun de Odun de: An Exhibition Celebrating Aspects of African-American Art and Culture in the Bay Area. **AKINTIUNDE** was born 22 June 1962 in Midwest USA. Interests include African/African American History; public speaking; chess; study and research of poetry and poetic forms (creator of the Eintou) **ELIZABETH ALEXANDER** is the author of *The Venus Hottentot* and *Body of Life*. **KAZIM ALI** has earned an MFA in poetry from New York University. **CAROL ALLEN** is a professor of English at Long Island University's Brooklyn campus. **JEFFREY RENARD ALLEN**, an Associate Professor of English at Queens College (CUNY), is the author of *Rails Under My Back* and *Harbors and Spirits*. **ARTHUR ADE AMAKER**, who teaches in Chicago's public school system, is coeditor of *Sons of Lovers*, an anthology of poetry by black men. **TA'SHIA ASANTI** was the first Black columnist for the *Lesbian News*. She is Managing Editor of *Gay Black Female Magazine* and an award-winning poet, filmmaker and journalist. **ASKHARI**'s work appears in *In the Tradition* and *Catalyst*. **JABARI ASIM**, an editor and book critic at *The Washington Post*, is author the of *The Road to Freedom*, and editor of *Not Guilty: Twelve Black Men Speak Out on the Law, Justice and Life*. **JACQUELINE P. BANYON (AKA *TADOW*)**, age 10, the precocious daughter of Sheree Renee Thomas, is a poet, rapper, and student in New York City. **HOLLY BASS**' work has appeared in *Black Prison Movements U.S.A.* **TISH BENSON** is a poet and playwright whose work has appeared in the anthologies In the Tradition, Verses That Hurt, Listen Up! and Bum Rush the Page: A Def Poetry Jam. **TARA BETTS**' poetry has appeared in Obsidian III, Dialogue, Mosaic, Poetry Slam, Powerlines, and Bum Rush the Page: A Def Poetry Jam. **MARLON BILLUPS**, co-founder and host of Third Floor Poets, has been published in Eagle and Egg: A Literary Journal. **DANIEL BLACK**, a professor of English and African American Studies at Clark Atlanta University, is author of Dismantling Black Manhood: An Historical and Literary Analysis of the Legacy of Slavery. **KRAIG A. BLUE**'s art appears on the cover of Black Prison Movements, USA; in The Black Holocaust for Beginners and In Defense of Mumia. **JANEÉ BOLDEN** is an MFA candidate at New York University. **S.R. BONAFIDE**'s poetry appears in Bum Rush the Page: A Def Poetry Jam. **SHANE BOOK** is the 1998 recipient of the Charles Johnson Prize in Poetry, and a New York Times Fellowship in Poetry to attend New York University. **LAWRENCE YTZHAK BRAITHWAITE** is the author of Wigger and ratz are nice. **CHARLIE R. BRAXTON**, author of Ascension from the Ashes, has been featured in the Black Nation, Catalyst, Cut Banks and the anthologies In the Tradition, Soulfires, Catch the Fire and Bum Rush the Page: A Def Poetry Jam. **SHARON BRIDGFORTH** is the author of The Bull-Jean Stories. **KYSHA N. BROWN** is a publisher and poet. She writes with NOMMO Literary Society, a New Orleans- based black writers' workshop. **ANTHONY BUTTS**, a Ph. D. candidate in poetry and gender theory at the University of Missouri in Columbia, is the author of Fifth Season. **KENNETH CARROLL**, author of So What: For the White Dude Who Said This Ain't Poetry, has appeared in In Search of Color Everywhere, Catch the Fire!, Spirit & Flame, and Bum Rush the Page: A Def Poetry Jam. **SHIRLEY CARTER**, a painter and print-maker living in the Bay Area, is also published in Erotique Noir/ Black Erotica, and Art Week. **ADRIAN CASTRO** is the author of Cantos to Blood & Honey. **JAMES E. CHERRY** has been published in City Stories, 360°-A Revolution in Black Poetry and Bum Rush the Page: A Def Poetry Jam, and City Stories. **FARAI CHIDEYA** is the author of The Color of Our Future and Don't Believe the Hype: Fighting Cultural Misinformation About African-Americans. **STACEYANN CHIN** has been published in Poetry Slam and Skyscrapers, Taxis & Tampons. **R. GREGORY CHRISTIE** is the illustator of The Palm of My Heart, Richard Wright and the Library Card, Passing Through and DeShawn Days.

THE ROLE CALL

THE ROLE CALL

CLAIRESA CLAY, a teacher and filmmaker, has been published in *In Defesne of Mumia* and *Bum Rush the Page: A Def Poetry Jam*. **ROSA CLEMENTE** is youth organizer for the F.R.E.E. Youth Empowerment Program of Central Brooklyn Partnership, an organizer with the Malcolm X Grassroots Movement and co-host of WBAI's *Where We Live* public affairs program. **HOWARD L. CRAFT** is the author of *Across the Blue Chasm*. **MORGAN MICHAEL CRAFT**, an avante garde musician, is the producer of the CD, *Adagio*. **QUASHELLE CURTIS** has exhibited at Ruth Hall Gallery, Morris Brown College; Rush Arts Gallery, African American Museum in Philadelphia, and King Plow Center, Atlanta, Georgia. **MICHAEL DATCHER** is the author of *Tough Love* and *Raising Fences*. **JITON SHARMAYNE DAVIDSON**, editor and publisher of *fyah.com*, is the author of the novels *Antiquated Journals* and *Lynchburg Grave*. **RENALDO DAVIDSON** has had his artwork published in *In Defense of Mumia* and Obsidian III. **EISA DAVIS'** work has been published in the anthologies *Step Into A World, Letters of Intent, To Be Real, The New Delta Review*, Cave Canem's 1999 and 2000 poetry collections, Rap Sheet and *The Source*. **NELSON DEMERY III**, an MFA student at the University of New Orleans, has appeared in *Drumvoices Revue* and *About Such Things Literary* magazine. **R. ERICA DOYLE'S** work appears in *Callaloo, Best American Poetry 2001, Other Countries: Voices Rising*, and *Bum Rush the Page: A Def Poetry Jam*. **TORKWASE DYSON** is a visual artist exploring the middle passage. She is completing a Masters of Fine Arts degree at Yale University. **KELLY NORMAN ELLIS**, an Assistant Professor of English and Associate Director of the Creative Writing Program at Chicago State University, has appeared in *Sisterfire, Spirit & Flame, Obsidian, Calyx*, and *Boomer Girls*. **THOMAS SAYERS ELLIS**, who teaches in the Department of English at Case Western Reserve University and in the Bennington Writers Seminars, is the author of *The Good Junk, The Genuine Negro Hero, and coeditor of On the Verge*. **STEVENSON ESTIMÉ** has exhibited at Meringer Gallery, Vienna, Austria; Times Square Gallery, Hunter College; Silvermine Arts Guild; and Art Lab Studio. **NIKKY FINNEY**, founding member of The Affrilachian Poets is the author of *On Wings Made Of Gauze, Heartwood* and *Rice*, winner of the PEN American Open Book Award in 1999. **MARILYN FLEMING,** an associate editor at *Black Issues Book Review* and a reviewer for *Ms.* magazine, is currently working on an urban sci-fi novella about genetic engineering and a novel about growing up black in xenophobic England. **JAIME "SHAGGY" FLORES** is the author of *Sancocho: A Book of Nuyorican Poetry*. **STEPHANIE MWANDISHI GADLIN**, former National Press Secretary to the Reverend Jesse Jackson, Sr, is a Chicago-based writer who focuses on cultural and socio-political issues. **AYESHA J. GALLION**, a first-generation St. Lucian in America and a 25-year-old, Morgan State University alumna, with a BA in Journalism, lives with her husband, Mutaalib, in New Jersey. **CALIDA GARCIA**'s paintings address the concept of identity and its relationship to love, sacrifice, hope and internal strength. Some of her most recent pieces contain Adinkra (West African) symbols to further express her own perception of their unique personal relationship to their social environment. She has exhibited her work at Cinque Gallery, Spelman College, Museo de Arte Contemperanio in Panama, and Camille Love Gallery. **DANIELLE LEGROS GEORGES**'s work appears in *Step Into a World*, *The Beacon Best of 1999*, *The Butterfly's Way: Voices from the Haitian Dyaspora in the United States* and *Bum Rush the Page: A Def Poetry Jam*. **BRIAN GILMORE** is the author of *Elvis Presley is Alive and Well and Living in Harlem* and *Jungle Nights and Soda Fountain Rags*. **THOMAS GLAVE**, an assistant professor of English and Africana Studies at the State University of New York, Binghamton, is the author of *Whose Song? and Other Stories*. **R.C. GLENN** is the author of *eyeseen: insights outward*. **TAJ GREENLEE** is an MFA candidate in the New York University's Creative Writing Program. **MICHAEL GUINN**, a Child Protective Services Investigator with the state of Texas, is the author of *Back Talk* and *Poetic Confessions from the Soul*. **DURIEL E. HARRIS**, a poetry editor for *Obsidian III: Literature in the African Diaspora*, appears in the anthologies *Spirit & Flame* and *Bum Rush the Page: A Def Poetry Jam*. **REGINALD HARRIS**' work appears in *African-American Review*, *Harvard Gay and Lesbian Review*, *Obsidian II*, *His 3*, and *Brown Sugar*. **THEODORE A. HARRIS** has had his work pulished in *In Defense of Mumia*, *Long Shot* and *The Hammer*. **YONA HARVEY**'s work has been published in *Catch the Fire!!!: A Generational Anthology of Contemporary African American Poetry* and *Bum Rush the Page: A Def Poetry Jam*. **SHAYLA HAWKINS**, a Cave Canem alumn, has appeared in *Obsidian II: Black Literature in Review* and *In Our Own Words*. **TERRANCE HAYES** is the author of *Muscular Music*. **ANGELA HODISON-MALELE** free

THE ROLE CALL

lance writes for the African American Newspaper, *The Kansas City Globe*, currently is engaged and is seeking her bachelors in elementary education. **ANDRE O. HOILETTE**'s work has appeared in the journals *Sideshow, Nexus, Ducttape Press*, and the anthology *Bum Rush the Page: A Def Poetry Jam*. **JOHNALYNN HOLLAND**, a film student at Howard University, has exhibited at Clark Atlanta University, Atlanta College of Art Gallery, New Visions and Spelman College. **LITA HOOPER** teaches writing at Georgia Perimeter College in Atlanta. She is a 2000 Hurston/Wright Fellow and holds a M.A. in Creative Writing from the University of Colorado at Boulder. **MELANIE HOPE** is a mother, a poet and a lesbian of African descent currently living in New York City. **ESTHER IVEREM** is the author of *The Time: Portrait of A Journey Home*. **MAJOR L. JACKSON** is the author of *Leaving Saturn* and coauthor (with Wadud) of *Back to Africa with a White Woman*. **G. WINSTON JAMES**, author of *Lyric: Poems Along A Broken Road*, is also featured in *Callaloo, Fighting Words: Personal Essays by Black Gay Men, His 2: Brilliant New Fiction by Gay Writers*, and *Sojourner: Black Gay Voices in the Age of AIDS*. **HONORÉE FANONNE JEFFERS** is the author of *The Gospel of Barbecue*. **TYEHIMBA JESS** has been published in the anthologies *Soul Fires: Young Black Men on Love and Violence* and *Bum Rush the Page: A Def Poetry Jam*, as well as *Obsidian III*. **JACQUELINE JOHNSON** is the author of *A Gathering of Mother Tongues* and *Stokely Carmichael: Leaders in the Civil Rights Movement*. **KARMA MAYET JOHNSON** is a poet, performing artist and teacher. She received an MFA in poetry from New York University and is a graduate fellow of the Cave Canem workshop/retreat for African American poets. **DOUG JONES** has been featured on Toni Short's WBAI radio program, *Person-to-Person*, from New York, and has written book reviews for *Black Issues Book Review* magazine. **ALLISON JOSEPH**, a professor at Southern Illinois University and the Poetry Editor of *Crab Orchard Review*, is the author *Soul Train, In Every Seam* and *What Keeps Us Here*. **KAGENDO** is a Kenyan feminist living in New York. **DOUGLAS KEARNEY**'s work appears in *Nommogeneity, Cave Canem: V, The Ethiop's Ear, The Amistad* and *The Publication*. **JOHN KEENE** is the author of *Annotations*. **JEREMIAH HOSEAH LANDES**, bandleader of Earthdriver, is producer of the CD, *No One's Slave*. **EMILY HOOPER LANSANA** is the Director of Education at Lincoln Center Theater. She is a member of the National

Association of Black Storytellers and her work in the Ethnic and Folk Arts has been recognized by the Illinois Arts Council. **TONI ASANTE LIGHTFOOT** is co-founder of the poetry collective Modern Urban Griots and leader in the national arts organization, Blackout Arts Collective. **KIM LOUISE**, former director of the New African Writers Workshop, has had her poetry and articles published in *Cathartic, Fine Lines, Papyrus*, and *The Omaha Star*. **ERIC MACK** has exhibited at Ruth Hall Gallery, Morris Brown College; McMillan Law Library, Emory University; Hammonds House, Atlanta, Georgia; Old Slave Mart Museum, Charleston, South Carolina. **KIM MAYHORN** has exhibited her work at The Bronx Museum, The African American Museum in Philadelphia, Here Art Gallery and The Whitney Museum of American Art, Independent Study Program. **SHARA MCCALLUM**, who teaches creative writing at the University of Memphis, is the author of *The Water Between Us*. **CATHERINE MCKINLEY** is the editor of *Afrekete*, and author *The Book of Sarahs*, from which her piece is excerpted. She lives in New York City. **MELISSA MCEWEN** was born and raised in Hartford, CT. A graduate from the University of Pittsburgh with a BA in English Writing, she is the mother of a five-year-old son, Izaiah Adrian McEwen. **NANCY MERCADO**, Editor-In-Chief of *Long Shot* literary magazine, is the author of *It Concerns the Madness*. **CHERYL L. MINOR** is a photographer and video producer in New York City. **GWENDOLYN A. MITCHELL**, author of *House of Women*, is an editor at Third World Press. **BRIGETTE M. MOORE**, founder of both Problackgrrrl-Feminism and Black Grrrl Revolution, Inc. has appered in *The Village Voice, Ms., Curve, Nylon, Jane, Y2G.Com*, and *The Chicago Sun Times Next Magazine*. **JESSICA CARE MOORE**, the publisher of Moore Black Press, is the author of *The Words Don't Fit in My Mouth*. **LENARD D. MOORE**, a professor at Shaw University, is the author of *Forever Home*. **LISA C. MOORE**, founder and editor of RedBone Press, is editor of *Does Your Mama Know? An Anthology of Black Lesbian Coming Out Stories*. **BRUCE MORROW** is the editor of *Shade: An Anthology of Fiction by Gay Men of African Descent*. Nigerian writer and editor **OKEY NDIBE** is the founding editor of *African Commentary*. His debut novel, *Arrows Of Rain* was released in 2000. **LETTA NEELY** is the author of *gawd and alluh huh sistahs* and *Juba* **NAVIN JUNE NORLING** has exhibited at Breer Library, Stanford

THE ROLE CALL

University;Isabel Percy West Gallery, California College and Crafts; Times Square Gallery, Hunter College; and Lynn House Gallery. **LISSETTE NORMAN** has been published in *freefall* poetry magazine, *Mosaic* literary magazine, and the anthologies, *Moving Beyond Boundaries* and *Bum Rush the Page: A Def Poetry Jam*. **MENDI LEWIS OBADIKE**, a Ph.D. candidate in Literature at Duke University, appears in *Collective Jukebox*, a travelling sound art exhibition, and the *Race and Digital Space* net art show. **DAEL ORLANDERSMITH** presented her first play, *Liar, Liar*, in New York in 1994, and since then has written several others, including *Beauty's Daughter*, which won the Obie Award in 1995, and *Monster*, which was presented to critical acclaim at the New York Theatre Workshop in 1996. **GREGORY PARDLO**, a recent graduate from the MFA at New York University with a fellowship from the *New York Times*, has appeared in *Callaloo*, *Hawaii Review*, *Lyric* and the anthology, *Bum Rush the Page: A Def Poetry Jam*. **G.E. PATTERSON** is the author of *Tug*. **WILLIE PERDOMO,** the author of *Where a Nickel Costs a Dime* and *Visiting Langston*, resides at the intersection of the street and the academy. **ROY L. PICKERING JR.** was born in St. Thomas, Virgin Islands, and moved to the Bronx, New York at the age of 5. Roy is now a freelance writer in New York City. He recently completed his debut novel, *Patches of Grey*. **PAMELA PLUMMER**, recipient of the Hughes, Diop, Knight Poetry Award from the Gwendolyn Brooks Center for Black Literature and Creative Writing, is the author of *Meditation on Ironing*. **KEVIN POWELL** is the author of *In the Tradition*, *recognize*, *Keepin' It Real* and *Step Into A World: A Global Anthology of The New Black Literature*. **ANTOINETTE PRESSLEY-SANON**, a Ph.D. candidate in African Languages and Literature at The University of Wisconsin, Madison, has exhibited her work at African Poetry Theater Gallery and York Community College. **ROHAN B PRESTON**, lead theater critic at *The Star Tribune*, is the author of *Dreams in Soy Sauce* and co-editor of the anthology *Soulfires: Young Black Men on Love and Violence*. **SHEILA L. PREVOST**, CEO of S.L. Prevost Design, has exhibited her work at the Caribbean Cultural Center, the Studio Museum. **KIM RANSOM**, author of *The Black House (from the kitchen to the closet)*, appears on jazz saxophonist, Ernest Dawkin's, New Horizon's CD, *Mother's Blue Velvet Shoes*. **DJ RENEGADE**, who has been published in *Callaloo*, *Asheville Poetry Review*, *Red Brick Review*, and the *GW Review*, and appears in the screenplay and film, *Slam*, is the author of *Shades of Blue*, *21 Blackjacks* and the editor of *The Red Rooster Social Club*. **JILL ROBINSON** is a marketing specialist who earned a BA in English from the University of Maryland at College Park and an MA in education from American University. The Cinnaminson, NJ native currently lives in Brooklyn, NY. **KATE RUSHIN** is the author of *The Black Back-ups*. **CARL HANCOCK RUX** is the author of *Pagan Operetta* and the spoken word CD, *Rux Revue*. **ALICIA VOGL SÁENZ**, a member of the L.A. Poetry Festival coordinating committee and the Women's Poetry Project, has been published in *Blue Mesa Review*, *Drum Voices Revue*, *Grand Street*, and is the author of the chapbook, *The Day I Wore the Red Coat*. **KIINI IBURA SALAAM** has appeared in *Fertile Ground*, *Dark Eros*, *Dark Matter*, *Father Songs*, *Men We Cherish*, *Essence*, *Ms.* and *Bum Rush the Page: A Def Poetry Jam*. **HANNAN SALEH**, a photographer based out of Philadelphia, mounts her color portraits on a variety of surfaces, attaching some of the work to worn plywood, spraypainting the wooden mattes with colors in the image. **FAITH SANGOMA**, the mother of two sons, Shango and Sowande-Ase, is a rape and incest survivor who is committed to using her art to break silences around issues of sexual abuse. **DARLENE ANITA SCOTT** recently completed her M.F.A. in creative writing at Virginia Commonwealth University where she edited the "elements" section of the university's news magazine, *The Vine*. **TIM SEIBLES** is the author of *Body Moves*, *Hurdy-Gurdy* and *Hammerlock*. **CHANGAMIRE SEMAKOKIRO** is a visual artist whose work has been published and exhibited around the country including shows at the Rush Art Gallery and the School of Visual Arts. **ANGELA SHANNON** appears in *Crab Orchard Review*, *Drumvoices Revue*, *Essence*, *Ploughshares*, *TriQuarterly*, *Water-Stone* and *Willow Review*, *Powerlines: A Decade of Poetry from Chicago's Guild Complex*, *Catch the Fire*, and *Step Into a World: A Global Anthology of the New Black Literature*. **NICHOLE L. SHIELDS**, author of *One Less Road To Travel*, has appeared in *The Iowa Review*, *Nexus*, *Rhapsody*, and the anthologies, *360°—A Revolution of Black Poets* and *Bum Rush the Page: A Def Poetry Jam*. **EVIE SHOCKLEY**, author of *The Gorgon Goddess*, has appeared in *The Beloit Poetry Journal*, *Callaloo*, *Catch the Fire*, *Crab Orchard Review*, *Dark Matter*, *New Sister*, *The North American Review*, and *Obsidian III*. **MICHAEL SIMANGA** is the author of the novel, *In the Shadow of the Son*

THE ROLE CALL

and the short story collection, *Tomorrow's Song and Other Stories*. **SHARRIF SIMMONS**, co-owner of MoorEpics: The Poetry Planet in Atlanta, is author of *Fast Cities and Objects That Burn* and the spoken word CD, *Sharrif Simmons and The Black Monsoon*. **BRYANT SMITH**, a member of the Gwendolyn Brooks Collective and the Chicago Writers Collective, has been published in *Warpland Journal*, and is the winner of the distinguished 1997 Gwendolyn Brooks Poetry Award. **CAROL SMITH PASSARIELLO**, who has appeared in *Black Issues Book Review*, *Honey* and the film, *The Best Man*, teaches in the English department at the State University of New York, Westchester Community College. **PAMELA SNEED**, who teaches at Long Island University's Brooklyn campus, is the author of *Imagine Being More Afraid of Freedom than Slavery*. **REBECCA STRAIT**'s work has been featured on *Kuma2.net*. **SHARAN STRANGE**, a founding member of the Dark Room Collective, is the author of *Ash*. **GINA M. STREATY** has been published in *BMa: The Sonia Sanchez Literary Review*, *In Our Own Words, Vol. II*, *The Saracen*, *FYAH*, *Voices*, *Black Arts Quarterly*, *The News & Observer Sunday Reader*, and *Windhover*. **MARIAHADESSA EKERE TALLIE**'s work has been published in *BOMB*, *Drumvoices Revue*, *Long Shot*, *Paris/Atlantic* and *Listen Up!* **NATASHA TARPLEY** is the author of *Girl in the Mirror: Three Generations of Black Women in Motion*, *I Love My Hair* and editor of *Testimony: Young African-Americans on Self-Discovery and Black Identity*. **SHEREE RENÉE THOMAS**, editor of *Dark Matter: A Century of Speculative Fiction from the African Diaspora*, has published short fiction and poetry in *KONCH*, *Drumvoices Revue*, *Obsidian III*, *FYAH.com*, as well as the antholoy, *Bum Rush the Page: A Def Poetry Jam*. **EDWIN TORRES** is the author of *I Hear Things People Haven't Said*, *Fractured Humorous* and the spoken word CD, *Holy Kid*. **NATASHA TRETHEWEY**, an assistant professor of English at Auburn University in Alabama, is the author of *Domestic Work*. **LYRAE VAN CLIEFF-STEFANON** has appeared in *African-American Review*, *Callaloo*, *Rattapallax*, *Shenandoah* and the anthology, *Bum Rush the Page: A Def Poetry Jam*. **DEBORAH VAUGHAN**, a law graduate who has worked as a political aide for the past ten years, has appeared in a number of anthologies, including *Obsidian III* and *Penguin: New Book of Black Writing*. **FRANK X WALKER**, director of Kentucky's Governor's School for the Arts and co-founder of the Affrilachian Poets, is the editor of

Affrilachia. **ANTHONY WALTON** is the author of *Mississippi: An American Journey*, *Crooked Weather*, and coauthor of *Go and Tell the Pharoah: The Autobiography of Rev. Al Sharpton*, and co-editor of two poetry anthologies with Michael A. Harper, *The Vintage Book of African American Poetry*, and *Every Shut Eye Ain't Asleep: An Anthology of Poetry by African Americans since 1945*. **ARTRESS BETHANY WHITE**'s work appears in *In the Tradition, Go the Way Your Blood Beats* and *Soul Survival: Black Power, Politics and Pleasure*. **MARVIN K. WHITE,** a member of the reknown poetry and performance troupe Pomo Afro Homos, is a poet, performer, and visual artist is the author of *Last Rights*. **ANGEL KYODO WILLIAMS** is the author of *Being Black: the Art of Living with Fearlessness and Grace*. **ANGELA A. WILLIAMS**' work appears in *Obsidian II, The Black Scholar, The Journal of African Journal-Writing* and *Obsidian III*. **JACQUELINE WOODSON** is the author a number of books for young adults, children and adults including *Autobiography of a Family Photo*, *Miracles Boys*, and *The Other Side*, and is the editor of *A Way Out of No Way: Writings About Growing Up Black in America*. **ANDREA M. WREN** has been published in *Eyeball, Drumvoices Revue, Young Tongues* and *In the Tradition: An Anthology of Young Black Writers*. **MTUME YA SALAAM**, former music editor of *The Black Collegian* and *www.black-collegian.com*, has had articles, interviews, music reviews, and profiles published in the *All Music Guide, African-American Review* and *Offbeat magazine*. **BRO. YAO** has been published in *African-American Review, Crab Orchard Review* and *Catch the Fire*. **KEVIN YOUNG** is the author of *Most Way Home, Giant Steps* and *To Repel Ghosts*. **SHAY YOUNGBLOOD** is the author of *The Big Mama Stories, Soul Kiss* and *Black Girl in Paris*.

THE ROLE CALL

AN EXPLORATION OF CURRENT CULTURAL AND CLASS BUSINESS IN POETRY, FICTION, ESSAYS, VISUAL ARTS AND THEATER-ON-THE-PAGE.

IV

Shirley Carter–**Girl Child, Paw Ain't No MLK** oil on canvas
    moneybags

This City Has a Broken Halo

from the notebooks of the Reverend Clarence James
on the eve of his fall from grace

I fear that God is just another woman that I have done wrong.
I was a master of conversion. The tender brains
of the uninitiated malleable blueprints at my fingertips.
She must have known a similar pleasure
peeled from the features of the first man
born beneath her approving gaze.

In the beginning, angels rode my soul like lampreys.
Led me to the fallen, the weak, and despised.
I filled their needs. Distributed
bite-sized philosophy, hip pocket grace
to carry them into salvation.

My soldiers were those that had known my
corporeal appetite. Recipients of the last
embraces of a godless man. Together
we grew my image until it eclipsed heaven.

I just want to tell her
It wasn't supposed to be like this.
I was the savior, one of the chosen.
My name and image billowing
against graffitied walls
a confirmation of my worldly kingdom.

Artress Bethany White

Catechism

He was a primer I must learn He was the Father trying
to break out all my teeth   make room for the Divine
I needed to be baptized in his piss   I should give
thanks for what he was about to do   what I had made him do
what I would make him do over and over to me
The Word only my death could recite   Fire tapping my scalp into ash
You walk too proud   I was a sin   You don't obey me I was a sin
You're nothing but a silly whore scratching your face
I was a sin   A praisesong in three notes
Did I believe in the holiness of fist
foot   cock   Yes I believed I was created to bleed for him
My womb was his and the direction of my eyes and the horizon was his
Say it My neck was meant to snap under his weight   Say it
I was never meant to be saved   He was my soul's
cantor   I better open up for almighty God

Honoée Fanonne Jeffers

118

Mother Love

I know what she knew
and when she knew it.
Standing behind her
in front of the stove.
My words still swirling
in the space between us.
The hem of my dress torn
below one knee. My hands
clutching and unclutching cloth
inside my pockets. The room
spinning darker and darker
like those nights she would leave
and the shadow would descend—
his greedy tongue lapping
up the air around my body.
But she kept sweeping the floor,
stoking the fire. Looked at me
only long enough to say:
Yu dutty little liar.

Shara McCallum

It's always the same. The white house. A little girl who cannot run,
cannot scream, can only take apples for kisses, gum for occupying
her tongue. It's always the same man, whiteyellowredbrown, his
hands larger than her mouth, crackedorsmooth, roughorsoft against
her lips. His lap is a hole. If she moves too close, she will sink. She
is never alone. Across the room, her sisters sleeporareawake. Down
the hall, she can still see them when it grows against her
handsfacebetweenherlegs. The mother is never home. Always that
same moonorsun staring on. The windows parted. The door ajar.
Bathroombedroomkitchen. Always, the same. When she wakes, the
moon still in its place. The water on the table.

Shara McCallum

Mama's Boy

What would his mama say? What would she think if she could see him now, about to do what he was about to do? She'd kick his butt good. Toss it into the streets with no more hesitation than if he were the garbage. His mother would be ashamed that he was her son. But she wasn't seeing this. And he didn't have a choice in the matter.

He had wanted to be down with the Crypt more than anything. Now he was. That brought responsibilities along with it. The lesson most stressed by his mother was that you live up to your responsibilities, no matter what. That was how she had managed to raise half a dozen kids in this neighborhood with no man around, and done just fine. Ricky was the last of those children to grow up, and the most difficult to get there. His older siblings had made Mama proud, graduating high school, getting jobs with the city, marrying before kids were on the way. They made things easy for their mother, because they bent to her overpowering will.

She had not been able to go six for six, however. Ricky had fought with his mother from day one, when he had to be forcibly removed from her womb. A clear omen of things to come. When his mother commanded that he eat his vegetables, Ricky screamed for candy. She told him to get to bed early, he wanted to watch late night talk shows. When she demanded he hit the books, he read comics. She insisted that he clean up his act and stop getting detention, so he got himself expelled instead. His mother had dreamt the impossible for all her children, that they go to college. Ricky was her last hope. He had not placed college very high on his list of priorities. But at age thirteen, he joined a gang.

That was six weeks ago. Since then he had done a lot of things his mother wouldn't approve of. He had consumed alcohol and ingested drugs. He had engaged in sex. Ricky had robbed, and fought, and hurt people foolish enough to resist. He had hurt people who didn't resist at all. If there was anything in his mother stronger than her will, it was the love she had for her children. Ricky knew that despite the things he had done in the past, she would forgive him. But after what he was about to do? He didn't think so. This crossed the line not even a mother's love would venture beyond.

Nevertheless, Ricky had chosen his path so now had to walk it. He wasn't willing to travel the long, arduous road his mother had tried to direct him towards. He was in too much of a hurry. Out on these streets is where he would stake his claim, where he would immediately be paid in full.

That's why Ricky was leaning against a fence, waiting to fulfill his latest duty as a member of the Crypt. Any moment now the guy would be coming home, basketball in hand, cap turned backwards on his head, one pants leg rolled up to his knee. And Ricky would make his first kill.

He patted the gun which was held securely in the waist of his jeans, hidden from view by his overlapping shirt. Ricky wondered what it would be like to kill a person. What else was there to think about at such a time? Would he feel like more of a man, or less? Would he feel regret and remorse? Or only relief that he had accomplished his mission? Would he like it? Would he like himself? Would he be able to do it? If so, would any of the other questions matter?

There he was. Ricky could set his watch by him. He was alone as usual. The sun was down, the nearest streetlight out, no witnesses to be found. Ricky moved closer. It was necessary to be as quiet as possible, because if seen, his intentions would be instantly known. But he couldn't be too far away. Missing was not a luxury he could afford. When his foot hit the discarded soda can, a dozen car alarms and a marching band could not have made a more resounding clamor. Surprise was no longer his ally. Neither was time.

Ricky raised his arm and fired. The bullet harmlessly flew over the left shoulder of its target, eventually imbedding itself in a wall of the tenement building behind him. The second bullet released sunk deeply and with finality into soft flesh. Its victim crumbled to the ground, his hands useless as a dam to hold back the flow of blood.

"Did you see that?" a voice asked. "He just smoked that nigga."

Apparently there had been people around. Ricky hadn't noticed them. Who could blame him? He was new to this. Killing was a skill like any other. You had to practice to get good at it. Doing it right, doing it perfect wasn't easy to achieve the first time out. Novices tended to be sloppy. They made amateurish mistakes like not observing witnesses; making unnecessary sounds that gave them away; missing their first shot, which could turn out to be their only one. Cause if your mark was wearing a piece himself, then he would get a chance, and you could end up lying on the ground bleeding your life away. Just like Ricky was.

He would never know what it felt like to kill a person, but he would learn how it felt to be killed. Voices around him slowly growing softer, the stars in the sky becoming fainter by the second. The pain, overwhelming at first, then fading as well. No chance to even be afraid, for Ricky had allotted his precious remaining moments to asking himself a question. The police would come, the news would spread, the sordid tale would be told. Ricky Tate, thirteen year old gang banger, tried to pop someone and got popped himself.

What would his mama say?

Roy L. Pickering Jr.

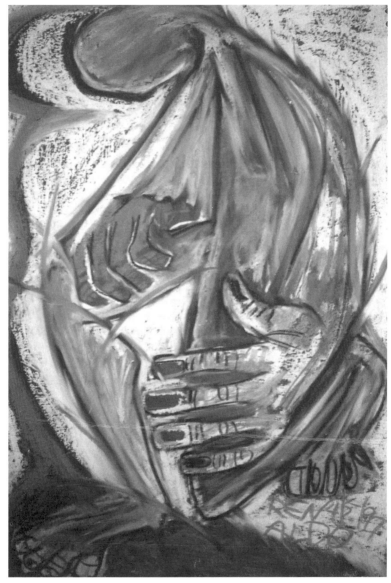

Renaldo Davidson—**Kneeling Figure** oil pastel on paper

The Sweeper's *Job*

INT. KITCHEN, DAY

Robin is standing in the kitchen area. Robin, an African-American in her late 30's is filling a bucket with water from the kitchen sink. Also, she adds cleaning solution to the water. She has an oversized night shirt on and her locks swing from side to side.

ROBIN: *(Voice over)*

I've been doing this for about
4 years now, almost as long as
we've been living here.

> *She walks to her bedroom to change into jeans.*

ROBIN: *(Voice over)*

It's a secret power or maybe a
world. I don't mess with it though.
I keep wearing the same clothes.
I think it comes from my mother;
she doesn't even change the dirt
from her window sill.

> *She slips jeans and a tee-shirt on. She ties her hair back*
> *with a bandana or spongy.*

ROBIN: *(Voice over)*

These things swing all over the
place. Every night twisiting, washing
and oiling them. I can't stand it, but
I can do it in about an hour now.

> *Robin walks to the door with the water bucket. She takes out the inverted*

sweeping broom from a bin of other brooms. She opens the apartment door 45 degrees and holds the door there.

ROBIN: *(Voice Over)*

Sometimes at this very spot, I
hestitate about my next step,
"It's just nerves hitting me,"
I say.

> *Robin prays.*

ROBIN: *(Voice over)*

Father, keep my family and me
guided and safe in our daily
endeavors. Protect my sons and
daughters. Guide them home safe
and out of harms way.

> *She closes apartment door.*

EXT. FRONT STOOP (STAIRS), DAY

> *Robin walks out the doorway and down the stairs.*

> *Robin splashes water on the ground. She begins sweeping back and forth.*

ROBIN: *(Voice over)*

Someone gots to do it. I hope someone
does it for me. . . Every night you can
hear them banging like they the only
ones with a gripe against life.

> *Robin is moving the broom back and forth. The ground is covered with spilled blood and a chalked outline body. Police popped banners, "Police line don't cross" are laying around.*

> **ROBIN (Voice over)**

I don't now how many more today.

> *Robin walks to the stairs and sits looking side to side with the broom in her hand and the water bucket rests beside her leg.*

Clairesa Clay

Shirley Carter—**The Month of May** oil on canvas money bags

seven

life promised her
played her
pimped her
ported her
here with me
more of the same
her funk thick
trippin' on a hit
to her vein

i'm seven.

most times i try not to see her
don't want to be her but
her condition is mine.
like fine wine she ages bitter, so do I.

i'm seven.

she sellin my christmas presents
to get high
a grade-A junkie
a first grade bystander,
keeping out her way
day in, day out
praying she won't miss me.

i'm seven.
can't comb my hair
can't teach little sis how
can't clean
i feel dirty
don't really knowing why

no one knows i got problems
f's in conduct
itching and smelling
reading below grade level

teacher say i lack concentration
can't focus
teacher wanna know

when she gone pick up
my report card?
teacher say i can't come
to school until she
pick up my report card.

Kim Ransom

126

Shirley Carter—**I Did Not Intend to Live Past the Knowing** oil on
canvas money bags

Eight

Smiling, he says I know you like me girl
and tries to coax me down onto the bed.
He slides his middle finger round the edge
of my blue shorts. I don't know if I should

shoot a bird at him, shoot him dead. At eight
what I know is Mama keeps bullets in
the bottom dresser drawer of this same room,
but I have never seen the gun. He smirks.

Don't even know what pussy is, do you?
I know more than I want to know. I smile,
and draw him to the game of war my brothers
fight with pillows against his sisters while

our mothers, off at prayer meeting for hours,
praise God. I've learned to call on other powers.

Lyrae Van Clief-Stefanon

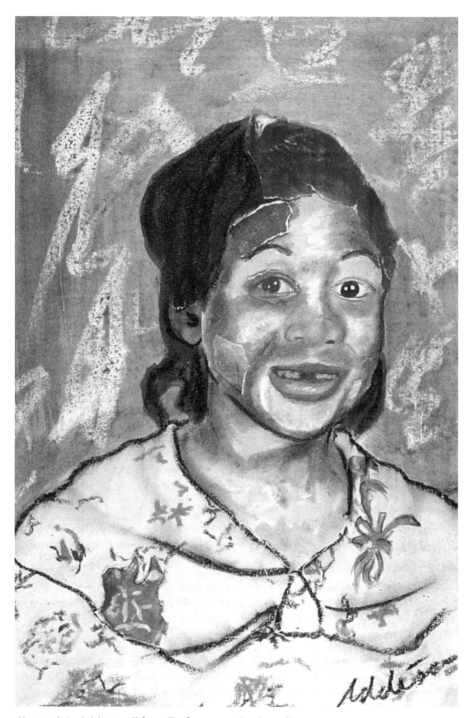

Kenneth L. Addison—**Blue Paloma** mixed media

A Father's
LOVE

In the darkness of the night daddy came. Softly, tenderly, quietly. Always at the same time. He was consistent like that, as though five minutes either way would have ruined the ecstacy. I could feel his presence in the dark like one feels a cold draft, never really knowing from where it comes. When the chills started, I knew he was on his way. His power preceded him and paved the way for his unobstructed entry. He tried to tiptoe, not to disturb the other spirits in the house, but it didn't matter. I could feel his approach. I would hide under the covers, praying desperately for God to help me, but maybe I hadn't known Him long enough, for He ignored me. Or maybe I just didn't speak loudly enough. But I couldn't. Daddy would have heard me and thought that I didn't want him to come anymore.

So I screamed silently. But my voice found no ears to fall upon, so he just kept coming. He said it was because he loved me so much and needed to know that I knew. I told him I knew, but apparently he needed more than my verbal confirmation. He needed the warmth of my breath close to his to be assured that he was a good father. So he slipped into my bed quietly every night as he whispered, "Shhh...It's just me." He wasted no time wrapping my 12-year-old soul with his much more mature one and entering my being despite the "No Trespassing" signs I had posted in places most visible.

The heat was overwhelming. I often wondered if Shadrack and the others in the fiery furnace had felt like I had. A fire most blazing although mine was within. My outer being could have cooled tons of hot tea instantly. That's another reason daddy came. He said I was too cool, too sweet, too soft. And he wanted to protect his gem. So he rubbed my back gently as he explored all there was to know about me. From the looks of things, I would never have guessed that he possessed anything as large as what I felt enter me. I thought that maybe he was a magician who knew how to make things other than what they really were. Someone who has mastered the art of distortion. For my pain, like that big thing that entered me every night, was so exacerbated that, after a while, I didn't feel it at all. It was too large to comprehend. I was numb. The first time daddy came though I was so tense that I was sure he would be turned off. But he came again. And again. Until his visits became routine. Then I decided that to be tense was a mistake. He enjoyed barging his way through me. It meant that I was all his own. It meant that we shared something most fathers and sons didn't. It meant that he had taken me places and shown me things that should have remained a mystery. It was all because he loved me, he said.

The blood seemed not to bother him. In fact, that's when he relaxed and let his hands come to know my private intimately—when he felt my warm blood ooze around his big thing. And then when he deposited that milky substance within me, he let out sighs of relief and sounds of satisfaction which always made me cry. He would grab me tighter during these moments of ecstacy, as though trying to capture a thing which he knew could only last a spell. As I got a little older, something within me began to rush to the tip of my private as he drilled me and often spilled over into his hands which always embraced it. Whenever this happened, he would mumble, "Ummmmm." I hated it because he enjoyed it. I tried to stop it from happening, but I couldn't. My body responded without my mind's permission.

That's when I knew it was all my fault. If I had fought him all the way, then he probably would have stopped. I'm sure he would have. But I had no plan of battle. So I just looked at him real hard with frowns of confusion and disbelief, trying to see beyond his being into the source of his pleasure. Trying to fashion not why he did what he did but why he did it without my consent. If I had asked though, he would have said it was because he loved me.

So in the darkness of the night daddy came. I had totally exhausted my life supply of tears, so after age 14, I just lay there in a trance. I always felt like a ship on the big seas as I rocked in response to his catalyst. Occasionally a high-pitched whine would find its way up my throat and into the world as we know it, but I would cut it off quickly, knowing that he would interpret this desperately lyrical moment to mean that I didn't want him to come anymore.

The night of my 15th birthday, I lay in bed looking at the shadows of the birthday cards plastered across my dressers and walls. And I waited. I had mounted posters of Malcolm and King, the faces of which now seemed to ask if I would please take them down. The moonlight coming through the window bore just enough light for me to see that they didn't feel right. They seemed to know that they were in the presence of a very evil thing, and they begged me to displace them. But I couldn't move. I was waiting on daddy. What was taking him so long?

I soon realized that daddy wasn't coming. I could tell because his spirit was not in the air. I began to cry. Didn't he love me anymore? I had been a faithful lover. Maybe he had heard me ask God to make him stop coming. I had destroyed a very good thing. How would I fix it? I began to get nervous. He was just doing it because he loved me, and he didn't come that night because I had not been appreciative. My ingratitude made daddy take his love away from me. He had probably told mom that I didn't love him anymore, and now she would hate me for disrespecting a good Black father. "You oughta be glad to have a father like yours, son," she used to tell me. "A good Black father is hard to find." I had made daddy feel bad about loving me. That's what he was supposed to do, wasn't it? He had given me his all, his everything, and in my selfishness I had rejected him. Mom had gone out of town later that day, so I knew daddy was lying in bed alone, feeling hurt and despised by his only begotten son.

So in the darkness of the night I went to him. I wanted him to know how much I loved him and appreciated his nurturing over the years. I wanted him to know that I wasn't a child anymore, that I was now prepared to reciprocate the love he had given me. The hatred I had shown in years past was simply my inability to understand the enormity of a father's love for his son. I hoped daddy would forgive me.

I rose from my bed, tiptoed quietly not to disturb the other spirits in the house, entered daddy's dark room, slid into his bed, and embraced him completely. "Shhh...It's just me, daddy," I cried softly.

Daniel Black

John Abner—**Allow Him to Parent** collage

My **Body** is **Bread**

I was dreaming in French...

The mother, tall and stout, stood at the double sink in the kitchen smiling ever so slightly at a sparrow eating crumbs she sprinkled on the windowsill, but she wasn't my mother. It was winter.

My mother dried her hands on the hem of her apron and sat down at the kitchen table next to me. She took my hands in hers and leaned in to whisper so my father wouldn't hear. "He was too handsome to be a husband." She stood, walked over to the back door and tossed bread crumbs out into the yard.

"Are you pregnant?"

The father, thick and rigid as a two by four sat stiff in a green velvet dining chair, caressing the body of a gun he used for hunting dinner rabbits, but he wasn't my father. Snow was falling.

"I never liked him. Did he touch you?" My daddy looked at me as if he could see underneath my clothes the bruises under my skin.

I couldn't speak. I shook my head. My father held me like he used to when I was

134

a little girl pulling me into his chest and stroking my hair while I cried.

"I'll kill him if he touched you." My daddy was born to protect me. He solemnly feeds the gun.

My small, trembling, blood stained hands were folded over my mouth. I wet the carpet with the water in my eyes. Footprints covered my body from head to toe. I stood on the stairs of a house that wasn't my house. "He kissed me twice" was only a song on the radio. After one night in Paris, I was dreaming in French.

The mother wipes her hands on her apron and turns to look at the me who is not me and she smiles, a sad smile that tries to comfort, but I know somehow that it won't last long so I cough and slap my face and I try to wake up, but the father who is not my father is pointing the gun at the mother who is holding me close so I won't take the pain. Salty dew on my lips. I swallow the grit of forgiveness as words, like bullets, strike us in soft, fleshy places.

I am thirteen years old and when I wake up I can tell that the witches have been riding me. My ribs are still sore from the pressure of their bony knees. I am exhausted. There are thin, ghostly trails of their footprints in the corners of my mouth and eyes. I feel bigger than my body as if my insides are growing into a much smaller vessel. I am rising like bread in a pan much too weak. My body holds new fluids. Tears spring from my eyes, blood from between my legs, mucous from the same place when I touch myself. There are two swollen places on my chest that hurt like the kiss of a thousand bees. I smell different. New wounds open between my thighs. My body is a blooming field of mysteries to be discovered at night, in the dark, under a tangle of cotton covers, quietly, quickly, over and over again. My eyes are windows. I wipe the damp weather from my eyes with my arms which are leafy branches.

My body is bread. My body is water. My body is a house on fire. voluminous breasts. thick, chewy nipples, my greedy mouth devours. a gun as big as my father's. taken from behind shamefully. pleasure. pain.

Imagine a world where mothers hold their daughter's hands and cover their eyes with kisses not tears or blood or dirt collected from beneath broken fingernails. When I wake up in the bed that seems to be a boat in dangerous waters I wipe the footprints from my face and turn in the circle of my mother's arms. Our bodies mold a new curve in the bed. With hot orange lips I kiss my mother until she melts away.

Many nights later my father sends me a piece of broken glass on which he has written, "I will miss the you that was." I wipe the bad weather from my eyes and take my new me down the carpeted stairs, out of the house and in the streets to find someone to feed on my feverish body like winter birds on bread.

Shay Youngblood

for Renée Orlander

This always happens:
sometime
after the day you
are born   somebody
does something
to you.

And it's cruel
and hard
to believe, maybe
leaves a mark. Not
visible
necessarily, but

something
like a scratch inside
one lung   that
burns a little
when you breathe.

───────────

A lot of times it's
been some time
since
it was, since

the thing
was
what it
was,
since the thing
was done   and over
the years you've
said I'm
okay. I'm al-
right. Could'a
been worse.

And, no doubt, it might
have been. No
doubt. And you are
fine now. You are. You
go days, weeks,
longer   with hardly
a trace. You
work, make
love, joke
around.

Like always, people
ask how you've
been   and you
flick it off
your bottom lip:
fine. It's so auto-
matic—as if, of
course, the
past
with its jagged
bulk could fit
into that
small word.

But when you
do   think about it,
your eyes mark
a certain

curve in the air
and inside you   a blunt
edge caught, a
stomach   full of
stomach and

whatever it
was   finds you and you
cannot stave off
the fact
that the human
world is
an unbearable place,
that once and for
all   nothing is
okay,
none of it, no
bones ever
knit.

And though it's
good to seem
friendly—nice
to let the
bygones go—right
then,
what you need
more   is to find the
one, the ones

who did what
happened   and do it
back to them,
give it
back.

Tim Seibles

Sex When I Don't Want It

I'm an enthusiastic participant in sex, most of it I eagerly initiate or encourage. A couple of times I wasn't really into it, but decided to do it anyway. And once I didn't want to do it all, but I couldn't find a way out.

I was alone in Santa Fe, New Mexico, sleeping over at the house of a man I barely knew so that I could attend my first Native American sweat. After talking of spiritual themes far and wide, sweating out toxins in the sweat lodge, and preaching from the heart when it was my turn to speak, I felt safe. During the car ride home, my host offered me his bed.

"No sex," he said. I had done that before, slept in the same bed with a man and had nothing happen; I took him at his word. My mother says never get into bed with a man you don't intend to have sex with. Mother wit may prove itself wrong twenty times, but in the end it prevails. When I felt his hands on my body, I literally heard a trap slam shut. I felt completely powerless.

Staring at the ceiling, I reviewed my options. I could roll onto the floor and run to the bathroom. I could scream, but who would hear? I could just say 'no.' Instead I went into denial. It's just cuddling, I told myself. Then when he was pushing away my clothes, I spoke up. "We're going too far," I said.

"We don't have to do anything," he whispered and continued undressing me. I lifted my arms and legs as if in a trance, while frantically trying to find a "cool" way out.

"Maybe we should stop now," I said diplomatically.

"We don't have to do anything," he repeated. In my head, I screamed at myself, What is wrong with you? Be a woman! Do something, stop it. Stop this from happening. I did nothing. I thought, if a spiritually in-tune man who can read my aura, doesn't listen when I say "this is going too far," what are the chances that he's going to listen if I say "no"? When he ripped my underwear, he was still swearing that we didn't have to do anything. I got the message—he had heard my protests and gave lip service appeasement to my hesitation. I could do what I wanted, but he fully intended to have sex. Then I lay there and let it happen, wondering if he noticed how stiff and uninterested I was.

I'm not a weak woman. I've traveled to five countries alone. I've fought a man who tried to rape me and a friend at gun point. I've also been alone in Havana, Cuba, spending the night in the house of another man I barely knew and woken up to find him in my bed with nothing on but a towel. I sat straight up in bed and said "I'm not interested in this," over and over again, until he crawled back out of the room. So, why couldn't I say no this time? In Santa Fe, I remember trying to convince myself that, although I didn't want it, it could be a good thing. You haven't had sex in a while, I told myself. Enjoy the sensations. My pep talk was futile. I would not, could not, did not enjoy it.

The next morning I was disappointed in him and furious with myself. I hid myself behind a sweet, silent mask. He woke thinking he seduced me. No matter how hard I tried, I could not persuade myself to set the record straight. He took me to breakfast and bragged to a friend of his that he was going to marry me. I smiled and reserved comment. Could he be that clueless? He dropped me off at the bus station, passionately reminding me to call him. I rolled my eyes as he drove away.

When I returned to my sister's house in Albuquerque, I lied. I told her I had had sex with the man, but I didn't tell her I didn't want it. I was ashamed to. Having sex against her will is not something a powerful, evolved woman of the 90s does. I felt guilty and stupid. But some small part of me felt justified. As the twisted logic goes, by having sex with this man when I didn't want to, I stopped him from raping me. If I have a choice between rape and having sex when I don't want it, the choice seems obvious. Nobody wants to be a rape victim.

Rape is huge, overwhelming, devastating, debilitating; sex when I don't want it is manageable. Manageable except for the anger and shame, manageable except for my fear of being playful and open with men, manageable except for the nightmare I had a year later. In the dream, a man was holding me down and I struggled to be free. I woke trembling and afraid. When I described the dream to my mother, she said: "Sounds like a bad experience you've had with a man." Suddenly the sensations flooded my body all over again: the self-hate, the anger, the blame, the shame. All the emotions I thought I had settled and buried a year ago assaulted me.

More unsettling than the man's callousness that night, was my collusion in his game of false seduction. I could dismiss the sex, I could dismiss his stupidity, but I couldn't forgive my weak reaction. In failing to take care of myself, I failed to live up to my self-image. My unwillingness to be honest with him and fight for myself haunted me. After a year of silence, I decided to share my story with a few women. Each of the women responded to my story with one of their own. All of them had a renegade sexual situation terrorizing their memories: sex they didn't consent to; sex they put up with rather than battle to stop; a sexual experience that was neither seduction nor rape. There was one common thread that ran through all of their stories: the fear of rape. In one way or another, each of them said: "I didn't want to get raped, so I just did it."

I was both saddened and heartened to discover "just doing it" was a common survival tactic. My self-esteem strengthened with each story I heard. This Sante Fe thing ceased to be just a weak moment in my history. It took its place as one of a million cases that together form an ugly social epidemic.

These women who shared my trauma were my friends—people I could relate to, women I respected. There was Cynthia. We studied abroad together. She was working on her law degree when she confessed that she had been raped. She told her story hesitantly, with a touch of nervousness. She was aware of all the reasons he could pretend it wasn't rape: there was no a gun or knife involved, he didn't beat her up, they were friends, she was attracted to him, it was late, they were in his house. None of these facts deterred her belief that it was rape. Although she couldn't explain why she considered it rape, she knew there was no other name for it.

"It wasn't physical," she explained. "It was psychological. He made it so I had no choice. I was in his house. I did like him, I had told people at school that I thought he was cute. I couldn't see a way out. He didn't listen when I said no, so I did it and left. He couldn't understand why I never spoke to him again. He thought it was all cool. I swear I said no about five times, but he wouldn't listen. He was so big, I didn't want it to get physical, so I gave in and then I went home."

There was Marielle. Funny and lively, Marielle quit her job to travel throughout Europe for six months. Before she left, she told me her "I just did it" story. She went drinking with a mixed group of friends. One of the guys insisted on walking her home. She invited him to crash on her couch. Once in the house, they shared a kiss, then she said goodnight. She got up and walked to the stairs. He stood and followed her. "Where the fuck do you think you're going?" he asked. She froze. The details of the situation—you're drunk, you invited him in, you kissed him, it's the middle of the night—flashed through her head.

She considered fighting him, but then she remembered her friend Diane. A month earlier, Diane chose to fight. The man blackened her eye and broke her teeth. Then he raped her anyway. She told the authorities and was consequently ostracized and ridiculed by men on campus. Rather than risk broken limbs or a tarnished reputation, Marielle returned to the sofa and allowed him to have sex with her. When he was asleep, she ran to a friend's house where she felt safe. Was she raped?

Monica, a literature professor and a passionate intellectual, simply said, "you don't want to hear my story."

"I want to hear it, if you want to share it," I assured her.

"Without burdening you with the details, I'll just say I got to that point you and Marielle got to, rather than shut up and do it, I decided I wasn't going to. I drew the line, and he crossed it." I was silent as I let her words sink into my body.

"That's exactly what those of us who don't draw the line are afraid of," I finally said.

"I know," she said. "The bright side," Monica went on to say, "is I know I've been raped. I'm not burdened with the questions and guilt you're wrestling with. I don't wonder if I could have stopped it. I tried. And he knows he raped me. He can't walk away pretending he seduced me." Suddenly I understood that we who "just do it" aren't only protecting ourselves from physical rape, but we are also attempting to avoid the psychological ramifications of rape. We have sold ourselves a false reality in exchange for a fragile peace of mind. "If I give in, then he didn't take it," we assure ourselves. "If I decide to have sex, then it wasn't rape."

If we had sex to avoid rape—unlawful sexual intercourse by force or threat (*Webster's Ninth New Collegiate Dictionary*)—then by virtue of the threat, weren't we raped? By current social definitions, we weren't raped. Certainly by the definitions of most of the men involved, we weren't raped. In many of our own minds, albeit by technicality, we weren't raped. But I can not ignore my mother's gentle reasoning. As I wondered and analyzed, defined and ignored, my mother asked me one irrefutable question: Did you give your consent? No, I said. Her soft and simple reply was: Then you were raped.

Unfortunately my mother and her simple wisdom are not the judge and jury. Society has a different set of standards to judge men and women in sexual situations. There is an invisible matrix of unspoken rules governing women's interactions with men. A look, a touch, a word, an article of clothing, any number of random facts can shade a woman's innocence and declare a man guiltless. These facts become more important than a woman's desire not to have sex. The possibility of court cases, destruction of character, and the loss of privacy weighs heavily on a woman's decision to have sex when she doesn't want to. These considerations shouldn't enter the picture, but they do. Society upholds the man's prerogative. Rather than support a woman in danger, society rears its head to judge, question, and punish her.

Assuming that a woman can negotiate her way through this invisible matrix, assuming she finds the strength to say: *Screw society, I don't want this*; there's still that other matter. The matter of men's size, might, and strength. In each conversation I have had about questionable sexual situations, the threat of violence is an active presence. The threat need not be spoken; it rarely is. We live in a world that says might is right. A man's presence, a man wanting something a woman doesn't want is enough to bring the threat of violence to the surface. I wonder how mindful men are of the threat of violence that lingers in their bodies. How aware are they of the power of domination given to them by history, biology, and societal mores? I wonder how intentional they are when they employ that threat to push women into sex.

When I started talking to my male friends about sex and sexual consent, they all said they only had sex with women's consent. When I explained the complex motives that might encourage a woman to have sex when she doesn't want to, some of them paused. "Are you saying that some of the women I slept with may not have wanted to sleep with me?" one of my friends asked me. "That's exactly what I'm saying," I replied. He lapsed into thought. Then he shuddered as the full meaning of my statement hit home. "You know, as boys, as men, we're taught to push and push to get what we want." We left the obvious conclusion dangle between us unsaid. I hope he thought about it later. I hope he considered that perhaps his pushing became force, perhaps once, without knowing it, he forced someone to have sex with him.

Quite a few of my male friends have a frightening definition of seduction. Joseph told me that "seduction is when you make somebody do something they don't want to do." In order to seduce a woman, he has to change her mind about sex. He says: "When they get to your house, they don't want to have sex. So you put on a little music, kiss her on the neck, do whatever to make her want to have sex with you." For me, this definition has less to do with seduction and more to do with force. In the realm of sex, "making somebody do something they don't want to do" is rape. If you start with the concept of changing someone's mind, how do you know when you've changed it? If, each time, a woman says she doesn't want to have sex, the man responds with another approach, another method of "seducing" her, where is the space for her choice? Is it possible for her to say no? Who decides how many no's consist of a sufficient refusal of an offer? When does seduction end and rape begin?

Across the board, my female friends agreed that seduction had something to do with persuasion, but nothing to do with force. Their collective comments define seduction as an invitation and rape as a demand. Marielle believes seduction is about "revealing hidden feelings," but "not [about] changing someone's mind." In other words, when there is no apparent desire or refusal, there is room for seduction, but when someone communicates through word or action that they don't want sex, seduction is no longer possible. Each attempt to make her change her mind moves the situation closer and closer to rape. Both seduction and rape transform the sexual environment, but seduction creates a yes from nothing, while rape forces a yes from a no.

Joseph has two categories for women's possible responses to his attempts at seduction. "There is the no-no," he says, and "the no-yes. The no-no is when she says no and she takes her hands off you. That's clearly a no, and there's nothing you can do about that. But there is the no-yes where she's saying no, but she's still touching you and kissing you. That's a no-yes. You know she doesn't mean no and you can make that go the way you want it to." But how does he know she doesn't mean no? Can he be sure that he's interpreting her signals correctly? How can anyone be sure what a no-yes really means?

The truth is, men are not the only ones confusing the matters of sexual consent. Adding to the chaos are women's mixed messages. As we women are busy backpedaling, trying to find a nonconfrontational way out of sex we don't want, we send out confusing, unclear signals. My conversations revealed a few other, less-than-noble reasons why a woman may give unclear sex signals. She might be wishy-washy about sexual consent when she hasn't embraced her sexual self. She might be embarrassed by her own arousal or may want to protect her reputation as a "good girl." Marielle admitted to me she played the no-yes game in the past. "With my first boyfriend," she said, "every time we started to have sex, I would say no. I didn't mean it, I wanted to have sex with him, but I would whisper, no, no, no, no. I don't even know why."

When a woman plays these games, she protects her own reputation at the expense of all women. A man who has had sexual experiences with a woman who said no when she meant yes, then has an excuse, no matter how hollow, to interpret another woman's no as a yes. He has seen the old adage—"when a woman says no, she really means yes"—at work and can use it to dishonor women who say no and mean it. The no-yes game also supports the fallacious belief that women need to be talked into sex. Women love sex and don't need to be pushed into sexual consent. But when we hide our desires behind the cloak of confusion and uncertainty, we support a dangerous tradition that destroys women's choices as sexual beings.

I admire my friend Sybil for her huge presence and take-no-prisoners attitude. She, like many women, has used the no-yes tactic often. More than once, she found herself in unwanted sexual situations. In each of them she was clear she didn't want to have sex, but was afraid it would become rape. "I didn't want it to get ugly," she says, "So I went ahead and had sex." "Do you think you were coming off as [confused] at those times?" I asked. "Yes," she said. Clearly, women's hesitations to say no—to cross their arms and flat out refuse to have sex—are founded on the very real climate of male intimidation that colors our world. At the same time, if we don't speak them, how can we expect our desires to be honored?

It is my sister's belief that we give men too much power in sexual situations by expecting them to rape us. She suggests that women should refuse sex as they would refuse the offer of lobster. Rather than experience it as a charged moment of fear, confusion and shame, my sister believes we would feel freer if we viewed unwanted sex as an invitation to dinner. We can say firmly, "No thank you, not tonight," with little trepidation. I like her theory because I know the mind is a powerful force in defining situations. I know that silent compliance will get us nowhere. Wouldn't it be worth it if we could avoid forced sex simply by relating to sex as a choice?

I still sit and wonder if the sex in Santa Fe could have been avoided. Had I grinned and said no thanks, would he have raped me or would he have let me go? Months later, I sent him a letter. In a few pages, I explained that I hadn't wanted to have sex with him. I also expressed astonishment that he didn't pick up on my disinterest. He wrote back with an interpretive spin on my words. He thought I was saying that I was so overwhelmed by desire for him that I had sex against my principles. Even after my detailed letter, he still believed he seduced me. He didn't (couldn't? wouldn't?) understand that I felt trapped, helpless, forced. Stronger than my written assertion that I didn't want to have sex with him was the fact that I "just did it." In his world, my actions spoke volumes, while my words were insignificant. My submission fed the vicious cycle that made him think he had the seductive power to convince me to participate in sex I didn't want. In the end, I didn't do the one thing that could have convinced him that I wasn't seduced: I didn't refuse to have sex.

This whole experience has taught me that men and women view sexual consent from two different perspectives. Women expect a man not to push for sex unless she has given her consent. Men believe sex is consensual as long as the woman goes along with it. A few no's along the way don't mean much to many men. It's getting to the sex that counts. One of my male friends says he refuses to have sex with a woman who is wishy washy with her sexual consent. If she isn't clearly interested, then he's not doing it. He gives me hope for future sexual interactions. There will be a day when all men view a woman's no as valuable currency. When her hesitation, discomfort, and fear are noticed and respected. When she can say no, without battling the threat of rape.

When that day comes, we can erase the no-yes as an acceptable response to seduction. All sex will be the result of a yes-yes. A yes-yes is usually accompanied by joy and enthusiasm. The hesitations and confusion of the no-yes are simply a mask for fear. A sexually interested woman does not hesitate. A sexually aroused woman is rarely confused. I know this because I have been there. I have been at the beach with a friend and her brother talking about nothing in particular. I have floated in the sea with this same brother feeling nothing in particular. After the beach, we all went reggae dancing. I wasn't interested in him, but I wasn't not interested either: I was just hanging out. Turns out that our hips worked together at just the right speed. Somehow we made magic on the dance floor all night. We held hands as we walked out of the club. I was surprised and amused. While driving me back to my house he reached out for my hand and seduced me. The seduction happened while he was tracing patterns across my palm and squeezing my fingers with his. I saw all the possibilities when he simulated sex with the meeting and separation of our palms. Soon he was kissing me and I was climbing out of my seat into his as we sped down the road at 60 miles per hour.

No was a foreign language at that moment. Had he not copulated with my hand, I never would have ended up in his bed at 3 in the morning. Sex wasn't my plan, but he seduced me. The seduction didn't involve him forcing me to change my mind. I was enticed into an encounter I hadn't considered. It was a thrilling invitation, I accepted without reservation. If I hadn't been interested, he would have had to find another target. The burden falls on the seducer—male or female—to get genuine consent from the seducee. As my mother says: no consent, no sex.

Kiini Ibura Salaam

sometimes there are
NO WORDS

She wanted her two dead-born babies
to live again inside her tired womb.
This time she would keep them safe, hold
them until birth, help them push their way to breath.

This time she wanted it:
the rounding of a protruding belly,
the fullness of breast,
the tender swell of nipple,
those nauseous early mornings,
frequent trips to the bathroom,
her ice-chip cravings.

She wanted no reminders, no pity, no explanations.
She wanted no *God's will be done*
to console her soul, fill the space left open.

She wanted it
not too late, not too early.
Gave her two dead-born baby boys
names of the living
so they might return,
so she might not forget
that after twenty-one weeks
they had reached their limit,
let go.

Gwendolyn Mitchell

A dangerous thing happens.
I run from men rattling chains.
Grope for air, turn a horrified face
toward the clock.
Vines entwine my soft brain,
squeezing until I fall unconscious
through a slit in the floor.

Every morning I have to reinspect
the nucleus, rebuild
my killer cells.
Every morning there is the twist struggle
of a rugged dance done with rugged feet.
A fight before daybreak.

Lately, the rat scurries away
long before I descend the steps
in the dark. It has become a game
and ritual: I descend and he runs.
I stomp my feet on the floorboards
to signal: this is my house. Get out!

The precocious green leaf of a nephew
dripping and shaking water
from his two-year-old limbs
asks when I will take my bath.
I look at him later sleeping, digital numbers
on the cheap clock have their limbs mismatched,
matching my midnight and morning red-eyes.
I must say to him, as my posture announces
every   time to these
morning   leeches,
that I haven't yet.
          I haven't yet.

But when I do,
it will be dangerous for them.

Esther Iverem

 Second Birth

Her voice is swallowed as the contractions push her
until her eyes cannot see
until her ears cannot hear
until she does not feel herself anymore.

Instead of being baptized by his touch
she is drowned
she gasps for air as his need rises his fear smothers her coming

There is no room for
                    her wonderment
                    her wide eyes
                    her open heart
                    her desire
                    her power

Before she learns to breathe
her breath is swallowed by his need.

He is frightened because if she is born again
                    whole—
          her soul will be able to fly and she will
          discover her own power in freedom

What if the second birth crushes your spirit?

When you move upon the earth—
                    you look before you step.

Afraid of what has been
pushed in
and afraid of release—
you wrap yourself in layers and cover the skin.

You listen for the silencers.

When your voice emerges it
fights to fly on wounded wings.

Emily Hooper Lansana

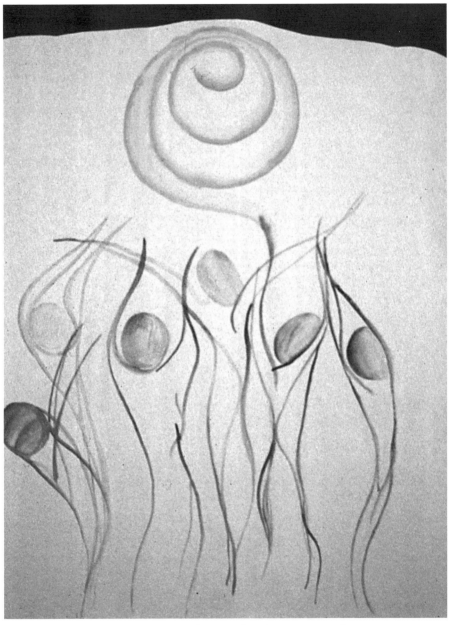

Antionette Pressley-Sanon—**Reach for the Sun** watercolor on paper

My Mother Left Me Long Before I Was Born

Her hands held rigid and away
from her own thickening body
she denied me more than my father's silence
she can no more hold me now than
she could paint me darker then
yellow my skin
not quite white enough
to make her stay

She had to leave
so I could grow
away from the shame of her
and the Chinaman in his family car
rutting in more than the turbulent seventies
crossing picket lines
they would never be able to go back
these choices would return in wild circles
to haunt the fruit of their tempered labor

have me marked for death
or this life with no borders

Rejecting hands
would never raise the fury of this child
the passing band of homes dragged
screaming into adulthood
fathers offered and refused
in the name of charity and guilt
an identity built by rage and rumor
There will always be stories
surrounding my coming
women's tongues will clack
children will remember me
their laughter echoing the sloped posture
of my father's shoulders
my grandmother would say my tongue
has always been my mother's
I never heard her speak before I became a woman
but felt the fear in her
saw her mother's stride reflected in the feet
running roughshod over the self
she always wanted to be
her father's porcelain daughter

My father's icy gaze tells me
I have always been my mother's child
full of dreams deferred and reams of tear-stained letters
written in haste, discarded in leisure

We are both too far from home to ever go back

Staceyann Chin

Jamaica
Farewell

I could not tell the moment the earth fell beneath me, cannot explain how, each time, returning here means I lose and gain myself. In the hotel lobby, an older black man in flowered shirt and straw hat strums a guitar and sings the old folk song, "Jamaica Farewell":

> *Sad to say I'm on my way.*
> *Won't be back for many a day.*
> *My heart is down,*
> *My head is turnin aroun.*
> *I haffa leave a lickle girl in Kingston.*

I see my father singing this song on a Jamaican television program and dedicating it to me. In our living room, watching the recording with him, I wanted to know how he could be inside that box and there with me at the same time. At five years old, the moment was both real and not real. Hearing the familiar melody and words, watching this man — his gesture, attire and voice — something again is not right or too right. The palms in the lobby, the peach rattan sofa. This man: singing for who? The answer I know and hand over four US dollars. He smiles and tips his hat. I am not a tourist, I want to say.

Reneé's friend, picking me up from the airport when I arrived two days ago said, "You don't sound American." "I know and not quite Jamaican either. Just some mixed-up accent," I responded. Later that same day, on the road from MoBay to Lucea, Eavon, the driver, and I talk politics and race: in the recent election, he didn't vote and I ask why. Like Papa, he is a JLP man: "It doh matter to me if a black man like Patterson sayin we should elec him and not the white man, Siaga. What he do for us but rob us, him own people, bline to set up himself in one nice house an see sey him friends taken care of. Same ting all de time. An is de poor people a get poorer an poorer. It doh matter who in power. Seem to me like we would a betta off to have a white man than black one like that."

We pass hotels, glittering in the setting sun, alongside shantytowns. And none of this is a metaphor. That people are poor and don't have money to buy food so they ben over in the hot sun at any age, to dig ground an live off the one, one cocoa an yam they plant is not an image I need to create for the benefit of art.

Visiting the residents at the Hanover infirmary in Lucea, I talk with a woman whose leg is covered in white pus, flies swarming around her open sores. I see a young man, maybe schizophrenic, wandering the grounds in torn pants, open at the fly, fondling himself and talking to voices in the surrounding air. *Why do you go there?* my grandmother wants to know. And I don't have any good way of explaining to her why I, sixteen years removed from the island of my birth, am recording the stories they tell me of their lives. Or why I am gathering their words even knowing that words do not feed an empty belly nor cure disease and that these words and any others will do nothing more or less than approximate truth.

The old man's song ends as the bus pulls up to take me to the airport. He puts down his guitar and smiles once more in my direction. I pick up my bag, turn to go. In one hour, on the same plane as the American tourists who don't leave the hotel the duration of their stay, I will be heading back to New York. Landing on US soil again, I will hear an immigration officer, this time with a different accent, say "welcome home."

Shara McCallum

Quashelle Curtis—**Babylon Queens** oil on canvas mixed media

ITTESISTIBLE InTenTions:
U.S.-based African LGBT Communities Organize

The variety of African lesbian, gay, bisexual, transgender, ("LGBT"), lived experiences, ideological perspectives, and political visions is as wide and complex as that which exists in any region's local movements for social transformation and justice. With the exception of South Africa, which provides constitutional protection from discrimination on the basis of sexual orientation, African states for the most part criminalize same-sex relationships and consensual adult sexual contact through the retention of latent post-colonial penal codes.

In the past six or seven years, the topic of homosexuality has been introduced into the public domain within African countries at an unprecedented level, though in a damning and sensationalizing light. Heads-of-state seeking to police local women's movements and to detract attention from pressing issues of national concern continue to conveniently scapegoat African LGBT communities via national newspapers seeking to boost their sales. The lives of African LGBT organizers, especially those living on the continent, have been placed under extreme jeopardy.

In 1995, just prior to the Fourth World Conference on Women, President Mugabe of Zimbabwe became the first African head-of-state to publicly denounce and ostracize African lesbians and gay men with such vehemence as to bring him infamy. Other African heads-of-state soon followed, especially after the highly sensationalized lesbian organizing at the Beijing conference, and a high-profile case in which former Zimbabwean Prime Minister Canaan Banana was convicted of sodomy for his rape of a former body guard, which was well publicized throughout the continent. Presidents Moi of Kenya, Museveni of Uganda and Nujoma of Namibia have each repeatedly weighed in with denigrations of homosexuality as "un-African," "anti-Christian," "opposed to African traditions," and "a disease of the decadent U.S. and West," increasingly calling for the arrest of all known and suspected offenders.

African LGBT organizers based in the U.S. have found it strategically useful to develop ties with LGBT organizers on the continent and other anti-heterosexist allies throughout the world, to mobilize timely responses to the anti-homosexual witch-hunts in our countries of origin. In the past few months, members of a New

153

York-based network of African LGBT people and their friends have collaborated with Africa- and Canada-based LGBT organizers and the New York-based Astraea International Fund for Sexual Minorities, to secure the freedom of physically displaced local activists facing life-threatening circumstances in their countries of origin as a result of their organizing work under increasingly dangerous local conditions.

Our successful trans-local initiative, supported by the cutting-edge philanthropy of the Astraea Foundation, helped mobilize enough funds to save the lives of five leaders of a local African LGBT organization. These courageous and resourceful men and women had survived detention, torture and in some instances rape at the hands of members of the local police force, acting in response to their head-of-state's calls just a few months prior, for the immediate arrest of all the nation's homosexuals. The significance of our autonomous agency in this instance is highlighted by the fact that outside of our initiatives, these comrades had no other immediate recourse despite the fact that their case was already well-documented by mainstream human rights organizations.

Human rights meta-narratives deployed in response to the current conditions of African LGBT people too easily obscure the agency of these very subjects. The decontextualized visibility of African LGBT people, in the absence of our sustained autonomous knowledge production, limits the potential of our local and trans-local organizing. While we remain exposed to all manner of personal policing, including the constant threat and reality of exposure and blackmail, we cannot afford to have our courageous life stories and initiatives erased, sidelined, or subsumed by the well-intentioned agendas of others. We must remain vigilantly conscious of our historical relationship to movements both in the U.S. and in our countries of origin, which have had broader visions for social transformation.

Our historical legacy as African LGBT people includes victories over slavery, colonization and apartheid; and centuries of experience with multi-pronged organizing for fundamental social, economic and political transformation and freedom for all. Our conceptual approaches to organizing draw from the multi-lingual, interdependent, inter-textual, intersectional strategies of African, Black and Third World U.S.-based feminist movements. It is essential that our progressive U.S.-based allies contextualize themselves relative to this country's history of genocidal war against indigenous peoples and enslavement of Africans, and recognize the function of white supremacist ideology to the maintenance of white structural privilege and U.S. capitalist expansion.

While current mainstream LGBT academic and human rights publications may provide some interesting and even useful perspectives on our lives and organizing, they too casually uphold white male structural privilege. The paternalistic packaging of African LGBT experiences without explicit and systematic consideration of our complex autonomous agency in perilous circumstances is rather a cynical and myopic action by the purported defenders of our existence and rights. The survival of LGBT Africans working under life-threatening conditions in fragile coalitions urgently requires demonstrated recognition from our allies that the eradication of white supremacy and male supremacy goes hand-in-hand with the eradication of heterosexual supremacy.

Our daily material realities and political economies as migrants, along with our ideological convictions and political alliances as Africans influence our social language, cultural expression and pragmatic parameters as agents for change. In September of 1999, a tri-continental coalition of African, Black and migrant LGBT people realized a timely cultural intervention at the first Africa-based International Lesbian & Gay Association (ILGA) Conference in Johannesburg, South Africa. With the support of the Astraea International Fund for Sexual Minorities, members of our New York-based African LGBT network, the Johannesburg-based "Gay & Lesbian Organization of the Witwatersrand (GLOW)" and the Amsterdam-based Black and migrant LGBT group "Strange Fruit The Real" planned and created a cultural FREE ZONE dubbed "Unifying Links," which centralized the experiences and needs of lesbian feminists of color in attendance at the conference.

With an outlook to inspiring self-expression amongst global lesbians of color, our friends and allies, a group of us drafted and circulated a list of goals and strategies for our multi-media intervention, and requested input and participation from our allies at the conference. Our explicitly anti-racist and pro-feminist agenda prioritized self-empowerment, visibility, autonomous and equal participation on our own terms, the creation of space for networking and creative cultural self-representation, monitoring and documentation of the conference itself, and good old-fashioned fun. To this end, we secured and decorated a room in the conference hotel, in which we screened independently produced videos reflecting our various communities, maintained tables and walls where allies could display their organizational materials and creative works, and sustained a critical dialogue on issues arising at the conference as well as issues crucial to local and trans-local organizing by lesbian feminists of color.

As LGBT Africans based in the U.S., we must boldly lay claim to our own ideological terrain, and continue to mobilize personal commitment, economic resources and political will in support of our work. Trans-national philanthropy continues to play a crucial role in the development of sustainable economic and technical resources by movements and organizations committed to securing human rights and justice in different countries. The commitment of progressive U.S.-based foundations to African organizing on gender and sexuality uniquely positions them to have an impact on current cutting-edge creative initiatives. Our U.S. location opens up the space for our strategic collaboration with U.S.-based foundations as part of our on-going work.

Our covert organizing, fragile visibility, contested legitimacy, and commodified existence need never obscure our analytical base or needlessly drain our energy. Here's to creative autonomous African organizing!

Kagendo

155

AULD LANG SYNE

ninety-six came rushing in
beside a road curled like a "s."
swirling between a football stadium
and parking lot,
behind the kentucky college
where i used to teach,
a black woman lay on frosted grass.   her throat
carved up for the holidays.

her live face made a pretty picture on the news.
they flashed her on then off again
at five and six and then eleven.
so young,
attractive,
brown,
familiar.
did i grade her essay in english 101 or brush
past her in the crowded hall?

two weeks later
a shackled brown man with a pudgy face
pleaded guilty to my tv screen. they flashed him on
then off again. head bowed, he whispered to the camera lens
"we were friends."
his voice like warm steam
through a radiator's leak.
they were old acquaintances
ushering in nineteen ninety-six.
a nugget of crack their champagne.
until that argument over precious rock
and he opened up her pretty brown throat

role call

just in time
for auld lang syne.

meanwhile
at the g-spot gentlemen's lounge
a white woman did bumps and grinds atop a bar
and some man watched how
her hips rounded, her breasts drooped, her calves pumped
up and down in cheap high heel shoes.   he dreamed her dead
on new years eve
left her slit along a highway's yellow, fractured lines.
just a trampled party favor in the road.
she lived
two blocks away from me
on fifth and lime.
i wonder if
i ever passed her on the street near progress market
or spalding's bakery? but there are too many white girls
around these places. i can't memorize all their sad
peeling faces.

that new years day i cooked a pot of black eyed peas
to bring good luck
added plenty of black pepper, tomatoes, a little curry and
rice
creating a recipe to distract myself
from a crawling fear
afraid of what the year would bring for women
i already knew.
two women i might have met
became bruised, punctured flesh balloons
ticker taped in the streets.
it takes a whole hesitant year to write this poem
but i do
for women murdered
three hundred sixty five days a year.
their faces faded
glitter
falling
confettied in the streets.

Kelly Norman Ellis

John Abner–**Daily News** collage

son RISE

at the intersection
of peachtree & auburn
between park place
and luckie street
an atlanta son rises
before the tourists
waiting to be kissed
by the light
at the foot of urban majesty
at the center
of commerce
marble, steel and glass
scraping the sky
while e-business
and olympic residue
embrace a silent Sunday morning
calvin clark
married w/children
54, able-bodied
blood shot eyes
reeking of alcohol
and homelessness
begs—no asks passers by politely
for a cigarette
mumbles that he dreamed about
kentucky last night
said it must have been
that nicotine callin'

I, so much a boy of bluegrass that I am
the color of tobacco
and bourbon
am suddenly attentive
not believing in coincidences
I put my amateur photojournalism
on hold
join him on the stoop
and try not to stare at his
tommy hilfiger shoes

and his crusty unwashed face
both equally out of place
together

I offer him two dollars
for breakfast
and five to take his picture
he accepts
apologizes for being needy
then volunteers
that his mind just comes and goes
and sometimes he just acts a fool
but that he is not himself
didn't use to stutter
done eleven years
on the inside
use to box and teach
use ta paint too
done three weeks, here
in this park
been robbed three times

all I did was pray for 'em
he said
figured they must need it
more 'n me
pointing upwards
he said
I talked to Him 'bout it
and He said
eva thang gonna be all right
so I ain't givin' up
I ain't neva neva givin' up

Frank X Walker

Social
security

The line is long and starts in Guatemala.
The Jamaicans came in a group of five
three passports between them.
There are six babies in line. Two
of them are crying. There are clever
people who stand in one
line appointments only.
Three hours is the standard wait
according to the form that takes
seventeen minutes to fill with facts
for nine essential digits.

*You tell me go to Sutphin   That security guard told me come   here   Doesn't he
know anything   He told me come here   My mother in law has her retire   I   went
to   Sutphin they told me come here   you tell me to go there!*
She is loud. The mother-in-law twists the end of her sari.

No one is at the Spanish window.

Come to Aunty if you so bad come come nuh Hit him if he bad hit him
The mother ignores her sister.
The Aunt fans herself with the baby's form.

*Oh Jesus I can't stand here all day like this   I too weak Lord yes Jesus   told me to
come here from Sutphin   no sweetheart you older than me sit down   got me
standing in this line Jesus those boys stole my card   half these windows empty
need my number Lord*

A man bumps gently dreaming against the windows   hands leather claws unfolding papers   his mouth whispers aubergine   the bureaucrat speaks another language

SIR   THE RED WHITE AND BLUE CARD SIR
LISTEN TO ME THE CARD
THE WHITE BLUE AND RED CARD SIR
YOU SHOULD HAVE THAT YOU DON'T
HAVE THAT BUT YOU SHOULD HAVE THAT SIR
YES SIR I WANT YOU TO TRY TO UNDERSTAND
WHAT I AM SAYING THAT DOOR IS LOCKED SIR
BRING THAT CARD WHEN YOU COME BACK
TOMORROW I WANT YOU TO LISTEN TO ME

The bureaucrat's desk.
Microphone snakes from glass to mouth Without this umbilical eel I am deaf to him
Excuse me?
He curls it to thin lips. ID floats like smoke. I give him three.
With this proof I am stamped. Numbered. Legal. Non-alien.

R. Erica Doyle

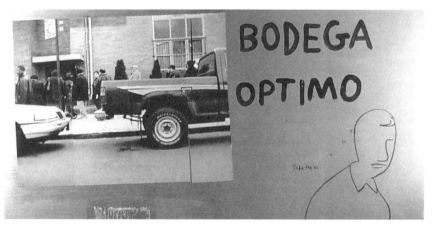

Steveson Estimé–**Bodega Optimo** mixed media woodcut

Why are there no coups in the U.S.?
Because there are no American embassies in the U.S.
-Haitian Joke

Crematorium

here we are now
lost   gone away
from that which
we once were

the rubble of us
decaying
                with time

here we are
scattered remnants
of a people
spread out
beneath bodies
and blood

blown apart
so many years
detatched
from one another

gasping
                for air
in the all
consuming
                blaze

Arthur Ade Amaker

dreamy **blues**

for barney bigard, arthur whetsol & lawrence brown

> you ain't been blue...til you've
> had that mood indigo...
> > **Ellington/Mills**

a young girl
is somewhere waiting on
the boy she loves; she
has seen him every day for the last
five years but today he will not come.

an old man
is down by a river
standing at the spot
where he saw his only son drown.

a woman who never knew her
mother but knew her
mother did not love her
is somewhere walking the
streets.

i travel to all these places,
long to capture that
which seems to be our shadow,
swells with absurdity
recalls jobs we can't have,
hotels we can't enter
restaurants which show us doors
instead of menus.

ours is a deep dyed emotion;
marching bands
ragtimers

banjo pickers
barrelhouse ballers
dangerous dance halls
segregated neighborhoods
too proud to weep what it lives.

we are that drama.
we are this
unusual arrangement
that speaks for the millions,
that is why this song is
full of our dreams

heard in
late hours on our radios
phonographs
we love ourselves more
sleep well at night
rise from our beds
to work hard
and fancy future
triumphs where
we are wide awake
in the middle
of nightmare,

this sound will
carry us forward
and speak to the world
in a language that does
not lie

just a ditty i wrote down
one day
before the show
while my
mother prepared supper,

and somewhere
we were living
this mood...

Brian Gilmore

HAIKU

empty bucket on her head
a woman walks to the Euphrates
in acid rain

Lenard D. Moore

Passing the Middle

folded funk flexed fear bent bones scraped skin
blood burst torn tongue blind mind good god heaven
help us hold together limp lungs spent spine
belly burn flux flow damp dark deep death wild waves
salt seep wet wounds rust rape rats cruel gruel
choke chains piss pain hell hold

Jabari Asim

Shelia L. Prevost—**Lynching** oil on canvas

Black men don't kill themselves

my boys rode up on me
and induced a new fright
because cats don't look the same in the dark.
i continue my silent trek,
my feet trying to make the skip to home.
but in their place is numbness.
i inhale the scent of my own piss,
never imagining it would come to this
little damp patch of dirt beneath my knees,
my jeans gathered in their bend.
i am a skeptical sight
fresh from a fight with my girl;
my whole world off balance.
journey seems long tonight.
i'm far from the pine chapel purgatory
where my ghost will tell the story;
painful chapters unfolding
as witnesses rewrite
and officers seal the scene so tight
the truth suffocates.
the air my people breathe will come out printed
bold and black
on pre-shrunk white tees;
they pledge their frustrated and skeptical allegiance.
black men don't kill themselves.
they die that way;
strangled by their pride when they talk too much;
choking on their balls when they're man enough.
i'm not the pillow soft, rock hard kid next door;
not the hustler tricking for small treats.
i'm about to tally my talents into a g.e.d.
i'm a year away from copping a legal brew;
one half of my momma's egg split in two,
i'm not any
single
man;
i'm history
and you know the crooked neck, the facts unchecked,
on display in conspicuous places
i peer out from the edge of the old south,
my mouth twisted in a pout.

Darlene Anita Scott

The First (and Last) Anti-Clinton Poem

i mean, even a huckster like slick willie got to be impressed
there's a sucka born every minute
even socks the cat is pulling three card monte hustles
even hip nigga liberals bow down to his righteous con

him slicker than owl doo-doo
him slicker than sperm sliding off Monica's perm
him slicker than greased okra

slick willie know we was blinded by reagan/bush
(dey was real bad masters)
but slick willie playing the cool master
him blow saxophone, shoot basketball,
eat at mikey-d's & chill in harlem
he down wit the people
& most of the people are down—

Kenneth Carroll

New Rules of the Road

Make
  No sudden movements
Like from your neighborhood
  To someplace you don't belong

Keep
  Your hands visible at all times
Above your head.   In these
  brand new handcuffs

Speak
  Only when spoken to
Or not at all: You have the right to
  Silence

Have proper ID on you at
  All times
You have no right
  To travel

Reply only to
  The questions asked
You have nothing to say
  We want to hear

Give the officer
  Only the materials requested
You have nothing to show us
  We want to see

Do not leave the vehicle
  Unless told to
You have
  Nothing

Go quietly
  When arrested
You are
  Nothing

Do not
  Resist
You are a
  Thing

Do not
  Run
You have
  No rights

Do not say you
  Do not fit The Profile

In America:
You are the profile.

Reginald Harris

A **Story** for **America**

Little Boy has nothing on
wants to have what Big Boy has
wants to flex muscles he doesn't have yet
wants to fly away from home
looks back after taking 2 steps
looks at his shadow
crawling up mountainside, up pyramids, up steps
back home

> Little Boy sees the sun casting its light
> & calls the sun: America
> America sees Little Boy screaming in playground
> & calls the boy: A Problem

Big Boy has left home already
doesn't see America as anything
sees everything as sunshine
sees into the sunshine
gets blind from the sunshine
& calls it: Tomorrow
Tomorrow sees Big Boy removes his eyesight
& calls him: Mine

Now Big Boy belongs to Tomorrow
has no one Today never Today
Little Boy has Today before Tomorrow
sees him, playing
in Central, South, & other Americas

> Little Boy sees Tomorrow
> & calls Tomorrow: Mine

Little Boy wants what Big Boy has
Big Boy wants what Little Boy was
they were two things marked the same thing
& everyone is happening everywhere
They were two, by any chance
anybody see anything with nothing on it?
By any hour, anyone see anything, by anywhere, see any place, we fill
this room with nothing, what?

> *They were anything*
> *anyplace, nothing*
> *with anything on*

Edwin Torres

Negative

Wake to find everything black
what was white, all the vice
versa-white maids on TV, black

sitcoms that star white dwarfs
cute as pearl buttons. Black Presidents,
Black Houses. White horse

candidates. All bleach burns
clothes black. Drive roads
white as you are, white songs

on the radio stolen by black bands
like secret pancake recipes, white back-up
singers, ball-players & boxers all

white as tar. Feathers on chickens
dark as everything, boiling in the pot
that called the kettle honky. Even

whites of the eye turn dark, pupils
clear & changing as a cat's.
Is this what we've wanted

& waited for? to see snow
covering everything black
as Christmas, dark pages written

white upon? All our eclipses bright,
dark stars shooting across pale
sky, glowing like ash in fire, shower

every skin. Only money keeps
green, still grows & burns like grass
under dark daylight.

Kevin Young

Eric Mack—**Vibrate Plain** mixed media on canvas

Clash of Denial: Black Homophobia and Gay White Ghettos

BEDFORD-STUYVESANT-BROOKLYN, NEW YORK: Pictures of knobby-kneed black children playing in streets littered with broken glass and lined with abandoned buildings; the inner city run amuck, crumbling under crime wave after crime wave and white flight born on thoughts of the new hopes to be found in the nearest suburb; timbs and sweat suits, sagging jeans and backwards turned baseball caps, sitting atop the doo rags or brightly-colored scarves on the heads of rod-straight black bodies bent to swaying, floating on the sounds of a rapper's lyrics matched to a heart-thumping bass beat. "Do or die, Bed-Stuy." These images do not emerge from a fictive perspective, but these are not the only images of Bed-Stuy that exist. These are the popular ones, warped into hyper-stereotype, the ones that make it into the mainstream of American consciousness.

Seventh Avenue, Chelsea, Manhattan, New York: Bodies, male bodies, white male bodies in unabashed lust for each other; block after block of pale-skinned, blond-, black-, or brown-haired male effeminacy moving in a world exclusive unto them; cropped hair and Log Cabin Republicans, combat boots and nipple-rings, spiked heels and grotesquely muscular bodies, swirling in unison to voices screeching club songs under a disco ball called the sun. "We're here, we're queer, get used to it!" Across millions of TV screens in America, an alarm sounds and the consciousness of an invisible minority erupts: How did those people get like that and how do we keep people like them from coming here? And these images, too, while derivative of the truth, may owe their final presentation to a retooling on the hotbed of American media; certainly "those people" are a bit cartoonish and are not representative of male, same gender-loving (SGL) people everywhere—particularly us black ones. But in a society that is quick to congratulate itself about the homage it pays to the image of diversity while still being very homophobic, these are the images that take root, evolving into a feeding frenzy of the ignorant and gaining a fantasy life all their own.

Lay these two worlds, one on top of the other, and they clash. Cumbersome does not begin to describe their imbalance to each other; the reality of one is inseperable to the other.

I find the circumstance of the gay white (male) movement interesting-it is a conundrum of white male dominance, more about continuing the uninte—rupted privilege of a particular subset of the population rather than the pursuit of universal rights for all. I find it problematic that the gay white (male) movement would dare to compare its struggle with what African Americans had to endure to secure (limited) civil rights; before I decide whether to announce the way I love, people can see the fact of my blackness and my maleness. In a racist America that fears blackness first, and black maleness most of all, the fact that I am a black SGL man-and that I chose not to prioritize any part of myself over another-figures prominently in my choices of where I live; how, where, and when I reveal myself to others; and how I interact with my community, family, friends, and acquaintances.

For the record, I grew up in Bed-Stuy, in a different Bed-Stuy than the one I've captured here that figures far too mythically in America's imaginings of the inner city. I hold two degrees: an undergraduate degree from Morehouse College and a graduate degree from Columbia University. My parents, my brother, and most of the relatives with whom I am very close know how I love. I still live in Bed-Stuy and I'm real comfortable moving through my neighborhood in my timbs, baggy jeans, and oversized hoodie-but I doubt anyone would confuse me for a "thug." As of this writing, I have not announced the way I love at work—I find no need and, strangely enough, I seem to have been excluded from general office speculation about my weekend's conquests or my dating status or the other usual musings that colleagues can have around one's bedroom activities. Strangely enough, too—especially for an office of eight colored folk (six black men, one black woman, and a latino woman)— whenever questions of which way so-and-so might swing or rumors about

who-might-bring-who to an office event do arise, they've been refreshingly pc. No mention of "faggot" this or "punk" that or "dyke" the other thing. And I'm hyper-tuned-in for it, ready to take offense and defend a reality I know is mine. If anyone at work ever asked, I'd answer honestly, but no one has, and I've found myself wondering whether or not that makes me "closeted," or "hidden," or on the "down low."

Most of anything I have to do is either right here in Bed-Stuy or a short distance away: The gym I go to is in East New York—Starrett City to be specific-and I've never felt uncomfortable amid all the hyper-masculinity expressed there either. Again, in a place that is filled with more than its share of black and Latino people, it's interesting to note the lack of overt verbal expressions of heterosexuality that usually take the form of braggadocios conversations about tits and ass, punks, sissies, and faggots. It's not that we aren't there. I've caught my share of eyes and I hooked up with one brother from there (and I'm no towering pillar of testosterone, one of those types who turn the heads of anyone everywhere I go), and I definitely don't think anyone is consciously monitoring their behavior so as to be less offensive, whether it's at work or the gym. There's a pharmacy within walking distance of my house, for those incidentals I might need, and I shop for groceries at the Pathmark at Atlantic Center (just about the "gayest" place I find myself these days). About the only times I venture into the city are to hang-out at the movies or grab a drink with my boys. I consider myself adequately equipped with enough intelligence, looks, and personality to accomplish what I want to get done. However, I do think I'm atypical when lined up against that word "gay." But then again, I think most black men are—at least to those who see that word as the construct of a reality and identity not of our own machinations—and as I move through my daily reality, watching brothers just like me do the very same thing, I wonder: in a racist America where perceptions about the inner-city can morph into a surreal concoction of the truth, where white gay culture is promoted as the exclusive playground of a hedonistic few, who decides what homophobic is and how did the African American community get slapped with the label, "Most Homophobic"?

I don't mean to suggest that the black community isn't homophobic or gloss over the reality that there is a definite stance within African American culture that is as virulently homophobic as it is misogynistic. However, the question must be asked: In context of what I've already stated, who defines black masculinity, its function within the black community, and how does its definition and function impact a mainstream American interpretation of "homophobic"? I point to the evidence of the sacrificial type slaying of Matthew Shepard, the rape, hunt, and subsequent execution of Brandon Teena, and the bombing of the popular Atlanta lesbian club, The Otherside, not as a way of exploring in whose community—black or white—lies the greater pathology, but as a way to examine what the mainstream means by the word "homophobic."

Whether it is a wild night of college white boys out on a nightly terror ride by a gay club or an epithet shouted at an unsuspecting individual from within the safety of a group or bashing the "right" individual caught in vicinity of the "wrong" place by a marauding band of perpetrators, there is a physical dynamic associated with the mainstream interpretation of homophobic. It is an active engagement in which one or, more accurately, a group of bodies prey on the perceived sexual difference, real or imagined, of another body without regard to bodily injury or the loss of life. The perceived sexual difference is the key here because it is the trigger: the meek and effeminate man, the butch and aggressive woman, the seemingly normal individual in close proximity to what is considered to be an abnormal place; all of these individuals require swift and exacting remediation. And these responses are irrationally violent physical reactions to the perception of a misunderstood sexual reality. This analysis can even be elevated to the anti-gay policy-making activities of the government and employers, albeit, they are less physical in execution, but the intent and overall effect is no less severe.

The black community requires a more psychic analysis of its interpretation of the word homophobic. In a country where the presentation of a black body, whether male or female, is already complicated by a media that expresses obvious fetishes only for certain aspects of both, the possibility that that community might have its body reflected back at it through the lens of a racist society under the influence of various exclusionary factions—themselves obsessed with the satisfaction of their own hedonistic pleasures—must be an intolerable idea. In short, as a friend put it, "I think that the black community is homophobic of a gay white effeminate construct that is associated with the term "gay." I think it stems from a fear that same sex behavior automatically makes us akin to them." The question almost asks itself, "Are you black first or gay first?"

I look back at my own life, to the moment when I told my parents about my connection with men. I'd been living in Birmingham (yes, Alabama) for a year or so after I'd graduated from Morehouse. My banking career was steaming right along—I had a phat apartment, my own car, was beginning to live less like a college student. I'd graduated and begun to expand in the role of "Dutiful Son" as had been laid out for me since birth. At that time—1991—Birmingham was still the south in the most conservative ways one can imagine: still grappling with its problematic history concerning race; class division between a black lower class that was collapsing into the decaying structure of the inner city, a slightly better-off black middle class that was striving to get to the next level, and a black upper-middle to upper-class that was doing its best to will the other two out of existence was so distinct as to be tangible; and the mention of anything "gay" or "lesbian" was met with blank expressions, whispers, or a stone wall of silence. Luckily, being the recent college graduate that I was, my jaunts back and forth to Atlanta, my frequent (male) visitors, my lack of a committed relationship, my exploration of the entire southeastern United States with my carousing bunch of (male) friends was seen as nothing other than the perpetuation of that fraternal rite of passage known as sowing one's wild oats by family and colleagues both. I had a rousing good time for almost two years until my mother noticed the absence of women from my conversation and women— their presence, the friendships, the few relationships—had been a consistent part of my life throughout college. She couched her question in what she thought was a joke, "I don't hear mention of any girlfriend—don't tell me you don't like women anymore." And my response: "Not like you think, Ma." I don't remember the rest of our conversation but I do remember my father was out of the house and Ma said she'd have to tell him as soon as he returned home.

There are a few things to understand about my father: First, he's a big man. Sure, I mean he's physically big, but he has a presence that matches his size. Big voice. Looks you in the eye when he talks and expects you to do the same when responding. Takes large strides when he walks and is as heavy-footed as he is heavy-handed. Thoughtful man in that he is intelligent, but a thoughtful man also in that he's considerate. There're numerous charities, both formal and informal, which have benefited from his generosity. Excellent provider—my brother and I wanted for nothing growing up. My father would describe himself as a country boy from North Carolina. I will go one step further: My father is a country boy who learned the games of the city kids and became very, very successful at them. His understanding of black manhood can be short-handed to this: A black man is the head of his family, he is both provider and protector and he makes all necessary commitments and sacrifices to ensure that his children have a significantly better start in life than the one he experienced. Period. As black men, that is how he raised my brother and me. As the eldest child in a family of six children, who succeeded challenging circumstances without resorting to drugs, violence, or any other crime, and produced his own family, that his eldest child could grow up to have an intimate connection with men was indecipherable. Period.

My revelation to my parents came a few months before Christmas and right before I was to leave Birmingham to return to Brooklyn for holiday vacation, I wrecked my car. Given that I didn't have the money to return home and fix my car, I thought it best to spend the holiday in Birmingham, perhaps visit relatives down in Montgomery instead of returning to New York. Instantly, my father sent money for car repairs along with his demand that I was to return home immediately. He needed to see me with his own eyes—he needed to see how I looked. At that time, for that moment, that was enough for me to return home and him to see me and recognize that I had not become physically different from the person he knew.

Not only did my father and I not speak for a year, we did not try to speak to one another. My mother later described that time in our family as one of incredible anger. "We were some pissed people." When my father and I finally did speak, there were things he made me understand about his childhood, about his own father, about his extended family and the promises that he made to himself and the way he'd raise his children. The way he knew he raised his sons. He did not raise a son to be a woman. He did not raise a black boy in America to be anything other than what he knew a black man had to be.

My father and I have an incredible relationship now and I am not being idealistic. There is still a lot about me he does not know, but I know he knows what matters: That I am the son he raised. When I think about what my family and I have been through, the is-

sue of black masculinity, how it is structured, and how black men have to move through the daily reality of America, I don't think any of us were conscious of labels and blanket misnomers; we were in a deeper place, a place where we had to analyze the circumstances of realities based on very real, lived experiences. It is a place where, intuitively, I know millions of black families, whether they are fathers and sons or mothers and daughters or brothers and sisters and regardless of their sexuality, have to travel to each day. As easy as it would be to buckle under the collective identity of the "most homophobic," I know that is not what we're doing—that is a foreigner's unsupported hypothesis. Too many of us live in too close a proximity to each other and even in places such as Clinton Hill and Fort Greene where large numbers of the black SGL community have amassed, it is still a different collective than a gay white enclave such as Chelsea. That the black community is more homophobic than the rest of America is conjecture by a siege mentality that has not ever sought to understand anything about African American culture save that which it could co-opt for its own purposes. It is a distraction that keeps us from understanding who we truly are and the myriad of strengths and weaknesses that encapsulate our multiple realities. And the gay white ghetto is the sideshow circus that makes that distraction possible.

Doug Jones

THE **House** of Dangerous *Surprise*

Suburban barbeques, late-night bid whist parties,
laughter and frying fish crackling the air,
I come from Chicago,
brought up on blues and beer
by men and women who worked the hard shift.
Descendants of the northern migration,
they staked their claim in the Midwest—
urban-drawn folk who gave up back porch tales
for fast promises of a greedy city.
They built churches and taverns side-by-side
and I was baptized in both.

I come from kitchens filled with cousinsauntsgodsistersplaybrothers,
living rooms where halos of smoke crowned steppers
who made love to Sam Cooke
while others nodded and snapped jeweled fingers,
tapped polyester knees.

I grew up with Bobby Blue Bland, Donnie Hathaway, Stevie Wonder
singing me into fantasy, blocking out
the hard clamor of parental love.
I come from chronic rage raised up by whiskied glances,
my mother's cries piercing my sleep as
the dog shits in the corner, too frightened by it all.
My sisters pretend to sleep, not smell
the sting of cigarettes and wine nudging the air
separating the white officer and my father
whose fist, a glistening cannonball, silences my mother.
And all the while B.B. King repeats himself, urging
them back to the blues of their youth.

I come from a house of dangerous surprise,
people made mad by desire and dream.
Factory workers, truckers, mechanics
who showed frightening love, made holidays and birthdays
divine spectacles. Then,
the timely blow. Still,

I grew straight, found peace in the inbetween.
And what of this? The hindsight?
I come from a people flawed and bruised
who loved me while
trying to love each other.

Lita Hooper

Soundtrack for Us

You and I lay
Make music
Match the stereo

You ride
My southern funk
The beat of Outkast
Rise with the bounce
Fall into the drawl
Dance to an eleven minute track
That loops on and on and on

When I trace rings around your spine
Sade's song circles me
With pure light
Pleasure emitted by her voice
Bliss echoed in the collaboration
Of our bodies

You begin the slow climb
Five steps closer to climax
And Lenny Kravitz is moaning
About belonging
I wonder about belonging
If that is an appropriate word
To describe my feelings
If it would be closer to the truth
If I omitted be

Leave this place
Long enough to join you
In a moment of joy
As we both collapse
Into the egg crate cushioned mattress
My only thoughts on the raw rich noise
The reassurance of Jill Scott to Black Thought
"You got me."

Janeé Bolden

The Inside

I cry my faces
into the fabric of your fingers
know that inside you
my breasts are the same as my feet

never had room to rollout all my skin before
but you know the naked of me
you have walked my prayers
and lit cranberry lanterns
where placenta should have been

stood in conference with God
and told Her I was worthy

sat at the bottom bunk of my childhood
and bore the child my first lover left behind

watched the slide shows of dysfunction
that told me my mother was human
and my father was someone she hated sometimes

you are my sister, I share the period stained panties
of my youth and crooked spine I have out grown

you are my fingers, I play in mud and lick the earth into myself

you are my husband
and forehead to forehead
we stare ourselves awake

Jenoyne Adams

Calida Garcia–**Berry** oil on canvas

On DaYS

Concrete burns and heat smells
the streets are thick long
Cadillacs shake with soul music
Foreheads and lips are Vaseline-d

Francesca and the Haitian twins hang out
on the corner of Albany & Main
in their so tight dark denims
rolled up at the ankles and their
our-mamas-are-at-work-so-we-
gonna-do-what-the-hell-we-wanna
attitudes

Miss Tullis sits on her stoop
legs split far apart,
Lamont between them
back towards her
hands move like knitting needles
through his hair

Men with dirty mouths gather like gnats,
mosquitoes in front of Corner Market & Deli
some bare-chested, some cigaretted, some ashy
black elbows connected to ashier black hands
that strangled paper bagged bottle necks

my bedroom is hot
even with the windows wide open
and the fan turned on high

the radio on top of my Bible spits static
the sun throws patches of light
onto the southwest corners of my bed

on days like this
i feel like parting my legs for you

Melissa McEwen

When Lost, Ask for Directions

I.

how
can we
end this tale

of two cities
on a map
with a scale surreal
where a few inches
between father and daughter
equal a million miles

I could trace
the line of your nose
and know
my own reflection

but these days
we touch
without feeling

I could look
into your eyes
and see myself
but even at our closest
we stand
back to back

II.

each time you left us
for letters behind
your name
I learned to forget

I loved you

each time
you returned
wiser of the world
to a household
of unlettered strangers

while you defended
your dissertation
I was bullied
on bus 29

but I guess
that wasn't
the committee's
concern

III.

I am
your failures
and aspirations

Can you love
yourself
enough
to know me

can we
mourn these miles
and cry

Kysha N. Brown

ROLE CALL IS A LITMUS TEST—AND A CALL TO ARMS TO A GENERATION GROWN FAT ON THE LIMITED FREEDOMS WON BY THE CIVIL RIGHTS STRUGGLE.

Shirley Carter—**Is Excess Sin** oil on canvas money bags

warning

It rises from the hard times that
Hide too long in a woman's smile.
How bloodshed occurs is not strange
Nor does it happen

By accident. Sleeping with one eye
Open, mining her soul for palpable
Images of survival, she will consider your
Death each time you mistake

Her for prey. She is vigil of the ones who
Intend to slow her down until she
Loses her meaning and who, even sooner, intend
To kill her faith until she loses her

Laughter. How bloodshed occurs is not
Strange at all. Nor does it happen by accident
And if it surges from a woman's compromised
Splendor, nothing can save you.

Lissette Norman

The *Escape*

i just remember my teeth
were bared

i couldn't stand there
a moment longer
i
i just couldn't listen/hear
another sound from her throat i
felt my feet frozen into the
frozen earth couldn't move couldn't
stay for another second

it was coming from her throat
that sound from her
eyes the way she
owned me
could make those noises could
look at me that way and my
teeth were bared
my feet frozen into the ground
my expression not known my
left eye meeting hers defiantly my
right eye on her throat

watching the muscles move up and down
as she spoke watching the
red trail of blood rising in her veins
to her face which brimmed over with it
eyes bulged with her anger
i was hers
forever

feet frozen into the frozen earth
as the rest of my body shivered

perfectly still
when time collapsed as
our bodies
as i felt my nails dig into her shoulders
as i felt no heard
teeth
ripping into and apart
red stinging in my eyes hot
stinging sprayed all over my body heard
felt the momentary quiet felt
heard the momentary absence
of that noise
of that look of that
neverendingness

and when time collapsed
back into itself
i was running

feet still frozen and
moving so fast it
didn't matter i couldn't feel em just
running
from the taste of her blood in my mouth
days and days of rivers, years of rain never
took that taste of blood from my mouth
running
sweating the frost from my face
wearing rocks in the soles of my feet never
leaving one place behind, taking it with me

hiding in bushes in day and in night
running for cover for safety for god
running from that sound those sounds those
eyes everywhere just
half existing but not dying as it might
slow down my running pace

falling down when i had to
eating nothing but grass / grass /
didn't know anything else didn't
know where i was couldn't
get the taste of her blood outta my mouth
her who is me there
is no me i was learned only
her she
owns me
forever running
from the taste of her blood in my mouth
glad for the silence
   for a minute
never escaping
the sounds or the eyes
never leaving behind that
blood that i took inside of me

and i was hers
forever
and ever
amen

Samiya A. Bashir

The **Ghost** of **Orpheus**

And Orpheus' ghost fled under the earth, and knew
The place he had known before
The fields of the blessed found Eurydice
And took her in his arms

I

Peel back the layers of God's skin
and we find the incandescent insides,
the cascading nuclei, of Hydrogen,
Oxygen and Carbon. This beacon so far
in the dark, a storm inside the body,
winks out this night like the seven legs
of a spider gone mad. God is dead
and we have killed him; daffodils also bleed
but not like you and not like my skin, rippling
in waves of heat and light like the wings
of a fruit fly lifting into the air.

II

We structure the universe in molecules
of contempt, in safe approximations
of the first lover, as if falling in love
were as seasonal as fruit. Atoms fly faster
at sunset, warm ions escaping the night,
the arc of buckshot into a dew-dipped
pond, and the bird, startled into flight,
its wings expanding heavier than before,
the lead dragging the body downward, its wet
paper wings just beneath the surface,
soggy in their release.

III

There was a shadow somewhere
drifting across walls and sidewalks,
fingering those surfaces, detailing

the fixed body of the universe.
We cannot separate our shadows
from ourselves, a naked singularity
from the reservoir of dreams. The cold soil
that glistens beneath the February sun
is my iced body dressed in its safest
desire until all I see are women,
until all I see are unmade women
disguised as men.

IV

We made a world of the strongest spells,
the belt-hook neurons trickling down
my shoulders like my last dead bat
or paper butterfly crushed beneath
the stuff that became mother.
To name my father means a gun
does exist somewhere.
The world now contains
just the primary colors, the safest ones
of all. I had few real options,
my parents like imaginary
gods above the displaced living room
furniture. I spoke endlessly
to myself to keep in touch
with someone actual and to reach
the true Deity. I kept many gods
close to me like the scientists
who make fruit flies from
a repetition of genres: one
was a furry ball of eyes, a multitude
of skins searching for mother.

Anthony Butts

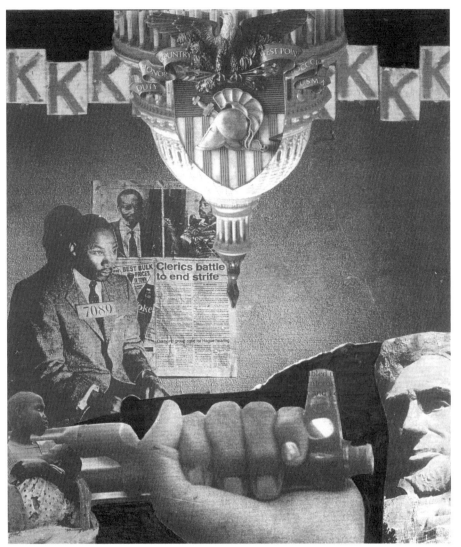

Theodore A. Harris—**The Bible and the Gun** collage

Irony of Negro Policeman

His inked arm-
proud, pea-
cocked, preening

like a teenager-
PLCMN
Placed above

PAW (LEFT),
a pawn.
Drawn

& quartered-
arm half-mast
a flag

-not a fist-
2-WAY
WRIST

RADIO-
cuffed,
resists-

Kevin Young

There Is an Emptiness Approaching

swallowing minds like light
eaten by hollow caves
surrounding the young like greedy snakes
poking at sleeping minds
a silent killer
moving like monoxide

a fading history wiping out
generations of fighters
weakening our memory of the dead
replacing them with images
of tilted brim Mac Daddy's

sparkling hot ice burns
broken minds crippled by emptiness
underpaid teachers push unused thoughts
onto cocaine streets

the drum beats
the bling bling
the falling change
the broken glass
and stinking toilets
scenting the hallways
of overcrowded schools
head masters and metal detectors
blinded by hatred
for hungry children barefoot babies
watch them die

yesterday will be just another day gone by
forgotten by rotten leadership with
pimping fingers, alcoholic memory
and the will to sell anything
in hopes of getting elected
to empty seats
empty promises
empty feelings

Sharrif Simmons

Navin June Norling—**Alive** collage

better **roses**
(Georgia, August 1999)

Driving back from Albany, I tell my father that I'd like a piece
of cotton to take back with me. We stop along the road. My
father has told me how he used to pick cotton every day after
school during the harvest. Five-and-a half cents per pound. The
most he ever picked in one day was 217 pounds. Forty years
later, he still remembers this number. Still remembers the
excitement of having seven hard-earned dollars in his hand.

I open my car door. I'll get it, Daddy says. Whatchu want? Just
a cotton ball? He looks across the field for signs of a shotgun-
toting, overzealous farmer guarding his crop. No one in sight.
He wades through high grass in dress slacks and good shoes.
I pray the ground is dry.

He pulls off three balls. From where I am, it looks like he
is picking small, white roses for me. He returns to the car and
places them in my hands. I examine these strange flowers,
turning them by the stem. The papery leaves crumble as I
touch them. The hard hull, pointed enough to draw blood,
dark as my own skin.

Holly Bass

John Abner—**What Now? Losing Communication** collage

P.S.

War has been declared in the awakening of arms
and touches—boundary of territories
the language we speak from your mouth to my eyes
will be decided in the casualty of mirrors and unrequited hurt
This soldier's strategy is to come to you with an unrecorded history-
      (I died there)
The cartography of my body is a natural secret, so when I say I love you
      I love you
            I love you
it is my weapon against you—to bear arms
press you up against the wall with
      something unfamiliar to most
My disaster...the blues
      a disastrous agent disguising itself in me and that of voices
...politically we are on two separate fronts,
      my face hidden behind the shrub,
      wondering if that is you aiming yourself directly toward me,
      (I love you this way)
      in the changing flags we plant between us
      ...in the wonderment I see in colors you become
      ...in the hate I inherited for the land of my body
      ...in the fraying dirge folded across my mouth
      (oh yes I love you)
            (I love you)
                 (I love you)
      as long as nothing has changed
      & one of us acquiesces in the end
      as long as there is an end in clear view surrendering

Carl Hancock Rux

excerpt from ATONIA

Katoska looked at her black uniform. She was still getting used to the curly mass of hair slowly rising out of her scalp's follicles. The X section housed women like her.

Her fair skin was no longer an attractive, on-the-fence mechanism she used to advance herself in the city, in the office, in the hair salon, at the gym. Her light skin was oddly ignored here. No one asked her if she was mixed, those questions were forbidden in the institute.

Katoska was confined for processing her hair and abruptly tossing it whenever she was in public. The abhorred hair toss. It was probably this trait that gave her away in the New Society.

When Katoska was captured she was forced to have the processed hair shaved off. Extensions and false hair were not allowed in the Institute. Many women walked through the institute's halls with heads of fuzzy new growth.

Every once in a while Katoska would toss her head, only to remember that her head of springy curls did not toss, move or bounce. It behaved according to her genetic makeup. "Whatcha doing, K?" asked the short woman, also in a black uniform, with shoulder length dreadlocks.

Katoska looked up from her desk, where she wrote daily in a journal.

"Regina. Regina Hornwell. We met yesterday at the group counseling session."

"That's right, sorry. I've just been trying to stay focused. The Change isn't easy for me and I guess I'm still pissed. I haven't even—"

"I understand the difficulty," said Regina, who invited herself into Katoska's room.

"At least they let me keep my hair."

"Yeah, I was wondering about that," said Katoska. "Why? They cut mine off the day I was confined."

"I'm in for Revolutionary Fraud, you know. I name dropped. A lot of Marcus Garvey, Huey Newton, Elaine Brown, Gil Noble. I would memorize a couple of books, lines from speeches. Super-soul sister number one," Regina chuckled.

"So because you were 'for the cause,' or at least you half-way were, they let you keep your hair? Shit, I should have taken African-American literature at Syracuse. Maybe I'd still have my hair, too," said Katoska, smirking.

"Oh, no. That's not why they let me keep it," Regina looked at the red, black and green tiling on the floor. "It's punishment. See, I wore loose-fitting dashiki dresses because I was too lazy to exercise. Of course, I ridiculed the women who wore shapely outfits. 'You're squeezing your wombs!!!' That's what I would tell them."

Regina laughed at herself.

"You know that holier-than-thou act. Anyways, I locked my hair because it was nappy as all hell and the perm had eaten away the sides of my hair. I was tired of doing it and so I locked it. It stank, had lint in it. I would try to cover it up wit those oils, but well, the Institute knows that I wasn't really into to keeping it up. Their punishment is that I keep it up. Gotta wash it every two weeks and twist all 343 locks myself. Ain't so bad."

Katoska couldn't understand why anyone would want to go for locks. Why not put on a wig? She forgot for a moment that she no longer had a silky waterfall of hair and tossed her head. Regina stepped back with widened eyes of caution. Katoska twisted her lips, embarrassed.

"Sorry. Bad habit," Katoska said.

"Well, you were born with that good ha—"

"Shhh! It's forbidden! You know you can't say those types of things here. They'll have you in Follicle Chamber so fast," Katoska's lips closed in a worried pucker.

The mention of "good hair" was non-existent in the institute. Those whose violated this rule were sent to the Follicle Chamber and confined to the madness within.

The bed's cover was made from a horse's mane. The false hair on the twin-sized comforter was a musty concoction of braided, twisted, locked, curly and strait hairs. At a quick glance one would think that it was a mating party for a hundred black, shiny worms.

The walls were made out of wooly, kinky hair, the handle on the toilet was made out of permed African-American hair and the carpet was made out of the same processed hair. Hair that was cut from the residents of the Institution.

The words on the wall read: UGLY. BEAUTIFUL. NAPPY. PRETTY. AFRICAN. MIXED. INDIAN. SILKY. BREAKING. BALD. THICK. STRAIGHT. There was no space on the wall without some type of adjective to rattle the violator's mind.

Ultra Sheen, Gentle Treatment and Hawaiian Silky advertisements were everywhere. On the ceiling, as if to play some sick Michelangelo joke-was a large mural of nude, Causcasian women with flowing blonde, red and brown hair.

The voices of black women who were ecstatic over their straightened or false hair played continuously, hardly leaving a quiet moment for rest.

Look, my hair's so much easier to comb out...Ouch mommy, that hurts...It's shiny and bouncy and Ryan loves running his fingers though it...I didn't know the real length of my hair until I got KOKA...It's so much more manageable...

By the time the violator would leave the Follicle, she (or he) would be in a state of shock. Hair strands that she once loved, hated, wished she had or wished she was never born with would cling to her feet as she left the room in a daze.

They must be fully rehabilitated before the New Society accepted them.

Ayesha J. Gallion

Kenneth L. Addison—**Goodnight California** mixed media batik

L.A. suite

for Wanda Coleman

Truant birds descend on the hotel's swimming pool
a hollowed–out sanctuary yellow and smoky with
saucer-shaped illumination

Silverware and rolled napkins arranged in
sunny kindness around shaded deck
some alien pagoda left behind
abandoned ship drydocked here in final resting

Behind sealed slated glass
I sip imported glacial water
black icy edges that gut me
shank organs free in bloody drift

A metallic sun flat as a butterknife
sections off the city into neat compartments of
leavened and unleavened life

Palm trees like shredded biscuits
Clumps of random bushes / film on cutting room floor
Wide-streaming freeways
Bright bold cars / painted war canoes
Two bands of glowing traffic
illuminated suspenders connecting earth and heaven

Haze starches funeral folds into coarse permanence
gray gauze mummified around some congealed ill
Swear it a smoky curtain draping a stage in flame

So this is what the city offers in short hours
Pitched here from Paris
a proud always where tourists graze under Mona Lisa's oily pose
to a backward no place glowing in the comfort of hot gain
the lustful symptoms of a never-been a never-done

Dear Wanda
I understand why fury is reactive and quick
soiled hand shocked by chilly basin
Sheathe words in the dry costly skin of your children
You have the right to shout
The death of a child—no tougher row to hoe

What is sown is not alive til it dies
I pry through fresh graves
where bullets stud black dress
I see honed carpenter sharpening strike
mittened hand stirring prehistory into blood
I see sorrow stamped in precise hours and voracious minutes
and worms intoning praise in contaminating mud
I see whys and wherefores and how-tos and thensomes
and mute interrogation and corroborated act
I see scaly devils that threaten to motherfuck this page

It's all lost to me now
as the plane rises above the clouds

Jeffery Renard Allen

Stevenson Estimé—**Cash, Media, and Math** mixed media collage

new RECIPE

Words were her blanket
color wrapped around her tongue
like new languages
she spoke in D minor
laughed orange chiffon
moved a collage of ballet and African
floated and rocked when she danced
sang when she slept
conjure woman with a cross
Elekes under choir robe
saying Hail Marys with an electric guitar
wild diva banshee
with the *Wall Street Journal*
and a three-piece suit

Come on y'all
you can't figure her
she's 13 divided by three
one and one when it don't equal two
Put away the calculator
look at her
like Alice Coltrane's wailing harp
or a blooming flower in snow
or sky under your feet

Stretch reach imagine dream
shed your skin
fly into the ocean
where stars swim
clouds shine like sun
and there are no ladders
because everything is in reach
even God

Mariahadessa Ekere Tallie

That Midnight Train to **Georgia**

It was Georgia where I met an artichoke
For the first time
In a restaurant born a train
I liked the music
I liked the Black
Slower country ways
I learned to scrape
Waxy meat along my teeth

Some cousin was graduating from somewhere
We who had fled were returning
To see if we'd left anything behind
a cat's cradle in the corner
All she really wanted was to marry

Another cousin would soon kill himself
Inside the car he could never afford
He had been whipped one too many times
By one too many of his mother's boyfriends
It was all behind him now
His charming dimples gray and stiff
His freckles cold

There are trains moving east to west
Dropping dreams on the rails
Like pennies to be smashed
There are people who don't know where they are
Slipping through dim cars
To piss there between the shimmy
From small windows rounded at the corners
In stainless steel

All they see is a disappointing reflection
Of themselves in the darkness outside
No beauty or true love
New dreams must be woven
As we come from these coasts
A people with an intricate past

Balancing on tracks we are thrilled children
Guessing when the next train will come

Melanie Hope

On Hearing of the Death of Gwendolyn Brooks

I first heard the news via e-mail.
Winter clouds had devoured the sun that day,
hanging low and heavy, threatening
to crash through windows, nailing me
to walls.

Reports from Chicago said she was dead.

And for a few moments
or maybe longer, I became disoriented.

For 83 years her presence was like a lighthouse
I only knew her from a distance: poetry
readings, TV.

Nine in the a.m. the work
piled upon my desk like a mountain
too strenuous to ascend, too solemn
to speak to.

With a click of a button my computer sighed its death.
I raised my office window, allowing waves
of December winds to drown this sense of loss
and teach me how to breathe.

James E. Cherry

1977

When Elvis said hound dog, he meant us. We made our own song from it, "I Make Black People Shine My Shoes." Even here in Birmingham, Elvis is on the hot plate, frowned on like a boy who crochets. My cousin, good with the needles, worshipped Elvis—then heard he lifted his blues from somebody bluer. The Parasite King, Elvis sweats on TV and I watch, sitting in front of our grandfather's gold velveteen La-Z-Boy. It's daytime, he's at the gas station, but I know my place. Light hangs in the almost white curtains, windows look in on veneer, Pledge. I am staring so hard at the screen that the day goes black, narrowing, leaving nothing of Elvis but one sequin, his crotch a light, serene as a song. This is magic I've never felt before and haven't again, my Graceland, this place where light dreamed itself awake, while blackness around always shone, shone, like a polished shoe, buck and wing.

Eisa Davis

It resisted extinction
on winter's tongue of earth
because, so long house-bound,
it burned to move. I felt for it
the way Michelangelo felt
for the figure trapped in stone.
On the six o'clock, I am the one gesturing,
heroic to be caught
on camera dancing behind the reporter,
now proud to see myself
transformed into light, my celebrity
like flint agitating emery
tongues of the envious.
Paparazzi of broken glass
on asphalt mirrored wet and jugular
with hose. Homeless, drunks
and the otherwise extraneous
witness the pomp of flame
persistent as graffiti.
Huddled like hostages
behind a yellow tape,
my audience shivering tiny plumes
into thin air as the critics pimp
wet canvas up the engine ladder
into that burning house.
O to make a wick of myself,
the hot stone in my gut threatening
to ignite up the length of my spine,
rattling my glottis like the lid
on a boiling pot.
Tap water sounds like a fuse.
Strikes the basin and sparks.
Steam rises from what's burnt away
on the occasion of a kindling,
making a child of destruction
dutifully wash hands
of the sooty ruined thing.
Now they're showing
when the structure began to kneel:
reverent, infantile, innocent, reborn,
revealing timbers like one coming
out of his skin and embers litter the sky
raining hell suspended in the dingy exhaust
of one failed step toward the animate.
Housebound now I
think of joining the swarming,
sifting through all of them,
those glinting wind chimes wincing
at the sigh of my arrival, to reside
aloft like woodsmoke in the night.

Gregory Pardlo

ARSONIST

Making **Foots**

Many a foot
was chopped
off an African highgrass runner
and made into a cotton picking
plowing peg
was burned away into
two festering runaway sores
was beaten around
into a southern gentleman's original
club foot design

They went for our feet first
for what we needed most
to get 'way

My papa's feet
are bad
bad
once under roof
his shoes are always
the first to go
a special size is needed
to fit around
ankle bones broken at birth

Sore feet
standing on freedom lines
weary feet
stomping up a southern dust bowl march
simple feets
wanting just the chance
just one
to Black Gulliver jump

role call

a Kress lunch counter
or two
and do a Zulu Watusi Zootsuited
step
instead of a fallen archless
wait wait wait
for the time to come

Him wanted to put his feet up
and sip himself some

Papa, how you say you'll take that coffee?
Oh Baby, just make it black and bitter like me.

My papa's feet are bad
they beat our feet around with billy clubs
and by our raggedy feet
had hoped to drag us all away

Country corners
and city curbs is where
they hold my
keepsakes
some of my brothers
who brush their I-talian skins off
on the backs
of steam pressed
pantslegs

Shoes first
they'll tell you
shoes above all else
they'll show you

Nikky Finney

I Was There Once

for my great grandfather

It was something to do,
something to crowd the vacant
Alabama afternoon. My friend Angie
drove the ten minutes until we crossed
the state line: Mississippi.

My great grandfather killed a man
I love him for it.

Had I known
I would have gotten
out of that car
caressed that soil
taken it home

I would have asked Mississippi what she saw.
How many lynchings?
How many rapes?
Did vengeance surprise her?
Did she whisperscream run,
when my great grandfather decided
Enough.

Mississippi saw
my great grandmother
go home beaten and torn
saw my great grandfather's eyes cloud
saw the water fall
Enough

He rose from his reserved seat,
the chair of terrorized skin.

sit quiet boy
i can spit in your wife
split her open and
send her home

Enough

Mississippi saw
tired clench-a-fist blood,
a fallen body, our line
leaving the state to escape .

I will go back.

Mississippi will tell me
she saw some kind of justice–
at least once.

Mariahadessa Ekere Tallie

To the **Winners**

marchers whose garments tore in the gnarl
of German Shepherds, who billowed in the white witching
of hoses, whose skin rose against batons and billy clubs.

For the lordly ladies, gingerly gentlemen who pressed
knees and elbows to pews, whose ironed garb bore the soot
and sweat of holy struggle, turning poison to passion,
malignity to medicine. For these alchemists,

miracle-deliverers, turners of hatred to hope, vice to victory—your feet
unwearying, your lips untiring, prayerful, determined. We cheer you
for your song echoing in churches, in jails, in homes, at the feet of
gallant statues. For Emmet Till, whose eyes swelled beyond seeing,
whose skin bloated beyond feeling. For Medgar, Malcolm, Martin,
gasping on blood so that we can draw

less shallow breaths. For the quartet of little girls missing
pecan pies in Birmingham, their dreams exploded like milk
in black coffee. For the saints who prayed us up, moving
stone mountains with voices rising like applause, roaring mighty
freedom. You who battered wrought-iron gates and shifted the world
onto fairer foundation, so that others—gay with merriment
and love, feminine beyond constructions, Chicano;

Borrinqueño, Asian—could rise in righteous boil, and be
heard and be heard. For you who stood and chanted, cooked
and planted, we honor you, feet and fingers in your prints,
hands clasping in just repose, so that a man will not
bounce behind a truck, his head attached to a rope like
a spiked pineapple on string, his entrails scattering
kike torn, berry-stained rags, so that a woman will not bear

the belly of some unwanted barrel of a man, so that
an immigrant will not come home late from work to a hot,
whistling wall, his skin burned holy like a sieve, the plasma
straining out of him. We honor you with work and struggle,
with song and study, you, known and anonymous, who crossed
bridges, who rode buses with reserves of grace, we spread
our gratitude like fans at church cooling with thanks
for giving us back our name.

Rohan B. Preston

Try to Remember
that *South African Man*
from "Slits"

Sometimes I try to remember the name of that South African man, who insisted on being called "Coloured," even though in this country he would have qualified as "black." He was more attached to that identification than any other, such as "older," "dapper," "tourist," "uncut," "speaks Afrikaans," "wears glasses." His hair ran under my fingers like the body of a lambswool sweater; he could tongue longer than any guy I've come across thus far. What did we talk about as we lay on the comforter in his hotel room? Getting around Boston on foot. How we'd both considered studying architecture. Apartheid over there, racism here, especially how Black Americans had achieved so much in comparison, how we seemed to take everything for granted. Back and forth. Imagine if just bitching about inadequate schools and lack of housing could land you at the bottom of a ditch, he asked me. But it happens here too, I protested. He smiled: I know, respect your elders, even if they're lovers. Be quiet, now, and then his palm covered my mouth and nose, leaving a small slit for me to breathe. This is how he held me before they began to beat me, he said, and then showered me again with kisses.

John Keene

Thoughts On Those Flags

I hear they want to remove that flag from the
capitol building. They say it drags them kicking and screaming
down memory lane, scarring on the jagged rocks and broken
glass of Jim Crow, Separate but Equal, and Dred Scott.
They say it hangs over their heads images of trees
bearing fruits strangely un-ripened, bruised and elongated; that it burns
into their memories pictures of german shepherds, fire hoses, and billy
clubs; and laws establishing subservient second class citizenship.

They feel that removing that flag will make it all
better, the wounds will heal and all will be right
in this so-called melted-pot, integrated, multicultural society. No one
notices or cares, it seems, that that flag does not
wave in New York, Chicago, Los Angeles. Diallo did not live and
die under its yoke, and it did not wave over
that trial's courthouse. No, they gather down there, around that
building calling for the sheriff to release that flag into
their custody—mobs drunk with hatred and vengeance, frantic to

drag its beaten, mutilated body through downtown streets. And no
one, no one notices Old Glory waving just a
few feet above. No one notices the malevolent twinkle in
those Stars, the sadistic smile hidden within the folds of
those Stripes—the smile of the older sibling who prodded
the younger into wrong doings only to step back, pointing
an accusing finger when the deeds attracted the attentions of
Morality and Decency. And as they gear themselves to punish
the younger, the elder quietly gets away with murder.

Akintiunde

217

The **Butt** of The **Joke**

for Caryn Whoopi Goldberg Johnson

You were that little girl stage
made from different pieces of us all
a one woman show
mobile awning of melanin and goosedown lips
with a long wavy towel propped for false dreamy hair
wanting life to be just as blonde and endless
asking God and anybody else listening in on the Act
for blue eyes please
and all the perfect moments that naturally come along

And everybody dark laughed
it was a real scene
from many played out little Black girl real lives
and everybody light laughed
cause a funny Black woman on a well lit stage fastly
becoming a rising star by remembering her real life
nightmares by making fun of her
Wish-I-Mays-and-Wish-I-Mights
Wish-I-turn-out-white-tonight out loud
is so funny especially
if you already are

Now here you are again stage right
a grown up rich and funny woman
who has come such a long way baby
the first Black woman
invited to be roasted by the Brothers of the Friary

You are not the first Black woman
to arrive at her bonfire
feet down instead of feet first
not the first who was not tied up and dragged in
screaming and kicking for help
to the Occasion of her Roasting
you are not the first who trusted
that these times and flames were new ones and better
believing everything they said
you thought these would differ from those
that engulfed the corps of Black woman before
You are not the first Black woman
who walked on her own
into the Occasion of her Roasting

believing a new kind of fire would be set this time
and took your seat up front in the reserved chair
wearing the ear chimes of the rich and famous
that could not no matter how hard they tried
shimmer up the illusion of blue eyed golden tressels

You were a Black woman
invited to the Occasion of her Roasting
who came not wrist bound in a croker sack
and gagged with shit but willingly
expecting cool laughter to wash you into
an even lighter hue and cry for the icing evening
lighter than you already felt yourself to be there
on his arm

And yet the evening was true
it proved to be exactly more than it promised
the same flames that your great mothers knew well
that licked and finally bit their skin away
at their own private roastings
licked and nipped you all night at yours
an alabaster firestorm peeling back the skin
and leaving your white bones bare

You are not the first Black woman
who ever arrived by caterer
walked in stylishly late
to the Occasion of her Roasting
nor will you be the last
but you were the saddest in recent memory

Enthroned there in the honor seat
while your fellow funny lover stood just above
melting all over everything in Black face
spitting out all the old white classics
asking you and your plush African mouth not to
nigger lip it as he kept rolling it out all over everything
spinning watermelon jokes at your feet
while the flames caught your hemline
and you jumped and danced whooped it up
trying to miss what was coming at you
and keep your balance at the same time
as he dearly delighted the crowd with everything
from a coons age   ago
including the description
of your inflamed private Black woman's parts
comparing the overused width of your womanhood

to the sacred birthplace shores of the first continent
and the Franciscan Monks of the Friary lifted
their glasses clinking in toast to the roast of you
and the vintage kerosene flowed red gold

And your white actor peers laughed
and your black model friends laughed
afraid they would be accused
of not being able to take a joke

worried they would appear to be overly sensitive
terrified they might be recognized as Black first
then whatever else   if they didn't
no more the colorless universal-grey characters
they had worked so hard to be

They say some people with memories got up and left
but most stayed   swallowing their nausea
only to ask us perpetually vomiting ones later
Can't we take a joke,
and further taking up the cause
of Blackface humor at home
by sporting more shoe polished faces at
private Hollywood parties by invitation only
in support of the freedom to laugh
and in the rich tradition
of roasting Black women in America
Here   Here

Can I take a joke   you ask
you say comedy doesn't go by the same rules
as real life
can I lighten up some you wonder take a joke

I can take a joke   I can even take an insult
if I bite the insides of my cheeks long enough
before I smell gasoline being poured about my feet
my blood always comes to a boil   to let me know
for sure
but in order to laugh at things that aren't funny
I would have to swallow both blood and words
and this neck that historically has been
broken re-set broken broken re-set can't
I would have to swallow my tongue and
I can't swallow my tongue
Just like I can't lighten this up
fire always leaves things naturally blacker

than they were

I won't lose my mind in a false laughter
because a not-so-funny white man
is waiting for his applause
as he shovels it in your soft Black face
and you swallow in a two step shuffle along
while he tapdances with spikes
on an old Black woman wound
and the mothers who brought you here
hold their faces down in their hands whispering
shame on you

I can take a joke but what I won't take is injury
disguised as laughter then coated with
marshmallows stuck casually over a flame

I can take a joke but he slung all the old white embers
and you opened up just like he said you had
and stoved it even smacked your lips
even said it was good
while Black woman ears in every creek
valley and river bed
had to be doused by real lovers
who couldn't find the funny either

Instead of getting up in your mother-mother's name
and walking out with the rest of us you sat
smiling with his dripping shoe polished face
not believing what you had come this Friar's Club far
and in his defense
you tell us you even helped him with it
You have taken on the image of the living ghost
I see you and your face is hooded
well roasted and lightly floured
this is the powdery cameo broach of power
what it takes to make it to their top
the highest paid in Hollywood
is a little Black girl   back on stage
with colored contacts and to-die-for eyes
modeling a long towel now for escaping Rapunsel hair
and even though I have turned my back to you
still I reach up for the soft terry end of it
to help wipe the egg and other white things
oscaring off your face

Nikky Finney

Shirley Carter–**Children of the Sun** oil on canvas money bags

Glory

At Old Sturbridge,

a rooster's bark helped lift darkness
back up, beyond angels & smoke, to where
all things, regardless of size & color,
weigh the same. A slipcover of dew
camouflaged blades no longer green enough
to hurt, and three hundred uniformed extras

played possum, fallen blue & grey stars
against a sky of grass, war's constellation
of bodies & limbs. The director yelled
"Quiet!" & "Action!" And the black men
we'd cast as gravediggers walked toward us.
No more than actors told what to do,
a dark cloud unable to ignore God.

It didn't take much to make Boston's South End
look like Beacon Hill—top hats, overcoats,
dewinged confetti, American flags draped
like smiles over the frowns of brownstones.
The regiment marched through, principals standing in.
My friend Noland was next to Morgan Freeman,
but the cinematographer knew how to frame a shot,

how to exclude a man with a camera.
Francine Jamison-Tanchuck was there,
stitching cloth to celluloid. A natural-born seer,
her hands hid matrimony & promise in hoop dresses
 & bonnets
so that each soldier witnessed a flash of cross
& ring, a small church, heaven on earth,
things thought worth fighting for.

Thomas Sayers Ellis

Pasadena City Hall, April 29, 1992
in which students
attempt to burn a flag

elsewhere
liquor stores swallowed bricks &
poured smog from their glass eyes

we fed no one

milling before city hall
smoldering
under the weight of sun

our newborn fists
a jumble of turrets
hemmed in by distant sirens

cockblocked from picket fences
we stood in our own piss
waiting for a sign

I don't recall what the megaphones told us
only what Rodney, face & shoulders folded
like wet cardboard, pleaded

I don't recall smoke in the city of roses
only that the bic was slow to spark
old glory slow to burn

Douglas Kearney

Kenneth L. Addison—**33 Fisher Ave.** mixed media batik

Have You **Seen** Them?

Little kids who don't take
No kinda stuff offa nobody
Cuss out police cars
Bop at six
Rap at seven
Have you seen that mean
Four-foot high one-arm lean
If you don't watch out
They'll look you dead in the face
Cuss you out too

(Mess with them?
Me?
Not me
Me and my Afro
African prints
Swahili

Pierced nose
Nigerian summers
Five earrings in each ear
Twenty silver West Indian bracelets and
Thirty shelves of Black Studies paperbacks
UHURU!
Not me!
Me
Mature and Realistic
Thinking of my Future
And my car note
Maintaining my lifestyle
I know how to act
I'm a Young Bright Black Professional
In other words
A nice cdolored girl
Is this what they mean
By planned obsolescence?

But when you have seen them in the museum
With their faces pressed to the glass
Did you hear them ask you to lift them up
Cause they couldn't see
Have you seen them
Look at you with their mouths hanging open
Trying to see if you do what you say you do
Have you seen them frown and not know what to say
When you tell them they can have
Hotdogs or hamburgers or both if they want
Cause the Culture-In-The-Schools-Abstract-Dance-Company
Is at least Something Happening
Have you seen the way they look at you
When you tell them they have a birthday too

Little kids who don't take
No kinda stuff off nobody
Cuss out police cars
Bop at six
Rap at Seven
If you don't watch out
Look you dead in the face
Cuss you out too
Little kids who don't take
No kinda stuff
Offa nobody

Kate Rushin

Boys Think

Boys think girls can't play basketball,
but when we go against them we beat them all.

The score is twenty to zip, they need to lock they lips,
cause when we play this sport it's like our court.

And we're bustin them moves, makin them shots,
looking real cool, make these boys jealous in school.

While the girls are shoutin, the boys are poutin,
all Mr. Us is doing is countin our scores-

Up on the board if you ask me it's like connectin cable cords.
And while the world keeps spinnin we just keep winnin,
look at the clock, the game is close to endin.

You better listen to me boys, you better forfeit the game,
cause if you keep playin with us, we gon mess up your name.

Chorus

You boys think, that girls can't be strong,
but when we play basketball you find out
yo game don't last too long

You boys think, that we can't do a thing,
but when we compare our game to yours
we agree on a chicken wing.

Jaqueline P. Banyon (aka "Tadow")

R. Gregory Christie—**George Washington** acrylic on illustration board

those innocent eyes once weren't

dedicated to de la beckwith and them others

innocent eyes &
doleful glares
              and no one was there
              and no one was ever there

painful dishonesty
              a picture framed to insist

 and no one seems to have ever seen nothing
              and nobody seen a thing
                   and it's much much too late
                        it's much too late to interrogate the old nazi's

too much time has passed
and all the fascists have fled
all the SS have woodworked   into the argentine villages

of 16th street

and when shall we have our nuremberg?
    and when will we get our nuremberg?
          and when shall we get our nuremberg
and when will we have a nuremberg?

some have found that the innocent eyes of doleful old nazis   are hard to

execute

r.c. glenn

ROLE CALL TAKES ON ISSUES OF R A C E, SEXUALITY, EDUCATION, NATIONAL- ISM, SPIRI- TUALITY, AIDS, GLOB- ALIZATION, HIP HOP AND THE PRISON INDUSTRIAL COMPLEX.

VI

Derrick Adams—**Untitled (from *The Consumer* series)** manipulated
digital print

Narcissus Sits By the River to Take the **S.A.T.**

Our two brains leave their stations at the same time,
headed toward each other with matching speeds.
Sparks will fly when they collide.

Yes, fatalities occur:
We carry biological entities that change
the ecosystems of each and the point of meeting
forever.

Does this new life with no name that we create
belong to a recognizable genus/species?
If it's not easily categorized, do we kill it?
Mark it as an historical find?

At the river's edge rest No. 2 pencils.
Erasers. From the forest's farthest end
wafts a drumbeat—a resistance song.
From the moss patch at our feet the timer ticks.

Samiya A. Bashir

Gesture of a Woman-in-Process

from a photograph, 1902

In the foreground, two women,
their squinting faces
creased into texture—

a deep relief—the lines
like palms of hands
I could read if I could touch.

Around them, their dailiness:
clotheslines sagged with linens,
a patch of greens and yams,

buckets of peas for shelling.
One woman pauses for the picture.
The other won't be still.

Even now, her hands circling,
the white blur of her apron
still in motion.

Natasha Trethewey

Calida Garcia—**Retaining Dignity** oil on canvas

Excerpt from *The Book of Sarahs*

Part I:

The spring of 1989, when I graduated from Sarah Lawrence, signaled a break with my family, and a break in my memory—the final push in my attempts at finding a comfortable identity, which seemed dependent on forgetting parts of myself.

At graduation, the campus was bristling with tension. Six weeks earlier, Henri and I, part of the lead of Harambee, the group we'd started our first year in college, and two hundred other students, had occupied the college administration building. It was our parting shot in a four-year struggle to get the administration to admit more students of color, hire more than the one tenured Black faculty member, advance the curriculum, and also intervene in the rising racial harassment on campus. We'd had a heady last semester, and we were high on the image of ourselves as Black radicals and the power our actions had actually had. At the end of our take-over we had been assured among other things, six full-time tenure track hires over five years.

I felt strong and joyous among Henri and my friends as we marched in our kente cloth-draped gowns, our fists raised when we received our diplomas from the President's hands. But after the ceremony, as I walked across the lawn to find my family, my old fear of being seen with them returned. My family was going to bust up my Black Power revelry. I had managed to hide that I was transracially-adopted to most everyone at school except Henri. So when I met my parents, I felt a wall of my own shame and anger rise. They were open-armed and smiling on the other side. I hugged them each uncomfortably, and relied on that an gesture of quickly detaching and trying to lose myself in the crowd so that I could avoid having to introduce them to my teachers and friends.

That afternoon, after their car was packed with my things, and we were saying goodbye until the following week when I would come home, my mother handed me an envelope. In it was a letter that tore at my shame.

26 May 1989
Dear Cath-
It's pretty early on your graduation day. The dogs got me up to take them out. While everybody else is asleep, maybe I can say some of the things I probably won't say very well later today. So often we let the big ones go by.

You have done so very well! Against heavy odds you have found a path that lets you live in a divided world with divided allegiances and still become a productive, in fact creative contributor. You've emerged from an unusually complicated adolescence into personal, emotional and intellectual maturity with tremendous promise for your own future satisfaction, and valuable contributions to make to our troubled society. And you love and are loved by a wonderful, various group of people.

Dad and I are terribly proud of you. We love you more than we'll probably be able to tell you today (I'll cry) and we wish you ever more love and happiness and success.

Take good care of yourself—and phone home.
Love,
Mom

My mother was offering her best to me. Through the whole year she had been my champion, coaching an activism and sharing the victory of our campus struggles. She did not know how much I was hurting. In her eyes I was growing ever sophisticated and adept at moving between worlds, I had begun to feel I was moving about in an airless room that was foreshortened on all sides.

It felt like there was no place my different worlds met. In the previous eight years at schools where I was never part of more than a very tiny Black and Latino student body, I had never had any white friends. I had led an isolated life at school, superficially friendly all around, some would even say highly social, but keeping everyone at great emotional distance. I was hiding who I was, my family, my sexuality, to my friends, to the teachers I respected, even to Henri, my best friend and the only other bi-racial, adopted person I knew well. I was too afraid of being excommunicated to risk anything else, but the concealment and the lying, the sartorial adjustments, the emotions and emotional dishonesty, had actually pushed me further and further outside. Meanwhile, my parents and brother stood in a world that was completely white; they had never sustained even a casual relationship with a Black or brown somebody.

I had a graduate fellowship to Cornell, a coveted summer job, the triumphs of the sit-in. But no one seemed aware of how much I was fighting terrible depression, feeling the effects of a severely fragmented self.

At the end of the month, my parents would be moving out of our house in Attleboro, Massachuseetts, to retire to working their Christmas tree farm in Vermont. I was happy they were leaving Attleboro; happy to be able to finally wash my hands of the place, but I was also losing my childhood home, the anchor of my memories, however intent I was on forgetting my somehow-roots. It was fine for me to reject home and hold it at arms length as long as it was a place I still had one foot in. But with this move, I felt the spilt between me and my family, that had been threatening for so many years, finally set in.

Since leaving for college, going home to Attleboro, or to my grandmother's house in Connecticut, had become difficult for me to do. When there was a call to go home, I would find myself stalling, missing trains, traveling days later than I had arranged. On the journey home, I would be gripped with terrible loneliness. I felt like I had been pulled back into a cipher and was about to lose who I was and everything that had been so hard won, in just that little physical distance. We often had family gatherings at my grandmother's house, and the first whiff of those Fairfield county commuters and housewives returning from shopping trips to the city, uncomfortably sharing the train cars with Black and Latino laborers, would set off my rage. When the train arrived in Stamford, I would take a taxi to my grandmother's house, waiting to see what revision of a familiar conversation the usually Black driver would have with me as we turned onto her private, deep-wooded lane.

> *Do you work here?*
> *No, I'm going to see my family.*
> *I thought only white people live up here.*
> *(So do I answer, "You got it!" Or wait and watch him crane his neck to see who comes to the door?)*

> *Do you work here?*
> *Yes.*
> *How did you get this job?*
> *It's been in the family.*

> *Do you live here?*
> *My family lives here.*
> *Oh, Black people live out here?*
> *Yes.*

The shifting and negotiating didn't always change much inside of my grandmother's house. The spring before I graduated from college, we'd held an 80th birthday party for my grandmother, and I had been mistaken for the coatroom help—once I was tipped—by more than a few of my grandmother's friends. At the party my mother gave my grandmother an album she'd made of photos that friends and family had sent her as remembrances of my grandmother's life. My mother had included photos of my grandmother, smiling in blackface at a sorority fete, and no one had been willing to acknowledge that there was something wrong with that; that even if it was just "the times," maybe they didn't have a place in that album now. It was this history, erupting in these small ways, that under-girded my rage at my family.

My anger would tinge our visits, and my family would return it with distraction. They were never pulled from their usual intense pace of work—work invaded everything—so that holidays were spent tending trees or the birdfeeder, or the indoor plants, or making repairs on the house. My brother would arrive and rejoin their familiar intense threesome, going over details and plans. They seemed to never relax from workday rituals, and conversations seemed focused on the universe of their work. I would find a place to hide in my books, or talk with my grandmother. But our conversations would always quickly tip into fights as I struggled with my anger and they struggled to understand me. We usually fought at the level of dislike of my hairstyles, or of what I was wearing ("Do you think you're an African?"). I often felt like a not-friendly organism that joins another body; the host accommodating, not bothering too much the effects of the invasion, mostly leaving the thing to nurse undisturbed.

When it was time to leave, I felt the nearness of relief. My mother and I would ride in silence to their train station, or she would use that twenty minutes before our parting to focus some of her attention on me. We'd have awkward conversations. As the train arrived and I'd turn to go, my mother's eyes would fill with tears, and it seemed like I was waiting for that moment to allow myself to feel anything like love or a connection with her. I would quickly hug her, always feeling conscious of how we looked to the people on the platform, conscious of being seen with her by other Black people. Then I'd board the train and from my seat, watch her stand there crying, her body, usually strong and lithe, suddenly unbalanced. She would look frail and vulnerable in a way I never experienced her and I would feel a kind of smug satisfaction. I felt mean and powerful in a small, despotic way. When I arrived home I would call her and we would say warm things about the visit, then relax back into our usual weekly check-ins.

My parent's move to Vermont seemed like a very final, pronounced line had been drawn between us. It was different than the lines I had drawn in the past, acting against the surety that they would be right there no matter how hard I drew and redrew the battle grounds.

In Attleboro, those lines were drawn like this: In our house, I built a haven for myself, constructing my bedroom the way I thought it would have been if I had grown up in a Black family. My shelves were filling with Black books, replacing the artifacts of a former self—the dolls from my grandmother's travels, the complete Laura Ingalls Wilder boxed library, the collections of Scottish verse, the Petersen's guides to wildflowers and the seashore. I'd stowed them in the crawl space under the eaves of the house. I moved my mother's copies of *The Black Child: A Parent's Guide*, the SNCC freedom movement songbooks, Amiri Baraka's *The Dutchman and The Slave*, the row of James Baldwin paperbacks, and Stokely Charmichael and James Hamilton's *Black Power*, out from between the Rachel Carson and Thoreau and Henry Beston books, the trail guides, and my father's engineering books in the den. I covered my walls with cut outs from *Essence* and *Ebony*, and turned up the dial on the "Civil Rights station" (read: Black radio, aired only on late night and Sunday slots, picked up from the Boston airways) to let everyone know who was living there. And I put a ban on my room. My father, who was my ally, if only for his silence and quiet amusement at my lobbies against the family, was the only one allowed in, so that he could tend the African violets he grew in shelves he built into my bedroom windows. I liked the flowers; they were African, despite how suspicious they seemed to me, sitting in every old white lady in town's living room.

The three feet of landing at the top of the stairs marked a great divide between me and the rest of the family. My brother's room, across the landing, was done over patriotically, with white walls and red and blue trim. I had helped to pick the American flag curtains and bedspread from the Sear's catalog, and my mother ordered him a red, white and blue shag rug. And the rest of the house, with new outdooring catalogs and wildlife magazines piling the tables and shelves and tops of toilet tanks; a spectacular assortment of containers and thermoses and utensils; NASA tubing to ration and pack food for our excursions; liquor flasks; insect repellent; ski wax; fly fishing lures in the cabinets; gauges; seed packs; cork and cat gut and kayak patch in every kitchen drawer. Dried foodstuffs, iodine tablets, a snake bite kit on the shelf above the liquor stash. There were shells and bones and feathers, moose horns found in a glacier in the Grand Tetons mounted on the wall, snake moultings and rattlers, porcupine quills, and owl pellets on the fireplace mantle, on the corners of living room tables and edges of bookshelves, in the hutch with the china, something surprising you rotting in a covered dish. And always a hint of the life and expectations of their education and family upbringing that they had put aside: the *New Yorker* magazines, a piece of furniture or a painting, a fussy something, the Abercrombie & Fitch suede coats in a closet full of overalls and Sears & Roebuck farm wear.

Other lines were drawn this way: It seemed that parallel spaces existed inside of that house. My parents and brother had developed an interiority, a language and an emotionality expressed through nature that I wanted them to carry outside of that closed world. As we moved about in our lives in that house, different longings and a different material life were possessing me. I had an argument with the woods and bird feeder watching, collecting lichen, fly fishing, animal track sniffing, and the sweet tang of sycamore leaves.

When we sat together at meals, I would imagine that I was at a table with the characters from my books—maybe Ntozake Shange's Indigo was eating gumbo by my side and a mother everyone called M'Dear was asking me about school. Max and my parents would eat and watch the suet sacks hung outside the window, a pair of binoculars and a journal in which they recorded the birds that came to feed on the table between them. My anger at their quiet pact would disturb my imaginings, and I would sit there, imagining I was Zora Neale Hurston, anthropologist, and make my own catalogs: He smells this way because he is white; I feel this way because I am Black; she burns her chicken and doesn't use pepper because she is not my Black mother.

I remember sitting at dinner one time—it must have been early in high school—cataloging my grievances with them in just this way. My anger got the best of me and I went after my brother over whatever I felt was one of his recent sins of ignorance. I cannot remember what the matter was, but I remember him saying to me something that sandwiched "...because you're half-Black..." and I launched all of the artillery of my rage at him.

"I am BLACK!" I shouted. "In America, if you have one drop of Black blood, you are BLACK!"

"Well, you don't have to..." he stammered.

"Don't tell me what to do! I don't have to do nothing but stay Black and die!"

From that moment on I pronounced some real separateness from them, turning inside my really desperate need for them to make our worlds a little closer. I wanted to be Black, to be a part of a Black world, and also a part of my family's world, and they a part of mine. Instead I was feeling more and more like I was an appendage to their lives. I needed them to see us all as part of a multi-racial family, which demanded our being attuned to particular things. I wanted them to recognize what was being asked of me—the daily splitting off, the psychic shape-shifting—so that I could try to contain the disparate worlds I moved between.

So, when my parents began to pack up the house in Attleboro, I felt like their move to start a life as farmers was a signal of some final undoing between us. I went to visit them in Vermont a few weeks after they had moved. I spent the time with them feeling mounting waves of sadness, that had begun at graduation. I remember moving in circles around their new house, sifting through the boxes in which all of our life in Attleboro had been stashed. I found my father's old steamer trunk full of darkroom equipment and hundreds of old slide boxes and photos, and I settled down on the floor in the hallway, trying to distract myself from the racing panic I had been feeling in my chest for several weeks. As I worked my way through the trunk, I found an envelope with photos of me with a boy my age—were we six?—lying next to me buried in sand. The photos framed our faces, with green and red sweat-shirt hoods making bright, spongy lines between our deep, sun-browned faces and the sand trapping our heads.

I called my mother and handed her the pictures. She looked at the photos curiously, trying to remember who the boy was. "I don't know who that is. Oh, well, that must be Jimmy," she sighed. My cousin. My mother's sister's child, who had stood in the same brown relief against the family as I did for two or three years and then disappeared. His disappearance was signaled by a call one evening where I overheard my mother and her sister in Kentucky talking about Jimmy being "sent back." A few days later my mother explained to me and my brother that my aunt and her ex-husband had decided to relinquish their parental rights to him because of the strains of single-parenting and her ex-husband's alcohol abuse. They had divorced a few years earlier; she took her own two children (it was never said this way, but the meaning was not at all lost for me) and left Jimmy with him. Jimmy had "problems with his feelings" and was acting out, and the situation became too hard for them in the end.

I had put Jimmy out of my memory, feeling frightened by his leaving and what it revealed about the adults in my life: That there was a difference between your kids and your own kids. (It was not a difference that seemed perceptible. In our family the cross-section of children were treated with what always felt like a sameness, but now it seemed distinctions could be drawn.) But the absence of my parent's out-rage—they'd explained what had happened without judgment—betrayed their covenant of Responsibility, No Matter How Difficult It Is, and made me fear that I could also be dropped off. Jimmy was no different from me; not even so different from my brother, since we were all adopted. I could pitch a wild fight with the whole family. The only difference between Jimmy and me, and maybe even my brother, was that Jimmy came "late" and was leaving early. I was beginning to feel confused by this and by the waffling of adult's ideas: To be Afro-American and transracially adopted was a special thing. (Didn't my school principal regularly pull me into the teacher's lunchroom, which was already a great privilege, to show me photos of her adopted Afro-American granddaughter?) To be Afro-American and transracially adopted was a special problem.

The photos, and my mother's slow memory and lack of emotion angered me, and it became a flash point for all of the feelings that were overwhelming me. I started to go at her blindly, and I remember her turning away from me and saying, "I'm tired of all this race business," while she walked out of the room.

I was stung by what she said. They had signaled more her exhaustion from playing the difficult changes we were all undergoing, but I allowed them to punctuate my sense of being utterly lost to her and to my family. I sat in the room for some time, feeling my chest hollow out, while my old grief resurfaced—wanting her pro-tection and wanting to let go. I decided to take her words at face value. I thought: I cannot love you. I cannot love white people. They cannot love me. She could be tired and turn her back. I was going deeper in. For the rest of my visit we barely talked, and then I left to return to my life in New York before leaving for graduate school.

And this is where I decided in some way that what she'd given me was freedom to remake myself. And I decided in some way that my search for my birth family would be everything by way of a remedy.

Catherine McKinley

Quashelle Curtis—**Nemsi** mixed media on canvas

Excerpt from *The Book of Sarahs*
Part II:

New York City is a mecca of mulattas, of half-breeds of every kind. I used to sit in the Village and in Soho and watch them, tracing the stories of all of the other mulattas I had begun to encounter by the end of my twenties. I wondered if New York City was more productive that way, or if we had all made exoduses there hoping to disappear into a certain hegemony of brownness. But even in the mix, we didn't seem to lose a kind of hyper self-consciousness, a desire to be seen, moving in and out of people's flashes of perception about who we are. Perhaps I was projecting my own feelings—but there was something in these women's body language that seemed familiarly studied, anticipating people's gaze—the by-product, I am sure, of often being especially different and often The Only One.

I was beginning to take sensuous delight in mulattas that I'd never allowed myself when I was first meeting the women of the Yellow Diaspora I always thought of mulattas—unless they were the Halle Berry/Dorothy Dandridge/Jayne Kennedy polished pin-up girls who represented another side of Black people's self-deprecating ideals—as funny looking, even ugly. I felt a sense of self-loathing in the face of other women who reflected me that many don't expect from light-skinned Black people. There was no popular story of a post-Black Power mulatta's self-hatred. No yellow girl's *The Bluest Eye*. But I had learned self-hatred and the idealizing of black Black women very well. I knew well enough that for Black people, loving one's color—God forbid it being "too dark" or "too light"—was socially punishable. I had also learned that there was the light-skinned Black woman and there was the mulatta. One had social swing, and the other had to clear a (white) taint. There was currency in one, shame in the other—although shame has currency all its own.

*   *   *

As I met other mulattas in New York in my twenties, I began to let myself love our skin—the flatted browns, the ivories and yellows. I was beginning to enjoy the oddities of how we were configured: a WASPy boyish face and a Black woman's waist and behind; brick red nappy hair against near-white skin; sandy blond, naturally straight Caesars; lavender cat eyes; no bridge in the nose of an otherwise Semitic face. Whiteness showed in these women and I still felt some discomfort, but at heart I liked it. I liked our crazy hair and being able to laugh at the trouble of having some nappy patches and some bone straight ends amongst curls, all on one head. And the ultimate problem of not really knowing how to take care of it and style it, growing up as many of us did with our white mamas. And just when you thought the jokes might not be fair, a white woman with her brown child would stop you on the train and ask you nervously if she could look at how you had styled your hair and want to know who your barber was. I was trying to let myself love these women with the same passion I wanted to feel for myself, with the passion I'd felt for darker-skinned Black women that Penda and the *Essence* girls, and all of my library of Black characters, and the women at John Wesley, had instilled in me.

During my final year in college I had started to come out as a lesbian, waking up to another complication of my identity that had quietly troubled my struggle of outsidership. As I made my way, over the next eight years, into gay communities in New York, I realized that I was meeting more and more transracially adopted mulattas—I was even happily surprised to find my comrade, Tony, the other transracial adoptee from Attleboro, in a men's bar in the West Village one night. Suddenly it seemed I was a part of what we could actually call a critical mass of "trans-bi" girls—the name we began to use for ourselves, playing on the language of the gay and lesbian community, and on our contested racial and family identities.

In 1994 I met Vanessa, another "trans-bi" girl who was born in Illinois and had grown up in a white adoptive family in rural Ontario. Vanessa had reunited with her white birthmother while she was in college, and a few years later, the relationship had wound down to anger and silence. When I met her, she was beginning to search for her birthfather, depending on her own leads because of her birthmother's cruel games about his identity. At the same time Vanessa was slowly reapproaching her birthmother again. My best friend from college, Henri, had recently married and had moved back to New York with her husband. She was on the verge of finding her birthfamily. They became two spokes on the wheel driving my search. I shared their progress step-by-step. Vanessa was helping me to find a sense of humor about our predicament. We would make lawless jokes about our birthparents and the treacheries of our muddled identities and white families. One day Vanessa and Henri and I decided to incorporate our threesome, and we began calling ourselves Friends of the Mulatta Nation (FMN), extending the territory of our claim of a community.

The next day Vanessa brought us both packs of Little Debbie's brand Zebra cookies to celebrate, and presented them with a Certificate of Mulattahood, with Thomas Jefferson's famous pseudo-science of race, the Theory of Hypodescent, which explicates the ontology of the mulatta, the octoroon, the quadroon, copied on it's back. Then Vanessa started to take the FMN Chapter News to press, copying down all of our jokes and inventions: Mulatta Yom Kippur. The Mellow Yellow Awards to Outstanding Mulatta Personalities. "If You Ain't Nappy, Don't Front the Edges" and "Afrocious Hair Watch" were our headliners. There were media watches on Mariah Carey's incredible morphing identity, and personal ads that read: "Treach! Are you my Daddy? My mom's white, hip, and with the band. I have your eyes and a special way with the ladies. Can you help me? Am I really Naughty By Nature?-Transracial in Trenton, P.O. Box #1212, c/o FMN." The newsletter was always punctuated: "Any complaints? Write me at Massa's. Signed, In the Name of Jasmine Guy."

For Christmas, Vanessa really took on our joking: I got a honey-brown, colored t-shirt with MULATTA across the front, and A BIG HOUSE PRODUCTION™ on its back. There was one for every day of the week. It took some time for me to wear the shirt outside of the house, but when I did, I got some funny replies. There were people who asked if it was a movie. There were mulattas who were uncomfortable with it, Latinos who got the humor quicker than anybody, Black people who asked for one, Black people who were angered by it—my friends, even. They thought it expressed shitty politics, but I reminded them that in subtle ways they had been calling me all kinds of half-breeds and yellow girls and brownings all along.

I was finding the deep eroticism of yellow as Vanessa and I worked our way into a love affair. I loved her half-breed, parchment-colored body, and when I lay next to her, or when people admired us together, I felt the beauty of my own body settling into my consciousness for the first time. And I was feeling guilty about reveling in it. I could not imagine ever being able to act like I knew I was cute—Penda's warning had stayed with me—or to hang out with my girls and publically swoon: *Girl, she's a yellow hammer!* And have people understand that it was a remark of love totally mindful of the history and social warfare of colorism, but, that it's a yellow girls' Black revolution too.

As I would lay with Vanessa, I would drift into technicolor dreaming and all of my old home movies would suddenly play. The childhood memories I'd excised would roll out, at first in jumpy, fitful images that would find pace and eventually relax into calm. I'd be eating Thai food with her and the smell of mulch from our backyard in Attleboro, MA would fill my nose. Or I'd see the corner of a room in our old house there. The name of a bird would suddenly come into my head. Or I'd recall the bruise of cold air when you open the zipper on the tent in the morning. Or remember the beauty and scare of a loon's whooping cry across a glass-still lake before folding suddenly beneath its calm. I'd fall off to sleep remembering paddling on the Bungay River, pushing over accidental rocks that would scrape and bump up my bottom in the safe, steady place behind my mother's seat on the floor of the canoe. Vanessa reassured me with her ice hockey champion, hip hop and country music playing, Canadian-trying-to-cross-the-border-to-where-the-other-African Americans-are Black girl self.

I could express ideas to Vanessa from that storehouse of memory in one breath, without faltering, and I realized it was probably the first time I had ever done this. Vanessa was the first person I'd brought my whole self to. She was allowing me to be a Black woman full of contradictions, and to admit to what was pleasurable and what I loved about the people I had left behind.

Catherine McKinley

Renaldo Davidson—**Girl in Crib** oil pastel on paper

Detailing
the Nape

Our first summer at Grandmother's house
Daddy navigates country roads too slow
and we arrive only to hear of preparations for bed.

After shower
Grandmother inspects
the dark
condition of my sister's
neck
and declares it
filthy   youre not cleanin right
            we've got to get that dirt off you

I peek through
cracked
bathroom door
she and sister wait over the tub
until running water grows
hot enough

Sister kneels under the rush,
Grandmother scrubs in a Saturday
toilet bowl cleaning fashion.

Grandmother breaks
to wring and squeeze
the purification
towel free
of new mixture
water, soap, and this
bricky, muddy

colored dirt   chile all that noise ain't necessary
              if you could see this
              nastiness
              you'd be thankin me
Seeing my sister's distress
I open the door wide
M'dea', I think that's blood.
Grandmother quiets and
bandages my sister
well   I'm sorry
          baby I didn't know
          you was
          that black.

Nelson Demery, III

Paper **Armor**

SYNOPSIS

New Jersey 1930: Langston Hughes and Zora Neale Hurston begin to write a play they never finish, foiled by love, money and the vagaries of race. New York 2001: Chaney, a sexually ambivalent writer with a drinking problem and a newly dead mother, slams into her denial head-first when she is sent to interview a 97-year-old Communist who served as secretary to Hughes and Hurston. A perfect day for metatheatre.

CHARACTERS

in the present:
CHANEY BLASS, 20s. Volatile.
SHALE ROGERS, 20s. A producer at a reputable Off Broadway house.
MATCH TANSEY, 20s. An investment banker turned writer. Delicate ego.
LOUISE ALONE THOMPSON PATTERSON, 90s. Frail but energetic lifetime
        organizer and activist for civil rights. Light enough to pass for white or
        Latina.

in the 1930s:
We also see Louise in her 20s, a recent graduate of the University of California and a former teacher at Hampton Institute. An idealist with a degree in economics.

LANGSTON HUGHES, late 20s. Not yet Harlem's poet laureate, a discreet man with strong convictions who mystifies all entrants into his personal life.

ZORA NEALE HURSTON, almost forty but you'd never hear it from her. Her popularity is local, but she is still riding her fame from the Harlem Renaissance, now peaked.

"GODMOTHER," Charlotte van der Veer Quick Mason. Old money, in her 70s. She turns to patronizing black artists when her interest in Native Americans wanes. A deep and forceful spirit.

Four actors are double cast: Chaney/young Louise, Shale/Zora, Match/Langston, Older Louise/Godmother.

SETTING

New York City and Westfield, New Jersey. If possible, setting and costumes should allow for seamless transitions between the 1930s and the present.

This play is dedicated to the memory of Louise Thompson Patterson (1901-1999).

PROLOGUE

CHANEY: Some of the most significant disasters of our lives, the events which scar our virgin forests, start with the smallest misunderstandings,

LANGSTON: the pettiest of remarks that prove an entire theory of our earthly punishment,

ZORA: the most private and personal of slights,

OLDER LOUISE: and even the unspoken insults echo like mother and child. But these injuries, in order to be seen in their epic grandeur, require a story of uncommon weight.

ALL: And that weight,

CHANEY: even if accumulated from something beyond the dust of detail,

ALL: never balances

CHANEY: the shame of having to tell this story to yourself, day after day.

SCENE ONE
The present. Match's apartment. A funeral reception is just ending. Chaney, drunk, is saying goodbye to guests in the hall. Shale remains. Chaney closes door and begins cleaning. Shale attempts to help her.

CHANEY: *(taking plates from Shale)* Don't, don't.

SHALE: It's no trouble.

CHANEY: You sit down. It's my party!

SHALE: But you could use some help.

CHANEY: I just won't take any—

SHALE: You should be sitting down.

CHANEY: I need to keep moving.

SHALE: Chaney—

CHANEY: I need to keep moving!

Shale sits. Chaney continues to clean.

SHALE: I never knew how much your mother did. I heard so many war stories from folks tonight. Where's Match?

CHANEY: He's at the monastery in seclusion. Order of the Soho Grand.

SHALE: He's not coming back tonight?

CHANEY: Why would he do that? It's such a nice hotel.

SHALE: He picked the right time for a break up.

CHANEY: We're not breaking up. He's breaking me in. We're doing fine.

SHALE: Really?

CHANEY: Yeah.

SHALE: Okay. *(Pause.)* Wedding still on?

CHANEY: Why don't you advertise your homewrecking services. Be your own boss. *(pause)* He's on deadline. Has to finish a masterpiece for the New Yorker.

SHALE: He could have stayed tonight.

CHANEY: She died a week ago. He already paid for the flowers, the embalming, everything. Tell me that wasn't beyond the call of duty.

SHALE: But not to stay tonight—

CHANEY: He gets the Purple Heart. And I get some solitude.

SHALE: *(standing)* Do you want me to go?

CHANEY: *(suddenly)* No. *(pause)* Not yet. I'm only starting to embarrass myself. You gotta stay for the good stuff—

Shale hugs Chaney, and in the movement knocks a plate off the end table. Shale moves to pick it up. Chaney reaches for a bottle of wine and Shale gently blocks her.

SHALE: Listen. I hate to do this now, but we've got to have a talk about this play.

CHANEY: Shale, do you think, by any strait of the imagination—

SHALE: Stretch.

CHANEY: Of course. Stretch. That's the very point I wanted to make. Do you think you could stretch, imaginate—that is, do you think you could give me a god damn break? Just tonight?

SHALE: I was just going to say—

CHANEY: Because we both know you commissioned this play from me back during, when was it, the New Deal?

SHALE: A while ago.

CHANEY: And people at the theatre would have every reason to wonder where it might be—

SHALE: Right—

CHANEY: —and having not one page to show the money men must be a moderate to excruciating torture for you, daily—

SHALE: Right—

CHANEY: —and telling them that I'm your lush-luscious best friend whose—

SHALE: —mother just died—

CHANEY: —is an excuse worse than fish piss on homework.

SHALE: Chaney—

CHANEY: So who cares if people die. You don't. Who cares.

SHALE: I do care. And I'm sorry. But the writing might help you.

CHANEY: I told you I'm not taking any help right now.

SHALE: I want you to write a great play.

CHANEY: *(angry, pouring wine)* That's all you want, I know.

SHALE: That's not all I want.

CHANEY: Don't hustle me right now! Vampira. Vulture.

SHALE: Do you want me to go?

CHANEY: No! *(pause)* No.

SHALE: I can't talk to you when you're like this.

CHANEY: I haven't seen you in a while.

SHALE: That's because you've been avoiding me.

CHANEY: You aren't around! You've been eaten by this play.

SHALE: If our friendship is making this so hard, I can get someone else.

CHANEY: You can't give away my first major production. I can't live off Match any more.

SHALE: Didn't your mother—?

CHANEY: She left me everything she had—the complete works of Marx and Engels.

SHALE: I really liked her.

CHANE:Y We were only poor below the neck.

SHALE: *(mimics mother)* "Our work must be completed. We must be reconciled."

CHANEY: She'd propel me from bed with that every morning.

SHALE: Last thing she'd want to see is you sitting on your hands.

CHANEY: Shale. I'm warning you.

SHALE: It's true. "Nothing else can lift your spirits like creation. Output. Production."

CHANEY: She may have said that but I think she'd give me at least one night to say goodbye.

SHALE: *(her patience cracks)* You've prepared for this day for years, so don't.

CHANEY: What do you mean? What do you mean? Because she was sick?

SHALE: I'm not going to sit here, with you in your cups and your mourning togs, and let you lie. She never loved you, how many times did you tell me, never loved you at all or not enough. She didn't die this week, you killed her off—

CHANEY: Shut up!

SHALE: Alright, you cut her off the first time you realized she was capable of making a mistake. So if you have the energy to grieve, grieve for yourself because if you don't write this play, you've made the mistake. Of your life.

Silence.

CHANEY: No need for histrionics. I'll write your damn play.

SHALE: When.

CHANEY: Tomorrow.

SHALE: Rehearsals start in a week. The designers are flailing. Marketing people have nothing to market but you and no one knows who you are.

CHANEY: Do I detect encouragement? I think you broke the scale.

SHALE: I don't have to tell you how good you are.

CHANEY: It's set in the Harlem Renaissance. Can't the marketing people use that?

SHALE: Can't you?

CHANEY: *(pulls out some sleeping pills)* I'm going to sleep. If you get tired, you'll find my mother's coffin very comfortable-

SHALE: *(yanks the pills away from her)* This is your chance. And against all reason, I am giving it to you. Because you need to write it. Start on it tonight.

CHANEY: Who are you talking to? Who am I talking to?

SHALE: Yourself.

Shale stands to go.

CHANEY: *(desperate)* Don't leave.

SHALE: I've outlived my usefulness.

CHANEY: I'll start. Just stay.

SHALE: Why.

CHANEY: Please.

SHALE: Why.

CHANEY: Stay.

SHALE: You're gonna work.

CHANEY: Yes.

SHALE: Or are you really asking me to stay up all night like we used to?

CHANEY: You're my boss now. There are laws against sexual harassment.

SHALE: I haven't spent the night since you moved in here with Match.

CHANEY: Probably why I haven't been writing. You always send me careening for a
pen.

SHALE: I've set up a meeting for you tomorrow morning.

CHANEY: With your hair stylist? Colon therapist? Freelance motivationalist?

SHALE: With Louise Alone Thompson Patterson.

CHANEY: She's still alive?

SHALE: Sweet lamb of God. Alright. Do you know the topic of the play you are
writing?

CHANEY: *(parodies a reporter's accentuations)* Langston Hughes and Zora Neale
Hurston write a play named *Mule Bone* in 1930. They never finish *Mule
Bone* because they have a spectacular falling out, permanently severing
their relationship, the nature of which remains unclear.

SHALE: Thank you.

CHANEY: Possible elements of *Mule Bone* friction include: their common patron,
Charlotte Van der Veer Quick Mason, and their still-alive stenographer,
Louise Thompson—now what was her full name?

SHALE: Louise Alone Thompson Patterson.

CHANEY: *(over the top)* What really happened???

SHALE: Maybe Mrs Patterson will tell you.

CHANEY: I just don't know why you chose this. It's an open and shut case. Langston
was gay, Zora wasn't. Artists have beautiful rumbles all the time and live
to tell—Gauguin and Van Gogh, Hemingway and Fitzgerald—and
Michelangelo and Rubens wrote the book about demanding patrons. So
what's all the froth about? Did Langston leave the toilet seat up? 'Cause
that's a story.

Shale hands Chaney a pen and notebook from desk.

CHANEY: *(pouring more wine)* Why don't you start.

SHALE: If I don't have pages by tomorrow in my office, I'm getting someone else to do it.

Shale is about to leave again, but Chaney intercepts her and takes the pen and notebook.

CHANEY: Alright.

SHALE: Match is why you haven't been writing.

CHANEY: You're so sure.

SHALE: You're prettier when you're happy.

CHANEY: How did you—my mother always said that.

SHALE: And I bet you would frown. Just to be contrary.

CHANEY: I'm happy when I'm writing.

SHALE: *(holding up glass of wine)* To your mother.

CHANEY: Don't leave me alone. Don't leave me alone tonight.

SCENE TWO

March 1930. Morning. Langston's room at 514 Downer St, Westfield, New Jersey. Langston enters. A private moment. He is fixing his disheveled clothing. Suddenly he notices Zora standing at the doorjamb inside his apartment.

LANGSTON: *(startled)* Oh! Zora!

ZORA: Don't get your knickers in a twist, it's just swank old me.

LANGSTON: What are you doing here?

ZORA: Ain't tryin to befuddle your respiration. Sip up some air before you use this floor for a cooling board.

LANGSTON: Zora.

ZORA: Langston. It's been almost three years and my cheeks are lying fallow. You better fertilize—

She prepares to receive a kiss.

LANGSTON: *(overlapping)* Goodness, if you don't know how to scare a chap.

ZORA: —and I don't mean manure. Get over here!

Langston passes without touching her, entering the offstage bathroom. We hear water running, teeth being brushed.

LANGSTON: *(offstage)* You caught me unawares here—I have to use the restroom first—sorry.

ZORA: Huh. Did I shatter your schedule? Coming back early from a late date?

LANGSTON: *(laughs)* Right. *(pause)* I'm just pleasantly surprised.

Silence.

LANGSTON and **ZORA**: You've gotten a little sun.

They both laugh.

LANGSTON: Where have you been?

ZORA: Bahamas. You?

LANGSTON: Cuba. Last letter you sent was from New Orleans.

ZORA: And I still got my catbone, so don't you ever try to cross me.

LANGSTON: Last thing I'd ever do. *(Comes out of bathroom.)* Oh my goodness, it is so wonderful to see you. *(Goes back into bathroom.)* How did you get in here?

ZORA: Told you. I got my catbone. And *(she fingers a velveteen pouch)* my John the Conqueror root. But I only use hoodoo for special occasions. The door was open.

LANGSTON: Did you meet the Peeples?

ZORA: Of course. How else would I collect my folk materials?

LANGSTON: No. Downstairs. The Peeples. The couple who own this house, rent me a room.

ZORA: Oh, sure. She told me another woman down the road got rooms to let.

LANGSTON: *(re-entering from bathroom)* So you're here to stay?

ZORA: If you'll have me.

He hugs her jubilantly, and both laugh with the joy of seeing each other after so long. They pull apart and appraise each other.

LANGSTON: Well durnit, you know I will. Can't think of anyone I'd rather share the bounty of Westfield, New Jersey with.

ZORA: You think Godmother sent us here for punishment?

LANGSTON: I think she'd prefer to call it the freedom of discipline.

ZORA: Your work been chugging along?

LANGSTON: Nope. Few poems. No steam here.

ZORA: Mr. Hughes, you are far too modest. Godmother told me you just turned in your novel, so I've baked you a peach pie to celebrate.

She pulls the pie from a basket.

LANGSTON: No you didn't.

ZORA: Had to set us out on the right taste bud.

LANGSTON: Peaches? Can't be ripe now, at the dead end of winter.

ZORA: Ripe enough to cut. I threw in enough sugar and spice that if you can't taste the peach you sho nuff will taste the pie.

LANGSTON: Where did you get peaches?

ZORA: I'm a tropical girl. Now are you peckish or not?

LANGSTON: I couldn't pass up peach pie with a Rolls Royce.

ZORA: *(smiling)* The crab's still got claws.

Langston looks for utensils.

LANGSTON: Forks or spoons? Wait. Did you make it juicy like that one you made summer of '26, right before I went back to school at Lincoln? That was really one of the best pies I have ever had.

ZORA: Now why would I make a dry pie? To wipe your eyes? While some criminals bake them hard enough to scrub a sidewalk in West Hell, I make it juicy like you like it Langston so you best bring the spoons.

LANGSTON: Yes ma'am.

He returns with plates, a serving knife, and spoons.

ZORA: Not their fine china, I see. *(notices his watch)* That gold watch! Forgot all about it. Godmother went to town on that one for you, didn't she?

LANGSTON: And I wouldn't take it off for anything in the world.

ZORA: *(begins to serve pie)* You had to go and remind me of that dinner, didn't you. And Everette's gator face with the—

LANGSTON: No, it is too early in the morning for my sides to bust.

ZORA: But when he took that napkin and—

LANGSTON: No please, it's too much, don't, please.

ZORA: You don't want to see me do it 'cause then you'll start laughing and then you'll start crying and then you won't be able to keep yourself in your chair and then you'll be rolling around like an old beagle with fleas doing the cake walk on your hide, you will.

LANGSTON: *(laughing with his mouth full)* That is not true Zora, I beg you don't—

ZORA: Who's legislatin, your will or your gizzards?

LANGSTON: I am already choking, what more do you want? No! No! Don't do that! *(Zora stares at him.)* NO-

Zora makes the face. Zora and Langston are paralyzed with laughter, then their bodies jerk convulsively. Some spoons and pie fall from Langston's hands.

LANGSTON: Oh my. Do you always have to make me act so silly?

ZORA: My brother Everette always gettin someone into a heap of giggles. Would get more money just sittin on the corner makin faces than he would as an African prince.

Langston mops up pie, still laughing. They continue eating intermittently.

LANGSTON Now you have got to tell me what you are doing here.

ZORA: Putting my volume of folklore together. Still. Tired of it. Two and a half years of collecting and she won't let me publish one sliver of it till the book is out of the oven. She's even tucked my manuscript away in a safe deposit vault. I'm working from my field notes, so I need some help. Someone who is organized and mean on an Underwood.

LANGSTON: Godmother owns all your material?

ZORA: That's what the contract says.

LANGSTON: But that's the words, the music of the people—

ZORA: In exchange for a car, a movie camera, and $200 a month. Godmother's bankrollin you, probably bought you that desk and that lamp too, didn't she?

LANGSTON: Yes.

ZORA: And you get your monthly pittance just like me, so you know how it goes.

LANGSTON: But she doesn't own my work.

ZORA: *(this is news)* Really?

LANGSTON: She guides it but she doesn't own it.

ZORA: Then you're lucky.

LANGSTON: No I'm not. I feel like I've been doused with lime and everything that was once vital and hungering in me has been slaked by luxury. In three years, what have I done?

ZORA: You've written a whole book. Graduated from school with a fine education—

LANGSTON: But I want to do something pure again, something for the gutbucket. I want my gut pulled by something again.

ZORA: Something she hasn't got her clean white fingers in.

LANGSTON: It's terrible to talk like this. I shouldn't talk like this.

ZORA: I know you're thankful to her. We both are.

LANGSTON: But here we are, stock market all crashed, people out on the street fighting pigeons for a crumb on the ground, and we are up here, warm, well fed thanks to you, every want provided for, and I am an ungrateful brute if I don't see from what certain death Godmother has saved us.

ZORA: Amen to that.

LANGSTON: So I am lucky. I'm lucky you're here.

ZORA: Well ain't you as sweet as summer corn. *(pause)* You know it kills me that we've never written anything together.

LANGSTON: Godmother said no to our folk opera idea.

ZORA: But all this language we're trying to get down in books really belongs on stage. You need a living body to express it.

LANGSTON: No play has ever come close to portraying real Negroes. I'd like to see a pickaninny with a savage wit. Or a professor with the backwater blues.

ZORA: We could do it.

LANGSTON: We can talk about it.

ZORA: We could do it.

LANGSTON: Now?

ZORA: What else you got to do? Write your Nobel Prize acceptance speech?

LANGSTON: Write a play without telling Godmother?

ZORA: Why not? Her sunburnt children got to grow up sometime. We do this and we won't need to tangle with her over money all the time. We'll have our own.

LANGSTON: But if she finds out we've been doing it behind her back—what will happen to your manuscript? And me, I've never been dishonest with her. I don't think I can.

ZORA: Don't forget, she's telepathic. You just think right over the Hudson to 399 Park Avenue and she'll hear everything she needs to know. (They laugh.) And think: if you don't write this play, you'll be drowning. In lime.

LANGSTON And why do you want to do it all of a sudden?

ZORA: You really want to know? The truth? You're Langston Hughes! And I'm just as plain as a pile a rice.

LANGSTON: Come on now.

ZORA: It's true. First time I met you, after I heard your poems, you just about coulda mesmerized me with the half moon on your little finger. Your poems made us feel the warmth of our native tongue like the sun was setting in our mouths. You showed little old pile a rice me what I could do. I just had to sit on the same plate with the chitlins and the shortnin bread, drink up all the pot liquor from the collard greens, soak up the juice of a roasted hen, and I'd become an absolute necessity. I'd take it all in, and talk it all back, and write it all down. And once I had the nerve to get to know you, I could see you weren't much different than me. You're a pile a rice too. And I think rice writes better than chicken. You and I are supposed to do this, I can feel it, no matter what Godmother may say. We can make something she doesn't own.

LANGSTON: When you put it that way, how can I say no?

ZORA: You can't.

LANGSTON: This feels just like driving up North from Mobile, Alabama—

ZORA: You and me in that old jalopy for a month and a half. When was that?

LANGSTON: You know when it was.

ZORA: Summer o' '27.

LANGSTON: Everything came together then, huh? Anything seemed possible. I never wanted that drive to end.

ZORA: It didn't have to.

Louise enters.

LOUISE: Langston, I've got your mail—oh excuse me, I didn't know you had company.

ZORA: *(to Langston)* I didn't know you did either.

LANGSTON: This is Louise. Thompson. She's been helping me with secretarial services, typing.

ZORA: Typing? Typing what?

LANGSTON: This is Zora Neale Hurston, Louise. She just got back into town.

LOUISE: Oh, Langston has told me so much about you. Mrs. Mason too. She says you're a marvelous person and a grand storyteller.

LANGSTON: *(to Zora)* Godmother is paying her wage as well.

LOUISE: *(hands him envelope)* Oh, here's your check.

LANGSTON: *(his litany upon opening envelope)* "For there are few beings purer than the pagan Negro. Alamari has arrived to save the people." *(realizes)* Louise typed my novel. Maybe she can help you. *(to Louise)* Zora's looking for a secretary to organize her folklore manuscript.

LOUISE: *(to Zora)* I could do that. I'm out here every day anyway. (pause) If it's convenient for you, that is.

Silence.

ZORA: Are you the Louise who married Wallace Thurman in '28?

LOUISE: Yes. Although we've been separated for some time now.

ZORA: Well of course. Wallace isn't the marrying type.

LOUISE: No.

Silence.

LANGSTON: Well, Louise, Zora and I may be visiting for a bit and I don't want to waste your day here in the outback, so feel free to take off to Manhattan if you like–

ZORA: What are you talking about, Langston? This girl is crazy.

LANGSTON: I wouldn't say so.

ZORA: She's crazy enough to marry crazy Wallie Thurman. That's my kind of peola. Sit down and have some peach pie, Louise. *(The tension has broken and they all relax.)* Now, listen, there's something else besides my dusty manuscripts that needs your skills in insanity. Langston and I been specifyin about writin a play. But we'll need someone to stenogra-fy. You think your digits can manage?

LOUISE: I hope so.

LANGSTON: *(to Zora)* But we don't have the money to pay Louise for overtime.

LOUISE: It's a play you want me to type?

LANGSTON: Yes.

LOUISE: Then don't worry about it now. We'll balance the book later, when your play is up and running.

ZORA: Really?

LANGSTON: Are you sure?

LOUISE: I'm sure. I'd love to be of help.

Eisa Davis

The **Storm** Beneath the **Bone**

I. And this thing
        Huge thing
                Appears before me
Thing of limbs & sacred
        Thing before me has no shape yet
           Most alive

Every timber strokes with purpose
Electric life at the core of its rung

           So alive
           So shapeless
This thing needs my hands
        To hold it
           To guide its mass
Bulk of sorrow infinite mass
        It takes my hands
           It brings together
Palms together - space between is
        Human electricity
           The space between
           My prayers
Is human mass - the air
A conjure of bodies flexed over themselves
        Arms in armlegs in chest over bodies
           In this air
           Between my palms...
Is all humanity

Waiting to be formed
      Unshaped wild humanity – waiting
      For the rough of my palms
      To guide them in prayer

II.   White feathered baby
     Serengeti split-misted island

Separated by ancient languages
All white to grow into colors – your color

Is animal
Black and white muzzle manes

Side-by-side shebra lines
Patterns of a widening rift <hebron>

Culture of disintegration, lived along
Wrinkles of an ancient planet

Was time of adaptation
Is age of separation, plants the seed
On wrinkled terrain
Of our plain
Exist–
hence the challenge of our asking
Lies naked in acres of exhibition

There is a tension to abstinence, it resides
In the sway between the continents
The ethnic regions of our countenance
In the resonance of our posture
In our feed to the spirit

The spirit we call between our hands

In nocturne torrent sound of calm
In storm of air - the past
Is present - spirits' prison
Found in air - I found a prison
In the air...between my hands...
The big bang BAM! Humanity saved...

We place our palms together–the wires connect
The corpse is charged–we blow
The bomb–the body bomb
We blast & breathe : O BODY BOMB
Me body bomb : O BODY BOMB
We body bond : IN : BODY BOMB
    The bones are born : O BODY BOMB
    The fossils formed : O BODY BOMB
    The spirit owned : O BODY BOMB
    The people torn : O BODY BOMB
        The feces flown : O BODY BOMB
        The famine grown : O BODY BOMB
        The rage is stored : O BODY BOMB
        Beneath the bone : O BODY BOMB
    The seed is sown : O BODY BOMB
    The tree is strong : O BODY BOMB
    The leaf is long : O BODY BOMB
        Belief is born: O BODY BOMB
        Beneath the storm: O BODY BOMB
        Belief is born: O BODY BOMB
        Beneath the storm: O BODY BOMB

Edwin Torres

Hannan Saleh—**Silhouette with Barbed Wire** black and white silver

You In AMERICA Now:
Caribbean Dreams
and Speaking in the I-and-I

Public School 181 stood at the edge of the marsh near John F. Kennedy airport in Queens, NY. From the playground we could see the planes landing and taking off, if we wanted. Usually we were too busy playing "Tweedle-ee," "Miz Mary Mac" or double dutch to notice. The fourth, fifth and sixth grade girls initiated us into the complex movements and poetry of playground performance. Membership was arbitrary and could be revoked for the discovery that you had peed—or, God forbid, shit—your pants in kindergarten. We stood in groups as large as twelve, hands flying up down side-to-side hips swiveling eyes and necks clicking on head stems to the beat girls taught girls. This was before cheers, before rap, before designer jeans, before Cosby, before crack, before Atari, before Black History Month and Martin Luther King Day, before before before.

As we went up in grades, the older girls taught us more complex rhymes with "nasty" words—like pussy fuck dick—and a studiously observed silence fell whenever a younger, ineligible group approached. Our intoxicating play in the fields of 1970's aviation and girl love was only interrupted by the sight of the Concorde, a beautiful white hawk among the 747 pigeons, whose sonic boom we felt in our bones.

Every Friday was Assembly, when we were all required to wear white shirts and dark bottoms: pants for boys, skirts for girls, and Lord help you if you felt differently about it. Our principal Mr. Aranoff, a German Jew like most of the teachers of our mostly Caribbean student body, would make grim pronouncements rendered unintelligible by the faulty and ancient PA system in the auditorium that also served as lunchroom and gym, depending on the weather. We mostly saw films, or some grade level's theatrical production, but in February we always saw the "Civil Rights Movie."

The "Civil Rights Movie" was a black and white affair that showed Martin Luther King, Jr. saying "I Had a Dream," Rosa Parks at a press conference, and black people being hosed by white police officers and bitten by attack dogs in the street. Afterwards, we went back up to our classrooms and that was it for black history. For some reason the debut of the "Civil Right Movie" in our school coincides for me with the fevered mid-seventies viewing of "Roots," something I was deemed too young to stay up and watch. At first, I thought this meant it had sex in it, but, as I gleaned from my clandestine sneaks into the vicinity of the living room, it mostly had to do with black people being whipped and otherwise abused. Even though I was not allowed to stay up and watch the most watched miniseries in the history of television in the United States (second in viewing audience perhaps only to the OJ chase) (second only in miniseries viewing to "The Thornbirds" which I did stay up and watch with my grandmother and which did, in fact, have lots and lots of sex in it), everybody talked about what had happened the next day at school. A lot of the talk involved boys saying defensively what they would and would not have let happen to them in a similar situation: "I wouldna ever let them whip *me* like that" or "I woulda *been* run away."

Perhaps, it coincides in my mind with the "Civil Rights Movie" for the similarity of reactions they both engendered in me. Seeing Kunte Kinte whipped by a black man saying, *You in America now, boy* and seeing those young black people mowed down by dogs and water, I felt a deep and abiding sense of shame and embarrassment. This was immediately followed by the thought that, well, I am not American, that didn't happen to us, it happened to *them*, and, right on the heels of that thought, remembering that in the seventy-five years too long of slavery in Trinidad, some of my ancestors had been slaves, too, and feeling a deeper shame at my shame. I felt also a sense of relief; relief that my history wasn't thrown in my face like that, and a suspicion that if *those* black people on TV, in the movie, were treated so badly, well, then, it must have somehow been their fault.

As we sat in our metal folding chairs in that antiseptically clean auditorium, smelling the poorer kids' hot lunch being cooked behind the cloth partition; as we shook our heads saying, "That's not us, that's *not* us, that's not *us*," the Africans of us, the Indians of us, the Europeans of us, the mixed-up every which way ones of us; as we stepped away from those black people on the screen; as we struck back at how we had been erased from everything that America gave us as an image; we blamed those black Americans, as our parents did, for their own misfortunes.

When I went home from school those days I ate callaloo and bake and accra and stew beef and curry goat and roti and plantain and saltfish and macaroni and cheese and franks and Hamburger Helper and TV dinners. I heard my male relatives comparing the latest newspapers from "home"—the *Bomb*, or the *Guardian*—and talking about development and CLR James and Eric Williams and VS Naipaul and the World Bank and where the oil money went. For a while our babysitters were cousins needing work visas (always pronounced vis-ay) until the old Jewish lady down the street took over looking after us, who told us about Germany and the Nazis and gave us books to read about girls from Poland and Minnesota. And Mrs. Andriolo, an elderly Italian lady next door, let my brother and me play in her dusty attic, and gave us cookies and lemonade on hot summer days. Tom was Italian too, and he was the ice cream man whose tinkling call had us running back when they only had soft serve and didn't sell candy at all. My mother's purse got snatched and my friend Diedre got mugged and robbers came in my other friend Nadja's house at knifepoint. And at the family barbecues at my grandmother's house they played calypso and one day one of my cousins put on Stevie Wonder, much to my grandmother's dismay, *can you feel it all over people?*

Then too we were always being shuffled to one old person's house or another where it was always too hot and where we drank strong tea and ate sticky rice and stewed chicken and some kind of pink or yellow cake. At Aunt May's house, there were saucers with open scissors carefully placed on them at every doorway, so spirits couldn't follow you from one room to another, and an ancient chamber pot in the room she locked us in at night to sleep. Not that we were going to pee in that thing, at least that's what we said. She regularly reported to my father her conversations with her dead brothers, and he just nodded and mm-hmmmed while my mother slapped our mouths shut. And someone was always being visited by ghosts or hearing their mother brother daughter call them in their minds. And home was somewhere you took a plane five hours to get to, at least. Brooklyn was almost as good, even though there was the problem of the "black nigger children."

The first time Aunt May warned us about them my brother and I nearly keeled over in shock. The only time before that I had heard the word nigger I hadn't really heard it, a little white girl mouthed it to me as I was smiling at her through the back window of our car. *Nigger* clear as anything, and it had burned me in my heart. I had read it snarling from white lips in *Sounder* and *Autobiography of Miss Jane Pittman*. And here was Aunt May saying it to us and eighty seven years old at that! We had no idea what she was talking about obviously, because we said, I think in unison, "But we're black!" "You are different," she qualified. "All'ya are nice pretty pretty colored children. These black American children are nasty and dirty and all'ya musn't play with them."

Fast forward to the future, my cousins in a jawing jam session: "They are so selfish, they disrespect their parents, their elders, they don't work! They think the world *owes* them." My aunt over the stove, "Them lazy you see, opportunity right in they backyard and them doesn't take advantage." A Trini friend newly on Wall Street, "Them does have a nasty atichude, yes?" And me, "You can't generalize about everyone based on some people. There are cultural differences, historical differences, you never know right now, maybe somewhere there are a group of black Americans sitting in a room somewhere talking about us. What's the point? Divide and conquer bullshit!" My cousins wave me away (I've got to stop ranting, it just doesn't work). Maybe my cousin who took a black (US) history class will chime in about the miserable things people here suffered and about the virtual apartheid system that exists in the country today. But somewhere underneath is, well, why didn't they all make it? And the larger question, what does it mean for us? Will this country chew us up and spit us out, too? When we see succeeding generations with less educational ambition and multiple employment capabilities (read having at least three jobs while going to school full-time) (read: less stars in their eyes?) than our parents, what does it mean for us?

Many of my oldest friends are second generation like myself: Cuban, Indian, Korean, Puerto Rican, Japanese. I count my allegiances with borderless grace. When you live two nations and multiple cultures at once, you know something about connections, and about distance. You were raised by people who for a myriad of reasons, some economic, some political, some personal, leapt off the edge of what they knew towards an imperfect dream. Does what they gained make up for what they left behind? Seeing the leap, it seems disrespectful to even ask. And what would make them come to a place where they were hanging people, dragging them behind cars, beating them to death with baseball bats, for the color of their skin and the shape of their eyes?

We push ourselves away from the madness and its implications with our words that distance us from *them*, the ones who are chosen to suffer for some dark mark against their destiny. Somehow, in the convoluted logic of America, the sufferers are paying for their sins with poverty, addiction, violence, imprisonment, and death.

As Amadou Diallo and Vincent Chin's tragic deaths proved, none of us are immune from the consequences of this country's race politics.

Two African girls were beaten up on the subway because they were holding hands, a common custom for West African school friends in their country—a crime in the eyes of the teenagers who thought they were dykes. None of us are immune from the consequences of this country's homophobia.

I am a woman whose lover is a woman. I am as Indian as I am Carib, as Carib as I am African, as European as I am African. I was raised by a man who beat me within an inch of my life and by other men who taught me my times tables and a thing or two about birds and politics. I was raised by generous women who didn't squander hugs or money or play second fiddle to any man outside of their home, and who did without so I could have and showed me the grace of forgiveness. I've always known that older girls could teach you a thing or two, if they thought you were ready, that a kind soul comes in the most unexpected packaging, and that what I do know is a fraction of what I don't. These are but a few of the simple facts of my history. I share some of these same facts with a lot of people, and no amount of erasing will change that.

Nor will a futile turning away from an illusory otherness into the folds of our own. Speak in the first person: I and I.

And the shame we pushed away all those years ago, in that little New York City school at the edge of an airport? That shame I bring to me and clap it away between our palms, beneath our stamping Converse and Keds singing Punchinella, our hands tapping *freeze* and running, I send it out into the sonic boom of that beautiful jet flying east, because it will not save us, it will not heal us, there is no bad mark upon us that pisses into the wind of our destinies, we do not have to deny each other, no, because we made it, look at us, we are making it, sankofa, give them back their shame, give it back.

R. Erica Doyle

Drive

Cool night, like the snap of peas or dry branches underfoot.
Someone's waiting for me: a photograph of my breath.
The moon is cropped stingy and my skin is a tethered shade of heat
drawn to outer darkness and the gentle sucking in the thick of it.

Looking for the turn. Dull stretch of road the weight
of any other. Rolling straight back into clannish trees
like a cinnamon woman, powdered cleavage, struck
dumb in the spirit, falls back trusting.

A dredloc creeps from behind my ear, scrapes my nose, yarn
between my eyes. I slip its tight coil into place with a motion
reminiscent of white girls' easy laughter and the prep school I hated,
tinged with the riddle of their dearness and my brown body unseen.

Looking for the turn. Sign posts become tar field scarecrows,
mute Colored, bowed heads at 3 a.m. wherever trees shoot up
in a clearing. And down a piece there's a church, one room sanctuary,
one paint-chipped iron rail at the front three steps. The doors

are swollen shut from rain; above them, a cross-shaped window
broken out, fist-sized, where Jesus' head would be.
Cool night passes through the jagged godhead whistling,
condenses on the stained glass pane the way a house settles,

the way our bodies soften into earth, the way our suffering
mists, seeps into the bloodstream and runs. My we,
us, we people breathing on both sides of the hold belly.

role call

Greed and our flesh trials nurse the second half of this millennium.

What I wouldn't do for a *bidi*. I turn on the radio.
There. And I'll turn again before I reach the leaf dense trees
to go where I'll spend the night. Haven, where someone's waiting
and smells like cornbread under cloth, like thighs, moist

armpits, is a double portion, ribbed, combed, and fastened.
At the end of it: a bell my fingers feel for.
Sometimes, I dream a lonely highway and wake up driving;
sometimes, I am wet and full and prone in the pasture.

While inside me, desire shepherds the hills swallowing night's crisp
center and loose pearls in the swayback of darkness until I
breathe, reaching, replenished, forgetting, palpable
and palatable like pulling smoke but more than momentary

shuttling lungs and ear drums, more than, until I am a dream
within a dream within a dream like electric organ humpbacks
and only-born-once Al Green's happiness squealing
eeeeeeeeeee moan for love *eeeeeeeeee* over road hiss

over dirt shoulder scratches over prairie far off trees and sky
darknesses taking up space until I am an ellipsis, spinning.

Duriel E. Harris

Evidence
A Sex Story

The rain on his skin; the petals behind his ears; the leaves down his shirt; the stain on his underwear, already, dark, wet in the front; the dirt on his shirt, back; the mud in his shoes; the mud on his socks, splashed on his shins, wiped on his heavy braided brow; his black hair, heavy with rain, cool to the touch, on his face, black against the blue-black sky; his thick, uncut cock, hard in my hand, hard to get a grip on, hard but soft like a firm mattress that contours to your body; his eagerness exhaled onto my shoulder; his desires whispered into my ears, aching, straining; his laughs tickling my nose; his eyes lunging at my mouth, fluttering, "Don't, not yet, don't, hold on"; we hold each other, we hug each other, we do what some might call embrace each other, beneath the dancing shadows of trees; in the park, in the woods, in the dark, our positions change—the first of many times; his sinewy thighs, legs, arms wrapped around mine as others, out on their long walks (the kind that gay men like to take), look with envious but playful eyes as they pass; the scratches on my back, my neck; the bruises already forming, scarlets, on his nipples, across his chest, still wet, in puddles, dry, in patches, here, there; the smells—of deodorant, of shampoo, of cheap cologne, of dead skin and the bacteria that lives off of dead skin-all over us; the smell of wet leaves and wet soil and wet trees and wet weeds that we carelessly trample, kill with our clumsy sex act; the probing of a finger, the tugging of hands—"you're hurting me, you're pinching too hard, careful—slipping across rain wet skin; the trembling leaves over our heads; the incessant scratching over there: "That rat scared the shit out of me"; the condom in my hand; my cock up his ass; the holding back of time, pumping, while watching the night evaporate; the rain on my face; the lack of air, everywhere; the sound of that rodent racing, squealing; the fear mixed with excitement as I grunt and he comes and we collapse together; and all I can see in the rising moonlight as we grunt and separate into he and me, are my fingerprints on his skin, all over him.

Bruce Morrow

What I Brought to the Family Reunion

A box of chicken
    and a case of beer.
Homemade banana bread.
A dozen "House" music tapes
    and Motown on CD.
My camera, loaded,
with three extra rolls of film—

And my Lover of ten years

So that later, after pictures
of The Matriarch and oldest connection to the past,
when we, "The Grands,"
the brothers, sisters, cousins gather
to form our lines and pose,
those with arms full of infants will not ask me
where my wife is, or whisper that my hands
                are empty.

Reginald Harris

Cousin **RITA**

My cousin Rita's
menagerie of menfolk
always stir up talk
among family

At seasonal gatherings
she is sure to be
accompanied

Rita's claimed to have known
close to a thousand men

Half true, says her sister Ruth
She's done over two!

Nichole L. Shields

Survivor Rememory

she learned early
male eyes on her
mean violation
ocular and physical
rape.
subsisting on
a child's fear she fades into
nothingness
escaping to that
hidden corner
of herself
behind the pain
under the guilt
beside the shame
wondering
when it will be
safe to venture
out again

Faith Sangoma

Faggot
Faggot

We nicknamed Robert
Robin because he played
With girls and memorized cheers,
Preferred Home Economics to Shop.

In Gym he switched like them
And could control his strength,
Hitting volleyballs with his wrist
To boys of his choice.

Like somebody's sister,
He rolled his eyes and fought
With his hands open, backing away,
Kicking & scratching, a windmill of self-defense.

For this we called him punk,
Faggot, sissy, whistling & kissing,
Whenever Miss Williams left the classroom
Or turned to write on the board.

In talent shows he sang "Baby Love"
Backed by girls we had crushes on,
Signifying he knew more about
The opposite sex than us.

He did. We were virgins.
Our big brothers protected him,
Saying we'd understand when
The fuzzy shadows under our arms

And between our legs
Turned to hair. When one
Of our rubber bands bruised his neck,
His father came to school

And beat the shit out of him,
Erasing our passion
Mark with marks
Of his own.

Thomas Sayers Ellis

She

fully exposing them
by her long-awaited arrival
this miniature form
a great threat
only by the tips
of her ears

All would know that
the evidence of the
morphine drip
of black blood in blue veins
would end their transparent
road to pass

but before a whimper
could escape
the little pursed lips
she was announced

still

Nichole L. Shields

Silent

 Languages

In a McDonald's line,
one man pulls a penny
from another man's hand,
gives too wide a smile, and pays
the extra change.

The boy behind the register
takes my look of jealousy
for one of disapproval
and shakes his head at me
to say: I hate faggots too.

Shifting my weight
of shame
onto one skinny leg,
I open my appropriate mouth
to order.

Nelson Demery III

BULL-jean slipn in

ever day
5am
deacon willie/clara's man
go git him
supplies umph
everbody know
nappy love
be the one filling him sack.

every day
5am
deacon willie/clara's man
slip out   bull-jean
slip in
          clara git her supplies too.
bull-jean say
one GOOD thirty minutes
lasts a Life-time
umph bull-jean and clara
got mo Life-times than a cat's times infinity i know
cause i been watching them bout that long.
          not that i'm nosey or nuthn/cause
          i got business of my own you see/but
every day
5:30am
bull-jean slip out
look ruffled/smile dusty
eyes rolled   tongue damn near wagging
close yo mouth gurl i say
she don't hear
jes float on down the way.

one morning
5:30am
i jes snatch her on in sit down/talk right-in-her-face
bull-jean when you gonn smell the coffee
that gal is married! i said

blam/slam her some coffee so strong
            it don't move in the cup.
bull-jean say
i been giving away tastes
piece by piece/samples
of my Heart/i
been giving for free   all my Life
it's almost gonn/my Heart
all i really want
is a kind word
and a smile

and that wo'mn is kind
and she Loves me   and
it don't matter if it's thirty minutes a day
or ONCE in the next Life
i'll go git her/smile
whenever she'll let me
have it!

bull-jean go back to looking drifty.
umph/seem to me they be doing more than smiling
ova there.

then one day
5am
deacon willie/clara's man
didn't slip out
but bull-jean slippd in
shiit
i got my gun
figured all hell would break loose ova there
and spread my way
i waited
and
waited

5:05am
deacon willie/clara's man come out
tail dragging

sit on the porch holding him head
till 5:30am
bull-jean come out the FRONT door
and nod him good-bye

struttn!

na/everbody know
the deacon was doing nappy love
but it turned out
deacon willie/clara's man
also been squeezing frosty jackson's onion
and frosty got mo sugga in him shorts
than the sto got sacks to hold it in
        so i guess that make the deacon
         semi-sweet.
bull-jean tole ole deacon
unless he want her to tell the wind/he better
go git some money from him honey
cause he was moving out
and she was moving in!

ain't no mo
slipn in/or out
ova there.
all i see is bull-jean and clara floating round
smiling.

ever na and then they come ova
sit wid me   looking drifty.
i give em some of my strong-ass-coffee
but they don't seem to smell it
and that makes me
smile.

Sharon Bridgforth

Cum. Cum.

cum the bustiered breasts entreat
cum, cum, come taste come
sample come try come
buy me I'm slick and
sticky as fly tape...gonna get you
stuck...come fuck this
pussy. All you got ta do
is sling the Benjees
and we can get down.
i see this ho/on a red bed
she on her knees
her legs and ev'ything showin
she kinda fat, got big eyes
her hair real

       why do my mama say
       i don't need to look?
       it's just a ho picture...i known
       what that is since the first time
       i was in second grade
       besides...it's like the ho girl
       lookin at me, tellin me
       cum, cum on, you

Betta snatch yo eyes
off that mess/not for children.
Wouldn't do no white woman
singer like that, make her get buck naked like that
to sell a album. They ain't even
makin records for music no more...just freak
video/phone sex wit a beat...
and they don't care who sees it.
Least put that shit up in the back if
you hafta have it. Or where you gotta ax for it...
not out here for my children to look at
comin out the Baskin Robbins. Know
they wouldn't put that shit up on they Madison Avenue.
Hold still and put on your goddamn hat!
       Sheeit, baby

        Everybody wanna get blowed
make somebody go low and mouth no
apology. It's all about the ground right about now...
who can crawl is who can make the money flow.
I don't owe nobody nuthin/my picture...my face
my titties...on every other block down 1.2.5/what?!
I'm a muthafuckin icon...y'all don't know...it's just 2
years I been off AFDC/now you tell me
Babylon ain't fallin/I'm on every other block
Anywhere, block...it's a continuum
        every muthafuckin
 block, I'm a symbol/it's a continuum
        driven by capital, black
it's a continuum, anywhere
block   I'm on the black
  symbolic anywhere block
     black bitch I'm here
on the block, stood there
on the block, black, block
  stood there on the
block/picture
  stood there on the/auction
black, stop...stood there on the
stop/black...auction
stood there on the block
stop/now you tell me
Babylon ain't/driven by capital, black
On every muthafuckin
block

Karma Mayet Johnson

bull-jean & TROUBLE

i knew
trouble had done left   when i saw bull-jean sitting at
the b.y.o. wid jucey la bloom
i knew
trouble was gonn

cause jucey don't drank
and bull-jean don't hang
lessn some wo'mn done broke she Heart/and baby
bull-jean musta sho-nuff been hurting
cause jucey had done drank the fat part of a rat's ass
jigg'd.
you see bull-jean and jucey la bloom
friends from last-Life/they so close
they feel one-the-other's pain
jucey say
i think
i'll begin life again   come back
a dog/cock my leg or squat   bow-wow-mafucka
folk gonn haveta deal wid MY shit
next time round
yessuh/they business jess skooch-ova to my table
          cause you know i ain't a nosey-wo'mn.
jucey say
she ain't nuthn but a periodic-ho   ain't even got sense nuff
to charge on a regular basis.
bull-jean sit
holding she head
low to the table   stream-a-tears
rolling down the left side she face/her
don't bat a eye/nor make sound.
jucey on the other hand
jesa howling/rocking backwards and forwards/eyes

rolling
why/bull-jean/why you git we in this mess gurl
why?
bull-jean raise up
say
trouble/came in
stood to the side
  made me
  sense her first
russling skirt/jiggling jewelry/clicking
heels   trouble/came in
smelt lik sunshine   lik
freedom on a bed of posies/trouble
made me want her
befo i ever saw her face   she
entered my Heart
and held me/trouble
came in   ass popping
from side to side
she carried me across the room in her gaze/i
got lost
haven't found my way back
from trouble/she holds me
in her smile   i fit
between the moist on her lips/i
fit between her ears/i fit
in the middle of her intent/i fit
at the end of her fingers
i fit
in the pressure of her voice/her
heat as it lifts me/at the tip
of her thoughts as they extend themselves/wid
the extent of her desire/i
fit   i done laid down wid trouble/and
cain't
git
  up!

role call

trouble came in
stood to the side
    and took me
home.

jucey la bloom
jes hugged she head and she bottle
and cried.

Sharon Bridgforth

The *Singer*

(*excerpt from* The Singer, *a novel in progress*)

The first time I saw the singer I was sitting in Washington Square Park smoking a joint with Colette. Colette's father was one of the biggest pot dealers in New York City and at the time was doing six to nine (months) for possession. The last time he'd gone to prison, he'd come home a boxer. All over Colette's house there were framed pictures of her daddy, who'd changed his name from Carlos to Tigre and in the pictures he's looking dead-on at the camera, his black boxing gloves close to his chin. Two times he'd won the featherweight championship and two times either the cops or another boxer broke his nose.

Tigre kept the pot in ornate porcelain vases set up high in the china cabinet. The china cabinet was right next to the dining room table and it was no big deal to pull a chair over to it and help ourselves to a couple of bags every now and then. Me and Colette weren't potheads but we liked to get nice every once in a while, mostly on Friday nights after a long week of school or our mothers had gotten us down. Drug laws weren't crazy stupid like they are now where a person could go to jail for life just by simply touching a joint. It was summer, July I think and Washington Square Park was filled with all the freaks it's notorious for. There were skateboarders with purple hair, Rastas whispering what kind of smoke you could buy from them, skinny white boys making out with skinny black girls—this was a long time ago before you saw that kind of stuff all over the place. There were brothers roller-skating with boom-boxes on their shoulders and I think that crazy woman who used to always come to the park with her three pink poodles was there. I think I remember me and Colette bugging out about those dogs. I mean, it was kind of like a hallucination. The woman wore all this pink makeup and it was like she was trying to look like her dogs. Yeah, I'm pretty sure she was there that day.

And in the center of the park, by the huge fountain that in all the years I'd been going to the park I'd never seen actually working, was the singer. The thing that struck me first about the singer was how butt-ugly he was. He was a little guy, no more than five three, five four at the most, with big bugged out eyes and a near bald head. He was black, blue-black and not in that black is beautiful kind of way either The black is beautiful people were all around us, skating and making out and playing guitars. This guy just looked a mess. His lips on his face were too thin and looked as though they'd been burned and his nose wasn't one of those nice full noses you see spreading across brothers' faces. It was like God had said "Oh I forgot to give you a nose. Here's one." and stuck the tiniest thing he could find on that brother's face then pulled it out long and skinny like. I squinted at him while I took a deep hit from the joint then handed it to Colette and exhaled slowly. The pot made my lungs feel like they were going to explode out of my chest and land in a million red and black bits of skin and blood all over the park.

"Damn, that mother is butt-ugly."

Colette nodded. She had picked her curly hair out into an Afro that moved slowly every time a breeze came by or she moved her head. Her hair was blacker than anything and people were all the time asking her if she dyed it. "Look at my eyes, stupid. You gonna ask do I dye them too?" Colette'd say and we'd both crack up in the person's face. Her eyes were as black as her hair—a matched set. She was the first and only person I'd ever known with absolutely black eyes. We had been friends all our lives, born two minutes apart at the same hospital. Our mothers had shared a room and discovered they lived around the corner from each other. They stopped being friends years later which wasn't our problem. I think they got it into their heads that since we were their only daughters, we were supposed to stand by them. It was a stupid fight—over a man no less—and there was no way me and Colette were gonna turn our backs on each other because they couldn't keep their stuff together. The way I remember it was this guy had been going door-to-door selling brushes or something. My mother says he saw her and his eyes just about fell out of his head. Colette's mother had the same story. They both dated this guy and then after a few weeks, both decided the guy had to make a choice between them. Of course the guy disappeared—he's probably in some other neighborhood causing the same kind of drama and my mother and Colette's mother each blamed the other somehow. I guess Colette and I were about seven when this all happened. Maybe a little younger cause I remember waking up one night with blood in my mouth and my front baby tooth on the pillow. I remember that brush-guy giving me a quarter while my mother stood beside him, smiling all proud. Then I fell back to sleep.

Thing about mothers is they figure daughters are supposed to be like extensions of them or something. We're not. Our mothers were fat. We weren't. Our mothers were old and getting older. Colette and I would never get old. Sometimes, I felt like I was standing on the outside of us, watching me and Colette grow tall and agile and elegant. Some mornings as we hung out in my front yard doing walkovers and cartwheels in our matching halters and shorts, I could feel the full-tilt heat of us, feeling like we had the power to make the whole world sweat.

I was young once too, my mother would often say as she watched me fussing with my hair in the mirror, combing it this way and that or pulling it up on top of my head and letting the ringlets of it fall down around my brows. But I'll never be old, I'd think but not say.

Most of all though, our mothers weren't beautiful. Some mornings, sitting in the window watching my mother walk to the bus that would take her to her job, I coveted her straight back and the proud way in which she lifted her head with a longing so deep, my throat would hollow out. But I had no desire for her massive breasts, breasts I feared mine were genetically destined to grow into. Nor did I want to inherit the frown lines above her brow and at the edges of her mouth. And while my friends often remarked on the sweetness of her voice and the beauty with which she delivered Carol King's "Way Over Yonder" into the world, I feared for the day my body would swell and curve into one whose arms, lifted into the air, revealed heavy sacks of hanging flesh. Me and Colette were not conceited, we were convinced. Convinced that we would one day walk right out of our stupid Brooklyn lives into a world as fabulous as New Orleans in Streetcar Named Desire—a sultry, sweet world full of men going crazy for a chance to kiss our throats and pull our hair. That summer me and Colette were both fifteen and burning up with all kinds of longing.

"Sometimes, I wish I was born with her eyes," Colette would whisper to me about her own mother whose eyes were vivid green and surrounded by long, dark lashes. The summer we were fifteen, our mothers were thirty and always warning of the trouble they'd gotten themselves into at our age.

"Don't believe it when somebody says I love you," my mother would often say. "It's always a lie." But I believed there was someone out there with eyes for me and me alone. So every summer weekend, Colette and I dressed in pale pinks and blues and grays - shirts that clung to our chests and shorts that our mothers fussed about until we took them off, snuck them into our knapsacks and re-donned them in restaurant bathrooms.

I stared at the singer. He had a small boom box with music coming from it. On one side of the box, a long thin black cord with a mike on the end lay on the ground all curled up like a snake. I hated snakes so I only glanced at the cord before it turned into a boa constrictor and chased my eyes back to the singer. He started pacing back and forth and sort of clearing his throat. I cruised the crowd for boys and saw a halfway decent one standing at the far end with his arm around a chubby girl with glasses. When the girl saw me staring, she gave me a fierce look and pulled the guy a little closer to her. I gave her a tiny wink and she turned away from me. I'd learned a long time ago that winking is the best way to fluster other girls because they never know whether you're flirting with them or conspiring.

A small group of people had gathered around. People always gathered around the fountain. There's a long low stone wall encircling it that's the perfect height to straddle or sit on the ground and lean against. There used to be this comedian that would perform at the fountain. He always told roach jokes and people would be on the ground laughing. Then he'd start in on different people in the audience, mostly people who looked like they came into the city from New Jersey. Everybody who wasn't from Jersey made fun of Jersey people. You always imagined them in their big ugly houses with lawns and tire swings and every morning they came outside in a good mood to pick up their Jersey paper and wave at their fellow Jersey neighbors. New Yorkers hated Jersey people. Later on, I learned that we hated them because they had gotten out and we hadn't. But back then I thought it was because they were stupid-looking and clueless and had to actually admit they rode that dumb-ass Path train. You could tell the New Jersey people because they were always just a little too neat and clean for the city. They always looked like they had spent hours dressing up to come hang at Washington Square. New Yorkers probably spent the same amount of time but we always did it so that it didn't seem like it. If our hair was messy, it was a mess that took hours to make. If our t-shirts fell sloppily over our jeans, it was because lots of turning this way and that in the mirror had rendered desired results. Me and Colette always called each other to find out what the other was wearing then we'd end up at either my house or hers putting on make-up and restyling our hair. Me and Colette were beautiful and we knew it—not in the conceited way of those girls who were always talking about all the guys that wanted them and stuff. Different. Every since we were about ten people had been staring at us. Men mostly. And when you're ten and men are staring at you it makes you feel two things—real scared and real powerful. Sometimes we'd pass a group of men playing dominoes and they'd just stop slamming those dominoes down on the table and watch us walk by. Ten! We were ten and we could stop a fast-moving game of dominoes! We didn't even have breasts yet!

Magic, this old man whispered one time when we walked by. Magic.

After that, me and Colette started calling things magic. Good things. If Colette bought a pair of jeans that gave her a nice ass, I'd say "Magic" and we'd laugh. The day I won my campaign for freshman class president, Colette made a big sign to hang in her window that said "Magic. And the first time that butt-ugly singer opened his mouth and began wailing, Colette and I looked at each other, the joint burning my thumb and forefinger, Colette's eyes already starting to fill with tears.

"Magic," I whispered.

And Colette nodded, echoing "Magic."

Jacqueline Woodson

where **the boys** are

i said goodbye to everything
my hopscotch destiny
my foursquare ambition
my tether ball hope
my red rover aspiration
everything
my jacks experience
my hide and go get it flair
my kick ball capability
my dodge ball knack
everything
my wall ball calling
my marble scholarship
my patty cake purpose
my blind mans capacity
everything
my tag savvy
my doorbell ditch dreams
my double pump fate
my monkey bar bent
my little dick
my high voice
my chin and chest hair smooth
everything
just like you said
to stop you
from outgrowing
this love

Marvin K. White

Period

for Judy Blume

I wanted blood.
I called Are You There, God?
It's Me, Margaret, read the words like
psalms, knew them like the lines
in my open palm. I read
the boys' version too,
the one about wet dreams,
its title no prayer, no supplication,
only the indecision that expresses
agency, engorged with
options. I understood
not one word of it,
the workings of
their foreign bodies, grown
before I tried to reason why
my brother might have been
touching me. I wanted blood
just like those white girls
praying for it:
so normal and so blessed,
them and their bleeding.

Lyrae Van-Clief Stefanon

First **Day**

My sister and I crossed the train tracks
after school and started back on the road,

gazing at the field of sunflowers, their stems
tall as giraffes reaching toward the possible.

Butterflies hopscotched on waving grass
while we skipped toward Miss Mae's biscuits.

And with every step, we disremembered
the National Guard pointing and ordering

the principal to open the doors,
the girl with sausage curls cursing and crying,

the teacher re-naming us pickaninnies.
We rose when the bell trembled,

straightening our faces and spines, wrapped
our arms around each other's spirits

and forgave God for being absent
minded and not meeting us that first day.

Angela Shannon

Snow
for Toi Derricotte

It came once, the year I turned ten.
That year they told us how we
would become women, and I began
my monthly vigil. But this was
the miracle, singular, unexpected.

The whites had finally stopped
resisting. Unwanted at their school,
we went anyway-historic, our parents
intoned, eyes flashing caution
to our measured breaths.

That first martial autumn mellowed
into a winter of grudging acceptance
and private discontent, a season of hope
shaped by fists and threats.
Then angels molted, pelting all

of creation with their cast-off garb.
We went home early, drifting through
a landscape of sudden ghosts,
the yard churning in frothy waves,
as if by an invisible tide of protestors.

What I remember most is its rude
coldness, stinging and wet. How we
mixed it with milk, sugar, vanilla,
into a poor child's ice cream which
melted before we could savor it.

Sharan Strange

role call

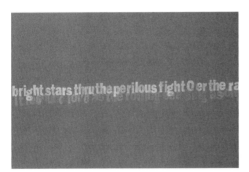

Kim Mayhorn—**Home Speech** photo essay installation

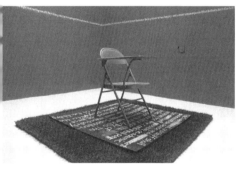

Plenilunium

I want this music and this dawn and
the warmth of your cheek against
mine. —Rumi

In St. Louis,
the moon hung
large and full,
red and harvest,
still bleeding its ritual
like my sisters on moontime.

Does she see a crimson globe in her view?
    Has the moon begun her flow;
            the dancing of menses?
Is she standing barefoot
in the midnight garden,
toes grasping the fresh soil,
looking up to the skyward goddess
chanting *blessings, peace onto you*
and twirling as the lilies open
in the brightness of this night?

Andre O. Hoilette

Scribulus

Scribulus, son of Medusa the beautiful Abyssinian. Of the time before she seduced Posiedon, causing Athena's rage to turn her skin from ebony to envy, her locks to snakes, her gaze to stone.

Scribulus, son of Zeus the titanic womanizer who spent time between thighs while Eternity swallowed his impetuous children. Never knew his Hera saved her worst anger for his darkest child.

Scribulus was supposed to grow into manhood knowing a mother's love, a god's strength. But how does a boy grow to know these from a mother who stops holding him, a father who never acknowledged him. How does a mother go the rest of her life without looking into the eyes of her son even if it will turn him into stone.

Scribulus feeling confused and angry went to the Sahara, slaughtered an elephant, uprooted a tree, dipped it in blood, created the first alphabet, then the first tragic poem. Showed his invention to Medusa, who turned to her son, wept tears we now call diamonds, kept him dusted and polished for years while herb women worked spells to free him.

Scribulus remained sleeping stone until Medusa found the Yoruba. Obatala's women children full of passion and miracles dripped honey on the obsidian man-child during a storm, bid him to teach the secret connection of mind and hand.

Scribulus is freed from jealousy and a mother's love when a woman calls his name seven times. He'll run naked through her dreams like sweat, weep poetics like blood from an open wound.

Toni Assante Lightfoot

LYRIC FOR a NEW LIFE

I died before you—
Took the plunge
Ran out the door of life,
I went on before you—
Stopped speaking
Turned my sight away
Closed off my hearing
Folded my body up from your touch before you—
I decided,
Before you—
Past away into another life
Met it head on like a new course of study—
People missed me before you—
They asked about me for a time
Wondered what became of me
Asked if I'd left anything behind—
They cried for me before you
They called my name out in vain
Wished they'd been better friends before you—
My soul grew weary of this life
My mind fatigued by lies
My heart riddled by deceit
My legs weakened with each blow—
I decided to collapse before you
To give way
To allow an ocean of tears
To sweep me elsewhere before you—
One day, I resolved to perish before you
Resolved to cut across the void
To come out at the other end with no one
Naked in a new world, unrecognized
Inching along from day to night
And day again—

I finally reached the promised land
I finally saved my self—

Nancy Mercado

Juking AT *Miz* ANNIE'S

blues beat four-four
memories/grayer than
rain soaked concrete/
into the tiny marrow
of my black hip bones/
while i grind in agonizing
ecstasy/trying to exercise
four hundred years of pain-
filled scars/my belly rub-
in sweet sticky sweat/into
the pores of brutally dethroned
queens/whose buttocks
swings/like poetry in
motion/to the nitty
gritty gospel/of deep
down home/rhythm & blues/
i lose/hold of my control
and scream/in the forgotten
tongue of my ancestors

Charlie R. Braxton

Microscope

In sixth grade, science was a puzzle
of shifting shapes—Africa, Europe,
and the Americas—fitting together
as we'd float wooden plates over
a background of blue. Small discoveries,
magnetic push and pull, dull rocks
breaking open to colored gemstone,
fool's gold, and stars—already dead
we were told—lighting the planetarium roof.

At home I'd find science in swampy ditches
teeming life—small worlds to swirl and multiply
in my petri dish—or an onion skin translucent
as dragonfly wings. In the World Book
Encyclopedia 1966, bought for the year
I was born, I looked for Rays of Light
and found, instead, Races of Man:
skull measurements and body equations,
chin to forehead, femur to tibia. Pictures
detailing Caucasoid, Negroid, Mongoloid.
Hair texture, eye shape, color. Each image
a template for measure, mismeasure.

I collected hair from everybody at home,
and offered up samples at school—my own,
straight and shiny, first; then my brother's
tight curls waiting in a plastic dish.
I've got it, but it's just a tad bit dirty,
the teacher said focusing, his face pressed
against the eyepiece, showing me how
anything—fool's gold, a dead star, my hair,
all of science, glittering and out of reach—
up close could lose its luster.

Natasha Trethewey

For the Distinguished Historian who would enter **"into the current-day lives"** of **Sapelo's People**—or, the *Long Walk* to FREEDOM that Lasted 2 $\frac{1}{2}$ Weeks

You would enter into a life
just once
just long enough
to reel in the words
fish-hooked from
local tongues
baited from the flesh
of others' labor
skinned and gutted
then wrapped neatly in
yesterday's morning papers.

You would take
a long 6-week walk
into freedom
a scholar's journey
but you settled
for 2 $\frac{1}{2}$ weeks
    instead
your friends up North on the island
warned you that the weather
would not be as warm
in the Hammock
but you didn't dress for
a chilly reception

Now back home
in your faculty chair
you think of them
Sapelo's People
reminiscing about
getting holy
at First African Baptist
finding Jesus
in a temporary tourism of
the souls of black folk

knowing full well
you could have done that
back in your hometown
uptown on 125th Street.

Yet you think of them now
when your colleagues
look back in wonder
on how you got ovah
at your distinguished prizes
won with words that paint
"a sensitive portrait of the
lives of Black Americans"

as if riding a ferry across the shore
were all it takes
as if riding a bike down a dusty dirt road
could bring instant insight
as if knowing folks by name, first & last
could release revelations
hidden histories trapped
in the pores of Geechee-black skin

You think of them now
Sapelo's People
"handsome" and "humble"
but never angry
You think of them now
when your CV wants color
when you have run out
of more subjects
in need of "the rehumanizing of history"

You go on with your book
Your "moving meditation"
on race & history
Keep signing copies
& evoking our names
but don't bother sending us
an extra crate
we still haven't found much use
for the first one.

Sheree Renee Thomas

Note: Sapelo is one of the Georgia Sea Islands. Established in the 1800s, Hog Hammock was one of five historic communities on the island, home to 450 African Americans. Once owned by wealthy families such as the Reynolds, 96% of the island is held by the State of Georgia. Of the five historic African American communities founded on the island, today only Hog Hammock remains Current population 70.

Who Is Black?

A Puerto Rican Woman Claims her Place in the African Diaspora

Yesterday, an interesting thing happened to me. I was told I am not Black.

The kicker for me was when my friend stated that the island of Puerto Rico was not a part of the African Diaspora. I wanted to go back to the old skool playground days and yell: You said what about my momma?! But after speaking to several friends, I found out that many African Americans and Latino/as agree wit him. The miseducation of the Negro is still in effect!

I am so tired of having to prove to others that I am Black, that my peoples are from the motherland, that Puerto Rico, along with Cuba, Panama and the Dominican Republic, are part of the African Diaspora. Do we forget that the slave ships dropped off our people all over the world, hence the word: diaspora?

The Atlantic slave trade brought Africans to Puerto Rico in the early 1500s. Some of the first slave rebellions took place on the island of Puerto Rico. Until 1846, Africanos on the island had to carry a libreta to move around the island, like the passbook system in apartheid South Africa. In Puerto Rico, you will find large communities of descendants of the Yoruba, Bambara, Wolof and Mandingo people. Puerto Rican culture is inherently African culture.

There are hundreds of books that will inform you, but I do not need to read book after book to legitimize this thesis. All I need to do is go to Puerto Rico and look all around me. Damn, all I really have to do is look in the mirror everyday.

I am often asked what I am — usually by African Americans who are lighter than me and by Latinos/as who are darker than me. To answer the $64,000 question, I am a Black Boricua,

Black Rican, Puertoriquena! Almost always I am questioned about why I choose to call myself Black over Latina, Spanish, Hispanic. Let me break it down.

I am not Spanish. Spanish is just another language I speak. I am not a Hispanic. My ancestors are not descendants of Spain, but descendants of Africa. I define my existence by race and land. (Borinken is the indigenous name of the island of Puerto Rico.)

Being Latino/a is not a cultural identity but rather a political one. Being Puerto Rican is not a racial identity, but rather a cultural and national one. Being Black is my racial identity. Why do I have to consistently explain this to those who are so-called conscious? Is it because they have a problem with their identity? Why is it so bad to assert who I am, for me to big up my Africanness?

My Blackness is one of the greatest powers I have. We live in a society that devalues Blackness all the time. I will not be devalued as a human being, as a child of the Supreme Creator.

Although many of us in activist circles are enlightened, many of us have baggage that we must deal with. So many times I am asked why many Boricuas refuse to affirm their Blackness. I attribute this denial to the ever-rampant anti-Black sentiment in America and throughout the world, but I will not use this as an excuse. Often Puerto Ricans who assert our Blackness are not only outcast by Latinos/as who identify more with their Spanish Conqueror than their African ancestors, but we are also shunned by African Americans who do not see us as Black.

Neely Fuller, a great African American sociologist, stated: "Until one understands the system of white supremacy, anything and everything else will confuse you." Divide and conquer still applies.

Listen people: Being Black is not just skin color, nor is it synonymous with African Americans. To assert who I am is the most liberating and revolutionary thing I can ever do. Being a Black Puerto Rican encompasses me racially, ethnically and most importantly, gives me a homeland to refer to.

So I have come to this conclusion: I am whatever I say I am! (Thank you, Rakim.)

Rosa Clemente

At the OLMEC EXHIBIT in Washington D.C.

In the third gallery I discover my lover
in a stone statue thousands of years
older than Tenochtitlán. Sitting,
he is my height, I could press my whole
body against his back. The stone is warm.
Shoulders lead me around, I unearth carved
face: broad cheeks like peeled avocado halves,
full upper lip: a cat's snout. On the wall:
Olmecs had the mouths of the jaguar, their nahual.

I turn and see my lover by glass case
becoming the clay jaguar on display.
His movements fluid as a leaf's rustle.
Squats to tie his shoe, thighs become haunches.
I envision him leaping over the glass case.
I circle the statue, memorize faint red pigment.
Suddenly, his breath grazes my neck,
tropical as moss hanging from a tree,
hair on my arm bristles.

We follow halls out of the museum
like trajectories of a river. At the hotel order steak,
juice running on the plate, we eat with fingers.
That night our sweat smelled like jungle:
moist earth, the sound of quetzal wings.
In the morning, under my nails, I find traces of clay.

Alicia Vogl Sáenz

My Love Affair
with **Jamaica**

has always been double-edged
two ends of a pimento candle
burning towards a slender middle
the indulgent heat pushing me off-center
on this island
there has never been safe ground

The flat-cut of Liguanea
contrasting with the fluid shape of indigo mountains
Gordon Town framing the blue-black faces cleaning
dirty windscreens on Hope Road
the hunger in their eyes eerie at twilight
the dead breathing wistful flames at night
rolling across childhood memories
the raspy sound of my brother's breathing
reminding me that I must never rest
the uneven iron bed was never big enough
to hold my dreams—my fears
sweating through the polyester nightgown
water will always find its own level
my grandmother whispers
sleep now—before the new day come find you
still looking into yesterday
Jamaica has always been harsh
hard words of rigid correction
connecting with the side of my head
two fingers of water above the rice
turn down the fire when the pot start boiling
gal pickney must learn fi wash them dirty under-clothes

The white uniforms hid the welts on my legs
the blue ties tempered the catholic purity
soft sister-hands encouraged the metal rosary

B+ is never acceptable in Math
you want to sell cigarettes on the roadside?
finish you homework
and come get a piece of cornmeal puddin'

The land has always been lush
coconut husks split open to the rush of a moody sea
Sunday afternoons on the endless sand
pre-adolescent belly bottoms slit to reveal the red fruit
pulpy sweet—but angry in captivity
Jamaica
has always loved me from a place of random beauty
women with wide cassava hips
and full star-apple lips
women with strong hands
reaching beyond their own fears
to give their children courage
teaching them to stand straight-backed
in the absence of fathers who visit
with the smell of white rum in their words

My father has never loved women
with soft hands—my mother will show you the scars
still wrapped around her solid middle
banning her belly tight against visibility
this child will never be silent
I speak now because my grandmother gave me tongue
I speak now because Jamaica has always given me
crosses I will have to bear alone
the only compass my mothers needle-sharp pain
shooting proud across my back
marked like a crab
Jamaica has always been able to find me
a thorn among the bloody hibiscus blooms
my Jamaica has always been
the hardest poem to write

Staceyann Chin

EVIL *Gettin' There*

Mamma was always evil gettin' to church.

That's what I kept thinking when I looked at Divine on the pulpit. I was delirious, and damn Mamma was evil gettin' to church. Jesus is the light and the way and your pleasure on earth can be multiplied tenfold if you just open up. Open yourself wide, let him in. I was fourteen years old and the songs from the souls made me want to shout. And I wanted Him. I wanted what Mamma had.

Mamma was always so evil gettin' to church that I wondered why she went and made us all go. Hair kinking up from playing in the tub or fantasizing and touching places untouchable. Mamma was so mad at me, had to press it again. I hated that hot comb. She screamed and stormed and shook all over and when Divine on the pulpit spoke of the devil, I saw Mamma's big "lady" hat with the flowers. We thought she was the devil.

Mamma was just so evil between humming hymns while Scrapple sizzled on the wood stove, gettin' popped by hot grease 'cause we had to get there, to church—in a hurry. My breasts had started to grow one at a time and the woman pain made me feel alive and afraid and connected and sinful. Divine said Eve did it, she made me have to curl up in pain and bleed. I was just so evil dealing with all of that and the boys popping the elastic in my little half undershirt. Mamma said I shouldn't stick them out so much.

I wanted to be baptized and have that bad part of me cleansed away. I wanted Jesus to take away my sins. I wanted what Mamma had. I would have gone and bowed at Divine's feet but Mamma had just been so evil gettin' there that I was delirious and I wanted to shout and the spirit was doing strange things to me. I thought I would cry. I wanted Jesus to save me, take me away from our hell.

The heat in church made my head swim. Mamma took my hand and her face looked like we knew something, like we shared something that there was no need to talk about and one of my brothers was dozing and two were giggling at the grandma with the wings of fat under her arms who looked like she could fly, screaming "Lord have mercy Jesus."

My favorite time of the week was when Mamma sang like Mahalia Jackson on TV and my brothers snored in the back of the station wagon and the evil was gone, at least for a little while. I'd look out the window and feel a tiny explosion every time I was reminded of something I wasn't supposed to be thinking about I knew it was wrong but I wanted to be touched and I knew it was wrong but I needed to know I was real and I just felt so lacking and evil. I didn't get touched till I was nineteen, I don't know when I became real.

Mamma's heart was lifted and I could tell it was full because the only man that loved her was the only one that mattered. And I began to understand how needing something so bad can make you evil gettin' there.

Jiton Sharmayne Davidson

Kenneth L. Addison—**Street Corner Revival** mixed media collage on batik

gawd and alluh huh sistahs

on dat great gittin up mornin'
  gawd and alluh huh sistahs
  wuz weavin theyselves a fyne tuesday
some fixin breakfast for each other
       and some still in bed bringin in da mornin' slowly/softly

one sistah said to another, its so much light in heah, we need some shade
      ummmmm hmmmmm, they all went, even the sistahs
who wuz lovin said, ummmm hmmmm and got off the clouds
  to join the circle that wuz forming

the sistahs all gathered round each other into a circle and began callin
colors into the sky
      chantin
        sunloveshe i found a place to lay my head earth deep resonant
      blackness empowering soulful blackness a happyblacksong pulled
        from blackness
           to blackness beautifulpowerful comfortinglovingblackness

            and one tall sistah started spinning round
          with her dreads flying round her and circles of
green and blue purple and blue
  wuz trailing round her with gawd and alluh huh sisters shoutin
     and clappin
its you my sistah, its you, you bettah go on girl wit yo bad self, its you girl,
         go sistaaah, go, go sistaaah go, go, sistah, go
    and that tall tall ebony sistah raised her hands through the sky and
     stretched her feets in the dirt till they became roots and
  she say
    sunloveshe i found a place to lay my head earth deep resonant
    blackness empowering soulful blackness a happyblacksong pulled
    from blackness
        to blackness beautifulpowerful comfortinglovingblackness

     and don't you know soon it wuz
        nightfall and alluh a sudden there wuz this sound of crickets and
         waves reachin
            all the way up to them clouds where gawd
         and alluh huh sistahs
       wuz braiden and twistin each other's hair and makin up songs
     for the second day we didn't git to read about in no
          bible neither

Letta Neely

The Good Lorde

I remember Sister Audre, she used to come to
Central Baptist some Sundays, always sat in back

on the left, next to Sister Gloria, with her hair
wrapped like she was African or something

Always Amen-ing, Praise the Lord-ing and singing
a little loud. Once I heard Deacon Jones

say she was a whole lotta yellow wasted but I
never understood that cuz she was kinda pretty

He ain't like her much cuz once in church
he stood up and said that black folks was

somehow better than everybody else. She
got up, looked at him real funny and said

"Remember, our sun is not the most
noteworthy star, only the nearest."

After service I asked her what that meant,
She told me "Never pretend to convenient beliefs,

even when they are righteous. You can
never defend your city while shouting."

One time nosy old Mrs. Hilliard asked her
if she had any kids, Sister Audre put

her hand on my head, walked her fingers
through my hair and said "My children are

wherever I find them." I remember that
all the stones in her necklaces was black,

one day I asked her "Why ?" and what kind
of stones they was anyway. "Coal" she said

when I asked her "How come?" she said
"I am black because I come from the earth's inside,

now take my word for jewel in the open light."
The thing I liked most about her though

was her voice. She sure could sing but never
did join the choir. Daddy say she was all

mixed up by that feminology stuff. One day
Sister Gloria came to church and said pray

for Sister Audre cuz she was ill. After awhile
she came back to church but folks started

avoiding her cuz she always wanted to talk
about being sick, describing it and stuff.

Ma said she had had one of her breasts removed
but there she was back in church, yes Lord-ing

and dancing like she still had two. Then she
got real sick, all skinny and bald but right up

to the end she kept on singing, her voice
never cracked. I miss Sister Audre who really

I barely knew except from church.
Sometimes on Sundays in the small spaces

Between the Reverend's sentences
I can hear her soprano still.

DJ Renegade

Kim Mayhorn—**"A Woman was Lynched the Other Day..."**
installation detail

Moontime &
Mezuzahs

I've always been skeptical when it comes to religion and the politics of salvation, and so I waiver back and forth from wanting to belong to a religious community and not being able to accept the teachings of any one religion as absolute truth. The "isms" inherent in organized religion have sent me wandering from faith to faith and one group to another for most of my adult life. No matter where I've been or what I've been taught, the core of my spiritual beliefs, the one's that never change, are those that have been passed on to me from my mother's mothers—healers who for fear of persecution would never profess any dealings with the power of ancestral, plant, mineral and animal spirits. The newest name for women like us is African-Amerindian spiritualists. That's a good name, and it's been a long time coming. Names like rootworkers, witches and heathens pushed many of us into hiding. Even now, spiritual work continues to be a veiled practice in my family. It's a shame when one must cover the beauty of a spiritual life in which everyday acts like eating, talking, walking, housekeeping, bathing—even sleeping—can have spiritual purpose, can become ritualistic and charged with healing power. A shame when one is afraid to herald a spiritual life in which there is room for all beings without exclusion and hierarchy.

Unveiling the mysteries of African-Amerindian rituals is considered taboo in my family, and no one—except me—ever openly keeps company with goddess worshipers, two-headed women, Voodoo devotees, spiritualists and Kabalistic pagans. We were taught to present ourselves as good Christians—never mind the seven-day candles burning in the corner of the room or the cup of coffee set out with tobacco and sweets for our ancestors. My mother had me dedicated at Second Reform Methodist, educated in Catholic schools, baptized at Union Baptist Church and otherwise saved more than once. I have been compelled to profess my acceptance of the Lord Jesus Christ as my personal savior—once in an actual church and once again while getting ready to attend my grandfather's funeral in Virginia. These were two of the proudest moments my mother ever had. We celebrated with jubilation every time someone got saved. I never really understood why I needed saving, but I wanted to please my mother, so I tried to sound sincere. Looking back, it seems my mother was using whatever was available by way of a spiritual community to us according to what was most acceptable in each time and place. We have been here always, gathering totems and medicine, adapting and adopting all that we need to survive from land to land, and while the words and images may change, the source remains the same.

Ours is a practice as private as it is peculiar, but I have come to know that synchronization is the common thread that ties together the spiritual traditions of many oppressed peoples. How else would my foremothers have come to cherish traditions, rituals and symbols from all over the world?

Adorned with objects and all manner of ritual tools, my mother's front entrance is a veritable shrine of varied practices and beliefs. All who enter are greeted first by a Yoruba gatekeeper, Native American smudge pots filled with Egyptian frankincense and myrrh, framed prayers from the Bible and a Mezuzah on the doorframe. There are hidden things like red bricks and camphor water under beds, herbal pouches stuffed in pillowcases, special oils and potions for bathing or washing floors. My Nana even has a Star of David clock hanging on her living room wall. It has always been this way with us. My home is much the same; it is what I know. There are many names and faces of God and goodness. Someday, my daughter's home may also reflect these ways.

Our amulets and totems: the Crucifix, Rosary beads, the Tree of Life, the Star of David, Mezuzahs, Orisha beads, crystals, stones, scarabs, sea shells, Medicine bags and a hard-shelled nut from Asia that I still can't identify were worn under our clothes according to need and circumstance. Each totem is considered sacred and powerful in our family-gifts that must be earned or offered by elders, never purchased or worn as adornment.

As I grew older and became more aware of my inheritance, attending church and upholding the Christian faith became increasingly confusing and unbearable. I just couldn't reckon the concept of a wombless trinity. I concluded that a womanless trinity was intellectually, instinctively and intuitively unreasonable. For me, the absence of the feminine in any concept of origin renders it fruitless and therefore finite, incomplete and undoubtedly insufficient, so I left the church altogether.

My mother and Nana ache over my absence in church. What's ironic about their dismay is that they are greatly responsible for my discontent with organized religion, and I honor and thank them for this. All that has created, guided, disciplined and nurtured me has come from them, the spirit-callers, the root workers, the crafters, the healers, the protectors, and keepers of the gateway to life.

My new spiritual language and imagery now include the feminine as an essential element of creation. I use language that affirms the feminine divine like Great Mother, and surround myself with images that reflect male and female energy in balance, connected in love and purpose. My spiritual revelation blossomed fully when I was finally able to recognize divine energy as that which generates in me the ability to live, to love and to give life.

My presence and my voice are no longer limited by the emotional and spiritual bondage of a community steeped in patriarchal doctrine based on the limitations of external power. Belief systems that impute and reinforce concepts of a male-only source of creation through the sole reference of that source as "he" and other male-centered descriptions, imagery and practices while relegating the concept of the divine feminine to either virgin mothers or conniving seductresses do not serve to connect us, male nor female, to the full wonder of creation.

Everything and everyone is made in God's image reflecting both the flow of the river and the smoothing of stone. Recognizing myself as divinely inspired, I don't want my daughter to wonder if it is true that woman was created as an afterthought. She attends church with her grandmother and great-grandmother almost every Sunday, so she too may face a confusing spiritual path, but I don't worry much about that because I embody the souls of wise-women with their private and peculiar blend of African Amerindian spirituality: crucifixes and candles, cowry shells and crystals, feathered stones and family bibles, holy hymns and healing hands, beating drums and breaking bread, sacred chants and sweet offerings, moon time and mezuzahs.

My salvation is remembrance. I shall have eternal life through the sacred act of remembering and passing on the truth of who I have always been—one in a continuum of wild daughters—questioning laws, eating forbidden fruit and consorting with snakes in the garden of all beginnings. These things I will pass on to my daughter as they were passed on to me.

Carol Smith Passariello

Antoinette Pressley-Sanon—**3 Market Women** watercolor on paper

When SHE Carried
a **Calabash**
for Katherine Dunham

They said the calm calabash will spill
I say the calm calabash will spill

There was no particular destination
these vines crawled
generously
defying gravity up
the textured wall up
la mata de paraíso
magically opening a venous path
curled like a juju-man's caduceus
un baston de Babalawo
Ifá ni Eromasunka- Hiinn
Mo ni Eromasunka- Hiinn

Subtle
hammocked below dense leaves
propped proudly
the amber calabash
(Not so many know
it was used to house the first lantern-
she packed it with nutmeg & myrrh
the herbs of maravilla & marilope
orozus romerillo rosemary
red palm oil spilled for fuel
She lit the path to the river
when they traveled from island to island
thirsty

Down the Tamiami Canal
she carried the calabash down Calle Ocho
beginning en los Everglades
balanced between braids & brass beads

she embraced with both hands
down the coral-lined trench
the muddy gun range
the erratic awkwardly placed sprawl
the concrete overpass
down the storefronts
the successive botánicas
the nostalgic cafés
with the thick ting of Chapotín's trumpet
snuggled by fertile matas de coco
she danced wave-like down NE 2nd avenue
diggin' the golden brown murals of the
days when boogie-woogie & big-band proclaimed the actual
story
like Melton with the crescent embouchure
Through Wynwood
still on NE 2nd
todo el mundo swiveling hips
frying bacalaitos
waves of abichuelas blooped
al son de Tito's timbal
Giovanni's secret hand
Eddy Gua-gua's cruise down baby bass harmony
When she carried a calabash in Buena Vista
only her named changed
Erzuli po' mago
they said through the clewon
the Rara drums walking thick on Bolu's hands
a constant tick-tock of skins jockeying
the echo of Morriseau-Leroi's exiled creolizations
bouncing through the mystical market of language
Ifá ni Eromasunka—Hiinn
Mo ni Eromasunka- Hiinn

And this here is an incantation
a wave arising from breath into sound into word
a wave altering the invisible like
when lovers kiss below a flowering canopy
Ifá ni Eromasunka- Hiinn
Mo ni Eromasunka- Hiinn

Now turning her way back home
she carried a calabash back home
down to the Oletta River
She stopped for the children of Abeng
those Jamaican conch blowers
who notified fish
wise fish of freedom
in an ancient tone she knew—
everyone was home
now
She collected some of our objects of sound
In the end
laced them side by side ensnaring them
In the end—
a net circling the calabash which when shaken
would sound of a call—
Ifá ni Eromasunka—Hiinn
Mo ni Eromasunka- Hiinn

They said the calm calabash will spill
I say the calm calabash will spill

Adrian Castro

The Eyes That Never Left Mine

As usual the Daladal was filled to capacity with people just getting off from work. This time of the day in Dar-es-Salaam gives new meaning to the word "chaotic." The blaring horns and the site of people trying to cross the street before possibly being run down by a gari or basi almost makes me laugh. Especially when the nearly injured pedestrian starts yelling obscenities to the drivers of these vehicles traveling along these dusty, badly paved roads. Each bump the basi drives over intensifies the soreness of my already overly fatigued body. At least today I was able to grab a seat. Usually, by the time I board it, the Daladal is beyond being overcrowded.

Passengers who are either sitting or standing make the decades old vehicle look like an over-stuffed dresser drawer with each person fighting to claim his or her own space. After years of riding it, I am no longer bothered by the various body odors emanating from all corners of the bus. Nor am I overly irritated by the leers and flirtatious gestures from the mabwana who seem to be all around me. For me it goes with the territory of living in Dar-es-Salaam, of being a Tanzanian bibie. This overcrowded bus is just a microcosm of what goes on outside of it. Across from me sits a man who often comes into the health clinic where I work. Wearing what looks to be a new pair of American blue jeans and a glaringly white t-shirt—the exact opposite of his near ebony colored skin—this bwana more than likely has HIV, an ongoing crisis here in the city and throughout Tanzania. Upon making eye contact with me, he gives a slight smile and then turns away. His eyes say everything that his mouth does not. That he is sick and if a cure is not found he will die from this disease.

Before I can say "kwaheri ya kuonana" to him he gets off of the bus. No sooner than I can blink my eyes, his empty space is filled by a gentleman who pulls out his copy of the newspaper *Nipashe*. As a nurse at the clinic, I see similar cases everyday. Most of the people who visit come in after months and months of feeling sick. Oftentimes when the symptoms are described: diarrhea, swollen lymph nodes, extreme fatigue, I already know what the cause is, but for fear of offending the patient who perhaps is already in denial about what is going on, I would remain silent. Silent just like many other Africans who believe that not talking about "it" will make the problem just go away, disappear like many of the shunned HIV/AIDS victims whose families want nothing more to do with them and their sickness for fear that such a revelation will bring shame upon their family. Not surprisingly, the other nurses, doctors and counselors at the health clinic remain in denial too. I will admit that until a few weeks ago I was the same way. That is until a mama brought her msichana who looked no older than 7 years of age to the clinic to be examined as to the cause of her child's symptoms.

By this time, the illness had obviously taken its physical toll on the deep coffee brown child whose sunken eyes and underweight frame revealed more than any story could tell (and if the truth be known, I believe that the mother was infected with the virus as well). Bursting into the clinic she yelled "nusuru msichana wangu!" The cry to help her child alarmed most of us who were winding down from an already long day at the clinic. After one of the doctors agreed to see the child and examine her, he sympathetically advised the mother to immediately admit her into the hospital, for our clinic could not provide the little girl with the care that she needed. With tear-filled eyes, the mother carried her daughter out of the building. Two weeks later the girl died. Not that this was any different from many of the other cases that I've seen, but there was something about this that caused me to lose sleep at night. Tossing and turning so much that mume wangu mpenzi shared in the suffering of my bouts with sleeplessness. Yes, my husband also became a victim of my insomnia problem. But I could not help it; there are just some things that cannot leave your mind. Perhaps it was the desperate look in the mother and daughter's eyes. Looks so hauntingly pleading it seemed as if they were trying to hypnotize me into handing them a cure. Yet we all knew it would have taken way more than that to make their problem go away. Ever since the day that I heard the girl succumbed to her sickness, I have committed myself to learning everything I can about HIV/AIDS and how I can make a change to educate my people. Whenever time allows, I go into one of the many cyber-cafes sprouting up throughout the city and read any website about this dreadful disease. It is my hope to be informed enough to pass along what I've learned to those in the clinic and outside of it. The willingness to change paves the way for actual change not silence. I think of this every time I envision the desperate gaze of the msichana whose deeply-set eyes never left mine, and the bwana with the stark white t-shirt and American jeans.

Angela Hodison-Malele

Through **It All**

It is not enough to say that I want to live
If there is a part of me, breathing and acting,
That secretly wants me to die
That leads me to felonious acts of lovemaking
In ways that cause me to cry out
From the guilt of pleasure
The subtle pressures of suicide

It is too often that my phone conversations
Are listings of friends who have passed
And those that are being frightened to death
Too scared to admit that their protruding bones
Are not the result of oral surgery
Their mottled skin not some severe lashing out
Of post-pubescent gay acne

It is heinous knowing that I and my company
Are like starving, beaten dogs
When faced with the idea of living
Seizing our days like neckbones and rotting pork
Too reticent to plan our lives beyond five years
Because we know what we have done
And with whom—may they rest in peace.

They, them and these are the greater part of my world
A place alive with hiding, seeking and needing
A fiction where hot touches are love
When the eyes are closed
Wholeness confused with being greedy,
Momentary and masked as we search subconsciously
For the hugs of distant fathers in disguise.

It is not enough, I know, to whimper "Someone, save me!"

role call

As I thrust against a lover's naked dick
I know in my heart it's the tiny child who prays for death
Because he's simply tired of hurting
Himself and the other boys in the bushes
Who learned better to tear than to mend,
To let die than to save one another through healing.

It is heinous knowing that through it all
Melancholy has been my madness
So much searching and wishing to be free
Climbing walls and scaling fences
Only to discover there is little room for love in my eyes
Since shame has been seated there longer than I knew
How society had hidden and killed me.

G. Winston James

Vellum

All torturers should write books
on how fingers can be curled into vices,

on the exact location of joints
in relation to a well-oiled machine,

on how to use pressure
to loosen tongues.

As writers formulate plots
using certain devices to best effect,

upon reflection, torturers should
direct their attention

to ensuring their details are correct
before writing the stories

of their victims—for perspective.

Danielle Legros Georges

A **REAL** Place

How Many are Swinging

HERE
  where it is very quiet
  a real place
Now it is very quiet   now he is no longer crying   now we are listening again   listening and listening   for yes he is talking   talking again about what happened   down
there in that place   so very far to the south and green   green with mountains with
rivers   where the people look like him   like us where the farmers fall off their fields
onto the mountains where the cattle still are lowing in the fires   and the people are
burning   and the trees are red like the sea   endless red like the sea   those rivers
endless to the sea   filled with the people burnt in the trees   filled with their hands
down there   so far away   so close   the memory   he is telling us   what happened to
the people   inside   outside   everywhere   a real place

Because yes he says I remember   remembering now but even now not wanting to
remember   there were so many different noises   the sound of cattle in the fields
the sound of children in the schoolyards   that came before they were in the trees
hanging black and red in the trees   and the televised executions and the bayonets
tearing inside   things you cannot remember   things you must not remember
the stench of flesh burning on the hillside   the ashes of hands in the earth   and
the smoke   and the screams   always the screams   and the sea

It is a whisper

I would like to remember the sound of hummingbirds
that sound   I would like
that noise
again
a whirr
and the color

there is nothing like it in nature

Now he is no longer crying   but yes he says once I was crying it was just that one
time in the room   the room where they brought you to answer questions   always
questions   that room always the shouting   that room   that smelled of rats and excrement   where the people were screaming   crying   choking a real place

A red river on the floor there
where the spiders were sleeping

red   sleeping

The room   always so dark   always so hot and the shouting in between the kicks and
the burns   always the shouting   we were swinging upside down there   the blind-
folds over our eyes the excrement smeared on our mouths   the red river that
smelled like skin   skin so soft before the burns   old people's skin   ours   the room
where they were going inside us inside us with their guns and their hands   always
shouting inside us with the pushing part that tears   when you tear you become part
of the red river   down   down down   you are tearing   down   down down   you are
screaming   but it's all right   all right they say all right   even when you're drowning
they bring you up again   they bring you around for more you learn   even when
you're drowning   swinging   you must swallow them   taste them   like excrement
taste them in the red

You tear forever then

And she   the little girl   she was screaming   in the next room she was screaming
saying stop   stop please   she was screaming they were going inside her with a cactus   then themselves

What you can't remember
what you have to remember
it is

Because memory he says   that is all of it and the end   the all of all life and feeling
where you live   where you die suspended   not like when you're swinging   that kind
of suspension   swinging upside down   your hands tied behind you   your face in
the piss bucket   it is not like that   the memory takes you away from it   even as they
prepare to go inside you   to open you up to the tearing parts   the memory it takes
you away   back to the time before their hands   before their guns and the tearing
parts

That's what I most want to remember he says   that time before them   was there
ever a time before them   when we lived simply beneath the sun   the sun on our
backs and we   alive and feeding the goats and cattle and we   tending the earth in
the highest hills   thinking there could be nothing more to any of it than the sea and
the sky   another place

The sound of hummingbirds
that whirr

That was before they came   they had been there before and had never left   that was
the truth   they had never left   always one of them behind an election   always one of

them planning an assassination   yet another siege   but that had never touched the
people in the hills   the people who held their goats and slept on leaves   the people
who knew the worth of pigs   will never touch us we thought   we're not important
enough   we   too much of the earth   we thought   another coup   another execution
and we'll still be here we thought   like the sea and the sky   ageless   still here

The sea has a blank face   not sometimes but always   its face is blank   telling you
nothing you can truly remember   the rivers flowing into it are red   now it is crying
and choking on excrement   choking on the bodies that have no faces   they are dark
swollen   have no faces   all of them are crying without their faces   the sea drives salt
into their wounds   the last place where the redness shows

If you walk into it it will tell you   it's all right to die   it will tell you   it told us when
we were swinging   our hands tied behind us   we were swinging   the electric shocks
and still we were swinging   the shit in our mouths and we were swinging even the
barbed wire beatings on our backs   we were swinging I didn't swing only once
when they cut me down and did that to me   nice and tight they said and   laughing
and filling my throat and   one by one they laughed and   too much to remember
when they open you up and   by that time you're already dead   in the sea   in the red
choking   you have no face   no throat   no hands

None of them who beat you are faces   only voices   always shouting   you hear their
voices so full of questions with the shouting   so full of   spit   always shouting   asking who you know and the shouting   who did this   and the shouting who went there
who signed this   who's working with this one   with that one   who is conspiring
who betraying even if you tell them lies still they go inside you   there are no stories
that are enough   you can't tell them you know only of goats   can't tell them that
when you're swinging   nothing is ever enough

Now the goats are burning on the hills
I see them

burning

the goats and the shacks

Now there can be no memory there

it was a real place
with faces   people
now it can be   nothing
ashes
no place

But yes he says   he who is I says   you don't have to touch me I'm all right   you don't
have to   touch   please do not touch no nor smile either   no smiles   not ever

Now he is no longer crying   now I am no longer   I can talk about her he says   I say
my mother   dead   now dead I am   she   I can talk about her   I   I can talk

I am talking

I can remember her   I can

She was the one there

The one I said was the little girl screaming   yes it was her   I'm fine you don't have
to touch me   please   don't   I'm sorry I was pretending   please forgive me   I was
pretending   there were so many little girls there screaming   so many of them
swinging upside down   screaming when I heard that voice yes   that voice   I started
to pretend

not her not her I said

Not her   not her   not in that room I said   no   they aren't going inside her   they
aren't putting a cactus into her   they aren't putting the tearing parts into her   I was
upside down swinging   the rope was hurting my arms   swinging   I was pretending
but the sea said yes   yesyes   it was her

That was another time they cut me down   not the others   just me   cut me down
we're going inside her now they said move it you son of a bitch they said   nice and
tight like a   why don't you watch us open your mother   open her way up in the twat
that might loosen your tongue a little bit they said   they were smiling   but I
couldn't speak I   had no face

It was all the sea
it was the river   it was
a real place

And she was screaming   hanging upside down she was screaming   when the first
one cut her down and went in her from behind she was screaming   you'll have to
break her jaw they said   and still she was screaming   beat her with the barbed wire
billy club they said and still she was   screaming   and the red river came pouring out
of her   out of her mouth out of her nostrils   she was in the river with a red face they
had only the voices left   she was opened up   gone

That was my mother

Why am I laughing   that's what the dead do isn't it they laugh the dead go dancing
on the sea and forget things   it's all right now you don't have to touch me   I'm dead
now you don't have to   touch   still I remember her river   I wish I could go on pretending forever   I wish I could   say it was another little girl they were tearing   I
wish I knew the currents of that sea it feels so good against the skin   against the
faceless face   when all you have left are the bones   and the sky

Now it is very quiet   now again he is remembering   he who is I is remembering   I
have to take back my face from the river now I am no longer crying   now we no
longer are   now instead we are walking   millions of us or more   walking across the
sea   across time and   out of that dream   out of that room   above the fields   above
the burning and the trees wetting our faces in the river   the red water is all you have
to drink   all you have to   take   the salt feels good in your wounds   it closes you up
where they went inside   where they opened   yes   I remember   a real place   down
there   where I came from   where I came from I say   that place of rivers and fields
and mountains   where still the machine guns are tearing the skin   another coup
another country   another man killing people in the national palace   only why is it
our people   why is it always   we

Now it is very quiet he says   I say   quiet   I want it to be for once   one time   very
quiet   listening to the silence   the memory   I might still have another chance   I
might not be dead yet   maybe there is still time to die   then the time to live   I think
that's right   it must be   must be   right   yes   I'm all right   all right I say don't
mind me   I'm trying hard not to remember   still   trying hard to remember   what
didn't happen   what always happens   down there   a real place   because look   do
you see   now I see them again   all of them   I see them   me   we   burning in the
hills   in the trees   and the soldiers   coming down again with the guns and now
now I say   the memory is not dead   we are not dead I say   in the memory she is not
the girls and the men but listen   you have to listen   you will hear it   yes   hear it
the soldiers   the guns   the fire   opening again   inside and now you can tell me
can anyone tell us   all of us   where is the truest memory   where is the death and
the sea   is it right here   inside   where they've already gone inside   where the spirit
sings and dies   O the spirit   singing   dying   the life and the creation   or is it still
there   down there   outside   inside   in that place so far away   so close   where
there are rivers and mountains   outside   inside   where there is red   outside
inside   down there   so far away   close   where they are tearing   where now again it
is very quiet now and always   here   all around   listen   it is quiet   in the sea   in
the river   in the red   the memory   the silence   outside   inside   where the spirit
swings   where it dies   where we all are swinging   all around   swinging   yes listen
now   we are here   all of us   swinging   a dark room   a red river   inside our lives
inside   in   always   a real place

Thomas Glave

Pest

I heard the terrible laughter of termites
deep inside a spray-painted wall on Sharswood.
My first thought was that of Swiss cheese
hardening on a counter at the American Diner.
My second thought was that of the senator
from Delaware on the Senate floor.
I was on my way to a life of bagging tiny mountains,
selling poetry on the corners of North Philly,
a burden to mothers & Christians.
Hearing it, too, the cop behind me shoved me
aside for he was an entomologist
in a former lifetime & knew the many
song structures of cicadas, bush crickets &
fruit flies. He knew the complex courtship
of bark beetles, how the male excavates
a nuptial chamber & buries himself—
his back end sticking out till a female sang
a lyric of such intensity he squirmed like a Quaker
& gave himself over to the quiet history
of trees & ontology. All this he said while
patting me down, slapping first my ribs, then
sliding his palms along the sad, dark shell
of my body.
                              How lucky I was
spread-eagled at 13, discovering the ruinous cry
of insects as the night air flashed reds
& blues, as a lone voice chirped & cracked
over a radio; the city crumbling. We stood
a second longer sharing the deafening hum
of termites, back from their play & rest,
till he swung suddenly my right arm then my left.

Major Jackson

statement on the killing of
patrick dorismond

a petty hoodlum (cop) shot/killed suspect (blackman) after hoodlum (pig) was told by suspect (haitian) that he (junglebunny) was not a drug dealer (nigga). the police commissioner (bounty hunter) referred to suspect (coon) as a "lowlife" (african) though his (aryan) comments were later proven false (white lies). the shooting (genocide) is the third (pattern) in thirteen months (institution) in which plain-clothes officers (gestapo) shot/killed an unarmed man (cheap blood). "i would urge (doubletalk) everyone (oprah) not to jump (dead nigga) to conclusions (acquittals)," mayor guiliani (watchdog) said, "and to allow (blind faith) the facts (ethnic cleansing) to be analyzed (spin) and investigated (puppets) without people (darkies) trying to let their biases (racial profiling), their prejudices (welfare queen), their emotions (fuck tha police), their stereotypes (o.j.) dictate the results (status quo)."

Quraysh Ali Lansana

Bone Memories

1. Bazaar (Dakar, Senegal)
Sendaga Market is a vortex, a black hole
trapping light. Thirty vendors swirl around
you, clockwise and counter, until you are
dizzy with negotiation and otter,

until bazin and bouba, silk and satin
are mainsails dragging crosses to
America. They would sell you the shirt
sweated to your belly and back, these men

who speak one hundred languages and will
exchange francs and marks, dollars and yen,
who take CIFAs against their bodies
like offertory papers, like passports

to Paris or passages to heaven.
Curry-colored dust peppers tears into
pearl-sized drops and their spittle salt sores.
Outside, buzzards have found a seal not yet

dead, but they jab and jook until it froths
with salt and old blood, until it caws
for air, surrender drying in its throat.
They would sell you the flies out of its

teeth, the pus welling in children's eyes,
and the tadpole-like children themselves.
They will sell you polio and amputations,
then tell you that you are welcome, brother,

returning from the no return—in through
the out-door—not a ghost, but upright with
a shadow. How about some pretty pictures,
made from glued-together butterfly wings?

2. Bruised Wind (Cockpit Country, Jamaica)

Into some jagged hurt indented
into the face of the mountain,
into some volcano pucker
which fixed so when it caught cold,

the moans did not come back
but left me here, in blood of the sun
and mournful rustle of trees,
retching, and seared as the dry leaves

dampened into Belafonte's throat.
Later, through a skein of spider-webs,
through the stitching hieroglyph
of cedar and sycamore bowing

to and fro, one hears them bat-hanging
between crags up in Cockpit Country,
dangling old rags and tatters—scarecrow
and bruised wind hosting duppies.

Through ribbon mist and smoke of some
cinnamon cooking, through whip-smacked wails
and chalk-boarding fingernails, swallowed
cries bound back now, unwearied, though

homed in the valley for a long- long
time—back in the muffled porch, with Niobe
weeping. And yet still not voiceless for
these stones cry on—these rocks cry out.

3. War-Bride (Queens, New York, 1990)

War-bride, without the battle
and without the wedding.
Her throat straitened in an iron ring,
the harder to tilt her hard head in.

War-captive spitting up blood

and semen ashy as grounded bones
as wolves turn over in their mud and muck
and wind blisters on in a brutal drone.

War-booty, oiled in the slapping
and beaten till skin slackens,
retched and stretched to a trembling cord,
riding red down the zodiac.

All she wanted was a pause
in that jig-jag, grunt-runt carriage,
the knife was not to gut him
just to null and void the marriage.

And the bite was just to zip up throats
chafing low in heavy battery,
the carved-out tongue a way
of hushing force-fed flattery.

And these shriveled implements,
desecrated earthworms and clothesline sausages
dangling like stringy earrings that show body
in the hair of his warrior-hostage.

And now that he is scattered powder
all loosestrife seeds and dustgrain gall,
she says that he now can claim he knows her
as wife and booty after all.

5. Grunt (Lakesie & Clarendon, Chicago)

Through drywall and plaster of paris,
through crumpled paperflesh and sunken wood-
binding, two rammers wade in the groan
of gored bulls, sloshing galoshes

in the muddy death-moan of a busted
throat, slapping and flailing in bony seethe.
And one edges to calling the cops

for spackling heaves with ritual

sacrifice. The floor tremble now
with a hollow hoofing, head-butt walls
squirting no, no. And closer as
the Taurus shakes, heavier as

the snorting sinks, one thinks to call
the ASPCA. Metal
chains clank and one sees them: stockyard
shadows lugging buckets of butchery

downtown, their side horses chewing steel
and neighing in the gelding meat that
will feet a hungry city. Another
thundering thud, another groan pulled

like tapeworm from the rectum up
through intestines, ripping into spleen
and arresting the lung—air breaks out
in hard wheezing until it kicks off

the tongue, curdling, then melting like mist
off a pane. In this room, in bass-rumbling,
lip-trembling knocks, the grunts pin me up
against wood-concrete, hard stones

bouncing off in orbit around my beaded
head, flint flickering fast. Slowly out
the window the lashing flutters down:
the beasts have drowned eating bog, blood

racing out of their tails; the butcher
has unzipped the belly, eyes rolled-up
in off-white moons. Somebody better
bring soap and some scrubbing towels.
The wet walls hang with slaughter.

Rohan B Preston

339

You Pay for What You Get,
But You Never Get
What You Pay For

Brooklyn-bound
and I left my heart uptown
with a Mexican mango sculptor.
I should have known
something was wrong
when Satan stopped
singing the blues
in front of the museum.

The queen of Sugar Hill
slipped into a new canopy
in the middle of the night
and ran off with the councilman
who never took his eyes
off the prize.
The next morning
buses disguised
as historic neighborhood tours
came and stole all her brownstones.
A homeless man went to see
if there were any leftovers.
He walked by a silver-studded prophet
who was standing at the corner, roaring,
pointing to a star that had six points
and the homeless man said,
Shit, even if God
did have an afro,
I still ain't got nowhere to live.
The corners have been
taken over by corn-row hustlers
and kente cloth syndicates
who refer to black people
as "you people".
Coffee chains, t-shirt clubs,
and ringing taco bells

got the magazines saying
that communities are safe and clean,
but the other day I kissed a girl
who was carrying a monster
and didn't even know it.

Wrecking balls are winding up,
aimed at the heads of housing projects.
The world is turning baggy
with brand names
and producers are being trained
in hip-hop speak
so they can keep it real.
There's an invisible billboard
on the side of the state office building.
It's a promotion for the platinum-selling single,
You don't have to go home,
but you got to get the fuck out of here.
The sidewalks on Lenox Avenue
are getting so small
you can hear whispers like
whatever happened
to that bookstore on the corner?
And a the homeless man
points to a gate and says,
like the sign says, post no bills,
for more information call the owner.

Brooklyn-bound
and I left my heart uptown
with a Mexican mango sculptor.
Now that the blues
Done gone
It's time to call
those poets who used to have bullets
stashed in their notebooks
because profit is being made
on top of plight
so they would step to the mic
and put one in us

Willie Perdomo

HUMAN-**Murderers**

they outlawed the drum
        still our hearts haven't
        stopped beating
living on the outside under
minimum security

it is hard to stand
on our wounds in flood
of alcohol and not scream
when you've seen
the shrapnel from the enemy
hit your children

and you haven't wiped
the dripping afterbirth off
their screaming faces

Theodore A. Harris

Theodore A. Harris–**We Wear Our Flesh Like Flames** collage

Hannan Saleh—**Girl in Flames** black and white silver

Death by Marriage

For the 10 Women Murdered by Their Husbands in Bangalore, India

after two decades of shallow breathing and silent footsteps, the fire consumed them. burned the innocence from their smiles. swallowed their sacred terror of impending i do. whole. hiding in one hundred and fifteen degree tears. this husband scribbled a memory into the hearts of their grieving parents. a river of blood screaming torture from knuckles and brooms. a generation of hope drowned in a flask of kerosene. the charge; an unfulfilled dowry. the punishment: death. mere arguments settled in flames and accidental poisoning. did she laugh at freedom bathing in the blue-orange heat? did her spirit rise above the human cauldron she was swimming in, with the belief that she had finally won?

Ta'Shia Asanti

The Runaways

I.

Hot runway dust stirred around shiny black shoes. wingtips and high heels shuffled along the line impatiently wanting to arrive in a world where they could dance and twirl on golden pavements. White ankle socks carried the soil from a world that was ending.

Men wearing Sunday's best anxiously handed their passports to the sweaty, brown-faced inspector. "The purpose of you' travel?"

To join my husband who 'as work and a place to live." The Inspector handed Agnes back her passport and she carried me onto the plane.

The women of my family buried my umbilical cord under the avocado tree. Planting my connection to a root I would not know again for twenty years. I was going to miss that tree where they lay me every day after my feedings.

Mum was happy to meet her childhood friend Darling, in the boarding line. She, like many other single women on the flight, wanted a piece of baby. My feet never touched the ground once in-between arriving here and leaving there.

When we landed there was snow on the ground. Our dark skin shivered against the icy white blanket. Dancing feet numbed at the extraordinary sight of frozen rain flakes falling from the black starless sky.

Our glow dimmed under the cold stares from unwelcoming immigration and customs officers, who pulled apart our hopes: stuffed barrels and suitcases bound with thick leather belts.

"You people are supposed to speak English. Show me your papers. Why are you here?"

The answer seemed so simple then. Nevertheless, over time we repeatedly asked ourselves the same question, like a mantra, without answer. We spoke English, our own indestructible lilt clipping the edges off "proper English" like a sharp machete against sugar cane.

II.

Every moment seeming real becomes temporary,
Like shadows changing shape,
Falling short of long drawn expectation.
Faces smash against walls built by limited
Beliefs about how far each soul can reach.
Like bonsai trimmed to augment another's design.

III.

It was dad's big day; he was showing off his brand new sun yellow '63 Ford pickup truck. Its shiny soft curves made us feel rich, but mum was not pleased. He used all the money he had from selling his jukebox bar business in Jamaica to buy it. Mum wanted him to buy us a house; she needed the security of walls that she owned around her. Want to never again beg racist people for a slum to rent. I held mum's hand as we walked in our new alien neighborhood, Brixton: a place West Indian immigrants live die.

Strange white men in sting vests looked to our difference with hostility. Why did they hate us so much? My first steps in this New World, slipped on frigid concrete molded in fear.

IV.

"Nigger go home!"

My mother and aunt stood their ground, protected me like towering oaks. Mum did not miss a beat. Her retort came in the Queens English.

"The only Nigger around here is under your mother's skirt."

For a moment time stood still. I thought mum might get us murdered. But the speechless youth slithered back into the shadows; scared away by the viper-tongued, four-foot-nine Indian women. On that day we shook off the soil saved in the crevices of our toes.

V.

We have no roots
to anchor our childhood joy.
Clarity fades.

Deep inside incidents spring,
breaking through the chrysalis,
one mighty stretch at a time.

New eyes see the world in spring green
old enclosures snap apart.
Rising to new heights,

we experience a forgotten substance.
Invisible secretions outside the average
constructs incinerate passion.

In the slow emergence of life
boundless wonders touch
infinite possibility like birds

who fly just because. Existing outside,
dislodged by waves of horror, dredged
up in the ebb and flow of life.

VI.

Dad put an extra shine on the already-sparkling side-view truck mirror, parked outside our mouse-ridden tenement flat. The next morning he went outside to resume his dream of being a contractor, an idea ahead of its time...but it was not there... they had stolen the truck.

The meager walls crumbled around us leaving us standing naked. Our reveries, turned into nightmarish aberrations from which we longed to be awakened. How they laugh at us now over pints of beer bought with broken dreams down at the local pub.

VII.

Years ago I swallowed a pebble the size of an eye,
it grew over time to the size of an apple.
Now the large object is lodged in my gut,
In the same way, I saw him that day.
The stranger, whom strangers ran to
for the fixing up of broken parts.
Meanwhile, I watched him snap apart
from the inside out.

VIII.

The optimism in my father's face dimmed and dis-ease in his heart slowly and quietly set in. Coldness numbed Mum's optimism, and bitterness at life's cruel hand set in. And I become invisible through their pain at two.

XI.

His face waxed and unwrinkled,
stretched tightly around his head,
awaiting burden-less-ness of the dead.
Where relief of belonging never comes
for the foreigner in a foreign land.

Marilyn Fleming

The List GROWS

They sent you back by boat
to a familiar shore,

your son and daughter with you,
your wife had passed safely.

You hid first in Mirebalais,
then in Port-au-Prince

where they arrested you,
disappeared you for two days.

Yvon Desanges, I know only
of your voyage,
and your image after:

your brow missing each eye
your mouth without its tongue
your left ear lost to a field,

your face mined. Your face
remains beautiful

and blazes to lay bare
your faceless assassins

who could not disfigure you.

Danielle Legros Georges

Note: Yvon Desanges—a 27-year-old youth organizer and vocal supporter of the democratic movement in Haiti, murdered in the spring of 1994 in Port-au-Prince.

Theodore A. Harris—**Resistance to Repression** collage

Free Trade, Free Cuba

I always thought the most popular drink on the island just south of Miami would be the rum and Coke Cuba libre, or Free Cuba. While visiting Cuba legally, unlike most of the 100,000 Americans who visit the island per year, I found that tourists at least tend to quaff the minty *mojito*.

Despite widespread evidence that the U.S. embargo against Cuba is out of line with our global policies, Bush administration officials don't seem inclined to lift travel and trade bans anytime soon, especially since our opposition to Cuba may have been a factor in the US being voted off of the United Nations Human Rights Commission, in May 2001.

America has built what techies might call a financial firewall against Cuba, one of our closest neighbors and the former site of all sorts of glitzy Americano gangster mayhem. After all, there's the Helms-Burton blocking trade with Cuba. It includes a provision that hasn't yet been enacted, allowing lawsuits in the U.S. against the European firms busy pumping billions into joint Cuban enterprises. They, of course, could choose to countersue us. But while we bar trade with Cuba, we are trying to give U.S. businesses a leg up with the Free Trade summit on Latin America.

Trade rights are a fickle thing. America rails against Cuban human rights

abuses, but we trade with China, which harvests the organs of executed prisoners, some of which may have, according to a recent investigation by the Village Voice, ended up in American bodies. We trade with Burma, which has put a Nobel Prize-winner under arrest, and with countries that do not allow women the vote. And we've staged several unsuccessful assassination attempts against Castro. But despite the pleas of the agriculture sector, among others, trade with Cuba remains among the most restricted in the world, affecting not just luxury items but basic foodstuffs and even medicines.

The effect on the flow of people is the most profound. A couple of million Americans, both Cuban expats and tourists, would likely flock to the island if the embargo were lifted. Somehow, an increasing number of Americans are ducking under the fading red curtain of the embargo—which Cuban officials call the "blockade."

In Cuba's capital last week, I met fresh-faced New Englanders who were spending a semester abroad at the University of Havana. Then a friend in New York told me her son's school, a public school, did a week exchange in Cuba. "I wish they went for longer," she said. And at the glitzy Hotel Nacional, where wealthy Cubans bring their daughters for quincinera photographs and foreigners smoke Cohibas and drink rum, photographs of Che and Fidel hang on the wall across from photographs of Naomi Campbell and Francis Ford Coppola.

This is not Nirvana, to say the least. Some of the tourists come especially for the jiniteras, or the women and men whose range of special services slide on a payment scale. As the Soviet Union collapsed, so did the Cuban economy. Only recently have ordinary Cubans, according to government statistics, begun again eating enough food to keep them alive. And, as a Habañero named Julio Cesar put it, "An American and a Cuban are having a fight about democracy. The American says, "I can go to the White House, knock on the door, ask for George W. Bush, and tell him what I think about him. The Cuban says, `Yes, it

is the same. I can go to the Plaza de Revolution, knock on the door, ask for Fidel, and tell him what I think about George W. Bush.'"

One official said the government was examining the impact of the tourist economy on their dream of what the French think of as liberte, egalite, fraternite. In America, we prize liberty—you can walk down the street naked covered in chocolate spinkles, but don't ask for health care. In Cuba, they prize egalite. Every neighborhood has a doctor. Of course, she or he is paid $20 U.S. per month, and has few medicines with which to treat patients, due in part to the ramifications of U.S. policy. Nonetheless, the Cuban infant mortality rate is lower than America's, and their literacy rate is higher.

America could learn something from Cuba. And Cuba, which has often been portrayed as being too proud or too foolhardy to change, is certainly learning something from America.

Farai Chideya

Theodore A. Harris—**Our Bones Have Numbers on Them** collage

Ten Pound Draw

On my first trip to London
I learned that the best way to see the city
Is from the top
of a red double-decker bus
If you want to be loved
on the first night
in more than one position
you have to promise
to be a gentleman
and help
with the cooking

On my second trip to London
I learned that the best way
to get your smoke on
was to first
find out
where the dark faces live
and ride the Underground
to Brixton Station
as always you find
that the dark faces
live at the end of the line

When I reach the exit
at the top of the escalator
I am greeted by acid jazz
and a trail of sandalwood incense
A scented oil peddler
with tinted blue sun glasses
talks into his cell phone
being righteous
might be his hobby
The black girls
The black girls
The black girls
on the block
smile and insist
that I'm Pakistan
Afghan
anything but

Nuyorican
so I talk como
like this
y como like that
y como like kikireecoo
tan linda
and no doubt
it's all good
right now
I am all of that
if you want me to be
but do you know where
I can find a ten pound draw?

I saw Roger in Reading
and he said I can't just ask for a dime bag
so I came to where the dark faces live
at the end of the line
where time lags six hours behind
depending on what side of the corner
you stand on
but the black girls on the block
don't know Puerto Rican
so I go to the peddler who can see
the search in my eyes
he sends a call to his brethren
and leads me to the smoke
for a small finders fee
I am willing to take these chances
in spite of the suspicious glances
but just in case
I buy a postcard of Big Ben
and send it to my boys
The Crazy Bunch
back in El Barrio
and write

> *yo, if I don't make it back home*
> *I was thinking about y'all*
> *when I went to this place called Brixton*
> *looking for a ten-pound draw.*

Willie Perdomo

AMERICAN Visa

This country is my co-dependent enabler.
The wife who hides my bottles, gives
credible excuses to my boss and children.
She steamrolls through my consciousness,
seeps in through unguarded gates,
lies prostate, flipping the channels
of my attention repeatedly
back to an esteem-seeking self.

She is not the victim here.

My compliance leaves plenty
of damning, forensic evidence.
She calls the extra rolls of flesh
at my sides (front/back) love handles,
brazenly flaunts a lack of knowledge
of the world outside of herself,
sends me to duel with
my own cavalier attitude,
sits a six shooter solidly
on each plus-sized flank.

Milady faithfully
tells me my station,
where I can get off,
and with whom. She
mispronounces my name
repeatedly while arrogantly
judging my phonetic compass,
while rudely pointing her own
miscalibrated needle in my face,
handing out directions like
one tourist who thinks
she's helping another.

Samiya A. Bashir

Sheila L. Prevost—**Afro-American** oil on canvas

Coming to *AMERICA*

On May 10, 1996, in a cavernous hall at the U.S. District Court located at 450 Main Street in Hartford, Connecticut, in the presence of a judge and a flag of the United States of America, I raised my right hand and, with appropriate solemnity, declared on oath my renunciation and abjuration of "all allegiance and fidelity to any foreign prince, potentate, state or sovereignty of whom or which I have heretofore been a subject or citizen," and other words along the same lines, and when I ended with the phrase, "So help me God," the judge smiled expansively and welcomed me—and many other oath takers—a brand new citizens of the American republic.

The event was deeply moving, in part because it was, for me, colored by paradox, some pain, even ambiguity. Its emotional glow enabled me to travel back in memory to the thoughts and sensations that marked my first encounter with America.

I arrived in this country on December 10, 1988. The Nigerian novelist, Chinua Achebe, had invited me to be the founding editor of an international magazine he and some friends had decided to publish. It was my first extended travel outside of my native Nigeria.

Apart from one suit case, I came loaded with tons of advice, remarkably from people—friends and relatives—who knew little or nothing at all about America. My parents' image of America was of mean streets where swashbucklers held sway, guns drawn, ready to wreak havoc at the slightest provocation—or none at all. (Come to think of it, this image is far less forbidding and misconceived than some Americans' impressions of Africa, including the example of a graduate student who believed that crocodiles ferried Africans across the Atlantic to the shores of North America!).

Devout Catholics, my parents' entreaties were short and direct. Hate and avoid sin. When you succumb to temptation, be quick to go to confession. Attend mass regularly. Say your rosary, faithfully. Never forget the meaning of your name. (Okey, the shortened form of Okechukwu, means one who belongs to God).

One aunt's greatest concern was that I not marry a white woman.

"Don't you think there are good white women?" I teased her.

"Yes," she responded in a serious accent. "Good women can be found in many different places. But goodness is not enough. We want a wife who understands your tongue. A woman who will not let you forget your homestead."

I emerged out of the artificial heat and intimidating vaults of JFK Airport and into the large arrival lounge, hoping to see a man holding up a piece of paper with my name scrawled on it. But the man who was to meet me was nowhere in sight. So, in my first misstep in America, I decided to walk outside and look around. I could not have made a graver mistake. I was embraced by a swirling, growling cold wind. The wind imparted a further chill to the 16-degree temperature. The cold stabbed through the light jacket I wore, for nobody had known enough to warn me that the cold tore through the body like a sharp knife. I ran back into the arrival lounge.

That first experience of the winter cold became an obsession in my first wave of letters home. The only way I could translate the cold for people who, year-round, lived in 80-plus degree temperature was to compare it to living inside a refrigerator!

After an hour's wait, a man approached and asked if I was the editor from Nigeria, then introduced himself as my caretaker for one night. Discombobulated at this time and feeling like abandoned luggage, I was grateful that he had come to claim me. He informed me that I had arrived on one of the year's coldest days. I took it personally. That treacherous gust of winter set my mood for the encounter with America.

The country had decided to welcome me, not with warmth and enthusiasm, but sullenly. I sat still, brooding, while my host drove through the light-suffused night. Taking in the scenes that whirled past, I had the sensation that we were headed into the vast violent belly of New York City. I felt a sharp sense of loss and danger, my chest tautly wound, heavy. The pilgrim's plaintive prayer rose in my mind: Home, sweet home; there's no place like home. I had read somewhere that President John F. Kennedy, following a particularly difficult summit with his Soviet rival, Nikita Kruschev, had declaimed, "It's going to be a long, cold winter," or words to that effect. Suddenly, I understood the archaic anxiety contained in that phrase. I had stepped from my warm, natal home into the friendless frigidity of an alien land.

That, then, was the beginning of my American rite of passage, an adventure which culminated in my adoption of American citizenship. From the outset, a sense of contrast has framed my American experience. I have viewed America through my African sensibility; through it, I sift, weigh, evaluate the multitudinous impulses that I experience in the U.S. everyday.

Much that was painful, hilarious, or humdrum has happened between the day I came to America and the day I became an American.

Ten days after my arrival in the U.S., I was standing at a busy bus stop in Amherst, MA when somebody tapped me on the shoulder. I turned to face a tall, muscle-bound police officer, his body a testament to hours spent in the weight room.

"Sir," he said, "do you mind stepping to the back of the bus stop?"

His very choice of words left me baffled. In Nigeria, no police officer (or anybody wearing any kind of uniform) addressed you as "Sir," or used such polite forms as "Could you..." or "Do you mind..." For a brief moment, then, I thought I had a choice in the matter, that I could say to this officer, "Well, I'm rather in a hurry today. Perhaps we could chat tomorrow." Yet, impressed by what I mistook as a reverential tone, I decided to make his acquaintance right away.

Once at the back of the bus stop, he brought up a business that left me reeling. "There's been a bank robbery," the officer informed me. "And you fit the description. Do you have any identification on you?" I didn't, I told him, because my only form of identification was my Nigerian passport, which I didn't think it wise to carry on my person everywhere I went.

"Do you mind if I frisk you?" he asked. Now the word frisk was not, at the time, part of my vocabulary. But I was savvy enough to know that, despite his seemingly polite tone, my choice in the matter was exactly nil.

"I don't mind," I said in a dread-drenched voice, still wondering what it was I had "permitted" to be done unto me.

The officer requested that I raise my hands, then he patted me down. Firmly convinced that I had no weapons of mass destruction, he put me in the back of his cruiser, then radioed his headquarters to say he had a suspect. He drove to my home where I showed him my Nigerian passport. By some strange means, that sufficed to absolve me. I insisted that the officer drive me back to the bus stop; I wanted the spectators at my arrest to see that I was not, after all, a criminal.

Everywhere I turned, America—Americans—intrigued me. How could people here walk past one another without exchanging a word, rather like dumbstruck waifs? Back in Nigeria, none but the notoriously evil or socially maladjusted lacked for friends. People live and have their being, largely, in a communal space. But in America, I learned of a thing called "personal space," quite highly prized. Seen from the angle of my African cultural background, the idea of a zealously claimed personal space seemed potent with peril, promising isolation, disconnection, pain and alienation. No, my American friends assured me, it's a wonderful zone to inhabit, an inviolable space from which one can "get in tune with oneself." In my mind, getting in tune with oneself is akin to holding oneself in ardent conversation. Now, that's a problem that, even today (twelve years into my sojourn in America), hardly makes sense to me.

I began to hear it seriously stated—by those who, it seemed, should know—that dogs were man's (and woman's) best friend. I had seen many dogs in Nigeria, but they were usually put to purposes less sublime and more practical than friendship, like guarding houses against thieves. One day, to my utter amazement, I heard one woman say to another that she and her husband wanted no kids, but had "two cute cats and a dog." Before then, I had never heard children and pets so brazenly mentioned in the same breath.

Turning on the television, I learned many disillusioning things. I saw talk show guests unabashed about dragging their best friends or family to the most glaring public forum to confess to all manner of secrets, from sleeping with two best friends to lying about their sexual orientation. News telecasts became a gory stew of drive-by shootings, suicides, arsons, assaults. I saw the ubiquitousness of sex; that a woman's body was freely used to sell everything from cars to soup. Watching comedy shows, I wondered if Americans were so humorless they needed to hire third-rate jokers to titillate them.

I became curious about certain idiosyncrasies of American public speech. On the debit side of Americans' impact on language must be added a humbling of words that used to conjure grandness and extraordinariness. I suspect that Americans singlehandedly removed the greatness from the word "great." And the awe from "awesome." I remember the first time I asked somebody "How are you?" and he said, "I'm great!" Great as Alexander the Great, I mused? Or in the tradition of Shaka the Zulu? Great as in an immemorial poem? As in Shakespeare's opus? Another time, somebody told me that a party he went to over the weekend was awesome. I instantly felt sorry that I had missed out on a monumental social event!

Less than a week after my arrival, an African American woman with whom I was discussing the travails and amazements of Africa asked if I had had lunch. When I answered no, she suggested that we go. In my mind I thought: here, my first generous American.

The lunch turned, instead, into a moment of cultural enlightenment, less food in the stomach than food for thought. In Nigeria, anybody who invites you to eat implies an offer to buy you the meal. Owing to that understanding, I had ventured to the restaurant without a dime in my pocket. After eating, we sat talking. Then the waiter, with that unfailing sense of propriety that is their peculiar gift, placed the bill at a spot in the table equidistant between my friend and me.

"We should go," said my friend, pointing to the bill. It must be a strange American custom, I told myself, to require that the beneficiary look at the bill before it was paid. So I peered at the piece of paper for a second or two, then turned to the woman and said, "Thank you."

We talked for a few more minutes, then she announced again that we ought to leave. At my assent, she once more gestured toward the bill. As far as I was concerned, I had fulfilled all my obligations by coming out to eat. Paying for the meal had nothing to do with me. But I already sensed that something was amiss, a small matter of cultural protocol perhaps. Surmising that the bizarre ritual called for me to unambiguously acknowledge my benefactor's kindness, I took the bill in my hands, then made a show of examining it for a few seconds. In the end, I put it down and said to the woman, in my most heartfelt tone, "Thanks for the meal."

Visibly upset by this time, she brought out her own portion of the bill and placed it on the table. "You are responsible for four dollars and seventy-five cents," she announced dourly. "Plus tip." How quickly my eyes opened! She didn't find it funny in the least when I confessed that I had no money on me. Her facial countenance told me all she thought of me—and more: I was the rudest, slyest, most arrogant freeloader in the whole of North America. No, make that in the whole wide world!

When I relayed the story later to a Nigerian friend, he had a good laugh at my expense, then gave a name to my experience. "Americans do Dutch," he said. Unimpressed, I vowed that day to continue to do "Nigerian." Since that day, whenever an American friend has invited me out to eat, I have told this story, and my resolve. Then I give them the option of treating me, or letting me pick up the check. In the interest of full disclosure, I might as well confess that, ninety percent of the time, I have had myself wined and dined at no cost to my wallet. For me, though, it is simply a matter of continuing to do things in a more culturally comfortable way.

The day I became a citizen, several friends rang me to offer their feverish congratulations. But the accent of delight was by no means unanimous. One friend said, in effect, that he hoped it was a good thing. Another asked how I felt inside, and was visibly disappointed when, rather than come up with a monosyllabic exultation, I offered a series of hedges, parenthetical asides, qualified happiness. Another Nigerian friend asked what I would do if Nigeria and the United States were to be at war. Dismissing my answer that I would lend myself as a peace-maker, he insisted that I choose one side or the other. "I don't operate by such bleak prognoses," I said testily.

When I called my mother on the phone and told her my news, she paused in a fashion that suggested a momentary incomprehension. Then, finding her voice, she asked in an anxious vein, "Why?"

Why, indeed. What did it mean, at bottom, that I had become, on that May morning, an American? Did becoming an American require that I "unbecome" a Nigerian? What deep significance was I to attach to the obligation to renounce and abjure all allegiance to my natal country? Had I become, by the fact of acquiring American citizenship, a human slate wiped clean of a set of sentimental, cultural, and experiential data, the better to make room for a new, uniquely American imprimatur? Was Nigeria and all that it meant to me now rendered somewhat ersatz? I wrestled with these questions in the months before I decided to apply for naturalization, a weirdly intriguing word in its own right. I still ask myself the questions today.

With the passage of time, however, the questions have taken on a far less anguished pitch. Perhaps there will never be full, adequate answers to them. But I do know that assumption of American citizenship has hardly vitiated my "Nigerianness," whatever ambiguous meanings that coinage might conjure. Nor has "naturalization" ever demanded of me, in the everyday experience of being an American citizen, that I erase Nigeria in order to enter fully and wholesomely into the patrimony of my American identity.

No, I have been able to cope quite well, even to thrive, by seeing my U.S. citizenship less as an invitation to gain the kingdom of America by giving up that of Nigeria than as a promising marriage of the two. As far as I am concerned, it is not a loss-gain dialectic, but a gain-gain proposition. In me, Nigeria and the United States don't find a battle-ground; rather, they consummate a coming together, a hyphenated conjunction: I am a Nigerian-American.

Yet, this celebratory insight came only after the fact; it certainly would be dishonest to invoke it as justification for my decision to take up American citizenship. What, then, inspired me in that decision? Quite frankly, a messy melange of factors.

Part of my provisional answer is rooted in Nigeria's historical experience. In 1995 when I applied for U.S. citizenship, Nigeria was in the grips of a bestial military dictatorship that had killed several political dissenters, maimed many, and sent even more into exile. Some of the casualties were my colleagues, or friends. It was deeply painful that, nearly forty years after independence from Britain, a cabal of ill-educated, morally inept military officers could hijack the affairs of my nation of birth and put my fellows and me at peril. From where I stood, then, the American promise of "life, liberty and the pursuit of happiness," whatever its verifiable contradictions, seemed quite appealing.

On another level, as a student of African American history, I had come to see this country as already mine in a sense, my claim to it more than established by the blood and sweat of the Africans who, for several hundred years, invested their lives in building a strong America—while getting neither material recompense, acknowledgement nor gratitiude. It was not difficult at all to imagine myself as an American citizen. The perplexing question was, what kind of American?

For there are, it seemed then and now, many different kinds of Americans.

For one, I decided that I would bring my African being fully into the lively equation of citizenship. Nobody who meets me, or hears my stories, or understands the values that animate me can mistake where I was born. Unlike the snake, I was not about to slough off my African skin in order to inhabit the American republic.

I came to citizenship with few illusions. I know that, whatever the color of the passport I carry, my skin always gives me away. I know about the perils of race in America, but I know of something even more potent and powerful: the grammar of values passed on to me by my parents—and passed down by all the ancestors before them. To be on the outside looking in, as is the lot of many African Americans is not an enviable position. Still, my reading of literature by African Americans as well as my familiarity with their sustained critique of America's contradictions, led me to believe that the marginalized often have a richer, more complex, as well as profoundly humane imagination. These, I have always felt, are attributes that the U.S. sorely needs as, daily, its economic prosperity misleads it into a false moral confidence and invincible certitude.

A more intriguing way to view my citizenship is to spell out the challenge other Americans have, the partial responsibility they bear, to meditate on what value and meaning to assign to my citizenship. In fellow Americans' eyes, how American am I deemed to be, with my African features, stories, accent and all? How much of my Africanness would they permit me to bring along, and what must I check at the door? What price, in other words, would they expect—require—me to pay in order to authenticate my American identity?

Okey Ndibe

Illegal Ingrate

what european sailed to shore
to find a native holding a sign saying:
no vacancy, food shortage, watch out for
run away arrows, vaccine and
immunization ports 2,000 miles
east, for colored only, crusade cruise
liners cannot dock here, all prisons
filled and whore houses burnt down?

what hopes were washed back
down the ocean's throat
when their ships came ashore?

Marlon Billups

Criticism of
Political **Rap**

The late Eighties political rap movement is often called "positive rap". But much of the music of the time had negative aspects including sexism, homophobia, anti-white bigotry, and "the myth of action." But some supporters of political rap would have us believe, at least in the cases of Boogie Down Productions and Public Enemy, that all was fair.

Regarding sexism, Hashim Shomari, author of From the Underground, makes the following claim: "Artists such as KRS-One, Chuck D of Public Enemy, MC Lyte, and Queen Latifah are examples of hardcore hip-hop artists whose lyrics do not disrespect Black womanhood." There are several clear examples of sexism found in the lyrics of Boogie Down Productions and Public Enemy. And, one would certainly hope that MC Lyte and Queen Latifah wouldn't pen lyrics that disrespect Black women, they themselves being Black women.[1]

In rating PE's Fear of a Black Planet the second best album of the Nineties, Spin magazine seems to make excuses for the holes in PE's social theories. Charles Aaron writes: "When Chuck D wrestles sexism on the anthemic 'Revolutionary Generation,' spits homophobic digs on 'Meet the G That Killed Me,' or stip-mines racist history on 'Who Stole the Soul?' he is voicing the weakness, paranoia, and betrayal that damned his family, in desperate hope of redeeming it." This (re)positioning of PE's sexist and/or homophobic lyrics as intentional attempts at redemption requires huge leaps in logic. One wonders what black women and gay men feel about PE's "redemptive" attacks.

In contrast to Shomari and Aaron, Greg Tate has penned some particularly biting critiques of Public Enemy's music. Says Tate, "To know PE is to love the agitprop (and artful noise) and to worry over the whack {sic} retarded philosophy they espouse." Tate continues, "Since PE show sound reasoning when they focus on racism as a tool of the U.S. power structure, they should be...intelligent enough to realize that dehumanizing gays, women, and Jews isn't going to set black people free." He concludes, "For now, swallowing the PE pill means taking the bitter with the sweet...."

Unfortunately, the political rappers are nearly unified in their disregard at best and contempt at worst for women. In fairness to Boogie Down Productions, KRS-One's treatment of women steadily improved throughout his career. As one might infer from the drastically different titles, 1993's "Brown Skin Woman" is a far cry from 1986's "The 'P' Is Free."[2] Public Enemy's "Sophisticated Bitch" and "She Watch Channel Zero" on the other hand, clearly indicate that when it comes to women PE has a lot of developing to do. As Aaron alludes to above, Fear of a Black

Planet's "Revolutionary Generation" attempts to showcase a bit of that development. But with lyrics like "It takes a man to make a stand / Understand it takes a woman to make a stronger man," it becomes clear that Public Enemy looks back to the Sixties for more than just their ideological heroes.[3]

PE isn't exactly illuminating when it comes to women, but at least they give it a shot. Others, like Brand Nubian for example, were unapologetically lascivious. Grand Puba in particular seems always ready to "hit the skins" of any woman lucky enough to cross his path. Puba was well aware of the contradiction between calling for civil equality for black men while relegating women to the bedroom. On the intro to "Wake Up," we hear the following exchange:

First voice: Hey yo, God. We need somebody to come drop some science on this track.
Second voice: Word up, word up.
First voice [continuing]: ...You know, tell it like it really is in the world today.
Second voice: Word up.
First voice: Hey, yo! There go that brother Grand Puba. What's up with that brother?
Second voice [contemptuously]: Aw, he don't know nothin', he don't know nothin'. He be talkin' 'bout skins all the time.
First voice: Aww....[4]

As for political rappers with a more Afrocentric slant (X Clan, Poor Righteous Teachers, etc.), their sexism was less blatant, but no less real. Jeffrey Decker explains: "Afrocentric [rappers] tend to limit the range of representations of black women to a set of rigidly coded sexist oppositions. Black women are either good or bad, mothers or whores, wives or gold-digging lovers." Afrocentric rappers do tend to talk about the "positive" side of Black women. But as Decker points out, since when was it up to men to define what a "good" woman is or is not?

X Clan was also aware of their critics. On the introduction to their 1992 album Xodus, X Clan includes the following question from a (presumably) black woman: "Are the women in the Blackwatch Movement leaders or are they a bunch of groupies dominated by your macho attitudes?" The woman's question is played over the whining of a baby. We may infer then that X Clan considers the woman's question to be just that, whining. X Clan then announces: "All you women...get behind the man [who is] the leader of the real X Clan—the Honorable Minister Louis Farrakhan." (Emphasis mine.)

Perhaps under the influence of Farrakhan's Nation of Islam, X Clan also tends to ridicule gays. Professor X ends nearly every song with an extended call of "Sissies!" and on "Funk Liberation" X Clan attack "faggots" and "dykes." Compared to X Clan's blunt bigotry, Brand Nubian member Grand Puba's style of homophobia is surprisingly prosaic: "Brother, you're wrong if you think crime pays / [I] don't like gays / And take vacations on the holidays."[5]

Brother J and Professor X also frequently refer to themselves as "pimps" and "pro-black niggas." They are obviously attempting to recontextualize the words—they certainly never advocate actual pimping or prostitution. Still, X Clan's use of words like "pimp" and "nigga" hardly seems consistent with their image of positivity and Black pride.

Any criticism of the sexism of political rappers should be tempered by the fact that these rappers are products of their environments. And I don't mean inner-city slums and ghettos, I mean America. Dr. Michael Dyson, the author of Between God and Gangsta Rap writes: "Attacking [rappers] is an easy out. ...While these young black males become whipping boys for sexism and misogyny, the places in our culture where these ancient traditions are nurtured and rationalized—including religious and educational institutions and the nuclear family—remain immune to forceful and just criticism."[6]

Sexism isn't the only shortcoming of Afrocentric rap. A wider range of historical perspective would've been welcome as well. As we all know by now (or should), Greeks and Romans didn't create civilization. But when rappers counter that Egypt is "the mother of all civilization," they are trading one dubious claim for another. Egypt may have been the first great civilization, but there are numerous non-European (and non-African) civilizations that predate Greece and Rome, including Sumerian civilization, the Hittite Empire, the Babylonian Empire, and the Indus/Harappa civilization. These civilizations, as well as ancient China and ancient Israel, all contributed greatly to the arts and sciences. Positioning Egypt as the paradigm of all civilization simply isn't accurate; as Jeffrey Decker says, it does nothing more than "allow blacks to occupy a category previously reserved for whites."

Decker also points out Afrocentric rappers seem to be under the impression that Egypt is the only great civilization of Africa. This is also incorrect. Ghana's empire lasted some 500 to 1,500 years, depending on one's source. Other ancient African civilizations—all of which lasted at least 300 years—include Mali, Benin, Zimbabwe, and the Swahili states. And finally, Decker notes that it is ironic that Afrocentric rappers decry America's history of slavery while conveniently overlooking the fact that Egypt's "enduring monuments" were themselves built by slaves.[7]

They say Sadat X is racist
Because I love the Black faces
—Sadat X (Brand Nubian / "Ain't No Mystery")

Following the lead of the Nation of Islam, early Malcolm X, and other militant black leaders, many political rappers use terms like "devils," "swine," and "cave people" when referring to whites. Just as X Clan took the lead in grass roots activism, they also took the lead in slinging racial slurs. They introduce "Fire & Earth" by telling "cavemen," "cave-women," "Neanderthals," and "troglodytes" to "hush."[8] Not to be outdone, on "Drop the Bomb," Brand Nubian reprises Trouble Funk's references to "Yakub" and "cavemen."[9] Public Enemy sometimes referred to devils and the like, but they are careful to avoid the direct association of whites with devil-try. PE is also fond of the euphemistic phrase "the other man." The word "other" doesn't exactly qualify as a slur, but then, that's what euphemism is all about.

From my numerous quotes, it may seem that the only critics of political rap were, well, critics. To the contrary, some of the most direct criticism comes from one of their own: BDP's KRS-One. KRS issued several stinging indictments, most notably 1992's "Build and Destroy":

> Pro-blackness is your solution
> But I don't know really know about that style you're usin'
> Too many teachers in the class spoil the school
> After a while you got blabbering fuckin' fools...
> The white man ain't the devil, I promise
> You want to see the devil? / Take a look at Clarence Thomas...
> An accomplice to the devil is a devil too
> The devil is anti-human / Who the hell are you?
> I lecture in rap without rehearsal
> I manifest as a black man but I'm universal
> - KRS-One (Boogie Down Productions / "Build and Destroy")

From time to time, Chuck D also criticized his political rap counterparts. But in this quote at least, Chuck is considerably less pointed than KRS: "...[W]e can work with [as opposed to for] anybody. Because we all have to live in this world together. Kids who are young and built up on pro-black rhetoric tend not to understand that concept. But they will as they get older. Or they'll suffer the consequences." (Notice that Chuck doesn't mention that PE is the source of some of that pro-black rhetoric.)

A quote from Otis Smith of the black Nationalist poetry group, the Watts Prophets, helps to explain some of the successes and failures of the political rap movement. "It's difficult for someone, no matter how brilliant or talented they may be, to have the wisdom and experience of a forty-year-old...when [they're] twenty." And Smith continues: "Similarly, it is very difficult for a forty-year-old to have the desire and outlook of a twenty-year-old."

In an interview with the authors of Nation Conscious Rap, the pro-nationalist rapper Paris illustrates both the idealism and lack of knowledge to which Otis Smith alludes. After telling the interviewer that one of his "rhythm and blues influences" is the legendary funk group Parliament, Paris says:

Back then lyrics didn't mean anything. [Quoting Parliament:] "I'm going to take my shoes off and kick up my heels." Brothers [and] sisters weren't nearly as conscious as they are now. Even though our people need a lot of work, we've come a long way.

Parliament—the band that Paris quotes as an example of "lyrics [that] didn't mean anything"—is considered by many music historians to be one of the more brilliant socio-political satirists of their era, or any era. And, it is quite debatable as to whether blacks as a whole were either better off or more conscious in the late Eighties, as opposed to (presumably) the Seventies.[10]

In addition to all of the above, some critics also contend that political rappers didn't really do much of anything, other than sell records, that is. Others counter that political rappers did at least force major labels to pay attention to Black concerns and problems. But as Hashim Shomari observes, "Any trend or style of rap that is lucrative [will] be promoted because the U.S. ruling economic elite is motivated above all by the profit margin." In other words, record companies sell what sells. The late Eighties proliferation of political acts shouldn't be seen as any sort of temporary shift in the moral fiber of record companies. The fact is, political rap acts were signed because they were popular.

Dr. Maulana Karenga's "myth of action" concept goes a long way to explaining many of the shortcomings of the political rap era:

> Politics was too often reduced to showing Malcolm X or Martin King in video...Too many rappers didn't even bother to make their lyrics, much less their actions, consistent with the philosophies or even the sound bites of these leaders and teachers... The hip-hop nation...promoted a "myth of action" whereby political responsibility, knowledge, and activity was garnered by proclamation and not by demonstration. This created a condition where people could practice one thing and preach another. This [also] created the prospects for disillusionment among hip-hop fans who witnessed the stifling of their "revolutionary" performers when [the performers were] called to task by their primarily white bosses.

In other words, Henderson is saying that many rappers weren't fighting the good fight so much as they were talking the good fight. An example of the "disillusionment" to which Dr. Henderson refers is the aftermath of the infamous Professor Griff interview. Many fans were disheartened when the biggest, baddest political rappers of them all, Public Enemy, appeared to be put in their place after they were charged with anti-Semitism. It isn't that PE's fans necessarily supported Griff's statements; the fans would've liked to believe that their heroes were indeed "too black, too strong" to be forced into an apology for anything.

As we have seen, the music of many political rappers had significant negative aspects. Despite the criticism, the political movement in rap was a vitally important, and often, musically successful, period in hip-hop music. For the first time, rappers explicitly called the ruling class to task, questioned authority, and as Public Enemy would say, "fought the power." Did "the power" win? Sure. But as Tricia Rose says: "The fact that the powerful often win does not mean that a war isn't going on."[11] And besides that, ask an older, wiser Chuck D, why is it that young people are being put on the frontline? "Black people in America are destroying themselves," he wrote in his autobiography Fight the Power, "And people are looking at today's youth as being the spokespeople. Youth should never be looked upon to be the spokespeople for the entire race. The youth may be the spokespeople for the sentiment and the expressions of rage being reflected, and they may be asking a lot of questions about what's going on, but you have to have adults who have experience...to be the spokespeople."[12]

In closing, one last quote, this one from Frank Kofsky. The way Kofsky tells it, political rap failed for the same reason that popular music's past flirtations with politics failed—because it had to. Kofsky writes: "It would be extremely naïve to think that any given set of purely musical innovations would suffice to emancipate black musicians from the grip of white entrepreneurial domination. To bring about a change of that magnitude would necessitate not only aesthetic revolution, but social upheaval as well...."[13] In the rap era, I can think of only two things that might qualify as social upheaval: AIDS and crack. Somehow I doubt that either is the sort of thing that Kofsky had in mind.

Mtume ya Salaam

1 Then again, with the popularity of female performers like Foxy Brown and Lil' Kim (both of whom seem determined to one-up male disrespect for women), perhaps Shomari makes a good point about Latifah and Lyte.
2 The 'P' is "pussy".
3 Perhaps the most infamous example of Sixties-era sexism by a civil rights leader is the often repeated quote by SNCC leader Stokely Carmichael: "the position in SNCC for women is prone." Apparently, Carmichael was kidding.
4 Five Percenters address each other as "God" because they believe that the Asiatic (original) Black man is, literally, God. In this context, "Word up," means, "Right, I agree." By the reference to "skins," Voice Two is saying that Puba talks about sex too much.
5 Quoted from One for All's "Grand Puba, Positive and L.G."
6 Also note that I take Dr. Dyson's quote out of context. His quote refers to gangsta rappers specifically.
7 The information in the previous two paragraphs is taken from Jeffrey Louis Decker's "The State of Rap" and Glovis Technologies' "Historical Timeline—Education for a New Reality.'" And while we are on the subject of historical perspective, please do note that our great civilization (the United States of America) has yet to celebrate its 300th birthday.
8 "Fire and Earth" is based on a sample of Jimmy Castor's "Troglodytes." The "cavemen, cave-woman" list is sampled directly from Castor's song. But Castor's tune is tongue in cheek and has no racial overtones. By inserting "hush" between the names (and using similar terms in a negative context at other times) X Clan changes the context of Castor's words from a joke to a racial insult.
9 Brand Nubian's "Drop the Bomb" samples Trouble Funk's go-go classic of the same name. In this case, however, there is no shift in context. Trouble Funk chant of "drop the bomb on the Yakub crew" refers to the "grafted devils" of Nation of Islam lore.
10 They recorded well into the Eighties, but Parliament is usually considered a Seventies band. When Paris says, "back then," he is probably referring to the Seventies, although the song that he quoted, "Agony of Defeet," is from Parliament's 1980 album Trombipulation.
11 From p. 101 of Black Noise.
12 Chuck D from Fight the Power, p. 177.
13 I happened upon the Kofsky quote in Brian Ward's It's Not About a Salary. It is originally from Kofsky's Black Nationalism and the Revolution in Music. And in my opinion, Kofsky's correct. Until millions of music fans replace their records with rifles and appropriate targets, I would imagine that the status quo is secure.

Color in My Life

BENAJA: The blues is a tricky, tricky thang there baby. It want you to moan and mourn and grovel and cry and laugh to keep from cryin' and moan and moan and moan and moan some more. And that ain't even the tricky part neither. The blues actually want you to sing the music—I mean sang from your gut and mean something by it. 'Cause the blues you can't fake, Jack. I'm tellin' ya, I tried and ain't nothin', nothin' happened. Da Dun Da Da Da. My baby didn't leave me. Da Dun Da Da Da. And I was still tryin' ta sang. Da Dun Da Da Da. My jain time got denied. Da Dun Da Da Da. And I felt the sunshine through the rain. Da Dun Da Da Da. *(Laughs.)* Da Dun Da Da Da. My "Oh me oh my" Da Dun Da Da Da became "Oh we oh us." Da Dun Da Da Da and my train to St. Louis Da Dun Da Da Da got to that station on time Da Dun Da Da Da. Da Dun Da Da Da. *(Laughs some more.)* Naw, you can't sing no blues if you ain't got them blues. Like you can't be absurd if your situation ain't already absurd.

(Two women dressed in beautiful evening gowns enter from opposite sides of the stage and sit at their individual vanity tables. There is no glass inside either of the mirror frames so that the audience sees their faces at all times. The women are preparing their make-up for their New Year's parties. Their eyes are bloodshot. There is a note and an old picture sitting amongst the make-up cases on each of the vanity tables. As the scene progresses, the women fill their faces with clown-like, grease paint make-up until there is hardly a clean surface left. They use no black or white make-up; only rainbow colors.)

WOMAN 1: I am a married woman

WOMAN 2: And I still love the way

WOMAN 1: Daddy tells the story

WOMAN 2: of my birth.

BOTH WOMEN: Mother and Daddy never really knew each other.

WOMAN 1: All they both knew is that they arrived at the dance at the exact same time.

WOMAN 2: Oh, how glorious a story. She was wearing a blue-black dress, short like a flapper, just above her knee

WOMAN 1: and he was wearing pants that didn't quite fit his backside, tight, hugging and exposed just below his yellow dashiki.

BOTH WOMEN: They arrived at the door just at the same time, mind you—

WOMAN 2: friends waiting invariably inside—

WOMAN 1: and they reached out their dollars just at the same time; his right hand brushing her left.

WOMAN 2: Oh, how marvelous. It was a college dance that Mother was crashing and that Daddy helped publicize.

WOMAN 1: But oh, when they touched, they felt sparks. Daddy says the cold air and the wool of the shawl Mother had draped over her left arm, her paying arm, caused the tiny series of shocks and neither of them jumped away.

WOMAN 2: They just said, "Excuse me."

WOMAN 1: And "Excuse me."

WOMAN 2: And then their eyes met.

WOMAN 1: Marvelous, simply marvelous and then their eyes met.

WOMAN 2: "Oh, I know you," Daddy said.

WOMAN 1: "No, no you don't, " Mother said.

WOMAN 2: "You're in my ..." Daddy said.

WOMAN 1: "No, no I'm not in any of your classes," Mother said.

WOMAN 2: Mind you, the lady at the table was getting quite upset since Mother and Daddy were holding up the line. "Come on people, you payin' or what?"

WOMAN 1: "Oh," Mother said.

WOMAN 2: "No," Daddy said before turning back to Mother and asking, "Will you come have coffee with me?" It must have been so marvelous.

WOMAN 1: Right out of a fantasy. He asked Mother again, Will you have coffee with me?"

WOMAN 2: And they departed from the party entrance right then and there—

BOTH WOMEN: that fateful night I was conceived.

WOMAN 1: That night I was wombed.

WOMAN 2: Mother quit work to womb me.

WOMAN 1: Mother left the college to womb me.

WOMAN 2: Mother denied herself contact with Daddy while she wombed me.

WOMAN 1: And now

WOMAN 2: it's 9 minutes

WOMAN 1: before my party guests arrive.

WOMAN 2: 9 minutes

WOMAN 1: and Daddy decides that now is a good time to reveal all of this to me

WOMAN 2: By giving me the note Mother left in my carrying basket when she finally returned to the college where she had been a janitor and where she found Daddy and plopped me down on his biology desk—me, my clothes, my carrying basket, my note, and my picture of her.

WOMAN 1: "Here black boy, take your baby."

WOMAN 2: "Here white boy, take your baby."

WOMAN 1: "Take your beautiful, beautiful white baby."

WOMAN 2: "Take your beautiful, beautiful black baby."

WOMAN 1: And then Mother left me with my 20 year old father

WOMAN 2: who brought me home to his mother

WOMAN 1: like the gift he says I am.

(pause)

BOTH WOMEN: And his mother accepted me.

(Pause)

BOTH WOMEN: Now I'm asking you, *(Pointing through their vanity table mirrors.)* you! Why would he decide to tell me all of this 9 minutes before my New Year's party *(Chuckling at the irony.)* after all these glorious years

WOMAN 1: of telling

WOMAN 2: and re-telling

WOMAN 1: the fly-by-night

BOTH WOMEN: chance-meeting

WOMAN 2: one-night-stand story

BOTH WOMAN: that ended with a mother's death in childbirth?

WOMAN 2: Though now I guess

WOMAN 1: I know she didn't really die.

WOMAN 2 : After all these years of being a white man's daughter

WOMAN 1: of being a black man's daughter. After all these years of being a black man's wife

WOMAN 2: of being a white man's wife, of being a white man's mother

WOMAN 1: a black man's mother

BOTH WOMEN: Mother! Mother! After all these years of being black/ white.

WOMAN 1: What do I do with my white self now?

WOMAN 2: What do I do with my black self now?

WOMAN 1: Now Daddy says that I've started to look like her, though she was only 18 or 17 or 16 or 19 when he met her.

WOMAN 2: I've started getting this olive, slightly tanning skin.

WOMAN 1: I've started growing paler and my hair has started falling straight with out chemical treatment like hers

WOMAN 2: And my hair has started curling like hers which fell coarsely around her neck.

BOTH WOMEN: *(Applying make-up with more force. In low voices.)* I bet they'll all be able to tell.

WOMAN 2: *(Pointing at the mirror again.)* Your mother is a black woman...

WOMAN 1: *(Pointing at the mirror again.)* Your mother is a white woman...

BOTH WOMEN: And that's all the note says. Your mother is a black/ white woman

WOMAN 2: who could only find a job cleaning a white college campus.

WOMAN 1: who could only find a job cleaning a black college campus.

BOTH WOMEN: Your mother is a white/black woman.

WOMAN 2: But the issue never

WOMAN 1: had the time to come up—

BOTH WOMEN: he just liked the sparks in her hands.

WOMAN 2: He had seen her before.

WOMAN 1: She washed the blackboards before a few of his classes.

WOMAN 2: He liked to watch her clean away the chalk with her bucket and rag.

WOMAN 1: He had enjoyed her all semester.

WOMAN 2: So he said it felt only natural to finally ask her out,

WOMAN 1: somewhere, anywhere away from the school.

(Pause and hold up the pictures and notes.)

BOTH WOMEN: What am I supposed to do with this now?

WOMAN 1: I am going to be the only white at the party.

WOMAN 2: I am going to be the only black at the party.

BOTH WOMEN: I am no longer the woman I thought I was. *(Pause.)* Oh, What if they can tell? *(Applying the make-up with ferocity.)* What if they all can tell? Oh, look how the black/white is beginning to show through. It's already showing through. *(Crying out.)* What am I supposed to do now, Daddy? What am I supposed to do now?

(The doorbell rings. They look toward their individual exits. They stand up, still holding the pictures and the notes, their faces completely covered with clown-like make-up, and they walk off. The doorbell rings again.)

BENAJA'S VOICE: Da Dun Da Da Da. Da Dun Da Da Da. *(Chuckles softly.)* It's the blues you can't fake, baby, 'cause they ain't fakin' you. *(Chuckles softly.)* Da Dun Da Da Da. Da Dun Da Da Da.

Angela A. Williams

Quashelle Curtis–**Hip-Hop Barbie** life-sized doll

wanda jean allen and the state:
A CAUTIONARY TALE*

let me tell you how the state knew that wanda jean should die
    she was a penny stamped
    with the state of the nation
    she grew bigger and bigger
    on a woman's bloody love
    she was nobody's mother,
    nobody's cause.

let me tell you what was wrong with wanda jean
    she was hit by a truck
    at twelve years old
    she was stabbed in her
    left temple at fifteen
    her invalid ideas had
    to crawl out of the wreckage
    of her shocked head

let me tell you what was right with wanda jean
    she knew who she loved
    her iq and the symmetrical
    shape of their lovemaking
    shared the same sweet number
    her body was brilliant
    deep inside where Gloria
    made the stars burst

let me tell you what wanda jean knew about love
>	she met her lover in prison
>	she fell in love with the sound-
>	track of oklahoma justice
>	ringing through the cell block
>	and the courthouse halls
>	her face was a canvas
>	her lover drew a rake across

let me tell you how wanda jean's case was heard
>	her lover's body was a theory
>	she shot full of holes
>	she tended to end her friend-
>	ships too permanently
>	she was dysfunctional enough
>	to kill but not dysfunctional
>	enough to save

let me tell you about wanda jean's final hour
>	she walked down the aisle
>	on the arms of two wardens
>	amidst bar-banging protests
>	she quoted jesus praying
>	for the folks who'd take her
>	death to their raging graves
>	she watched a woman sign
>	i love you with three
>	trembling white fingers
>	then closed her eyes

Evie Shockley

Wanda Jean Allen was executed by the State of Oklahoma on January 12, 2001 for killing her partner, Gloria Leathers, during a domestic dispute. The sentence was carried out despite arguments by her lawyers that she was borderline mentally retarded. She was the first black woman put to death in the U.S. since 1954, and only the sixth woman to receive the death penalty since it was reinstated in 1977. Oklahoma executed 11 people in 2000, making it second only to Texas, whose 40 executions in a single year set a U.S. record.

Kim Mayhorn—**Black Boxisms:**
Visiting Room
photo installation

Dear Mama:
Remember That Rose Water

Dear Mama:

In less than 48 hours, I'll be dead. And nothing's going to stop death from coming. You know how it is down here—a brother checks in, but he ain't checking out.

You been a good mama to me. I'm sorry that I couldn't have been a better son. But this world ain't hold nothing for me but misery. For every cup of hate I got, a bowl of hate I gave. You done the best you could for me. Believe that.

Tell Pastor Johnson and all the rest that I really appreciated his efforts. I heard the rally drew more than 500 people. For me! Even though I know I should be grateful, I'm not. Seems to me people always wanna rally for a person when they know they ain't got nothing to lose. Seems like if Pastor Johnson and those 500 people had done something for me when I was coming up in this world, things would be different. You can tell him that I'm "saved" if that'll make him happy. Tell him I found Jesus in my last hours, and that I know he's my "friend."

I heard some other people said they was gonna be out there protesting until the end. That's all well and good, but maybe those people can get together and go help somebody who's living. Tell them to hire some of those young black males hanging out in the Fifth Ward. I heard the protestors mostly white folks, too. Ain't that something? Where those kind of white people been all my life? They wasn't at my school, was they mama? They wasn't the ones with the jobs, or the ones you could go to for help? They sho' wasn't the ones wearing that police uniform on that night. Seems like those kind of white folks only turn up at the very end, when a brothers' got no chance at all. Maybe they from Mars or Uranus or something like that.

They say death's angel has a way of making a liar into a true believer. I guess somebody was right, because I can't tell a lie, even now. Even when I know I ain't got nothing to lose. I'm sorry for all the lies I told you. I regret every lie I told myself.

Mama, like I told you three months ago when I asked you not to come up here no more, I don't hold nothing against you. You done all you could for me and Ronnie and Beverly. And out of all three of us I guess Beverly the only one who made something out herself. I'm proud of Beverly with her singing and all and I know Ronnie be grinning up in heaven every time he hear that voice. I know he can hear it way up in heaven. She always did have the voice of an angel.

I just don't want you sitting up the rest of your days thinking you done something wrong with raising us. You didn't. You give me all the love a son could ask for. In fact, you gave me more than I ever deserved most times. When I was low, Mama, sometimes I'd look up in the sky, and all I could feel was your love coming pouring through. Sometimes when I was out there on the streets doing my thang, I'd think about you and I'd settle down. I know it's hard for you to believe, seeing all that love you give me over the last 32 years ain't save me from this.

But it did. In a way it did save me. All that Jesus talk and preaching you used to do, finally making sense to me now. Too bad its when I'm at the end of the line. I wonder what Jesus was thinking up there on that cross, if he thought of his mama too. I wonder if he felt sorry for something he might have done. I wonder if he was scared even just a little.

Mama, I want you to know that I done prayed for forgiveness. I want you to know when they strap me down and stick that needle in my vein that I'm at peace. I'm on my square. That I know'd I was loved. Even when I was so full of hate, I knew I was loved. They can't kill love, Mama.

I been fighting these words for all six years I been sitting up here. But when I'm done, and I'm buried, and your soul is comforted, I want you to go find that lady Mrs. Brommel and tell her I regretted what I did. I wish I hadn't taken her husband's life. But, it was his or it was mine. In the end, I guess death got us both. When they ask me for my last words, I'm just gone say that scripture you give me the last time I saw you. I'll let this note say everything else.

In case you wondering, and so to put your heart to rest, I ain't lie about nothing I said about that situation. You don't know what it be like to be a black man in this world. Police ain't never showed up at our door unless they was there to arrest us. So like I said on trial and in all my appeals, that cop was gonna kill me, Mama. I just got him first. I guess its no such thing as self-defense in the ghetto, unless you killing another black. You don't wanna know what my eyes done seen.

Still I'm sorry. Maybe I could have run off and let him live another day. Maybe I could have did what they call Sambo or something and make him feel sorry for me and put that gun up. There's a whole lot of maybes I been thinking about. I guess I never will know. I just don't want his wife going around saying I was a "cold blooded" killer like she been doing. I know she'll be glad to see them pull that switch, but if she's a mother, like you is, I know she sorry for what she said about me. I'm somebody's child too.

You gotta know in your heart Mama that I ain't tried to be this way. I don't care what them scientist say on TV, it ain't nothing in my DNA. I wasn't born criminal-minded, society just gave me the mind of a criminal. That's about all. I had to survive out here. I just didn't know no other way. Lets see now, I been in and out of the system ever since I was 12 years old. I guess it started with me busting out that liquor store window. Remember that? It seems so long ago. After I did juvey home, it got easy after that. I figure that at least you ain't have to worry about where I was no more, or if I was getting three square meals a day. I just adjusted to the life, and now I know, I done realized this wasn't no life at all.

They got this cloning going on now. Whatever you do, don't let them bring me back. Not to this place. Not in this skin. Not with the things I done seen. Seem like white folk always coming up with ways to mess with nature. Now they want to make people who never die. Ain't that hell, Mama? Never dying. I guess, they can't leave well enough alone. And they never leave the black man alone. Everything he is, they claim ownership to. No wonder they think God is white.

If God turn out to be white when I get there, that'll explain everything. That'll be the answer to every question I ever asked. When I find out, I'll figure out some kinda way to send you a sign that maybe we ought to go the other way! If hell is hot, and heaven is cold, you tell me what black folk like cold weather? (Okay, Mama, don't start clutching your chest and calling on the Lord, I'm just trying to make you laugh.)

I ain't blaming God for nothing I done. And I ain't blaming my life on that daddy I never had either. I used to wish you ain't name me after that cat. Now you see why I insisted you call me by my nickname "B-Love." I used to get mad as a mutha when you said my whole name.

In the spirit of truth telling though, Mama, I gotta admit, I done sat up here many a night thinking about if daddy ever thought about us. I wondered when he slept at night, if he ever dreamed my face. I wondered when he ate his breakfast in the morning, if he wished your hands had prepared it for him. Stirred the batter that made his pancakes, laid his bacon down on the hot plate just right, so it wouldn't shrink up into tiny little strips. When the holidays came around, I wondered if he thought of me, if I had toys, if I learned to defend myself against the schoolyard bullies, if I liked my first kiss.

No lie. I wish daddy had of been there for us, Mama. But I understand now why he couldn't. He ain't have nothing to give us. Not even himself. Like me. I ain't have nothing to give, so I just gave hate. I gave back everything I got. Misery point blank.

That's all I ever owned. This world got a way of owning poor folks. It's ironic too. We ain't got nothing, and we don't even own ourselves.

How many times we sat up in that welfare office feeling like we was State property? I shouldn't tell you this, but you gotta know. I hated being poor. I heard some records talking about how deep life is in the ghetto. Hell, Mama, do they really know? Seems like poverty followed us wherever we went. Even when we left Chicago and moved down here—who was waiting on our doorstep. Poor, his sister Hungry, his cousin Pain and they granddaddy named Hate. Seems like that family lived in our house.

And I remember every word of what them caseworkers was saying to you every single time we went down there with those letters. Remember that time, I think I was three or four, and we was in the aid office? We was still in Chicago. You had on this pretty red sweater. Your hair was down and you were looking so beautiful to me. You was pregnant with Beverly. Ronnie was at school or something, cause he wasn't there. I remember you smelling like sweet rose water.

We stood in that line for three hours and when we got up to see the caseworker, she took one look at your stomach and she said something like "don't think you getting some mo' money cause you done went and got yourself knocked up. You nasty ass girls need to close your legs!" I remember that as plain as day, and I remember you crying too, and somebody laughing at your tears. Then I remember you hugging me real, real hard all the way home. It was the winter and we was riding the bus and my coat was two sizes too big and the air was getting up under it and my fingers hurt every time the wind blowed. When we got home you made me a cheese sandwich and gave me a glass of milk. Then you just laid in your bed and cried.

Man, its funny how much a mind can hold. I been thinking about that off and on for the last couple of years. Sometimes I change it around though. Sometimes when I get to the part when that caseworker is fixing to disrespect you, I imagine you slapping her across the mouth. Sometimes I see myself as bigger and I punch her in the stomach. Sometimes I see daddy coming in to save us—'cept he's rich, dressed in a nice suit and with a nice car. My fingers don't hurt and I got on the right size coat.

Man, the mind is a funny thing.

Mama, I wish I could say something in this letter that will let you know just what I'm feeling right now I just don't know all those words like that. And I don't write no poems. But I want you to know I ain't scared of death's angel. And when he come for me I'm gone fight him till the end. What you used to call me, "yo little champ." Well I'm still gonna knock him out mama. I'm still yo champ.

You know how they say rest in peace. I think I know what that finally mean. See when you alive, you constantly at war. Your mind is at war. Your soul is at war. Your heart is at war. All the time. You never, really find peace—at all. Even rich people got problems. You know there's a white boy in the house with me who used to make $250,000 a year. He lost some money and snapped and took out his whole family—including his six-month-old baby. There's this other white cat who always talking about how he hate his mother, how he hate women. He raped and killed three college girls about fifteen years ago. I spit on the ground every time he opens his mouth or I hear his name. I think of Beverly. I don't think that man got no soul either. He say he looking forward to the cocktail—that's what we call the dose they give you. I think he's lying. No man really wants to die—not again anyway.

Then I hear there's some young, black dude about 17 coming to the house. Talk say he killed three people in some robbery or something. I wish I could be around to hear his real story, to let him cry with me, to let him say everything he needs to say to the world. Maybe I could be his big brother, and at night when he slept he could find his heart and a way to love.

I guess we all at war one way or another. I'm running out of paper Mama and the man'll be round here to get my last meal. I think I'm a make the State do me one up right. Some steak, fried chicken, shrimp, greens with ham hocks, butter beans, and a piece of cobbler with ice cream. But I know them prison cooks can't touch your cobbler. Not that butter crust!

I ain't got much of belongings, 'cept the few thangs they allowed me to have. I wrote something in my bible for Beverly. Make sure she get it. And the other books and thangs you can do with them what you like. The little statue of Jesus on cross I got from that Congresslady, that's yours. Its going to be the last thing I'll ever kiss.

I hope you can read my scrawny writing. No more tears Mama. No more tears.

Me and Ronnie gone see you in heaven, Mama, with that pretty smile, smelling like sweet rose water.

Love your son,
Robert J. Ashford, Jr.
Huntsville, Texas
April 13, 2001

Stephanie Mwandishi Gadlin

Libations for PHARAOH

A Play in Two Acts

CHARACTERS:

OMARI CONSTANCE	18-YEAR-OLD BLACK MAN HEADED FOR COLLEGE
RALPH CONSTANCE	Lawyer, father of Omari, husband of Ashaki
ASHAKI CONSTANCE	Professor, mother of Omari, wife of Ralph
PAPA CONSTANCE	Father of Ralph
SHANI	16-year-old sister of Omari
DETECTIVE HOLDEN	Black police detective

ACT I:

SETTING: Constance family living room, evening.

Ralph is reading the newspaper. Ashaki is grading papers. A knock on the door, Ralph looks up, looks at the door, and looks back at Ashaki who has not moved. She continues to do what she is doing. Another knock and Ralph looks at Ashaki again, then folds his paper and gets up from his chair. He opens the door without looking out. Detective Holden is there.

DETECTIVE: *(holding up his badge)* I'm looking for Omari Constance.

RALPH: I'm his father. What is this about?

ASHAKI: *(looking back over the sofa to the door)* Ralph, what is it?

DETECTIVE: Sir, is your son home?

RALPH: *(to Ashaki)* I'm not sure. *(to Holden)* No, he isn't home. What is this about?

DETECTIVE: Do you know what time he'll be home? I need to talk to him.

RALPH: Maybe my legendary communication skills are failing me, so I'll ask you once again. What is this about?

ASHAKI: *(rising from the couch and walking to the door)* Ralph, what is going on? What does that man want with Omari?

DETECTIVE: I heard you the first time, sir.

RALPH: So what are you saying? You chose to ignore me?

DETECTIVE: I'm just doing my job.

ASHAKI: *(stepping around Ralph so she is between the two men)* And what is it that is causing you to do your job here at our house?

DETECTIVE: I'm here to talk to your son.

RALPH: Do you know who I am?

DETECTIVE: Sir, believe me. I'm very aware of your standing in the community.

RALPH: You know I'm a lawyer.

DETECTIVE: I am aware of that, too.

ASHAKI: Why won't you tell us what you want with our son?

DETECTIVE: I need to talk to him.

ASHAKI: About what?

DETECTIVE: Here's my card. Have him call me.

RALPH: *(reading the card)* Lieutenant Scott Holden. Detective, 2nd precinct. Homicide.

ASHAKI: Homicide?

DETECTIVE: Have your son call me when he gets in.

RALPH: You'll be talking to me, not my son. So you might as well tell me what this is about.

DETECTIVE: When the time comes.

Holden walks away. Ashaki closes the door and she and Ralph walk back toward the sofa and chair.

ASHAKI: What could this possibly be about? Where is Omari?

RALPH: I have no idea.

ASHAKI: Where's Shani? Maybe she knows where he is.

They sit down in the same places they had been. Just as they get seated there is another knock on the door. Ashaki jumps up and looks at the door, then back at Ralph who turns around sharply. He stares at the door, too, but does not get up. After a couple of beats, Ashaki goes to the door and swings it open. Standing there is an elderly black man, nattily dressed in a suit and hat.

ASHAKI: Papa?!!

PAPA: *(glancing back over his shoulder)* What did the police want?

ASHAKI: *(still shocked)* Papa what are you doing here?

RALPH: *(going to the door)* Papa? Did I hear you say "Papa"?

PAPA: Yes son, you heard right.

Papa comes into the room. The two men embrace, then sit down. Ashaki stands behind them still trying to get over her shock.

RALPH: Dad, when did you get into town?

PAPA: Just a few minutes ago.

RALPH: Is everything all right?

PAPA: You tell me, son. Is it?

ASHAKI: *(finally sitting down)* Why didn't you tell us you were coming?

PAPA: Didn't know 'til last night.

ASHAKI: What happened last night?

PAPA: I got a feeling that I should come up here and see about Omari.

RALPH: Did you have one of your dreams? Is something wrong?

PAPA: Don't know. That's why I decided to get on a plane this morning and come on up here.

ASHAKI: What is going on here? First, the police, now you.

PAPA: What did that cop want?

RALPH: Says he's looking for Omari.

PAPA: What'd you tell him?

RALPH: The truth. He's not here.

PAPA: He's not?

ASHAKI: No.

RALPH: He should be here soon.

ASHAKI: Probably out making last minute visits to his friends before he leaves for school next week.

PAPA: So, he's going off to Harvard. That's what you said in your letter. He's going to Harvard.

ASHAKI: They came after him. Offered him a full scholarship.

RALPH: He was lucky.

ASHAKI: It wasn't luck. He had his pick of any school he wanted.

PAPA: I hoped he would come down south to one of the black schools. But I guess Harvard's ok.

ASHAKI: I'm sure it'll do.

RALPH: Can I get you something to drink?

PAPA: Just some hot water and lemon.

RALPH: You know that's what Duke Ellington drank every night.

PAPA: I told you that story.

RALPH: I know. I'm just saying...

Ralph gets up and goes off stage to the kitchen to get the water and lemon.

PAPA: *(looking at stack of papers in Ashaki's lap)* Ashaki, you still teaching?

ASHAKI: Papa you ask me the same thing every time I see you. Yes, I am. Probably will be for another twenty years or so.

PAPA: Harvard? How many blacks they got on the faculty up there?

RALPH: *(still off stage)* I don't know.

ASHAKI: Quite a few.

PAPA: I guess Harvard's ok.

RALPH: *(returns with the water. Sets it down in front of his father)* How long do you plan to stay?

PAPA: Depends.

ASHAKI: On what?

PAPA: What I need to do up here.

RALPH: Like what?

PAPA: Don't know. Have to find out what's going on with my grandson.

RALPH: I mean, this is the first time you've been to see us in 12 years.

PAPA: You know I don't like to travel too much.

RALPH: But 12 years.

ASHAKI: Then you just show up at the door.

PAPA: I didn't think you'd mind.

ASHAKI: Oh, Papa, we don't mind. It's just so unusual. After all these years...

PAPA: It has been a while.

RALPH: It has been.

PAPA: You still the only blacks on the street?

RALPH: Naw. All the whites left. This whole neighborhood is black.

PAPA: I thought you moved out here to integrate it.

ASHAKI: We moved out here to give our children a better life.

PAPA: How much are these houses going for?

RALPH: That's not important.

PAPA: *(squeezes lemon into the water and stirs it around with his finger)* I'm just curious.

ASHAKI: Ralph, tell him.

RALPH: On the low end, two hundred fifty thousand. On the high end, maybe four fifty or five hundred thousand.

PAPA: And those white folks just gave up this whole neighborhood.

RALPH: Yep.

ASHAKI: Within five years after we moved out here, most of them were gone.

PAPA: So who lives out here now?

RALPH: All kinds of professional blacks. You know, doctors, lawyers...

PAPA: Professors. *(He looks over at Ashaki and smiles)*

ASHAKI: Preachers. *(She looks back at him)*

RALPH: By the way, how's the church going?

PAPA: The church ain't going nowhere.

RALPH: You know what I mean.

PAPA: Everything is fine.

The old man folds his hands, rests them on his stomach, then leans his head back and closes his eyes. It is a way of cutting off the conversation.

RALPH: Are you going to sleep?

The old man says nothing. He doesn't move. Ashaki looks over at Ralph as if to say, "What are you going to do." Ralph shrugs his shoulders. She shoots him another look.

RALPH: Dad, do you want to go lie down in the guest room?

PAPA: *(without opening his eyes)* I'm not a guest.

ASHAKI: Of course you're not. You're family.

PAPA: Then I'll just sit here and rest my eyes.

RALPH: Fine. I'm going to look for Omari.

ASHAKI: He's probably at The Church.

PAPA: *(eyes still closed)* What church?

RALPH: It's a place where the kids hang out.

PAPA: What kind of church?

ASHAKI: It used to be a church.

RALPH: Now it's the Oak Grove Community Center.

ASHAKI: But the kids still call it The Church.

PAPA: But it ain't got no preacher?

RALPH: It's not really a church.

PAPA: No, I suspect you're right.

ASHAKI: Shani should be home soon.

RALPH: You want to wait here or come with us down to the—

PAPA: Church. That's not really a church. Don't think so. I'll just wait here.

RALPH: Fine. We'll be back shortly. If Omari comes in, tell him not to go any-where.

Ashaki and Ralph leave through the front door. Papa Constance remains on the couch with his eyes closed for a minute. Then he sits up, squeezes the lemon into the water, stirs it with his finger, picks up the glass and looks around the room. He spots a large plant in the corner, walks over to it and pours a few drops of the water into the soil while muttering something inaudible to the audience. He closes his eyes and says something else, then spills a little more. He walks around examining the room while sipping the water. The front door opens and Shani walks in carrying a purse and a backpack. She closes the door behind her and turns around to see her grandfather standing there.

SHANI: Papa? Papa Constance is that you?

PAPA: Of course it's me, young lady.

Shani drops her bags and runs and embraces him. She steps back. They are all smiles as they both examine each other from head to toe.

SHANI: *(rapid fire delivery)* When'd you get here? They didn't tell me you were coming? Have you seen Omari? You know he's leaving tomorrow for Harvard? Are you staying long? Please stay a while. It's been so long since I've seen you. Where's Mom and Dad? Do they know you're here?

PAPA: I see that you still got a million questions.

SHANI: I'm just so glad to see you. I mean, my God, I was just a little girl the last time.

PAPA: How old are you now? Wait. Don't tell me. You must be 15.

SHANI: No I'm 16, almost 17.

PAPA: I can't believe it. I haven't seen you since you were 4 years old.

SHANI: It's been a long time. When you left the last time, I thought I'd never see you again.

PAPA: I wasn't worried about that.

SHANI: I mean, you just left without saying anything.

PAPA: Your daddy and me had talked it out already and it was time for me to go.

Ashaki and Ralph come through the front door. They spot Shani at the same time.

ASHAKI and **RALPH:** Have you seen Omari?

Shani stops and gives them a strange look.

SHANI: *(to her parents)* I'm glad to see you, too.

ASHAKI: Shani, I'm sorry. But we really need to speak to your brother.

PAPA: *(sitting back down on the sofa)* How's my beautiful granddaughter?

SHANI: I'm fine Papa Constance. Just fine.

She plops down on the sofa next to him. Papa smiles as she gives him a hug and a peck on the cheek. Ashaki and Ralph watch them for a minute as Shani and Papa ignore them.

PAPA: *(to Shani)* Look at you.

SHANI: What are you doing here?

PAPA: Just stopped in for a quick visit.

role call

SHANI: *(turning sharply to her parents)* What's wrong? Has something happened?

ASHAKI: No baby. We were as surprised as you when you grandfather showed up.

RALPH: Do you know where your brother is?

SHANI: I just saw him over at The Church.

ASHAKI: When?

SHANI: About 20 minutes ago. He said he was on his way home.

RALPH: About 20 minutes ago?

SHANI: Yes.

ASHAKI: He should be here soon then.

SHANI: What's wrong?

RALPH: We need to talk to him.

SHANI: About what?

PAPA: How's he been doing Shani?

SHANI: Who?

RALPH: Your brother.

SHANI: The same.

ASHAKI: What does that mean?

SHANI: It means he—

The front door opens and in walks Omari. Everyone looks up at him. He stops just inside the door. He spots his grandfather but feels tension in the room so he doesn't respond to seeing him.

OMARI: What?

RALPH: Son, are you in some kind of trouble?

SHANI: What?

OMARI: *(sucks his teeth and rolls his eyes)* What are you talking about?

ASHAKI: A detective was here looking for you.

PAPA: Are you in trouble?

OMARI: Papa, what are you doing here?

PAPA: I came to see about you.

OMARI: I'm fine.

RALPH: Why are the police looking for you?

OMARI: They aren't looking for me.

ASHAKI: Then why were they here?

OMARI: I don't know.

PAPA: Omari, you think you're smarter than everybody in this room?

OMARI: No, sir.

PAPA: Then why you talking to us like we're stupid?

ASHAKI: Omari, we're just worried about you.

RALPH: Son, if you're in trouble let us know.

Omari looks at Shani, who looks down at the floor.

SHANI: Daddy, what'd he say?

RALPH: Who?

SHANI: The police.

RALPH: He wanted to talk to Omari.

PAPA: About what?

OMARI: Some kids got shot earlier today.

ASHAKI: What?

RALPH: Where?

PAPA: Who?

OMARI: Pharaoh Williams.

ASHAKI: Oh, my God! Little Pharaoh from down the street?

SHANI: He got shot outside The Church.

RALPH: Is he all right?

SHANI: He's dead.

PAPA: Why do the cops want to talk to you? Were you there?

OMARI: No.

SHANI: Some other boys got killed, too.

RALPH: What? Who?

OMARI: The two who killed Pharaoh.

ASHAKI: Did you know them?

SHANI: Everybody knew them.

RALPH: What do you mean everybody knew them?

SHANI: They were in a gang called the African Warrior Disciples.

PAPA: Disciples of what, the devil?

ASHAKI: Do you know something about what happened?

OMARI: I know they killed Pharaoh and now they're dead.

RALPH: What is wrong with you?

OMARI: Nothing.

ASHAKI: Son, are you ok?

RALPH: Look at me, Omari. What did you do?

OMARI: Nothing.

PAPA: Then why do the police want you?

OMARI: I don't know.

RALPH: The police know you aren't involved in any gang activity. Don't they?

OMARI: I don't know what they think.

ASHAKI: Why would those boys kill Pharaoh?

SHANI: Over a girl.

OMARI: You don't know, Shani.

SHANI: That's what everybody's saying. Pharaoh was talking to Shenita Taylor and she used to go with one of those boys.

RALPH: What? How long has this been going on? Who are the African Disciples?

OMARI: Everybody around here knows them.

RALPH: Hell, I'm around here and I don't know them.

ASHAKI: Omari you're not in a gang are you?

SHANI: They're not a gang.

RALPH: Who are they?

SHANI: O and his friends. They're a social club.

PAPA: Ralph, you know how boys hang together.

RALPH: Papa, with all due respect. This ain't South Carolina. This is Detroit.

PAPA: I don't care where it is.

OMARI: I want to go to my room.

ASHAKI: What is wrong with you? Omari this is serious. Do you understand that?

OMARI: It's more serious than you think.

RALPH: What does that mean?

OMARI: It means...

RALPH: Tell me. I want you to tell me what that means.

OMARI: I'm trying to tell you.

PAPA: Let him speak, Ralph.

SHANI: I don't like this. Why are you attacking him?

ASHAKI: We're not attacking him.

SHANI: Yes, you are.

RALPH: Shani, be quiet, this is serious! Omari, what did you do?

OMARI: I told you.

RALPH: No, you didn't.

There is another knock on the door. Everyone stops and looks slowly toward the door. Ashaki moves to answer it. She opens it slowly to reveal Detective Holden.

ASHAKI: Yes?

DETECTIVE: Is your son home now?

ASHAKI: Why do you want him?

Ralph comes up next to her and pushes the door all the way open so that the Detective can see everyone assembled.

RALPH: Come in Detective.

DETECTIVE: Thank you. (looks at Omari) Are you Omari Constance?

OMARI: *(looks at his father who nods)* Yes.

DETECTIVE: I need to ask you a few questions about the shootings today.

OMARI: I don't know nothing.

ASHAKI: Anything.

DETECTIVE: You knew Pharaoh Williams, didn't you?

OMARI: Yes.

RALPH: They grew up together.

DETECTIVE: Do you know who shot him?

OMARI: No.

DETECTIVE: Then you don't know that two of the African Warrior Disciples were killed about an hour later.

OMARI: I heard about it.

PAPA: Is he a suspect?

DETECTIVE: Sir, who are you?

PAPA: I'm the one asking you the question.

RALPH: This is Omari's grandfather, Reverend Lincoln Constance.

DETECTIVE: Reverend, I'm just trying to do my job.

PAPA: Well, then answer my question.

ASHAKI: Is he–

SHANI: a suspect?

RALPH: Well, is he? Or do you want him as a witness?

OMARI: I don't know nothing.

DETECTIVE: You knew Pharaoh, and you knew the two other boys who were killed today. Do you know why?

OMARI: I just heard about it like everyone else.

DETECTIVE: Are you in a gang?

OMARI: Naww.

DETECTIVE: Are you a member of the Masai Nation?

RALPH: Is he a suspect?

PAPA: The what nation?

OMARI: Naww.

DETECTIVE: Do you know who shot Hannibal?

OMARI: I already said. I don't know nothing.

ASHAKI: Anything. *(to Omari)* Why are you talking like that? *(to the detective)* He doesn't know anything about this.

SHANI: Why are you asking him all these questions?

PAPA: What is it with you? Don't you hear? Is he a Goddamned suspect?

DETECTIVE: Sir, I'm just doing my job. Just checking certain facts.

RALPH: What facts?

DETECTIVE: Your son knew Pharaoh Williams. He knew of the African Warrior Disciples. He knew there was some conflict between Williams and the Disciples.

PAPA: He didn't say that.

DETECTIVE: I thought he did. I thought I heard him say—

OMARI: You heard wrong.

RALPH: *(to the detective)* What kind of game are you trying to play here?

DETECTIVE: It's not a game, sir. It is definitely not a game.

ASHAKI: Detective, can you understand that we are upset? You come in here with all these questions. Can you understand?

DETECTIVE: Yes, Ma'am, I can.

ASHAKI: Our son is an honor student. He's going to Harvard in a few days. He comes from a good family with good values. He's not like those young black men you see on the news.

DETECTIVE: Three young black men are dead. What kind do you think they were?

RALPH: Look, is my son a suspect in this case or not? Give me an answer or get out of my house.

DETECTIVE: I'm a black man just like you. Got a son about Omari's age. You think I like this? Do you have any idea how many of these cases I've worked in the last few years.

SHANI: The police interviewed all of us down at The Church.

RALPH: What?

ASHAKI: When?

SHANI: Two hours ago.

OMARI: I told them the same thing then. I don't know nothing.

DETECTIVE: Son, were you involved in this? I know Hannibal was your best friend.

OMARI: I ain't your son.

RALPH: Do you know anything about this, Omari?

PAPA: If you do then be quiet.

RALPH: What? Certainly he had nothing to do with the killings. That doesn't mean he doesn't know something. He has nothing to hide.

ASHAKI: I'm sure Detective Holden is trying to do the right thing.

PAPA: Why? Because he's black?

OMARI: It don't make a difference whether the cops is black or white.

ASHAKI: What are you saying?

OMARI: They come around here now after Pharaoh is dead.

DETECTIVE: We do what we can.

OMARI: Now they want to act all surprised somebody got killed. Either they don't know what's going on around here or they know and just lying about it.

ASHAKI: Why do you say that?

DETECTIVE: Do you know anything about these killings, Omari? Were you involved?

RALPH: Is there something that you should be telling the police?

OMARI: I ain't got nothing to say to the police.

RALPH: *(Incredulous)* What? Son, your friend was murdered today.

OMARI: What are the cops going to do? Huh? What? They ain't been doing nothing.

RALPH: You mean to tell me that you will not tell the police what you know.

ASHAKI: Son, is there something you can tell us that would help the police arrest these people.

OMARI: Mama, I'm not talkin' to the police. I'm sorry.

RALPH: So you're willing to just let them get away with this?

OMARI: That's not what I'm saying.

ASHAKI: What are you saying?

RALPH: What are you saying? You plan to do something yourself? Were you involved in killing those other boys?

OMARI: I just don't have nothing to say to the police.

RALPH: What do you plan to do? Are you some kind of gangster now?

OMARI: Naww, I ain't no gangster, but I ain't no punk either.

RALPH: What does that mean?

ASHAKI: Shani...what is this about?

PAPA: It means the conversation with the detective is over.

ASHAKI: Detective, you can see we're upset.

DETECTIVE: I can see that.

RALPH: Is he a suspect? Is he...a God damn suspect? Can you tell me that? Is my son a suspect?

DETECTIVE: You have my card. If you want to talk, call me.

RALPH: Talk about what? You won't even answer my question.

DETECTIVE: I might want to talk to him again.

Detective Holden leaves. The family stands there frozen, each pondering what just happened. It is quiet and still.

ASHAKI: *(after a few beats)* Son, what did you do?

RALPH: You know who did this, don't you?

OMARI: It's not what you think.

SHANI: Tell them Omari.

ASHAKI: Tell us what?

Papa sits quietly listening, watching, studying his family.

SHANI: Tell them what goes on.

RALPH: What goes on where?

OMARI: Everywhere.

SHANI: Everywhere.

ASHAKI: What are you talking about?

OMARI: You think we're safe out here. You think things have changed.

RALPH: Of course they've changed.

ASHAKI: That doesn't mean they're perfect.

OMARI: You think things have changed.

RALPH: What are you talking about?

SHANI: They have to protect themselves.

ASHAKI: Who has to protect themselves?

OMARI: Everybody.

RALPH: From?

OMARI: Everybody.

ASHAKI: What are you talking about? You have everything. What are you talking about?

OMARI: You just don't know. You don't understand. Now Pharaoh is dead.

RALPH: And you blame us for his death.

ASHAKI: What did you do? You didn't do something awful did you?

OMARI: You just don't understand...

PAPA: It is time to make a decision.

RALPH: About what?

ASHAKI: Papa, please. We're trying to find out what happened.

PAPA: I know what happened.

RALPH: What?

PAPA: It's time to go. Omari, are your bags already packed for school?

OMARI Yes.

PAPA: Go get them.

RALPH: Omari, don't move.

PAPA: We need to get out of here.

ASHAKI: And go where.

RALPH: What are you saying? Omari should run from the police?

PAPA: He ain't gotta run, cause he ain't done nothing wrong.

ASHAKI: How do you know?

OMARI: He knows.

RALPH: Knows what?

SHANI: Why are you running?

OMARI: I'm not.

PAPA: He's going home with me. Harvard can wait for him.

ASHAKI: Have you lost your mind?

PAPA: What do you want to do? Do you want to lose him? Turn him over to the police? What? What do you want to do?

ASHAKI: I...I don't know how it came to this.

RALPH: He can't run.

OMARI: I'm not running.

SHANI: You didn't do it did you O?

RALPH: The police son, what about the police?

OMARI: They can't touch me.

ASHAKI: Did you do something awful?

RALPH: We didn't raise you to act like this.

ASHAKI: You didn't kill those young men did you? You're not running because of that, are you?

OMARI: I'm not running.

SHANI: What about school? Your scholarship?

RALPH: What about your life? What are you doing to your life?

ASHAKI: You can't run, son.

OMARI: I'm not running.

Omari walks off stage to get his bags. Everyone is frozen again, silent, still. He returns in a minute with a suitcase. His grandfather opens the door and they exit together. The mother, father and sister stare at the door in silence. The lights fade as the music from the beginning comes up. End of Act I.

Michael Simanga

Johnalynn Holland—**Less** black and white silver gelatin print

public   school

runny nose	hormones
anxious reason	tense laughter
jigga what	man size
sagging light	vacant lot
long fuse	short trigger

Quraysh Ali Lansana

Casualties

CEDRIC BLAKE, A 50-SOMETHING, BLACK MALE, DREADLOCKED AND DASHIKIED, MEDITATES IN THE FRACTURED BEAMS OF SUNLIGHT THAT SHINE THROUGH THE BARS OF HIS PRISON CELL.

DEBORAH: Good morning.

Cedric opens his eyes.

DEBORAH: I am Deborah Vanwa, your solicitor.

CEDRIC: Miss Vanwa, I was meditating.

DEBORAH: Our appointment was for 9:30am.

CEDRIC: I like to start my day with a clear mind, a focus. It is important therefore that the meditative process is not frustrated.

DEBORAH: It is 9:30am.

Cedric jumps up, grabs a pair of binoculars, stands on a chair and Peers out of the bars.

DEBORAH: Mr Blake!

CEDRIC: There she goes.

DEBORAH: We need to talk about your case.

CEDRIC: I have yet to see anyone, anyone (!) so absolutely alive. Come and look.

DEBORAH: I...

CEDRIC: Quick before she's gone. Pull up the other chair. Quick!

Deborah scurries over to cedric and stands on a chair next to him.

CEDRIC: Look beyond the courtyard.

DEBORAH: Who am I looking at?

CEDRIC: A running woman?

DEBORAH: Yes.

CEDRIC: Isn't she fascinating?

Deborah participates in the exercise under duress.

DEBORAH: Yes.

CEDRIC: I imagine her running into the arms of her lover.

DEBORAH: Quite.

CEDRIC: There's something familiar about her.

DEBORAH: *(Irritated)* If you would prefer, we can reschedule this meeting.

CEDRIC: I can't even remember asking for a lawyer.

DEBORAH: So you don't need my help.

CEDRIC: Cool down sister. You're here now, talk.

DEBORAH: Mr Blake, you have been charged with murder...

CEDRIC: I know....

DEBORAH: and you are facing a life sentence....

CEDRIC: The police haven't enough evidence. And there's no one to corroborate.

DEBORAH: On my way, I read a statement given by a gentleman called Maxwell Samuels...

CEDRIC: See it dey. Man safe.

DEBORAH: He's a friend?

CEDRIC: A brother in the struggle.

Cedric starts dancing, a calypso in his mind.

CEDRIC: 1959. We met on the boat coming over. We link up just like dat. (Does black power symbol fist thrust in the air).

DEBORAH: So he knows you well?

CEDRIC: There's not much we haven't shared from living space to women. We been fighting the system from time.

DEBORAH: What kind of man is he?

CEDRIC: Max is good people.

Cedric goes into his wallet and pulls out a photograph and shows it to deborah.

CEDRIC: That's me and that's Max. We just arrive in England. You see dem suits, made to measure, no off-the-peg rubbish.

DEBORAH: Very nice.

CEDRIC: Dem was the days. Rum, pom pom and dominoes.

DEBORAH: *[Sarcastically]* Very interesting.

CEDRIC: *[Proudly]* We were revolutionaries. We set up the first black organization—Justice for Africans.

DEBORAH: I wasn't aware that in your younger years you were a politician.

CEDRIC: A politician? A politician! That's an insult. I was and am a revolutionary. Politics is a business. Politicians put profits before people.

DEBORAH: Quite...

CEDRIC: A big difference.

Deborah tries to control her exasperation

CEDRIC: Black people ain't militant again. You know what our problem is, Ms.?

DEBORAH: Vanwa...

CEDRIC: We get little ways in life and we forget who we are? You understand?

Deborah nods

CEDRIC: Always talking about changing the system from within. (Shouts) Bullshit! But when we get within, we so glad for the scraps from Massa's table, we forget. And the subject, instead of the object, is reformed.

DEBORAH: We'll start by writing down your statement of what happened.

Cedric walks forestage. Cedric talks to the audience.

CEDRIC: She thinks I'm stuck in the interior.

DEBORAH: We'll start from the beginning.

CEDRIC: She feels I'm out of touch.

DEBORAH: The date, time, place and then I want you to detail what happened.

CEDRIC: This is a war! Can't she see that?

DEBORAH: Date?

CEDRIC: Preoccupied with the minutiae.

DEBORAH: Mr. Blake!

CEDRIC: She cannot see it's a war because the casualties are still on their feet. It's our minds and souls that are expiring.

DEBORAH: Mr Blake, the date!

CEDRIC: Why did you bring up Max. He alright?

Deborah does not reply

CEDRIC: Something happen to him?

Deborah still does not reply

CEDRIC: So what?

DEBORAH: *[Hesitantly]* He's giving evidence for the prosecution.

CEDRIC: You lie! Max wouldn't do that to me.

DEBORAH: *[Sympathetically]* No one with a modicum of intelligence wants a life sentence hanging over them.

Cedric is temporarily paralysed by his feelings of hurt and anger.

DEBORAH: Mr. Blake, Mr Samuels says that you killed Loraine Martins.

CEDRIC: No!

DEBORAH: He said that you were a party to…

Cedric shakes his head. His expression settles in the mode of a sad englightenment.

CEDRIC: Maybe.

DEBORAH: Maybe!

CEDRIC: I did not inflict the fatal wound but I may have helped create the tragic circumstances that led to her death.

DEBORAH: *[Dispassionately]* Is there blood on your hands? If there's no blood on your hands, you're innocent.

Cedric nods but is clearly unconvinced by Deborah's assertion.

DEBORAH: We need to prepare your defence. We need to discredit Maxwell Samuels.

CEDRIC: Revolutionaries stick together.

DEBORAH: *[Unsympathetically]* In revolutions. It's peacetime, Mr Blake. And in peacetime, it's every man for himself.

Deborah puts down the pen and waits for Mr. Blake to cooperate

DEBORAH: If you use your wits….

CEDRIC: *[Coldly]* Wits!

DEBORAH: *[Sarcastically]* Your ingenuity.

CEDRIC: *[Shakes head]* Lie? Lie!

DEBORAH: No.
CEDRIC: I am a man of principle. With me and mine there is a code of conduct.

DEBORAH: I understand, but...

CEDRIC: I don't think you do.

DEBORAH: *[Nonchantly]* The choice is between liberty or goal.

CEDRIC: A man of honour is always free.

DEBORAH: *[Uncharacteristic tenderness]* I realise that this has come as a great shock
to you.

CEDRIC: *[Glares at Deborah]* I don't believe you. I would have to hear the words
come out of his mouth. I would have to see his hand transcribe
his duplicity.

DEBORAH: Mr. Blake, I want to help you and I can, if you let me.

CEDRIC: Hmmm.

DEBORAH: I can come back when you have given the matter further thought.

CEDRIC: No, I don't think you understand what you are asking me, Cedric
Cleveland Oswald Blake, to do.

DEBORAH: I can be contacted on this number. Or on my mobile.

CEDRIC: I won't do it.

DEBORAH: As I said, get in touch when you've made a decision.

Deborah foists her businesscard into Cedric's hand. Cedric throws the card to the ground

CEDRIC: I don't need people like you.

DEBORAH: *[Implores]* Mr. Blake...

CEDRIC: When you get outside, you can spray on more of your expensive scent. It
will be as if you never came here.

DEBORAH: Goodbye, Mr. Blake.

Cedric stands intimidatingly close and circles Deborah while he delivers his onslaught.

CEDRIC: You black women. You get a bit of education and you can't even relate to black men.

DEBORAH: There's no need for that. I'm trying to help you.

CEDRIC: You feel sey you too nice, too special.

DEBORAH: I...

CEDRIC: You marry some tired white man for money and status. But your fantasies are full of black men with big dicks and long tongues.

Deborah's calmness/aloofness is now seasoned with contempt.

CEDRIC: Listen to your voice, your received pronunciation. You can't even speak your people's lingo.

DEBORAH: You don't even know me....

CEDRIC: You are a fine example of how the white man's education alienates black people from themselves and their own. You learnt well, too well. You've forgotten who you are, what you are.

DEBORAH: How dare you? You don't even know me. I am proud of who and what I am.

CEDRIC: No heritage, lost to Africa....

DEBORAH: I am proud of ...

CEDRIC: People like you wouldn't understand about commitment to the race. I won't do it. *[Pause]* I won't do what you want me to do. I won't sell out.

Cedric stands very close to deborah and almost whispers in her ears.

CEDRIC: There are enough coons in this world.

DEBORAH: *[Angrily]* Before destruction, a man's heart is haughty...

CEDRIC/DEBORAH: ...but humility goes before honour.

Deborah knocks on the door.

CEDRIC: Proverbs 19. I haven't heard that saying in a long while.

DEBORAH: Guard?

CEDRIC: Ann-Marie Jackson.

The sound of the name stops deborah in her tracks and she indulges the old man's reminiscence.

CEDRIC: She came from Barbados. A parish called St. Andrew. [Reminisce] I used to tease her, call her small island girl. She could dance, whoa! And she was sweet, all woman.

Yeah, Ann-Marie Jackson. Got pregnant for some guy and ran away. No note, no nothing. She just disappeared.

I thought about looking for her. But what was the point. She left me be cause she didn't want me.

DEBORAH: She talks of you in her more lucid moments.

CEDRIC: You know Ann-Marie?

DEBORAH: She heard a news report on the radio.

CEDRIC: Who is she to you?

DEBORAH: Said she knew you from the old days.

CEDRIC: Are you her...

DEBORAH: She's never begged me to do anything before.

CEDRIC: Her daughter...

DEBORAH: Said I should help you.

CEDRIC: Why?

DEBORAH: She still cares about you.

CEDRIC: I don't want to hear...

DEBORAH: Sometimes when she's well, she tells me about the old days: the blues parties and the dances you used to do.

Cedric shakes his head

DEBORAH: You could call her one of life's casualties.

Cedric walks forestage to create distance between himself and Deborah

> She had a nervous breakdown when she was pregnant with me. So I've never known the Ann-Marie you knew.

CEDRIC: Does she ever dance?

DEBORAH: I've never seen her dance.

CEDRIC: And run?

DEBORAH: Not anymore. She sits by a window watching the world go by and listening to the radio.

Cedric sighs heavily and tries to hold back his tears.

DEBORAH: Surrounded by symbols of the past. She is caught in a timewarp. *[Smiles sadly]* Some days she doesn't even know me. She laughs when you think she'd cry and cries when she should really laugh.

CEDRIC: I never knew. I thought she'd gone back home.

DEBORAH: I have to leave you Mr. Blake. My next appointment is due.

CEDRIC: And what about your father?

DEBORAH: Goodbye.

CEDRIC: Your father?

DEBORAH: I've never met him.

CEDRIC: Who was he?

DEBORAH: An unsavoury sort. Not a man of honour like you [Pause] Please get in touch with me if you need me.

CEDRIC: What was his name?

DEBORAH: I can't remember.

CEDRIC: That is one name a child always remembers.

DEBORAH: It doesn't matter.

CEDRIC: Deborah, I loved your mother for a long time. Years after we parted I would dream her. Maybe, it's vanity. Maybe it's just a man thing. I just want to know who was worthier than me.

DEBORAH: Ask your friend Maxwell Samuels.

CEDRIC: He doesn't know. If it wasn't for Maxwell, I don't know what would have become of me. I stopped eating, started drinking, couldn't think straight.

DEBORAH: Mr. Blake...

CEDRIC: That's why I can't turn on him now.

Cedric touches Deborah's arm.

CEDRIC: For us, it's all about survival. And in order to survive we have had to stick together.

DEBORAH: Yes.

CEDRIC: We're the walking wounded. But we still here. And that's saying something.

DEBORAH: Yes.

CEDRIC: You say yes, but do you understand?

DEBORAH: Yes. I do. But *[pauses]*

CEDRIC: Go ahead.

role call

DEBORAH: No, I better leave.

CEDRIC: Please...

DEBORAH: The running woman, she understands the expanse of her own freedom. Her eyes are open and she can see not only what is ahead, but what is to her left and right so that she can overcome any obstacle or danger in her path.

Maxwell sighs and suddenly seems very old.

CEDRIC: Why did she leave me?

DEBORAH: Your friend Maxwell Samuels knows everything.

CEDRIC: *[Surprised]* Max?

DEBORAH: He raped my mother and I am the product.

Cedric starts screaming

DEBORAH: She tried to tell you. But you wouldn't listen. So she left.

CEDRIC: All these years. You never really know a man, do you?

DEBORAH: If we're honest, I think we do.

CEDRIC/DEBORAH: "Understanding will guard you; delivering you from the way of evil, from men of perverted speech, who forsake the paths of uprightness to walk in the ways of darkness, who rejoice in doing evil and delight in the perverseness of evil; men whose paths are crooked, and who are devious in their ways.

Cedric grabs his head and starts to cry.

Deborah Vaughan

Sheila L. Prevost—**Imprisonment** pastel on canvas

Ten Precepts of
a **Zen Peacemaker**

Being mindful of the interdependence of oneness and diversity, and wishing to actualize my vows, I engage in the spiritual practices of:

1. Recognizing that I am not separate from all that is. This is the precept of non-killing.
2. Being satisfied with what I have. This is the precept of non-stealing.
3. Encountering all creations with respect and dignity. This is the precept of chaste conduct.
4. Listening and speaking from the heart. This is the precept of non-lying.
5. Cultivating a mind that sees clearly. This is the precept of not being ignorant.
6. Unconditionally accepting what each moment has to offer. This is the precept of not talking about others' errors and faults.
7. Speaking what I perceive to be the truth without guilt or blame. This is the precept of not elevating oneself and blaming others.
8. Using all of the ingredients of my life. This is the precept of not being stingy.
9. Transforming suffering into wisdom. This is the precept of not being angry.
10. Honoring my life as an instrument of peacemaking. This is the precept of not thinking ill of the three treasures.*

*The Three Treasures: Teachers, Teaching, Community

Angel Kyodo Williams

VII

ROLE CALL IS A JOURNEY THROUGH TOPICS OF BLACK LOVE, BLACK RAGE AND BLACK FIRE.

BLACK LOVE

Theodore A. Harris—**Meditations for Betty Shabazz** collage

What **Love** Is

my brother was love
always looked like a peace dove
in white shirts or straight jackets

brother turned himself into a harbor for voices
when a toke of weed laced with lsd
broke free the paranoid schizophrenic in him

he came home to break all the mirrors
never again looked at anything reflecting him
my mother never saw his living eyes again

the city came to pick him up
put him in a coat meant to make him safe
made him hug himself tighter than we ever had

he was love
love knows when to come when not to
when to play it sane to make my birthdays happy

though he lived in a rubber house
if tears hit my pillow at night
his smile greeted me by dawn

he held me when he told me
i have to do everything for love
my type knows honor is doing all love requires

so when part of him uncontrollable by him
told him to do things unthinkable to the sane him
when i became target of a lunatic living inside him

he released himself from his mental ward
turned the bridge named for a free flying duke of jazz
into launch a pad

he looked at the heavens when he
turned from man into angel
crossed over from brother to ancestor

when the back of his head hit a rock in the creek
the demons broke free
possessed, surviving brothers and me

we found our art and science of living
our parents stricken by the "we should've done" virus
forgot what they still had to do had to do with us

catholics told me pray for his unforgivable sin
but my brother was more jesus than judas
deserves more heaven than some ministers and fathers

my brother michael,
angel, dove
knew all about love

Toni Assante Lightfoot

Love Bigger Than
Yankee Stadium

The kitchen smells of
scrambled eggs and cigarettes.
I sit in the dark
on the kitchen chair
olive vinyl peeling,
scratching and digging
into the backs of
my thighs.

Jason is on the floor
With his head on my leg
His face round and glossy
Like a wet plum.
He tries to sleep off the heat.

My hands play in his
cornrowed hair.
I want to tell him
That he reminds me of Stevie
Wonder. If only
He had the beads.

Thinking back
Jason and I met at the A&P
in the fruit & vegetable aisle

He followed me
Told me his name.

He was darker than Coke.
Voice thick with the Bronx.
He worked at the Laundromat
From 8 to noon

He said I got love
For you that's bigga

Than Yankee Stadium 2
And that made me smile.
He used to talk
About the Bronx
Like it was his girl.

He was in love with it
Like it was some pussy
or Puerto Rican rum.

Now, I want to wake him;
remind him of those days
and tell him about the Hathaway
record that I got for $3,

But he'd start talking
About his boys at the bar
On Vine St.
And how Rodney got kicked
Out by his wife
And about how Black women are
Always bitching,

Our thing used to be
so sweet
The one thing I remembered best
Is when he parked
His two-door Honda in the back
Of Concetta's pizza house
On the South End.

We did it once.
We did it twice.
And our skin shined
like a woman in labor.

He sounded like a blues singer,
the way he moaned;
I wanted to do it all
night, But Jason,
he had to be to work
in the morning.

Melissa McEwen

Kenneth L. Addison—**Sins of the Father** mixed media collage on batik

Labor Poem #2

around noon she leaves her desk
first she goes to the cuchifrito on Broadway
for rice and beans and plantains
then to the Mr. Softee ice cream truck
parked on the corner of Spring
carrying her brown paper bag
with Isla Gorda stamped on the side
the bottom corners are spotted with oil
where the pinto beans are leaking because
the lids for the already-flimsy Styrofoam cups
were a deal from a second cousin
sometimes they put on two
she feels patient today and careful
not worried that the oil may stain
or the beans may spill
she sees her friend
from the twenty-four hour deli
who has been slipping a free extra piece of cheese
every morning on her egg and cheese on a roll
because it makes him happy to see her belly so big
it makes him remember his woman's belly
which is why he is here in the first place
many mountains from Mexico
behind the hot grill
every morning at six
he moves quickly to deliver someone's lunch
she moves slowly
toward her chocolate cone with chocolate sprinkles
her reflection in a shoe store window surprises her
she watches herself pass by
notices how easily her body maneuvers
the forty pounds it has welcomed
churns to keep her two hearts beating
the ice cream is everything she expected
everything she wanted right then she
decides to go one more block for six wings
from the Chinese take-out restaurant
the kind that are fried and fried again
she slides her money into the rotating bulletproof box
the smiling woman on the other side says good luck
then spins her change and the wings back to her
she thanks her, trying hard not to think about birth.

Melanie Hope

Cheryl L. Minor—**Nile & Onan Sitting on a Stoop Eating Ices**
digital photography

Illuminata

It was too dark the night she went
into labor, the moon standing guard
outside the tiny house. Mississippi nights are
dark and so full smells are hard to ignore,
sounds nudge you forward and what one sees
could be flashes of imagination burning
through coal sky. But it wasn't

a flash or streak we saw, peeking through
the window, too young to know how wrong we were.
It was life beaming between the scuffle of bodies
moving back and forth, room to room, one side
of the bed to the other, as we stole glimpses of
the mother and child. This is how we came to know

the contrast of light and dark. Not from fireflies or stars,
but tiny houses that dot the wide open fields
of Mississippi's Delta.

Lita Hooper

Dream Child

You are spiritchild
Floating on wind anticipation
Dreams and downdraft wishes for you
to escape modern and now, fly
free into tomorrow

Dream a minute ahead
Fill yourself on reality's spoonfuls
Let us break down the impalpable
unpalatable into bites of joy for you
to digest leisurely among colored blocks
hugs, things loved by the tender

Dream spirit, child
Imagine touchable destinies
solid follies, fragrant afternoon laughter
Wonder at the puffiness of clouds
not the gravity of future finance
Terrestrial weights anchoring
our once feathery frames

Drift in subconscious
enjoy thoughts of violet delight
over the daily simple
Sip tea cups of innocence
until you are full

Dance Twirl Spin
Giggle until the world is kaleidescope clear
dizzy vivid filled with rose and sky blue
at every gaze

Soar into night's bliss
Embrace the darkness, your darkness
Fold it into you like fresh sheets
of summer and candied laughter
sweetly spread over a mashed
childhood sandwich

Claim your birthright and fly
into the hour before dawn
where creation cries and craves to become
under dim shadow and stifled light

You are spirit, child

Bryant Smith

The **First Time I Saw** *Flo-Jo*

for Florence Griffith Joyner (1960-1998)

I almost died when I saw those Nile-nails,
bright as your neon spandex, tacky
& beautiful too.

Flo, girl

you ran like the Boogieman's
worst fear—a Black woman with God
all up in her. Ran so fast you caught
the Boogieman on a tail wind
& boogied his ass back.

> Someone said the Devil
> must have gotten in you
> for you to run like that.

But, the drums of your feet cried
war & eyes were husks
around your calves; were heavy
with memory; exploded with freedom
each time you burst. We thought: The wind
ain't got a chance. Do it like it ain't been done,
girl. Run like you gotta run, girl. Hotdamn,
look at our sister fly!

& Nail salons got rich,
Spandex was never so chic,
Kids poured strawberry Kool-Aid
on dirt, stirred it up & took off
running in ghettos everywhere,
exhaling: jojojojo flojojojo

& in those moments
when you ruptured the wind,
the drums of your feet crying
war, girl, we rallied
we rallied damned
if we didn't rally.

Crystal Williams

Let This Cover You When You Sleep

what do i owe love
that is not arms in motion

fill a vase with flowers
sing lovely stare into my eyes
what is done will not rest

the clothes are dirty again,
love, the trash must be taken
to the street again, love i
saw in your eyes the tired
that makes a man feel useless

late at night when we breathe
together, you will not lie
and say tomorrow is easier

though i know that is what love
wants, the touch of silk
a small pleasure what do i love
you for pressing against me
when my body is thorns

what can i sing for you
that is not blue

Bro. Yao

The Last **Moonsong**

I hear Daddy and Aunt Christy fighting again.

I don't know why they act like I'm not here, like I don't have ears and eyes and can't see what's going on. Usually they're whispering and carrying on like they the only ones Mama left here on the other side of a locked room, staying up late every night too tired to sleep 'cause you feel so bad. Daddy blamed Aunt Christy for not coming home sooner, not canceling her trip to India and coming to see Mama when she was feeling better, but Aunt Christy blew up. She said it ain't her fault and she wasn't going to stand up there and let him tell her it is.

Actually, she said "It's not my fault, William, and I'm not going to allow you to stand here and blame me for something that was beyond my control or yours, *blah blah blah....*" Aunt Christy speaks real proper, "propa" as Mama would say. She got a million degrees and has traveled all over the world collecting "data": oral folktales, the stories people tell themselves and their children. Aunt Christy don't have no children. She says that when she can sit still long enough she will.

That used to make Mama laugh, 'cause Mama say Aunt Christy like a humming-bird, her thoughts always in motion, whirring, whirring, never can be still. But Aunt Christy say *Mama* is the hummingbird, she always whirring, too, in her head-*worrying* about one thing or another. I heard her tell Daddy one day that Mama can't see where she going 'cuz her head always turned way back in the past. She say Mama ought to change her perspective, see her world in a new light. Aunt Christy try to get Mama to travel with her sometimes, but Mama wouldn't go. Said that was part of Aunt Christy's problem: she always ripping and running so she can see what she want to see and not what is. The last time Aunt Christy brought traveling up, Mama say that that one trip was enough for the both of them. Then they both got real silent.

Sometimes when Mama got mad at Aunt Christy, she'd say she was so busy stealing other folk's tales 'cause she didn't have enough imagination to tell her own. Sometimes I wondered if that was true, but I never had courage enough to ask Aunt Christy. It's not that I thought she'd get mad—Aunt Christy not like most grown folk. She always had a way of talking to me like I was an adult, her equal and could under-stand anything she had to say—*but*, she also asked a zillion zillion questions, and with something that juicy, I'd be looking at listening to her talk for at least three or four days.

Not that Daddy would mind. He always seemed to like listening to Aunt Christy's tales about 'the talking jaguars of Peru' and the time she nearly broke her neck hiking down Machu Picchu, when a shaman guy with a condor's feather sang her down. Daddy would sit up for what seemed like hours while Aunt Christy talked about Ti-Malice and Boukie in Haiti, and the time she heard a new story on the way to bless herself in some sacred waterfall, or how she got lost and wandered into the temple of the blue-skinned god of India, and the folk thought her name was Kali, one of his many girlfriends.

To tell the truth, I was surprised to hear Daddy saying those mean things to Aunt

Christy because when Mama was here, he was the one usually defending her. I don't know why Mama never got along with her big sister—except on the rare times when they were cooking holiday dinners and we were about to eat. I guess fixing all that heavy soul food made them think about Grandmama and how much she loved them, but now Mama is gone and Aunt Christy has been cooking a lot for us lately, since she came back.

The other day, Daddy tried to cheer her up and tell her that her food really ain't half bad. Aunt Christy just smiled that sad smile of hers, like Mama's. Mama to used to laugh and say Aunt Christy didn't know how to cook anyway, that she didn't want her burning up her kitchen. No matter how much they got on each other's nerves, they always used to laugh about that, somebody burning up stuff.

Mama was going to teach me how to cook, too.

Yeah, well, they fussed and fought like me and my little knucklehead brother Boney do, and they loved each like I guess sisters suppose to.

Our neighbor, Miss Beasley, says that love is going to see us through this.

But I wonder what kind of love she talking about.

We suppose to love each other, alright but everything so mixed up now. I've never heard Aunt Christy raise her voice like she is now. Unless you count the time L'il Boney and I were playing hide and seek in Aunt Christy's big ole house and wasted Kool-Aid on her oriental rug. We were visiting her and Uncle Crib in El Paso. Mama was so mad at us. She said Aunt Christy had gotten that rug from some old family up in the mountains in northern India, said they'd been hand weaving rugs for generations. She said the rug was damn-near priceless, cuz the family had worked for six months weaving a special pattern just for Aunt Christy, and the elder who had trimmed the rug had Passed On. Hers was one of the last rugs his hands touched. While Mama was hissing all this, Aunt Christy was sputtering and huffing and puffing so much and dabbing at that rug with a little wet cloth—I never seen her so mad—that Mama nearly tripped rushing us out of the living room. I thought she was going to whoop us, and L'il Boney was whimpering and whining like a l'il baby. "I ain't do it," he said. "I ain't do it! Reba push me!" Little tattletale. But it was true. I did push his butt, 'cuz he always peeking when he's supposed to be counting. When I finally had the courage to look up at Mama's face, I saw that she wasn't mad anymore, just shaking her head, sadly.

I think she took it worse than Aunt Christy did, and Uncle Crib, he just laughed it off. Uncle Crib is a big ole man, about seven feet tall and he always makes us laugh. He even makes Aunt Christy laugh, even when she don't want to. He made her laugh that day. I guess that's why she married him. Later, Aunt Christy gave us all a big hug, and told Mama not to worry herself about it, said she took things way too seriously, that it was just an old rug, something to walk on, and that Mama and us meant more to her than any ole rug.

That made Mama smile, but I could tell by the look in her eyes that she was filing that away as just another thing she'd want to repay Aunt Christy for. She had the same look in her eyes that Aunt Christy did, that "it-ain't-alright-but-it-will-be" look.

Now that I think of it, Mama and Aunt Christy more alike than folk say they is.

True, Mama was tall and graceful with a head full of bushy black hair, and Aunt Christy wasn't 'knee-high to a duck' as Big Mama used to say, and just as knock-kneed. Big Mama say Aunt Christy used to trip over her own feet, trip going up the stairs, but she always carried herself like a queen, since she was very little. And when she got old enough to be on her own, she wore her hair in long, thick dreadlocks that made her even look like an African queen.

Aunt Christy say Mama could have been a singer or a dancer, if she wanted to, said when they was growing up, Mama had the sweetest voice in the land and could kick her big ole long legs up in the air like the most graceful of Alvin Ailey's dancers. That when she was little Mama would always sing to the moon, 'cuz that's where Big Mama told them their daddy was. That he died right after Mama was born, and that he always loved to hear Big Mama sing gospel, or the blues, or whatever, it didn't matter. He loved music. She said it made him smile so wide, with his teeth all bright and shiny, like the moon. So when Mama missed her Daddy, she would sing, she would sing beautiful songs that she made up herself. She would gaze out their bedroom window in West Memphis and sing to the moon, imagining herself dancing and gliding and smiling with her Daddy.

I loved to hear them tell me this story, of Mama and her beautiful moonsongs. Sometimes Mama would sing for Boney and me. She'd just make up something and sing, and we'd laugh and she'd dance, then she'd pull us out of bed and we'd all dance with her. One day Daddy snuck up on us and recorded us singing, L'il Boney cracking notes, me holding my own (if I do say so myself), and Mama dancing to her own special moonsong.

I bet she could have been a dancer, if she wanted to. But I came pretty soon after Mama met Daddy, who had already finished high school. One day when I asked Mama why she didn't go on and dance like Aunt Christy said she wanted to, she just laughed and said she was always more of a homebody and that Aunt Christy was restless. I wonder about that now. Seem like they spirit the same. They just chose different ways of being. Maybe that's why it was hard for them to get along.

I'm thinking this, trying hard to think about something else when I hear heavy footsteps down the hall. A door slams. The echo seems to bounce off my walls a minute, then, after a while I hear Mama's voice.

Man Why does he have to do this? Every night, he keeps playing that stupid recording. I don't want to hear it. I want to run downstairs and tell him to turn it off. *Turn it off, Daddy! She ain't coming back, she ain't.*

Mama's voice is sweet and high, then it gets low, like those old Mahalia Jackson albums Big Mama used to play when she was dusting or mopping, or just looking out her window. I'm laying up in this bed, pillows squooshed around my head, trying to pretend like I'm sleep, like I don't hear what I'm hearing, but what I really hear is my mama dying, Mama leaving me, leaving me with nothing but these hateful thoughts and all these stupid, stupid questions.

I bury my face deep into my pillow. The pillowcase smells musty, like it ain't been washed in a million million years. Daddy ain't done no housekeeping since the funeral, and he ain't let nobody in here since that day Boney freaked out. People call or drop off food and stuff, but none of us have no appetite, and poor Boney. Usually he gets on my nerves, with his little ign'ant know-it-all five-year-old self, but I ain't had the energy to mess with him. It's been three days since the funeral, and L'il Boney still won't take his suit off or those stupid cowboy boots. They look silly and they too little anyway, but he won't take them off and Daddy won't make him. Aunt Christy don't say nothing 'cuz we all know why.

First he wouldn't go. Said he didn't want to say bye-bye to Mama 'cuz she didn't say bye-bye to him...

Crap! I can't think about this anymore. I'm tired. I can't sleep and I don't want to eat nothing, and all I can think about is Boney freaking out, screaming like somebody killing him 'cuz Cousin Glenda said he couldn't wear those crusty old black and yellow boots. "You want to look nice for your mama, don't you?" she asked. "No!" But she kept asking him, trying to say it in a different way everytime, but Boney ain't crazy, just worrisome. He didn't want to go so he hit her, then ran into his room, screaming. He wouldn't come out until Daddy told him he could wear what he wanted.

But when Boney came out in those little cowboy boots Mama had given him the last time we visited Aunt Christy in Texas, *I* didn't want to go. He was trying to look so brave, like he didn't have a hole in his chest just as wide as mine or Daddy's. He got them boots when he was four years old. They was too big for him then, but Boney had picked them out himself, and Mama went ahead and got them 'cuz he said they made him look like 'a big boy.'

Boney's five and a little small for his age. The other kids in school (my old school) seem to tower above him. Mama used to tell him not to worry about those 'Similac babies,' said he would grow in his own time, when he needed to.

Thinking about Boney, all alone asleep in the room next to mine, makes me cry even harder. I bite into my pillow and tear at it, tear at it 'cuz I don't want to cry. I want to rip this stupid pillow into shreds, like I feel inside, like this whole empty house feels. I don't want to cry and I don't want Daddy or Boney or Aunt Christy or anyone to hear me. But then the door cracks open, and a little light spills into my room, and then I hear Mama's voice, singing, Mama's voice, laughing. I don't look up. I know who it is.

Daddy sits down heavily on my bed, sighs and pats my back. He keeps patting my back like I'm not eleven years old and will be in the sixth grade in less than two weeks. He keeps patting my back like I'm a l'il bit, like Boney.

"Babygirl."

I don't say nothing. I don't want him to see my face.

"Babygirl," he gulps air. "Babygirl, I'm sorry. I know you heard me and your Aunt tonight, and I just want to say that I know your mama wouldn't want us to..." His voice gets high, like he's going to sing or something and I can't hold it in. It's too much.

I yank the pillow from my face and turn over. "Why?" I ask him. "Why she leave me alone like this? If she love me, why she do it, Daddy."

In the dim light I see Daddy's face become still, and it's like a glass, all slow-motion and brightness before it falls and breaks into a million sharp pieces.

Seeing him looking like that, seeing my fear reflected in his eyes scares me. I see his body shaking through my blurry tears and then I lose it. I just start yelling.

"If she loved me, why she kill herself? She didn't love me. She didn't love nobody but herself..."

Daddy pulls me close to him and I let him hold me, I let him hold me like he did when I was really little. I let him hold me 'cuz now he's the only one left to.

"It's not true," he says, but his words don't sound so sure. He says Mama loved me, loved Boney, and all of us more than anything but . . .

"But..."

His voice breaks.

See that's where I get tripped up, too: *but.*

"She loved you, and she loves you still ..." he says, slow and quiet at first, then louder, like he got to convince me and himself. "She did, it's just that ..." and he pauses.

I wipe my eyes and wait, wait and watch him struggle for the words. My Daddy's always been soft-spoken, at least as long as I've known him. He's the peacekeeper in the family, the one that got between Big Mama and her two handful-'o-daughters, and later, between the two sisters themselves. If something went down between L'il Boney and me, it was Daddy we'd run to because we knew Mama would be looking for the first one to whoop. Daddy would listen to whatever crazy excuses or half-truths we had to tell about who hit who and who took what and when and where, but Mama? Mama would whoop first and ask questions later. By the time she got through, wasn't nothing left to be said. But Mama didn't whoop us that much. She mostly threatened a whole lot and made us go to our rooms if we clowned too much. Daddy is the softy.

So I'm sitting here, in the middle of the night, after a whole week of sleepless nights, feeling my Daddy shake in my arms, waiting on him to stop my tears and be strong. I pull back and look into his face. I can tell he's tired, too. He looks like he hasn't slept in a zillion years, and he has that look on his face, the one he gets when he is thinking real hard. The pulse point on the right side of his chin quivers and turns up, and right now he's looking as if he's trying to make up the most fantabulous ending to the most fantabulous bedtime story.

I wipe my nose with the back of my hand and wait for him to collect his thoughts. I want to tell him that it's alright, that I'm eleven now, too old for those neat bow-ribbon fairytales he and mama used to tell us. And as Mama's voice drifts into my bedroom, from the stereo downstairs, I wipe my eyes but the tears keep coming, and I can't breathe, and I can't see, and I don't want to feel, but I'm mad, real mad and I want to tell him that he can save that moonsong mess for Boney, that I don't want to hear any stories anymore.

I don't want to hear any stories ever again.

Sheree Renée Thomas

Johnalynn Holland—**My Grandmother's Camera** mixed media
photo collage

Mr. Pate's Barbershop

I remember the room in which he held
a blade to my neck & scraped the dark
hairs foresting a jawline: stacks of *Ebonys*
& *Jets*, clippings of black boxers—
Joe Frazier, Jimmy Young, Jack Johnson—
the color television bolted to
a ceiling like the one I watched all night
in a waiting room at St. Joseph's
while my cousin recovered from gunshots.
I remember the old Coke machine, a water
fountain by the door, how I drank
the summer of '88 over & over from a paper
cone cup & still could not quench my thirst,
for this was the year funeral homes boomed,
the year Mr. Pate swept his own shop
for he had lost his best little helper Squeaky
to cross fire. He suffered like most barbers
suffered, quietly, his clippers humming so loud
he forgot Ali's lightning left jab, his love
for angles, for carpentry, for baseball. He forgot
everything & would never be the same.
I remember the way the blade gleamed
fierce in the fading light of dusk & a reflection
of myself panned inside the razor's edge
wondering if I could lay down my pen, close up
my ledgers & my journals, if I could undo
my tie & take up barbering where
months on end a child's head would darken
at my feet & bring with it the uncertainty
of tomorrow, or like Mr. Pate gathering
clumps of fallen hair, at the end of a day,
in short, delicate whisks as though
they were the fine findings of gold-dust
he'd deposit in a jar & place on a shelf, only
to return Saturdays, collecting, as an antique dealer
collects, growing tired, but never forgetting
someone has to cherish these tiny little heads.

Major L. Jackson

Gwendolyn Brooks
1917-2000

Sometimes I see in my mind's eye a four-or-five-
year-old boy, coatless and wandering
a wind blown and vacant lot or street
on the wind blown South Side. He disappears
but stays with me, staring and pronouncing
me guilty of an indifference more callous
than neglect, condescension as self-pity.

Then I see him again, at ten or fifteen, on the corner,
say, 47th and Martin Luther King, or in a group
of men surrounding a burning barrel off Londale
everything surrounding vacant or for sale.
Sometimes I trace him on the train to Joliet
or Menard, such towns quickly becoming native
ground to these boys who seem to be nobody's
sons, these boys who are so hard to love, so hard
to see, except as case studies.

Poverty, pain, shame, one and a half million
dreams deemed fit only for the most internal
of exiles. That four-year-old wandering
the wind tunnels of Robert Taylor, of Cabrini
Green, wind chill of an as yet unplumbed degree—
a young boy she did not have to know to love.

Anthony Walton

a tribute to
MS. GWENDOLYN BROOKS

somewhere brooks bubble with black power
haiku float on lily pads
waterfalls rage with clarity

sonnets shimmer like rainbows over rivers
their spectrum separates the night
thunder creates trembles and shivers
Splitting sadness with its might

listen

gwendolyn is crying colors again

listen

to the splash of a million tears
trickling down ebony faces
like spiraling Negro anthems

like black rain
time showers day with an opus of song
leaving prints upon the face of our future

listen

its
flowing freedom

Michael Guinn

Hydrangeas

for Gwendolyn Brooks

Great-Mama took such care tending

the teal hydrangeas—their massive heads,

full of petals like impulsive thoughts,

could fly apart in any spring breeze

and they would be left scattered, half

of themselves, and still appear full-headed.

Great-Mama nursed them with formulas,

whispered names and lullabies

under her breath patted and cooed

the soil at the roots until her palms

were caked black. And oh, how they blossomed

and sprouted, framing the front yard

as if to say, she is ours, ours, to touch her

you must cross the cool blue blaze.

Angela Shannon

Speaksong

for Gwendolyn Brooks

Syllables dancing so clear
speaksong reverberates deep
into our eardrums
strumming word-strings
songing black blues inside us
like the sun blazes air with fever,
never altering the majestic faces
that cry through earth-shadows

Syllables gather feelings
on air that clings in our nostrils
breathing grace notes, the simplest song
writing itself on the street.

Fine word-prints left behind,
form the language of jazz,
patient, yet urgent, track
the glinting streets while
healings move us into other lives.

Lenard D. Moore

peeling away
at my tempting
surface
twisting my mind like
a long brown stem
cutting me in half,
saving pieces of me in
the fridge for when
you're hungry a little
later.
I'm a popular fruit, but
you can have your
pick.
you peel. you bite. you
lick.
fulfill all my
needs

Apple Seed

tenderly you
eat me up
I plant my apple seed
wonder if you'll have
a craving once again
a sugar substitution
for a healthy freak
maybe next week
you'll pull me out of
that cold square box
apple juice on the
rocks
I love it when you
take the lead
searching for my
apple seed.

Jessica Care Moore

I REMOVED your picture from the BRASS FRAME on my nightstand

I removed your picture from the brass frame on my nightstand

Removed the hairs from your goatee from the grout
between my bathroom tiles

Thrown away the blue socks you left
and scraped the I love You
sticker from my rear window

Changed my phone number
pulled up the carpet
sold your record collection
started and stopped going to the gym
duck taped the toilet seat down

I do not miss your kiss or remember that you kissed me

But your touch

If you would remove it from my back
your knuckles pressed into my spine

I have burned the old bed sheets
changed the lock combination
and the porch light 7 times
I don't use Tabasco sauce on fried chicken
or fry chicken anymore for that matter

You are still here

I have cut my hair and it has grown back

I just can't forget how you held my skull like a rock
and threw me into the wall
like you hoped I'd go through it

Your touch
you know that touch from six years ago
the one you said I was responsible for
that touch and every other one you gave just like it

I am not a murderer
Erase yourself from me so I can stop
killing you in my dreams

Jenoyne Adams

Calida Garcia—**Woman** oil on canvas

I Hate Your Guts

but your ass has
a life of its own;
nothing to do
with anything about my total disgust,
disregard and ambivalence towards you.

It speaks on its own,
breathes on its own,
moves and sways on its own,
sits round and tight.

I hate how fine you are
how sassy you walk,
how the sight of your ass
alone can make me fall
back in love with you.

I continuously let you go, yet
you constantly reappear as if
by magic or
divine order.

Rebecca Strait

Renaldo Davidson—**Nina** oil pastel on paper

SARAH NELL

HE WALKS TO THE CORNER OF LENOX AND SOUTH MAIN, takes a right, and then she waits. She is going to meet another one. I follow her because lately she hasn't been bringing them home. I want to see what this one looks like. All the others were big and filled doorways. All were dark-skinned. Oh, except for one. People call him Tang (short for Tangerine) because his skin is the color of an orange. I don't know why people just didn't call him orange. I guess it didn't sound right. He was the first, after my father left.

The sun makes the plum tone of her skin look lighter. She looks more like the Sarah Nell from the black and white photos instead of Mama. Today, Sarah is made up of braids going back that barely reach her neck, big hoop earrings, and red-framed glasses too big for her round face. Men whistle at her as they pass on their way to work or on their way to see their mistresses. I like to think that I can read minds, and I guess they whistle and honk and stare because they like the way the warm wind pushes her skirt between her thighs. She looks at her watch. I am sure she is thinking about the men that didn't stay or thinking about trying not to think about the men that did not stay.

There were two, though, that stayed for more than just a little while: Marvin and Kenya. Marvin was married and that's all I have to say about that. Kenya wasn't and it didn't seem like he was planning on getting married either. What a petty man he was. I guess it's because he has been dealing with small things all of his life. All of his women were small; so is his mother and so was his pay. That relationship between Mama and him was built out of order. She went up to him first. She called him first. She turned him on and turned him out first (I know because I heard them and she tried so hard to be quiet). However, he wanted out first. I think he got tired of acting grown and so he ran along. He wanted to chase the girls in the clubs downtown, but Mama was giving him what the girls downtown giving him, but still he didn't stay. Mama is clingy. She clung to him like how she clings to her purse. When he wasn't around, she wondered where he was. And when he was around her, she was always following him and touching him. He would read a magazine and she would be on the arm of the sofa, pointing out the girls that she thought he would like.

She talks to herself—and most people do—but she does it all of the time. You got some nerve doing ME like that she said to the mirror once, perhaps pretending that her reflection was one of those men that did not stay. I was peeping through the cracked bedroom door and her fingers tugged hard her uncombed hair. Why don't men stay? she asked herself. This incident happened after Marvin, but before Kenya. She was seeing this singer who called himself Maggie, but his birth name was Yusef. He was known around the neighborhood as Magnet, Maggie for short. I remember he had thin wrists like a woman (but he hit like a man). That one, too, got away from her even though she wanted him to stay. He said she was too passive for him and so he ran off. When he comes around sometimes, my Mama spreads her legs easy for him. I pray at night that some man's love for her someday will be more than spread legs and oh baby.

She looks so little, now, standing and waiting. Look at the way her fingers fumble with her purse strap. I know her hands are sweaty from the tight grip she has on her purse. She looks at her watch again. I wonder if she is used to this by now. She seems to not be in any hurry for change because she continues with the same routine over and over again. Maybe she hates being lonely. But I'm there in the house with her. She can talk to me. I want to go up to her and tell her what I've learned from books and magazines about relationships and about men and women. What her problem is is this: She is too clingy! She's happy when a man is around, but when he leaves the house to go about his business, she is frustrated and anxious. I want to walk over to her and tell her this, but she'd say: Mind your business. I'm a grown woman! and I'd say: I'm grown, too. And she'd look at me with that If-you-don't-get-the-hell-out-of-my-face-I'm-going-to-slap-the-living-daylights-out-of-you-look and I'd know not to say another word to avoid making a scene. I'd just stand there and stare at her. She'd roll her eyes and pretend I wasn't there. This is the way it is with her. I know that she loves me and that she likes being around me, but a daughter can't touch a Mama the way a man can.

Melissa McEwen

The Future as Evaporation

Some afternoons I spend posing for Margaret
who is still composing what she calls a self
portrait using my body. Nice days,
we walk to Rhittenhouse Park and she positions
me by the fountain. She sketches standing
beneath the bough of the tree that sprawls
like the tree in my mind, hung with names
instead of fruit and painted along
the wall of a maternity ward—a wall
I imagine just as I imagine
the unfinished likeness of her
gestating the unfinished likeness of me.

The days are hot & so, occasionally I lean
backward onto the water surface enough
to wet my shirt on the sunlit
side of me. The hot air drinks
what it wrings from my back. An inch of water,
she says, can drown you. And I picture
my body sinking to the bottom of that inch,
my breath first like foil balloons, then a string
of beads. The surface stills
as I, submerged, hold knees against my chest
and breath the fluid that contains me.

Then Margaret lifts me from the water
by my tiny hands and rests me on her shoulder,
rocking a little as we go. I am unaware
of the man, now fetal, small as a wish
in the fountain. I will come to know him
as what goes unsaid between two people,
a face nearly recognized in a cloud.

The weather will doubtless return
me to some drowsing fountain, where I'll remark
the age of things and how we age
and the standing water left to blazon
a vast Narcissus of sky. I will
lay my cheek against the water.
I will lay my ear against the belly
of the water & eavesdrop at that humble
altitude. Listen to it purl and thrum.
It means to say *drink of me, let*
this reflection dry
on your lips.

Gregory Pardlo

choices

i.
i looked in the book of questions
asked would you rather be killed
painlessly or maimed for life?
maimed he answered.

ii.
i fell for his safe harbor of a chest
arms built up like a carpenter
like a chain gang member.

iii.
i dreamt the gods gave him armaments
chiseled his hands from granite
taught him to break soft earth with them.
i didn't know how to interpret my dreams.
i just knew i wasn't his enemy.

iv.
the last argument got personal
big egos erupted wounds left by
daddies who left us
by mothers still mad at them
his ain't tell him
never yell at crazy girls
mine never taught me how to duck
a sucker's punch.

v.
linoleum lay cool on my back
ceiling glittered with the stars of a concussion
he reached to help me
screams of pain separated us.

vi.
my mother hovered at the end of my bed
her face arid, eyes rueful
three uncles turned cerebus watched the door
story-line scripted skate, stairs, 'accident'
momma done been that playwright before.

vii.
ghosts of aunts pointed toward daddy's brothers
reminded me vengeance is divine and
their bulk is to be used for god's work.
my goose-bumps became braille reading
handle yo bidness gal or the men folk will
and we ain't gonna stop em.

viii.
been well for 21 days.
don't love him no more.
don't want to see him dead.
thank him for showing me how much he cared.
offer to cook him breakfast.
fool's too young to know—a woman you've wronged
can't be trusted in the kitchen

ix.
i scramble eggs, prepare a pretty plate.
hope he appreciates i'm about to save his life.
aunt fanny's ghost leans into me
whispers 'do this for us'
i serve a skillet backhand to his head.
watch him slump to the floor where i
rested in agony weeks earlier.

Toni Asante Lightfoot

a terrorist's prayer

lord
  have pity
    on those
      who
have no pity
   on me
     'cause if i
       ever get
         my hands on
           a gun or
           a bomb
           their ass is mine

Charlie R. Braxton

Changamire Semakokiro—#6

The Availability of LEAD

The mental health expert spoke about war toys in an unbroken string of facts. Boys must somehow work out their violent tendencies, and war toys provide an inexpensive but highly effective channel of expression. Far better than therapy. Believe me, Bobby Blast Bob and Shank Slash Sam will ensure us of fewer violently repressed males years down the line.

Ward sat bent forward in his chair, watching and listening, the world in the TV screen clear and cold. He sucked his teeth and began. There was this young crewcut footsoldier, and he had the misfortune of getting the top of his young crewcut head ripped off by enemy fire. His young crewcut comrades stuck the brain matter back in place, covered it with the scalp, secured a bandage, and fitted a helmet. They overran enemy lines and took charge of a truck that the fleeing enemy had left behind. They sat the wounded soldier perfectly upright in the back of the truck, one soldier on either side of him to keep him firmly in place. Several hours later they reached fire base. They were stepping down from the back of the truck when one of the crewcut fellows lost his footing and slipped. The injured comrade's helmet fell off, and his brains spilled into the helmet. Now, why doesn't that psychologist—Ward pointed at the screen—talk about that! He turned his head and looked at the landlady, who was watching him with small round eyes from the other side of the small, wooden, thin-legged card table—within call, within reach (touch). She had a round flat face troubled by the first lines of aging, a small flat nose, and weak brown skin with pale color underneath, like a repainted wall in need of another top coat.

Just like strawberry marmalade, she said. Yummy. She smiled.

Ward took it full in the face. This landlady day in and day out. This cramped, shuttered room.

The newscaster—the measured rhythm of his voice, words with no hint of accent or geography—reiterated the day's top story. Ward watched and listened, something heavy in his stare, the dead sameness, sight and sound grown deep, rooted, like his feet to the floor. No change in the hostage situation. Hatch will not budge from his unreasonable demands.

Ward shook his head in disbelief. I wouldn't tolerate it. Not for a moment.

I'm one with you there.

In the mugshot Hatch was a short, thin man of forty. A small amount of hair on an egg-shaped head with eyes that didn't catch much light placed wide in a pointed face.

Bullshit walks, Ward said.

You know him?

Is that so hard to believe?

The landlady rubbed her legs and arms, without looking up.

The Police Superintendent said that everything was being done to see to it that neither Hatch nor the hostages met harm. We are doing everything in our power to bring closure to this situation.

Ward snarled at the screen. The eye is the first circle, he said. The ear the second.

The landlady rolled her eyes. Cast a supplicatory glance at the ceiling.

The Police Superintendent moved his stupid face into close up and opened his official mouth to begin again. Ward spat on the screen. The saliva moved downward in a slow, slug-like streak.

The landlady just sat there for one telling moment, watching the small table. Then she placed her palms against the edge, pushed her hard wooden chair slowly out from under her, twisted to her right and away from Ward, and stood. Without the television to light it, her face was shadowy oval, but her dark brown hands, caught in the dancing glare, glimmered blue against the flanks of her white housecoat. She quit the room with slow steps, her bare feet noisy on the spongy kitchen linoleum—a soft wind tickling his cheek as she brushed past him—but silent on the hard bathroom tile.

Ward alone in dim blue light. A long sentimental song flowed from the screen. Gurgling bubbles rising to the ceiling, an aquarium filter. Ward listened but hung back from seeing. Looked at the feet he knew were his. The curved screen like some big glass forehead intent on butting him.

The landlady returning—rapid recoveries of ground—the rag dangling from her thin fingers, the landlady positioning herself before the screen, swirls of blue light on either side of her, this landlady bending at the waist, then playing the rag in slow arcs over the glass—the soft circular motions of her hands, as if cleaning a baby's bottom-the landlady righting herself, still for a moment, then easing around to face him, her legs braced and the rag clenched in one fist angling into her hip, Ward feeling her constricted face. Avoiding it, watching the table.

Fading footage—images faint as pastel or watercolor—showed the Police Superintendent and a reporter lying bellies to the ground under a low cement fence (or was it a broken wall?), chins covered by tufts of grass, noses almost touching, microphone between them. A steady stream of thick black smoke whirled skyward from the east end of the street (right screen). Red flakes airborne, too. A small silver object zigzagged from the screen left to screen right, halted, spurted red flashes in the direction of the cement fence (wall?), then disappeared, only to be followed by another silver object. Elevated voices. Crushing noise.

A light curved around the smoke-obscured building corner, and moved forward, slowly but without pause. The camera following, stumbling. The light close enough now to reveal its source: a flashlight taped to the top of a pith helmet, a tall lean white man, hair draping his shoulders and his hollow face with eyes clear large and round. The sleeves of his dark blue serge blazer stopping not far below the elbows. The jacket pulled tight and buttoned once at midriff, exposing a yellow-white shirt and the uneven ends of a red tie. Pants cuffs inches above white cotton socks and red high top sneakers.

The landlady laughing, the landlady laying her thin hands across Ward's shoulders, and Ward watching her white even teeth, the way tears intensify the glint of her eyes.

Funny huh? Ward turning away from her to face the jerking screen.

The white men close now, center screen, the cement fence just above his knees. The Police Superintendent and the newscaster absent from the frame. The light from the pith helmet momentarily blinding the camera. Then the white man looking directly into the camera, hard eyes, unblinking glass, a large square of cardboard pressed against his right flank, its long brown edge like a second pants seam. Elbow locked, the white man raising his arm straight out to the side and lifting the cardboard square dumbbell-like to shoulder-height. The white man spinning the cardboard in his fingers, edge to square. Words smeared in charcoal:

MELTING   POT
OR
CROCK OF   SHIT

Ward sucked his teeth, a rodent-like squeal.

Go ahead and say it, the landlady said. Go on. It'll probably do us both some good.

Ward bit back the words, but they would not be stilled. Pounded at the enameled gates of his teeth. The wheel of history! He screamed.

Uh huh.

The vicious circle of human existence!

The landlady clicked off the television, the dead screen a sinister mask.

In the dark, Ward directed his eyes where the landlady's back should be. Bare feet moving against the linoleum, then a bulb flicking on and Ward quick to shield his eyes. Once he had adjusted to the glare, he removed his hand and saw the landlady standing with the white plaster wall behind her. The landlady and Ward's eyes fixed in reciprocal staring. She didn't say anything. Stood there a while. Then she drew in a deep breath, exhaled, and shook her head

You're hungry, she said.

Probably so.

It's good that we're about to eat.

Ward kept his jaw rigid.

Men act strange when deprived of meat.

She spreads a cheap cloth over the small table, ranges the wall to the stove. Returns, balancing on her hands bowls and plates of brown rice and lentils and yams. Leans over his shoulder and sets the food down on the table. Quits the room. Returns. Black-eyed peas, greens, cornbread, and chicken. The wheel of history, Ward says. The landlady pausing in her arranging of the dishes. The vicious circle of human existence. Those words pushing her upright and into action. Placing a fizzling glass of soda on the table, and Ward's mug of swampy aloe vera juice. Then sitting down in her chair. Ward watching the plate of chicken but not saying anything. Chicken glaring back. His getting some of everything but the chicken, food steaming up in his face, and with mouth full, kiss me, baby. The landlady not saying anything, the landlady, eating, watching her plate, fine black hair loose about her shoulders.

Get yourself some more of those beans so that you can blossom into a nice fat juicy mammy. Ward waited. Then we'll screw and have us five or six nice fat juicy pickannies.

The landlady looked at Ward, a chicken breast halfway to her mouth. White man, we call those black-eyed peas, not black-eyed beans.

Fat black mammies have nice big fat black—

Well, go ahead on, white man. Eat them yams!

Kiss me, baby.

Where would you prefer?

Ward finished the contents of his mug.

The landlady grinned. Hey, Ward, you put some of that stuff in a bottle, stick a rag in the top, and set fire and you've got yourself a Molotov cocktail.

Ward sat his mug on the table. Squared his shoulders, then gave the landlady a mean look. Just relax, he said.

The landlady cut short her grin. Ward watching her. I, I bet that silly kidnapper might know a thing or two about—

Just relax. Ward continued to watch the landlady.

The landlady smiled. Black men like to cook indoors while white men like to eat out. She darted her tongue slowly in and out of her mouth.

Ward stands there, immobile.

The Landlady set down the breast of chicken and averted her eyes. Little ceremonies.

I see where this is leading, Ward said.

I don't think you do.

You think—

Well, you know more about it than he does.

Ward's chair flew backwards as she stood. You just had to say it, didn't you. Ward.

A burning urge. Isn't that right? Ward.

TWO FOUR SIX EIGHT! WE WON'T PROCREATE! Is that what you mean! The landlady watched Ward. That's not what I mean. You know that's—

HEY HEY! HO HO! MR CLEAN HAS GOT TO GO! HEY HEY! HO— I'm tired of your shit, Ward.

HO! MR. CLEAN HAS GOT TO GO! Ward gripped the edge of the table, positioned his flank beside the landlady's shoulder, and began shoving the table towards the television, plates and cups rattling, the clatter of forks and knives, these instruments of consumption stampeding across the table, the table colliding into the television, falling backwards off its stand and smashing to the floor with a loud hiss, plates and cups disappearing over table edge, glass shattering, utensils arrowing off into the distance, and a river of beans, yams, and cornbread flowing into the televison's broken eye. A diaphanous gown of smoke floated through the room. Sparks buzzed in the quiet. A fried chicken wing spun a greasy circle near the landlady's feet.

Ward clutched his stomach. (Punched?) Slapped his hand over his mouth and rushed for the bathroom in a low crouch, a running back.

Not long after, he comes back into the room, weak, his face white, legs undulating—there seems to be no floor-a hand towel at his mouth. The landlady, barefoot, standing where he had last seen her. The landlady, holding back something behind her face. Wobbly, he squats down to right his chair. Can't do so.

The landlady shakes her head.

Ward, a single side-long glance. He waits, a long clearing pause. Then he tries—silent twists and turns in the near-dark-for the chair again. Manages to do so, and seats himself, towel around his neck like an exhausted athlete. From the shelter of a corner he watches the landlady, and she returns his gaze, the two of them silent before the trashy mound as if at a campfire.

He clicks his teeth. Shuts his eyes. Defeated. This landlady day in and day out. These four walls.

Jeffrey Renard Allen

Apocalypse

across the sandy dry plains
of the good old wild wild west
the thunderous din of dead buffalos
hoof beat out a desperate warning
to one and all
beware
beware
jesus
is a big mean assed black man
painted smokey grey
and boy is he mad upset pissed off
dressed in a camolflauge shroud
a three day beard and packing
a steel blue jammie
last seen kicking asses
and calling names
headed for the second
coming

Charlie R. Braxton

Eric Mack—**MVB-57** mixed media on canvas

BLACK RAGE

Jah Witnesses

ASHES FELL FROM THE JOINT INTO THE BOOK OF CORINTHIANS.
With both hands, Darnell raised Chapter 13 even closer to his brown face, and blew
the charcoal dust from the crease. A squadron of the airborne specks settled on his
Coke bottle bifocals. Darnell passed the joint to Mel.

"We have to keep love at the center of this shit, dog," Darnell said, pulling off
his glasses and wiping them on his XXL white t-shirt. "We have to keep our hearts in
the right place. We can't be out here judging motherfuckers."

Smoke rushed out through Mel's nostrils. "My friend regardless of our well-
intentioned desires," Mel said, in his measured cadence that seemed much too de-
liberate for a young man of twenty-three, "our very presence in these streets suggest
a level of judgment that is both obvious and unavoidable."

The unusually hot morning sun baked the backs of their necks. The fountain's
mist offered insufficient relief. Darnell wiped the sweat from his nape.

"Mel, you speakin for yourself on that there. I ain't judging nobody. I'm just
tryin to love these punk ass niggas."

"But in identifying their need for your specific brand of love, you're identifying
their shortcomings, their character faults, their moral missteps. You're making an
inference about the quality of their humanity. You're judging these motherfuckers.
And so am I."

Mel blew puffy circles toward cloudless sky and passed the joint back to Darnell.
The marijuana served as both truth serum and exit door from his father. Mel had to
find rebellious activities to balance out all the other areas of his life where he had ca-
pitulated to his father's demands. He had led the teen ministry even though he did-
n't understand how God could have allowed black children to starve to death in
Botswana before they could even become teenagers. He majored in business. He
gave in again and agreed to get an M.B.A. because his father said, "I need someone
to keep an eye on the church's money and keep a hand off the same."

Mel hated that he looked and talked like his father—and dressed like him too.
Everything from his light-brown skin and hazel eyes, to his preference for tailored
slacks and dress shirts, to the collection of Stacey Adams he chose from that morning.

"My conscious is clear, dog," Darnell said. "It's clear cause I've been comparing my love against what the Word says about love. Check this, here in 1 Corinthians 13 and 4, 'Love is patient, love is kind. It does not envy, it does not boast, it is not proud. It is not rude, it is not self-seeking, it is not easily angered. It keeps no record of wrongs. Love does not delight in evil but rejoices with the truth. It always protects, always trusts, always hopes, always perseveres. Love never fails.'"

Mel smiled. "Darnell, my friend, your conscience is clear because, in your biased opinion, you think your life meets the standard described there in 1 Corinthians. What if I told you, in my opinion, as a person who knows your life well, you're falling woefully short of the bible's definition of love?"

"I'd say, 'I don't give a fuck what you think.' Nobody knows my life better than me," he said, and passed the joint back to Mel.

"Exactly. Now what's different about you forwarding your unsolicited opinions, your unsolicited judgments on the people who you're purportedly trying to love, which is to really to say, who you're purportedly trying to help?"

"The difference is that I'm not a punk-ass nigga? Now pass the joint motherfucker."

After almost a decade of almost turning the corner, Nickerson Flats was losing steam. In the early 90s, the gritty Los Angeles neighborhood had come together around Rodney King. It was as if the momentum of swinging batons had brought out the fight in the Nifty Flats residents.

Like a lazy heavyweight who needed to be knocked down before he'd really fight, after Rodney, the neighborhood pulled itself off the mat and tried to win again. Darnell observed it first. He noticed other residents stopping to pick up Taco Bell wrappers and 7-11 Big Gulp cups in the middle of the street. He stood on his front steps and applauded when he saw one of the young Crips confront a man who dropped an empty Doritos bag in front of their apartment.

"Nigga don't be droppin trash in front of my crib. I live here fool. Pick that shit up fore I put my foot in yo trifflin ass."

Mr. Dequa opened a coffeehouse on the corner of Third & St. Charles. The rickety tables and chairs he got from the Salvation Army, and put in front of the café, began to draw Nifty residents out of their apartments for conversation and chess. Before Dequa's opened, the residents didn't have a neighborhood place where they could go and sit down face to face. A place where they could look into each other's eyes and see the souls of black human beings, not the caricatures they saw on the 11 o'clock news. Before Dequa's, they had began to believe what the world was saying about them. That they were all dangerous. That they were not worthy of fresh produce and respect from the police. That they could not be trusted playing chess after dark on the street corner of Third & St. Charles.

"It's approaching 8:30 a.m. and David is still missing in action," Mel said. "Of all the unprompt young black men I know, David is the tardiest and most shameless. I don't think he's figured out how rude it is to keep us waiting Sunday after Sunday like this."

"He know what he doin, dog. He just think we won't leave him cause he got the music. Watch though, he gone slide up here one Sunday at 8:30 and we gone already be in the wind."

David bobbed up Third Street, the bottom of his long dreadlocks dancing like marionettes. Since his childhood, he had listened to so much Bob Marley that a comment or a street sign could cue up a Marley song in his head. The green Third St. sign at St. Charles had triggered, 'Three Little Birds." This is our message to you/ Don't worry/ about a thing/ cause every little thing/ gonna be awright. The sight of his two friends in the distance caused an unconscious quickening of his pace. He smiled. Wearing baggy army fatigues and an acoustic guitar slung across his back. David looked like a revolutionary folk singer.

"Here comes the Watchless Rasta now," Darnell said to Mel. "When he walks up, pull off your Movado and slap him across the forehead."

"Good brother, you know I don't support black-on-black violence, especially when my Movado is placed in harm's way."

"Shit, that's not violence that's a crash course on act right."

David stopped 10 feet from the Nickerson Flats Fountain and thrusted both palms high above his head in a pose of faux guilt for his tardiness.

"Beloved, who among you is without sin, cast the first stone or weed sack," David said. "Can you believe Mr. Late Long Hair is still trying to smoke too?" Darnell said to David, though looking at Mel.

"Don't tell I, you took the sacrament without I?" David replied.

"That's right, there was not I in we this Sunday. This work is too important for you to keep disrespecting it, and us, by coming late every week," Darnell said.

"Beloved, no disrespect intended. I and I ruled by Jah time and Jah plan not always found on man-made devices. All things shall come to pass in their destined order."

"Listen man, I don't wanna hear that shit. Eight-thirty a.m. is the time we all agreed on, and I and I and I and I and I needs to keep his fuckin word too, so—"

"Brothers, brothers, please," Mel interrupted. "let us not forget the spirit in which we are all gathering this morning. Dissension cannot further the work that God has placed on our hearts. We're all here now, right? Let's be about the business at hand."

The three men started walking in silence down Third Street. Darnell wished he had handled the situation better. He didn't like to go out with tension among the ranks. His father had taught him that. He often thought of the lessons his father had drilled into him. So many of Darnell's friends had grown up without a father, but he literally had been his father's pupil since birth. In the 70s, home-schooling was still controversial in the white community and almost unheard of in the black community. Yet, when Darnell was born, his father took a job as a night watchman so he could educate his only son at home.

"Only a fool would allow his boy to be educated in a school that systematically tells him he's inferior," Darnell would often overhear his father trying to convince his own friends to home-school as well.

"Even the picture of the Egyptians in those children's textbooks are white. I've been to Egypt, twice, and you can plainly see on them temple walls that those are black people. The white man's own father of history, Herodotus, said it too. But y'all niggas wouldn't know nothing bout Herodotus cause ya wouldn't pick up a book if it was taped to a hundred dollar bill. That's why ya sorry asses in the situation ya in today. Now that white man, though, he know the truth. But to let y'all know that the greatest of the ancient civilizations was created by the same people he attack as inferior, would blow his whole game. Man, it would be child abuse to let these motherfuckers educate my boy. If y'all had any sense, you'd be thinking the same way bout ya own kids."

Darnell's father, DeeNell, had grown up with Bunchy Carter, the leader of the thousands strong Slauson Gang. When Bunchy started listening to the teachings of Malcolm X and decided to use his influence to start a Los Angeles chapter of the Black Panther Party for Self Defense, DeeNell was set to be his first lieutenant. But they fell out over the girl who would become Darnell's mother. DeeNell's pride wouldn't let him join the Panthers but he followed them closely, and raised his son on the Party's 10-Point Platform.

"Awright, let's stop here for a second," Darnell said. "The house is the green crib there with the Lincoln parked in the drivel. Let me do most of the talking on this one cause Richardson knows me from the Gang Truce committee we worked on before he got elected to the City Council. I still can't believe how much this motherfucker has flipped. Anyway, imma run this one, but if the spirit places something on y'all heart to jump in with, do it quick and with conviction. Richardson is smart and slick and there really is no telling how he's gone respond to this shit. Awright, yall ready?"

Darnell, Bible in hand, led David and Mel up Councilman Richardson's slate stone walkway to the front door. He raised and slammed the gold knocker down hard and fast three times.

"Who is it," Richardson's gruff voice shot through the thick wood door.

"Councilman, it's Darnell Jackson from the Gang Truce committee."

After a few moments the door opened.

"Mr. Jackson, how can I help you this early Sunday morning," 5 foot 6 and balding Councilman Richardson said, warily eyeing the three men through replicas of the black horn-rimmed glasses Malcolm X favored.

"Councilman, you can help us a lot," Darnell jumped in, talking fast and forcefully. "But that's the problem, you're not helping us a lot. In fact, you haven't been doing shit lately and you know it. You—"

"Hold on I—"

"No, you hold on," Darnell said aggressively, planting his right foot into the doorframe. "God has placed it on my heart to give you a message cause this neighborhood needs you Councilman. You know we're on a dangerous, slippery slope and, as our elected public representative, you're in the best position to stem the tide, but you're acting like a bitch-ass nigga: cock-blocking important projects that could bring jobs to the neighborhood, shutting down the jazz festival. All cause you got some petty beef with some other bitch ass niggas. We need you to be bigger than—"

"Get your foot out my door or I'll call the police," Councilman Richardson grunted, tying to force the door shut. Ignoring him, Darnell opened his Bible. David swung his guitar from back to front, and began strumming feverishly, head tilted skyward, eyes closed.

Darnell shouted loudly above the music, "Revelation 2 and 4 says, 'Yet I hold this against you: You have forsaken your first love. Remember the height from which you have fallen! Repent and do the things you did at first. If you do not repent, I will come and remove your lamp stand from its place."

The Councilman began kicking at Darnell's foot, still trying t o close the door, he turned his head and screamed, "Marguerite call the police, call the police right now, call—"

"The police can't help you repent fool. You need to call on the name of Jesus, turncoat nigga. You—"

David, strumming into reggae rhythm frenzy, burst into Marley's "Heathen."

"The heathen back, yeah, on the wall/ the heathen back, yeah, on the wall/ the heathen back, yeah, on the wall/ the heathen back, yeah/ on the wall."

"Marguerite, Marguerite!"

Darnell screamed, "Repent nigga, and do the things you did at first. Let's get out of here y'all."

Darnell removed his throbbing foot and the door slammed shut. Mel and Darnell followed David back out the stone slate walkway, joining in—

"The heathen back, yeah, on the wall / the heathen back, yeah, on the wall / the—"

The three men made a left at St. Vincent, and continued down the middle of the street southbound. They faded toward the curb, when they heard cars coming down the one-way thoroughfare. They found that walking down the center of the street emboldened them. It was a symbolic act of commitment. They literally were taking to the streets in the name of defending their neighborhood.

David loved these times. He felt like he was actually putting some action behind the theories he was learning in UCLA's African American Studies program. The lack of action was his biggest complaint about the armchair nationalist that the program attracted. He was tired of all their big talk and little movement. That's how he had met Mel at a black grad student mixer during the first week of classes. Both second year students, Mel seemed as disillusioned about the MBA propaganda as David was by the black big talk.

David's father, Agbotui, had been a man of action. Or least David had always been told he was. His mother told him stories about what a brave and respected man his father was. How back in the early 1950s, when Ghana was still called the Gold Coast, Agbotui had worked closely with Kwame Nkrumah to fight for independence from British colonial rule. How proud she was watching her husband at the podium introducing Premier Nkrumah at the first All African Peoples Congress in Accra in 1958. "That's when I really knew Jah was real," she once said, teary eyed. "Because good had conquered evil, just as I had prayed for so many years."

Meri told David of his father's, and her won heartbreak when they had to sneak out of the country in February 1966 because of the military coup led by C.I.A. supported General Kotoka. The family threw a few belongings in the car and drove to Togo and caught a plane to New York. "Many of your father's friends, also supporters of brother Kwame, had no option, no way out. They were murdered in land they fight so hard to free. Your father never got over it. I wished you had known the man we all knew back in our homeland," Meri said. David was two when his father died of a massive stroke in 1979. Though his mother said, "He died of black men in white mask." Meri moved him and his two older sisters from Brooklyn to Westwood. She never took another husband. "How can I respect this American black man when he let white man boot stay on his neck and do nothing? Your father were a real man, a revolutionary. I rather be lonely than share me bed with man with no courage," she said.

Meri started each morning playing old Marley records because they reminded her of her husband. She stayed married to Agbotui's memory. David tried to live up to the same. He found memory elusive when he tried to model its invisible nature. Instead, he secretly modeled Don Johnson's walk and his penchant for sexy brunettes with something to say. When he brought his first white girlfriend, Kristen, home in the 11th grade, Meri just broke into tears and walked slowly out the living room. David had a bohemian undergraduate experience as a UCLA music major. After his symbolic break up with Heather on graduation day, David had decided it was time to come home again, in more ways that just starting the African American Studies program in the fall.

David swung his guitar forward and began to softly strum the melody of "Duppy Conqueror" as the three men walked.

He stopped abruptly. "Beloved, maybe it would be wise to take a back street to our next visitation. Brother Councilman Richardson, seemed serious about calling the beast on us," David said.

"What could that fool tell the police," Darnell said. "That we pulled a bible on him? He was the one assaulting me. He kicked me at least 30 times. All I gotta do is pull my shoe off. Fuck him and the beast."

"Why you so quiet over there Mel? You having second thoughts? Like I told you last night, dog, it doesn't even have to go down this way."

"Brother, don't confuse meditation with fear," Mel said with a peaceful grin on his face. "You have to pull the bow string inward for the arrow to fly outward."

Mel had always been good at hiding his nervousness—and his fear. He had learned his quiet confidence from watching his father run Mt. Zion African Methodist Episcopalian Church for years. Melvin, Sr. had started the small storefront worship hall on Peach St. and driven it into a 5,000 seat cathedral on Buckingham Way, with his steady but immensely charismatic hand. Mel watched his father hold off creditors and root out corrupt accountants with an easy smile and an iron will. Like the other assistant ministers, Mel called his father "The Velvet Hammer" behind his back.

Mel's inherited poker face was especially useful last year when he walked into his father's office to hand him the tallied offering for that Sunday, to find Mother Blatt's gums greeting him. Mother Blatt's mouth was wide open like her eyes. Her false teeth, seemingly on the verge of trying to say something, were cheesing on the edge of the desk. Mother Blatt's hands and knees were on the desk too. The pink floral dress that Mel had just seen her in behind the piano about an hour ago was now raised onto her back, as his father, Rev. Melvin Roscoe Jenkins, Sr., thrust himself aggressively in and out of her. Mother Blatt's had just celebrated her 80th birthday with the entire church, during the morning service.

Mother Blatt and his father were in the process of coming together. Mel was disgusted, but his poker face was in cruise control. Mother Blatt, clutching the front of the beveled desk, gray wig tilted forward and to the left by the pounding, released a deep, guttural, shuddering, "Ooooooooooooooooohhjeeeeeeeeeeeeeeesusssssssss." Still pumping in the trance of orgasm, all his father could do was close his eyes.

The sensation in Mel's stomach reminded him of the time he broke a 5-day fast at Killer Shrimp, and the bowl of giant prawns had been rancid. With his left hand still on the gold plated doorknob, and one foot inside Rev. Jenkins' office, Mel could feel the bile rising from his stomach to the back of his throat. He dropped the battered black suitcase full of money (they used to transport the Sunday collection) to the floor. He stepped back calmly pulling the gold handle with him. Mel walked over to the trashcan near the stairs and retched up the remainder of the respect he had for his father. Descending the stairs to go pick up his mother and drive her home, Mel wiped his mouth with the back of his hand without once touching his poker face.

Darnell, David and Mel stopped and huddled at the corner or 5th and Pleasant Lane. The July sun behind them and the foot travel had each of their shirts stuck to their backs.

"Okay, good brothers," Mel said, smiling. "This one's mine. If you must contribute, please be brief. Allow me to dictate the flow of the interaction. Is everyone fine with these parameters?"

Darnell and David nodded yes. They followed Mel up Pleasant Lane to the three-story brick house toward the middle of the pine tree-lined street. A waist-high brick wall dipped and rose a perfect square around the meticulously manicured green lawn. Two lions, each of their right paws raised, guarded the gate. Mel raised the latch and led his two friends down the brick walkway to the 14-foot colonial doors. Mel turned to Darnell, "Hand me the Bible." Darnell forwarded the Bible and stepped back with David. Mel pushed the illuminated cross to the right of the door. The sound of chimes cascaded through the large house. Darnell began to tap his right foot, the way he did when he was especially nervous. David bowed his head, as he slowly brought his guitar from back to front.

"Heh son, I didn't know you were coming by this morning. Your mother must have told you I was only preaching the evening service this Sunday. Heh Darnell and David it's good to see—"

'Rev. Jenkins,' Mel said, his trembling voice rising, "the precious Lord, Jesus Christ, who I serve and owe my salvation to has brought me to bear witness on this day that he has made. That same Lord speaketh through me now with a message about the sinfulness of the wicked." Mel snatched open the Bible to where his fore-finger had marked. His father opened his mouth to speak, the smile falling from his face in the process. No words would come.

David began to hum, swaying gently side to side. The bible shaking in his hand, Mel shouted, "Psalm 36 and 1 says, 'An oracle is within my heart concerning the sinfulness of the wicked: There is no fear of God before his eyes. For in his own eyes he flatters himself too much to detect or hate his sin. The words of his mouth are wicked and deceitful; he has ceased to be wise and to do good."

Everything about Rev. Jenkins was stiff, motionless, except for his quick flut-tering eyelids, shooting out a streak of tears like a Pez candy dispenser gone berserk. David began to hum louder. Rev. Jenkins mouth was still open.

"Son—"

"Don't call me that," Mel screamed, breaking into tears. Rev. Jenkins col-lapsed, sliding down the doorways frame as if his legs had turned to Silly Putty.

"Son, please—"

"I said don't call me that," Mel, leaning over, screamed down at his father.

Darnell raised both of his hands above his head and began to pray in tongues. Eyes still closed, David tilted his head back, and began to strum the chords to "Guiltiness." Rev. Jenkins was weeping uncontrollably in the doorway. He leaned toward Mel's legs, pleading,

"Pleeease."

Mel reared back his black Stacey Adams, and began to viciously kick his father in the chest and neck and face.

David sang, "Guilt-I-nessss/ rest on their conscience/ oh yeahhh/ woe to the downnpressor/ they eat the bread of sorrow/ woe to the downpressor/ they eat the bread of sad tomorrow."

As Mel began to aim the pointy dress shoes exclusively for his unconscious fa-ther's head, the broken bones of Rev. Jenkins cheek and jaw, swelled his face into a cantaloupe-sized tomato. Blood squirted from his ears onto the open white door. Darnell opened his eyes, tapped David on the shoulder, and began to back down the brick walkway. David, eyes still closed, walked back one step at a time, singing,

"Guilt-i-nessss/ rest on their conscience/ oh yeahhh/ woe to the downpresser/ they eat the bread of sorrow/ woe to the downpressor they eat the bread of sad to-morrow."

Darnell added his bass voice to the chorus. His right leg tired, Mel began to kick his father with is left shoe. Neither of their poker faces would survive this visitation.

Michael Datcher

Nat Turner Dreams of Insurrection

...too much sense to be raised, and if I was,
I would never be of any service to any one as a slave.
—The Confessions of Nat Turner, 1831

Drops of blood on the corn, as dew from heaven.
Forms of men in different attitudes, portrayed in blood.
Numbers, glyphs, on woodland leaves, also in blood.

Freedom: a dipperful of cold well water.
Freedom: the wide white sky.
Dreams that make me sweat.

Because I am called, I must appear so, prepare.
I am not conjurer. Certain marks on my head and breast.
Shelter me, Great Dismal Swamp. A green-blue sky which roils.

Elizabeth Alexander

In Elijah's Fields

The grass, even the trees
inhale our blood
like winter air.

In this hallowed place,
we were whipped and raped, and stood
where sheets still dry on sagging lines

In these fields hope bathed our tongues in
Psalms beneath the coiled roots of Sycamores,
our sweat aged in gravel, dried in tilled fields,
our lives marking back roads to corn stalks,
and the old white barn where some were

conceived. In Elijah's fields
I walk our breadth and length,
follow our whispers eastward,
sing our pain, pray on sodden ground.

Our farm leans on 160 years
of rust-red land, birthed manna
for slaves, folded stilled bodies
in its womb.

Gina M. Streaty

Kim Mayhorn—**"A Woman Was Lynched the Other Day..."**
installation detail

WHAT'S PAINTED ON THE WALLS INSIDE BESSIE'S WAIL

Yoruba
feet
in
cold
Carolina
sand

chained
ankles
clanking
on
the
ocean
floor

a bale a day
like a hump on her back

Anansi
spinning
her
wisdom
web

the
brutal
sun
of
an
overseers
gaze

thin pink lips on
her nipple at dawn

the crack
of a
whip's smile

a
bad
nigger
scowling
behind
his
eyes

freedomcreep
crawling up
the neck of
the woods

a
ringshout
rhythm
rocking
down
by
the
swamp

the smell
of a new boss

dust in her mouth
spit on her feet
cuz a nickel
could never
be a dime

the scattered shards of her consent

something
slowly
swinging
in the
southern
wind

"3o dollars
can I hear 40,
40, can I hear 50?
50, on the right
60, on the left

jump-down
dip-twist
Praise the Lord

geechee tongues
chattering gumbo
talk

60, going once
60, going twice
60, to the gentleman in the white hat"

a worksong purpling the setting sun

DJ Renegade

475

mercury & THE monk

she's unsleeping now, the mattock dug
  between her chin & breasts, between her clenched
  knees, its length warmed by a silent growth-

her rage. It's beaked, the mattock.
  one day when its head plumes, the mattock
  will rise & dive into the gravestone

of her grandfather, those hands took her
  crying head, screaming head, agape head
  into his sin, his lap, he bent her &

now when you wake, you find her Mercury,
  rippled shaking beneath your once swift
  tenderness, carry this here or there, but

mornings now after love the bed is
  wet from her face sketching the details
  again & again in a working word, no.

   *   *   *

I cross from my cloister, the quiet walls
  lead to you, a rare night finding you there,
  on the phone, curved back pushing

pleases into the receiver; she's not listening
  just driving, somewhere near the beach
  & we are locked in the piedmont of ourselves

& the mind is a conscience explosion, worn
  underfoot, tread upon my way toward you,
  but my arms are functionless, the ambit

unsure. She says she driving to Europe,
  she'll hold her breath all the way
  & park behind our spot on Dorsett

near Baker St. where the detective resolves
  the matter of the mattock, dusty in her passenger
  seat from crackling the gravestone of an old

dead, dead man.

Taj Greenlee

Sheila L. Prevost–**Broken System** oil on canvas

Grind

-WHAT'S WRONG W/ YOU-

Jerry sat in the station wagon, riding next to his father. A camping wknd and drive. The drives/He watched the road pass underneath him, under the headlights. The woods/the roadkill.

-I knew you were a rotten [rattin] kid, that something was wrong w/ you. Your eyes; you'd break things: bottles, plates. You'd spill your milk. There was something in your eyes. Your mother got nothing [nothin']. You were so selfish. She has only one dress to her name. You just got everything; not while I was there, not as long as I'm alive.-YOUDTHROWYOURMOTHEROUTONTHESTREETSANDSELLTHE-HOUSEANDTAKEOFF, if I wasn't there. You're rotten [rattin], all you kids are rotten [rattin]. You were born rottin [rattin]...-

He remembered spilling milk. He was four. He shouldn't have tried to carry it, like the full plates and glasses.

His dad would challenge him to boxing matches, like a boxer he'd pose. Those fists, very close to his face.

-Comeon, you think you could take me, comeon-

He'd have to slump real low to meet Jerry's eye level. He had a pin hole in the center of his head that came from shrapnel during the war. Dad saved the real contact for Erin, who was retarded and insane. Apparently she fell down the stairs on her head as a child. Mom and Dad took her in because no one wanted her. She still tries to study and live alone, despite her inability to become unretarded and nonviolent.

Jerry once saw her body fly across the room.

-...as long as I have money in my pocket, I'll keep you away from me...-

(dad gave him a good bash to the head w/his elbow)

He'd be sitting in front of the television in the dark watching a program. Jerry would go to his room and lock the door. He knew the television wasn't on.

There was a clipping about the death of Montgomery Clift. A boy was lying on the bed, his body burned w/ the blunt end of a Popsicle stick. He had taken several of those pills that his mother and dad kept on their dresser for their nerves.

-I'm the victim-

she said.

There was a noose in the basement, two weeks later, after his release from the hospital.

-Comeon you think you can take me. You f-cker, you little sh-t. Someone's going to die tonight-

And dad went to the phone and called someone.

-Yeah, Tony, comeover-

And he hung up.

Lawrence Ytzhak Braithwaite

Trees on our backs

(inspired by a series of "Beloved"-related paintings by Renaldo Davidson)

They done paralyzed our tongues with vinegar and a garlic noose
    swept the men away with a fractured mirror and a half-broom
    bolted the women to the cargo criss-crossing their bosoms
    buried the children alive in the feces of a dead dream
    kidnapped that old preacher and bid her to cast her gut
        in the 'cane field
    canceled our mass therapy session and told us not to dance no more
    inhabited our hands, urging us to slit the souls of our kinfolk
    sucked the life from our bodies and watched us confront the sun
        for more time
    painted the earth red and laughed as we vomited the blood
        spraying from our rubbery limbs
    soaked us in the atlantic, then dried us with a mule whip-

We say:

They done put trees on our backs.

Kevin Powell

smolder smolder smolder

aunt 'ree has lived
through the mississippi
of sheeted heads
soiling family hands

she say
he got a white face
but he got blood
just like mine

she prays for better days
in the ashes of 1996
while a cross burns
the saints' meeting place

Quraysh Ali Lansana

The Sound of
Burning Hair

Osage Avenue, Philadelphia, 1985

Dropping a bomb
Is not the same
As throwing it
One can be
A nervous mistake
The other   a dead intention
So they knew when they leaned
Their ticking arms
Out their flying doors
That bullets would never be enough
That bullets could tear
And nightsticks
Could render unconsciousness
But what would debone
Tough dark meat
From nimble arrogant quick healing joints
They knew when they threw it down
That bullets might slice a path
Through some unruly moppy untamed heads
But that would singe it off
Beyond skin and scalp
Under hairshafts and past regeneration

Fire would
Fire could

So by all means
Let us throw fire

Nikky Finney

Drapery Factory,
Gulfport, Mississippi, 1956

She made the trip daily, though
later she would not remember
how far to tell the grandchildren—
Better that way.
She could keep those miles
a secret, and her black face
and black hands, and the pink bottoms
of her black feet
a minor inconvenience.

She does remember the men
she worked for, and that often
she sat side-by-side
with white women, all of them
bent over, pushing into the hum
of the machines, their right calves
tensed against the pedals.

Her lips tighten speaking
of quitting time when
the colored women filed out slowly
to have their purses checked,
the insides laid open and exposed
by the boss's hand.

But then she laughs
when she recalls the soiled Kotex
she saved, stuffed into a bag
in her purse, and Adam's look
on one white man's face, his hand
deep in knowledge.

Natasha Trethewey

BLACK
FIRE

Quashelle Curtis–**Love Punany Bad** oil on canvas

Cakewalk

> *"The cakewalk started among American slaves*
> *as a high-stepping promenade that poked fun*
> *at the haughty ways of plantation masters...*
> *Whites began to dance the cakewalk about 1890..."*
> —from the World Book Encyclopedia

Isn't this how it always begins?
How rape is ravaged and beaten into submission?
How theft descends into the swamp of euphemism
And emerges as
Crossover appeal?

When the small mind flaunts
the strong soul as if its own,
When the beat of the determined heart
is tapped on linoleum floors
by shoes strapped to ivory ankles
and christened by ivory tongues
"Cakewalk," "Charleston," "Jitterbug"
When the screams of the Middle Passage
are strangled by ivory hands,
then chiseled into Broadway box-office,

Isn't this how genocide always begins?

If they took our fire to mobilize their beetles,
to shape their rolling stones,
to plaster their Madonna,
If they charged the world to despise
the black bastard God and worship
a white pagan,

Won't the death march follow?
Won't they take us away from us?

Shayla Hawkins

John Abner–**The Plan** collage

Identification
PLease

I am
everywhere. I am
rhythm. I am
blues. I am a B-flat abruptly blown
from a street corner saxophone
I am light and shadow. I am
joy and happiness, peace and prosperity
gentrified and ghetto, vagabond and vainglorious
slick like mercury, quick like lightning. I am in
His image with His power
residing in me

Moving with the strength of a thousand
thousand-fold footfalls drumming the earth
in unison

Speaking with Zulu fury
praising and chanting
my destiny to the universe

Thinking in 360 degree completeness
nine times over, forever giving knowledge
through life, creation
The Creator

But I Am
much more than that

role call

I am interstellar intergalactic space
infinite in possibility limitless
un-quantifiable

I am the umbra of man
the dark of the sun, an eclipse
with a blinding corona overshadowing
all others

I Am King
I Am Truth
I Am X

I am a man on Calvary
carrying a cross, the weight
of the world resting on bent and bleeding back

See, I am
the beginning. I am
the origin. I am Adamson
forged in fire, cast in bronze
born of the Lazarus Heart
forever rising higher and higher

Bryant Smith

Autobiography of a
BLacK Man

Who has not
On occasion entertained the presence
Of a Blackman?
Raymond R. Patterson

All the ladies feeling luck at love
ask me if I like jazz, want to go out
and kick it at some club they know. I nod,
being a man who never disappoints.
Every white man I've known has wanted me
to join his basketball team, softball league
or book-discussion group. They invite me
on week-long, fly-fishing trips to Montana.
One day I might say yes. They think
they admire my superb athletic skills
and my broad education, but it's nothing
more than my color. I am The Black Man
the whole world mythologizes and envies.
I can get cats to march like boot-camp soldiers.
No dog ever dares ignore what I say-
sit up, fetch, play dead-the whole fucking routine.
Even New York roaches know to behave,
scurrying and hiding when I say, Scat!
I'm big and too damn powerful. The boss
on the job gulps hard and fast while I piss
into the cracked urinal. His hand shakes
as he follows me out, making small talk.
I will appear in his dreams 'til he's dead.
Black brothers, too, hurt themselves to get near me,
like crabs trying to climb out of a bucket.
The Latinos up in Harlem yell, Jesus!
when they see me. They fall down on their knees.
Am I the Messiah? Might be. Might be.
Koreans behind fruit stands bow their heads,
treating me like Buddha. That's alright. Let 'em.
My father wants us to be better friends
as if father and son weren't close enough.
My mother loves me more now than before,
since I grew up and became a Black man.
I'm twenty-three, and I'm king of this world.
Everyone fears and worships me. I know
I'm the motherfucking object of envy.
I'm the be-all and end-all of this world.

G.E. Patterson

As for the Body

But let's say the body is not ready to go.
A brother I knew, never a lover but almost
so felt himself again and again on the edge
of that precipice-first thrush which stilled
his tenor, then lymphoma that left him too exhausted
to lift his head from a futon, finally CMV that bored
a swift and endless tunnel to blindness each passed
in turn—and each time his body, more vengeful
soldier than he, admonished, not yet: you must go on.

But what if you're sure you've reached your time?
Your mind, worn out by hourly trials that would still
Torquemada, shuts down; and your spirit, primed
by the strife-years, the struggles to wake, breathe,
submit to life, awaits its moment of flight; but your body,
insistent warrior, trudges forward, advances into the next
war, brazenly fielding needles and CAT-scans,
pills and fevers, battles cancers so rare no medical text
has fully described them, crying heroically, you must go on.

What if it will not tender its resignation, surrender?
All those years of being offered up to whatever chance,
opportunity or fate distilled as experience, the nights
we and others opened it up, filled it, emptied it;
caressed it, punished it, pushed it far beyond its limits
so that rhythms, patterns, traumas forged its independence;
thus when another hour of strength finds us ready
to press through to pain again, having been left for gone
the body accepts our complicity, urging softly, we must go on.

John Keene

Long Days Journey

O.J. is holding a can of tuna to his head. He's in the back of the white Ford Bronco, threatening to take his life. The cellular phone rings off the hook. Rodney King is driving and, if it were not for the .40 in his one free hand, he'd slam the phone down hard on the receiver to kill the ringing. It is suspected that Jimmy Hoffa's in the trunk. But we are reminded that a Ford Bronco has no trunk. So we figure the foul smell is coming from the glove compartment. Then we hear the weird pop and fizz and don't want to believe that some one as famous and admired as O.J. could emit such a powerful and obnoxious odor. We tried to sneak a glance his way and were relieved to find that it was just the can of tuna split open in the vice grip of his nervous, clumsy King Kong palm. Tuna water dribbled down to his elbow as he sweated profusely, praying that the split open can would not cut his pretty face. When this is all over, I still want to be able to get a job, he told us. Just above our heads propellers chop away at the air. A helicopter lands on the roof of the car. Come out with your hands up! comes the cry from a bull horn. Jimmy Hoffa, sautéed in John F. Kennedy's blood in the glove compartment of the white Ford Bronco, suddenly turns into James Cagney. He is animated. Ooooh... You'll never take me alive...Ooooh! Rodney King takes the .40 of Mad Dog and douses it onto the hood of the car, flicking his cigarette out the window to make a fire just in case they send SWAT men down onto the hood. The helicopter is immediately engulfed in flames, the SWAT team trapped in a flying open furnace. It hurls away into a ball of flames, shooting out like a meteor, landing like a godsend in Compton, its parts to be picked away like meat off a turkey bone at a homeless shelter on Thanksgiving Day. Rodney King continues to drive, tapping the bottle for leftover drops. Jimmy Hoffa roasting on a spit in the glove compartment. The heat from the hood of the car basting him. Damn! Smells like ribs in there, King groans, fussing with the doorknob of the glove compartment. He loses control of the white Ford Bronco, crashing across guard rails. O.J. nicks his face with the blade of the split open can of tuna. Fuck! he yells, blood spraying all over the inside of the white Ford Bronco. Miraculously enough, we end up in front of O.J.'s house on his front lawn. The car engine is dead. It grows cold inside. Ice starts to form on Jimmy Hoffa's body parts. Cops spring out from everywhere: behind bushes, parachuting off the roof, vehicles skidding up onto the lawn, blocking us in. Within minutes we are in Mai Li. I awake to find myself in the glove compartment, shivering. Jimmy Hoffa lies next to me sautéing in the blood of John F. Kennedy, smelling of day-old tuna. Outside, King is dragged out the driver's side of the car. Hundreds of cops appear, turning his head into a percussion instrument as nosy pedestrians begin a euphoric rumba off the sounds the knight sticks make against his skull. The cops continue this until they capture the rhythm of the crowd's dancing. By the time I stick my head out of the glove compartment of the white Ford Bronco to see what's happening, O.J. is whimpering because no one's paying attention to him. (People no longer cared whether or not he pimp-smacked a Barbie doll in a window display case at F.A.O. Schwartz.) His large frame broken down into an endless bouquet of sobs. His tears overflow the can of tuna, flooding the car and raising the temperature while Jimmy Hoffa melts away into John F. Kennedy's blood until a pool of it spills out onto the lawn, washing away the dancing euphoric crowd as Rodney King is being lifted up on to the hood of the car with knight sticks. For a second, in mid air, just before hitting the trunk, he looks like the good thief, or the bad thief (both of whom stood on either side of Christ on the cross), or Christ himself, innocently pleading, trying not to look surprised when they begin to douse him with gasoline and press a cigarette into the air.

Off in the distance, people will steal TVs and stereo equipment from O.J.'s house. No one will go near the refrigerator.

Tony Medina

The Receptionist–
Part One
after Wanda Coleman

The air was adrenaline
& knots pulled tight.

She was 40ish
with auburn-dyed hair
& a ten dollar cut.
Eyes frigid as snowy
Ohio, she traced
the length of my locks
with the haughty business
of once-over.

I was struck

when her paperclips flipped
to the floor, when her file folders
smacked the desk. Her crumpled mouth
asked May I help you?
in the key of another meaning.

After I complained
she called me at home,
her manager looming
in the background.
She asked in the voice
of those mistaken girls
I remembered from grade school
for one more chance

I hated her more for that.

Yona Harvey

the algebra of

let x = *what I have not said.*

the equation of which is Power
which gives *height* to the merciless
but strength to the bleak

let x approach the axis of Power
and y = *at what point will you open your mouth?*
and y^2 = *at point will you open your hands?*

graph Power against the axis of x and y

solve for wealth
solve for speechlessness

you are the equation of Power and Comfort

solve for x

solve for X

Kazim Ali

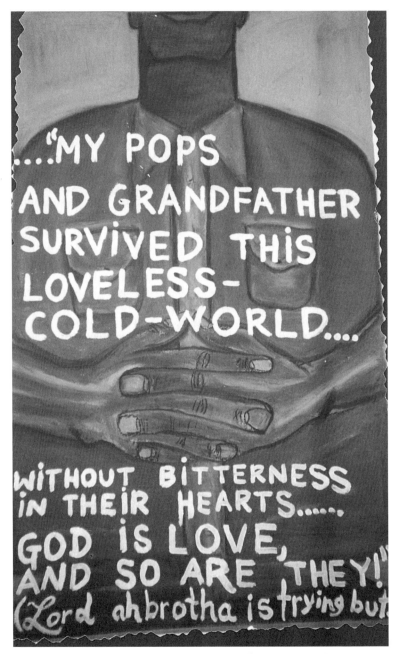

Renaldo Davidson—**God Is Love So Are They** oil pastel on paper

Future

Four Hundred years of ostracism, hazing, hostility with only
Partial reprieve in the solace of family and true friends.
Heavy years with little hope,
Clinging to work and making,
Knowing in the end and from the start that it
Would never be enough.

So I/s migrate, the soul feels its way to Babylon,
my ancestors and me go way from this
arid place,
Stopping all memories that do not sustain
Forward motion.

Some of past moves pass before my eyes,
And I learn.
I draw in reserves-fewer this time-
And wait for our moment to jump.

Home in our ten generation's absence has grown vague,
Only felt at moments close to the bone.
Perhaps, this time we will freeze
Perhaps this time our jaws will lock
And our drums grow silent.

But we go, keeping down
The desire to document every pain,
Every attack, every rape, every lie,
Every utter disappointment with the
Beast.

Instead, we tell war stories of the
mind
And victories and trade zany loopy hymns that
Vaguely praise God because
WE are uncertain.

Carol Allen

Struggle

Nobody said
this life would
be easy—that it
would take
shooting hot hate
into our blue veins
to smother the
archaic wails
of people
sprinting from
steel gangplanks
to iron waters
to cotton trees

Nobody said
that those cotton trees
would hang us
by our eyeballs,
demanding us to look
at the soul sores
pockmarking
our red, restless rivers

Nobody said
this life would
flow like a red, restless
river, or that that red river
would be an unhurried suicide:
as unhurried as molded syrup
crawling, like a cockroach,
down the face of a
nameless
junkie who gums death
because life has blown

his teeth away

Nobody said
we couldn't smile
anymore; or that
a smile, now, had
to be a wooden mask
forged with the blood
of a face we cracked open,
like a watermelon,
this morning in the mirror

Nobody said a face
like yours is but
a face like mine:
a wrinkled roadmap
slouching toward
a mother, a father,
who have never
hung themselves
with love, who
never pulled their
parents from that
spiritual wreckage
called history, who
never asked the
dead for relief,
and who never, never
pondered why ghosts
who don't smile
wage their civil wars
between our bone
and our flesh

Kevin Powell

Hold Up,
Motherfucka!

You think you can
Build yr death machine
On top of my yams
My sugarcane
My blackeyed peas
And live prosperously?

You think you can
Stick your science project
Inside my pussy
Sterlize my roots
Pull my unborn babies
Out from under
Rocks and trees
Live happily
Ski the alps in march
Sun on yr yacht
Poison my air with chemicals
Kill me
Enslave me
Open my legs
Dry my milk
Steal my land
Force my teeth to smile

I will take my eroticized body
Out yr hands
Take my children

Off the sick diet
You provide
Take my brother
Out the nigga clothes
Out the jail

I will pray to Dmballah
Kill the goat
Spray its blood
Conjure all the magic
You've been trying to kill for centuries
I will call upon
The spirits of revolutionaries past:

We will wash yr hair in fire
We will quench yr thirst with voodoo wine
We will bury yr cancer beneath the tree of life
We will topple yr lies with poetry
in the brilliant light of one billion cowries

Until yr computer rejects its creator
Until yr technology bows to the ocean
Until yr last vacation home slides off the cliff
Until yr tv broadcasts to no one
Until yr filthy U.S. dollars mean nothing

Starr Aché

Stevenson Estimé—**#9** mixed media collage on wood

I still do feel that a poet has a
     duty to words,
and that words can do
          wonderful things,
and it's too bad to just let
     them lie there
without doing anything with
          and for them.

—Gwendolyn Brooks

SHOUT OUTS

"Smokin' a phat sack right here on the station that plays only platinum hits, WBALLS."

"Caller my dick's in your ear, you wanna say what?"

"Uh, hi. okay. my name is todd. and i live like, you know, like, like almost by the east side, but not really in the east side, and i just don't really understand it man. i mean, like, i love everybody man, you know, and i like drive thru there and they like, you know, you know you know how those black guys, you know, with the pants hangin on down...i mean, don't get me wrong, i mean snoop dogg rules man, but, you know, it's like i just don't understand why they would like, you know, wanna beat ME up, you know ... but ... you know, i just wanna say i like the song man, and i give it the big bow wow.."

—The Dogg Pound

We say all that to say that the history of the Shout Out is, well, long. But its reasons are pure: to connect, to give respect, to offer thanks, prayers and love, and a lot of times just to hear yourself talk.

The list of people we owe our greatest thanks to, without whose help this project could never have been completed, is long and illustrious. When we sent out The Role Call—by mail, over the internet, by telephone, and by sitting up day and night for months on end going through libraries, personal collections and bookstores all over New York City pouring through pages of books, journals and magazines to find the representative social and political work of our generation—we had plenty of preconceived ideas about what the response might be.

We sought out the best, the finest, the most meticulously thought-out and created work our generation is producing. We wanted to cover POLITICS, which means something completely different to just about everyone. For some it's rhetoric, for some it's bloodshed, for others it is healing, spiritual, for all of us it is personal. It is love. What we found, what we received through every medium available, all those e-mails, postings, phone lines—where those without access to technology were able to recite their poetry to us themselves—the stacks of mail, the publications, the people who just walked up to the house, by the table at the café, was all of what we were looking for and so much more. For that, for all of that, we thank each of our contributors.

We'd like to thank our publisher, Haki R. Madhubuti, for having the foresight and faith in our vision, for (perhaps dangerously) allowing us virtual free reign to create the book we knew we had to create, for making room for the inclusion of so many voices and visions, for being a calm, supportive presence even when all forces seemed against our ability to get this into print. Huge thanks also go to Gwendolyn Mitchell and Rose Perkins at Third World Press for your help with all the details. We thank Jiton Sharmayne Davidson for her vision, her long, long hours, her personal, psychological and intellectual contributions, her elbow grease.

Janée Bolden gets a whole Stevie Wonder dedication hour for being the

Editorial Assistant that wouldn't quit. Through the drama and the laughter and the silliness and the slave driving she, and Laini Madhubuti who jumped in and offered her time, energy, keen eye and positive energy when it was most needed, worked and laughed along with us, helping to keep the ship running tightly.

Our deepest appreciation goes out to all of our family and friends, with special shout outs to Emily Hooper Lansana, Nile and Onan Lansana, Sheba Baby Bashir, Fofie Amina Bashir, the Medina, Hilliard, Bashir, Hooper and Myles clans and all of our friends, loved ones and would-be loved ones who put up with the so many dates we had to cancel, gigs we had to say no to, parties we missed, books we couldn't read and shows we couldn't come to, the stuffiness of our brains and our long-term physical absence.

Special thanks to Camille Banks-Lee, Kamili Bell & Carol Smith Passariello-for providing insight, raw goods, laughter, levity, realness checks and a certain element of scandal, and to all of our editors, coworkers and overseers for whom our work was always late. Thanks also to Chris Jackson and Laura Atkins, for putting up with the *Role Call* mafia interjecting into their other editorial projects.

Big, loving thanks to June Jordan for opening her heart even further when it didn't seem possible. Thanks to Liz Randolph for her watchful, copyeditor's eye, Quashelle Curtis, Jeremiah Hoseah Landes, Sheree Renée Thomas, Gabriel Stover, Lisa C. Moore, R. Erica Doyle for hooking us up with necessary info and helping us to reach out even further. Thanks to Fatima, Bassma and their Sudanese Hair Liberation Army for coming through the headquarters to keep our naps tight, to the Fantastic Lesbian Sewing Circle who provided respite, inspiration and fine fashion, to Saunders baby #2 for being born while this was going to press, and to Jacqueline Woodson and Juliet Widoff in particular for helping us fly to the diner with the good food in Beautiful Downtown Brooklyn.

East 116th Street, the Corn Man, Tei Okamoto, Martín, Yolanda, Kerri Thompson, and everyone in the dusky allegro nation for keeping us sane, and the beautiful and large smiling waitress at that roach motel diner where we burned so much midnight oil. ("I'll have the roach cakes." "Yeah, lemme get som'a that roach pot pie." "Could I try the roach a la mode?" "Pardon me, do you have any roach poupon?"—it is in part because of her mercy that we are still alive today.)

Finally, to this book's designers, Michele Y. Washington & Emily Punjavilasluck of Washington Design, who took our vision, our pile of work, and our constant nagging and turned it into a thing of beauty. From the bottom of our hearts, to everyone who made this project the completely wholistic experience it continues to be, we give you our thanks.

With love,
Tony Medina, Samiya A. Bashir, Quraysh Ali Lansana
Brooklyn, New York

Acknowledgements

Jeffrey Renard Allen, "Harbors & Spirits" originally published in *Harbors & Spirits* (Asphodel Press, 1999). Reprinted by permission of Jeffrey Renard Allen.

Samiya A. Bashir, "Berneatha's Story," was originally published in *The San Francisco Guardian*, 1996. Mama's quotes are used from "Crack Annie," by Ntozake Shange, published in *The Love Space Demands*, 1987 & 1991.

Lawrence Ytzhak Braithwaite, "Grind," originally published in *Wigger* (Arsenal Pulp Press, 1995). Reprinted by permission of Lawrence Ytzhak Braithwaite.

Charlie R. Braxton, "The Bird Cage Bunch," "a terrorist's prayer," "Apocalypse," and "Juking At Miz Annie's" originally published in *Ascension from the Ashes* (Blackwood Press, 1990). Reprinted by permission of Charlie R. Braxton.

Sharon Bridgforth, "Bull-Jean in Trouble" and "Bull-Jean Slippin In," originally published in *The Bull-Jean Stories* (Redbone Press, 1998). Reprinted by permission of Sharon Bridgforth.

Kysha N. Brown, "Survivors," originally published in *Fertile Ground: Memories & Visions* (Runnagate Press, 1996). Reprinted by permission of Kysha N. Brown.

Anthony Butts, "The Ghost of Orpheus," originally published in *Fifth Season* (New Issues Press/Western Michigan University, 1997). Reprinted by permission of Anthony Butts.

Farai Chideya, "Cheney and Mandela: Reconciling the Truth" and "Free Trade, Free Cuba," originally published by the *Los Angeles Times* Syndicate, © 2000. Also appeared in *popandpolitics.com*, 2001. Reprinted by permission of Farai Chideya.

Rosa Clemente, "Who Is Black?" originally published on *Black Radical Congress— General News Articles/Reports* (BRC-Press list, 2000). Reprinted by permission of Rosa Clemente.

Nelson Demery III, "Detailing the Nape" originally appeared in *Drumvoices Revue*, Summer/Fall 2000, Vol.9, No.1 & 2.

Thomas Sayers Ellis, "Faggot," originally published in *Learning by Heart: Contemporary American Poetry About School*, edited by Maggie Anderson and David Hassler (University of Iowa Press, 1999); "Glory," originally published in *The Genuine Negro Hero* (Kent University Press, 2001). Reprinted by permission of Thomas Sayers Ellis.

Nikky Finney, " Butt of the Joke," "Making Foots," and "The Sound of Burning Hair," originally published in *Rice* (Sister Vision Press, 1995). Reprinted by per-

acknowledgements

mission of Nikky Finney.

Thomas Glave, "A Real Place," originally published in *Whose Song?* (City Lights Books, 2000). Reprinted by permission of Thomas Glave.

r.c. glenn , "on the use of charliebrown/teachatalk" and "those innocent eyes once weren't," originally published in *eyeseen: insights outward* (Big Drum Press, 1999). Reprinted by permission of r.c. glenn.

Duriel E. Harris, "Drive," originally published in *African American Review* (Winter, 2001). Reprinted by permission of Duriel E. Harriis.

Terrance Hayes, "What I Am," originally published in *Muscular Music* (Tia Chucha Press, 2000). Reprinted by permission of Terrance Hayes.

Esther Iverem, "Every Morning," originally published in *The Time: Portrait of a Journey Home: Poems and Photographs* (Africa Wolrd Press, 1994). Reprinted by permssion of Esther Iverem.

Major Jackson, "Mr. Pate's Barbershop," originally published in *Boulevard*, Spring, 1998. Reprinted by permission of Major Jackson.

Major Jackson, "Pest," originally published in *Callaloo*, Vol. 22:3, Summer 1999. Reprinted by permission of Major Jackson.

Jacqueline Johnson, "Celebration," originally published in *A Gathering of Mother Tongues* (White Pine Press, 1998). Reprinted by permission of Jacqueline Johnson.

Shara McCallum, "Poem Where My Mother and Father Are Absent" and "Mother Love," originally published in *The Water Between Us* (University of Pittsburgh Press, 1999). Reprinted by permission of Shara McCallum.

Bruce Morrow, "Evidence," originally published in *Callaloo* (Spring 1998, Vol. 21, No. 1). Reprinted by permission of Bruce Morrow.

Letta Neely, "gawd and alluh huh sistahs," originally published in *Juba* (Wildheart Press, 1998). Reprinted by permission of Letta Neely.

Dael Orlandersmith, "Monster is an excerpt originally published in *Monster* (Vintage, 2001). Reprinted by permission of Dael Orlandersmith.

G.E. Patterson, "Autobiography of a Black Man," originally published in *Tug* (Graywolf Press, 1999). Reprinted by permission of G.E. Patterson.

DJ Renegade, "The Good Doctor Writes," "The Goode Lorde," and "What's Painted on the Walls Inside Bessie's Wail," originally published in *Shades of Blue* (Karibu Books, 1995). Reprinted by permission of DJ Renegade (Joel Dias-Porter).

acknowledgements

Kate Rushin, "The Coward," originally published in *The Black Back-Ups* (Firebrand Books, 1993). Reprinted by permission of Kate Rushin.

Carl Hancock Rux, "P.S.," originally published in *Pagan Operetta* (Fly By Night Press, 1998). Reprinted by permission of Carl Hancock Rux.

Angela Shannon, "First Day" was originally published in *Drumvoices Review*, Summer/Fall 2000. "Hydrangeas" was originally published in *Water-Stone*, Fall, 2001. Both poems are reprinted here by permission of Angela Shannon.

Sharan Strange, "Promise, in a Southern Town," "Barbershop Ritual," and "Snow," originally published in *Ash* (Beacon Press, 2001). Reprinted by permission of Sharan Strange.

Natasha Tarpley, "From *Girl in the Mirror: Three Generations of Black Women in Motion*," excerpted from and originally published in *Girl in the Mirror: Three Generations of Black Women in Motion* (Beacon Press, 1998). Reprinted by permission of Natasha Tarpley.

Natasha Trethewey, "Gesture of a Woman-in-Process," "Microscope," and "Drapery Factory, Gulfport, Mississippi, 1956," originally published in *Domestic Work* (Graywolf Press, 2000). Reprinted by permission of Natasha Trethewey.

Angel Kyodo Williams originally published in *Being Black: Zen and the Art of Living with Fearlessnes and Grace* (Viking/Compass, 2000). Reprinted by permission of Angel Kyodo Williams.

Crystal Williams, "The First Time I Saw Flo-Jo," originally published in *Kin* (Michican State University Press, 2000). Reprinted by permission of Crystal Williams.

Andrea M. Wren, "Dear Daddy," originally published in *Young Tongues: A Poetic Exchange* (First Civilizations, Inc., 1992). Reprinted by permission of Andrea M. Wren.

Kevin Young, "Guernica," originally published in *The Nation*. "Irony of Negro Policeman" and "Negative," originally published in *To Repel Ghosts* (Zoland Books, 2001). Reprinted by permission of Kevin Young.

Shay Youngblood, "My Body Is Bread," originally published in *Every Woman I've Ever Loved*, edited by Catherine Reid and Holly Iglesias (Cleis Press, 1997). Reprinted by permission of Shay Youngblood.